KU-242-110

THE
IRON DUKE
A MILITARY BIOGRAPHY OF
WELLINGTON

For Martin and Eve

LAWRENCE JAMES
THE
IRON DUKE
A MILITARY BIOGRAPHY OF
WELLINGTON

BCA
LONDON · NEW YORK · SYDNEY · TORONTO

This edition published 1992
by BCA by arrangement with
George Weidenfeld & Nicolson Limited

First published in Great Britain in 1992 by
George Weidenfeld & Nicolson Limited

Copyright © Lawrence James 1992

All rights reserved. No part of this publication
may be reproduced, stored in a retrieval system,
or transmitted in any form or by any means, electronic,
mechanical, photocopying, recording or otherwise, without the prior
permission of the copyright holder.

British Library Cataloguing-in-Publication Data.
A catalogue record for this book is available from the
British Library.

CN 5634

Printed in Great Britain by
Butler & Tanner Ltd,
Frome and London

CONTENTS

CONTENTS

ILLUSTRATIONS

Between pp 182 and 183

Infantry in a square (Weidenfeld Archives)
Prince William of Orange (Author's Collection)
Wellington at Waterloo by R. A. Hillingford (Private Collection)
After the battle: the field of Waterloo by Denis Dighton (National Army Museum)
Wellington's apotheosis (Author's Collection)
Wellington: a daguerrotype, 1844 (National Portrait Gallery, London)
Wellington discusses his statue with M. C. Wyatt the sculptor in 1846 (Mansell Collection)
Wellington's catafalque, November 1852, by Louis Haghe (H.M. The Queen)

Maps

PREFACE

The Duke of Wellington is the best known and probably the greatest of Britain's generals. He was also a great man who, during the second half of his long life, was honoured and respected by a nation which usually applauds its war leaders when there is fighting to be done and forgets them afterwards. He was more than a victorious general; his campaigns in the Peninsula and his defeat of Napoleon at Waterloo raised Britain's prestige to unprecedented heights. The long peace which followed that battle was a fruitful period of progress and expansion, and contemporaries were grateful to the man who, above all others, had made it possible.

Wellington was an aristocrat who held that men of his stamp and talent were alone fitted to rule nations and command their armies. He was a creature of the *ancien régime* and waged war in its defence against the egalitarian forces released by the French Revolution. His successes did much to preserve the principle of aristocratic leadership in public life.

This biography is almost entirely concerned with Wellington's career as a soldier in the Low Countries, India, Portugal and Spain. When he was not fighting, and sometimes when he was, he served as a diplomat and civil administrator and after 1818 he was a central figure in British political life. I have concerned myself only with his political interests when they were interwoven with his activities as a general and have therefore given the briefest account of his later life. To some extent this separation is artificial, but it can be justified on the ground that from 1794 until 1815 Wellington was preoccupied with war.

This is also the story of the men who served in his armies and learned to have confidence in a general who, while he possessed none of the charisma of Napoleon, compensated for it with a strict, paternal concern for his men's welfare. In time they came to trust his judgement on the battlefield, where his caution, quick thinking and good sense saved lives. Where possible I have allowed these men to speak for themselves.

At the same time I have endeavoured to place the wars Wellington fought in their ideological and political context. I have also, in the narrative of the Peninsular War, paused to examine the human and material resources available to Wellington, how he used them and in particular his vital intelligence system.

I am indebted to many friends and relations for their suggestions and encouragement. My special thanks are due to Dr Sonia Anderson, Dr Ian Bradley, Dr Martin Edmonds, Michael Ffinch, Professor Ray Furness, Bernard Mitchell (who allowed me to fire a Brown Bess), Professor M. R. D. Foot, Hilary Laurie, Andrew Lownie, David Roberts, Sam and Maria-Teresa Reid, Dr Nick Roe, Peter James, A. V. Williams, David Vernon-Jones, and to my wife and family. I have received great help and kindness from the staffs of the British Library, the National Library of Scotland, the Scottish Record Office, the India Office Library, the John Rylands Library, the National Army Museum, the Public Record Office and the University of St Andrews Library. Quotations from the Crown-copyright records of the India Office Records and the Public Record Office appear by permission of the Controller of Her Majesty's Stationery Office.

ST ANDREWS, JUNE 1991

Part One

1769–1793

1

A Sprig of the Nobility
1769–1790

In March 1787 Arthur Wellesley, third son of the first Earl of Mornington and at the time a few weeks short of his eighteenth birthday, was commissioned as an ensign in the 73rd Highland Regiment, for which he paid the regulation price of £400.

He was, and the evidence for this is largely anecdotal, an agreeable but torpid youth who, at Eton, had shown neither talent for nor interest in academic studies. Faced with his languid disposition and lack of intellectual curiosity, his mother Anne, dowager Countess, and eldest brother Richard, the second Earl, decided to place him in the army, where his shortcomings would pass unnoticed. Army officers enjoyed social prestige despite the common opinion that soldiering was 'an idle profession, that requires little intellectual ability'. So wrote Lewis Lochée, whose experience teaching aspirant officers at a military school in Chelsea convinced him that a regimental mess was 'the sure retreat of ignorance'.[1] He was more or less correct; the junior, and for that matter senior, ranks of George III's army contained an ample sprinkling of dunces, idlers and fops, many of whom would give Wellesley much trouble later in his life.

Wellesley was better prepared for his profession than most. During 1786 he had attended an international finishing school for gentlemen, the Royal Academy of Equitation at Angers on the Loire. There he had studied the rudiments of military science; practised riding and swordsmanship; acquired a fluency in French; and absorbed those niceties of conduct which distinguished a gentleman. It was a year well spent. He always rode well, whether out hunting or on the battlefield – where his horsemanship once saved his life – and his manners were perfect, at least on those public occasions which demanded precision of etiquette.

The arrangements for Wellesley's education and his entry into the army had been supervised by his elder brother Richard. After their father's death in 1782, and following his deathbed wishes, Richard (b. 1760) had taken over the direction of his three younger brothers, William (b. 1763: he later took the surname Wellesley-Pole), Arthur and Henry (b. 1773). For the next twenty years he dominated their lives, chose their careers and in the process made them the partners of his swollen ambition.

Hitherto the Wellesleys had never amounted to much outside Ireland. For generations they had collected their rents, dispensed justice from the bench and loyally supported king and government in a variety of minor offices. Garret, the first Earl, had devoted his life to music and established himself as a noted amateur instrumentalist and composer. He was also an active patron who, in 1757, founded Dublin's Musical Academy, which admitted 'no mercenary performer' and whose elegant players entertained their peers with monthly concerts in aid of such good causes as the Charitable Loans Society for the Relief of Distressed Ladies. Arthur shared his father's love of music and inherited some of his skills as a violinist. Fiddle-playing was, he imagined, an inappropriate pastime for a soldier and so, in 1794 on the eve of his departure for the Flanders campaign, he destroyed all his instruments. He continued to enjoy music, although deeply conservative in all matters: he insisted that Mozart was the last composer whose works were worth listening to.

For all his musical accomplishments Lord Mornington, like his ancestors, remained a provincial backwoodsman. His eldest son Richard was infinitely more ambitious. He was determined to project himself and his brothers into the forefront of British political life. All shared a powerful sense of public duty which, in Richard, was flawed by a craving for admiration and reward; he died full of regret that he had never been offered the dukedom he had always coveted. A prima-donna's temperament and vanity made him exaggerate his talents and political usefulness, neither of which ever outweighed his personal deficiencies. Mornington was an indifferent Parliamentary orator in an age when a flair for rhetoric counted, and he had no appetite for routine committee and administrative work.

Nevertheless Mornington's charm, vision and superficial brilliance made it easy for him to penetrate Tory circles at Eton and Christ Church, where he won the affection and goodwill of two influential sponsors, William Grenville and his kinsman William Pitt. These were felicitous attachments, for Pitt became Prime Minister in December

1783 and needed all the support he could get in both the Westminster and Irish Parliaments, in the latter of which Mornington controlled the borough of Trim. Grenville's influence was employed to secure Mornington's return as a British MP for the pocket borough of Bere Regis in Dorset early in 1784.

His subsequent advancement was sluggish and unspectacular. In 1784 Mornington joined the Irish Privy Council; two years later Pitt appointed him a junior lord of the Treasury; and in 1793 he entered the British Privy Council and was given a seat on the India Board. The trouble was that Mornington suffered intermittent ill-health which he tried to alleviate by regularly taking the waters at various English and continental spas. From late 1787 until 1791, he undertook a series of prolonged tours of France, Italy and the Low Countries. Often absent from the Commons, his political prospects were not helped by his marriage in November 1794 to his mistress, Hyacinthe Gabrielle Roland, who had already borne him eight children.

Mornington saw his brothers as useful political allies who, distributed in the British and Irish Parliaments, could strengthen his power base. Within six months of purchasing Arthur's commission in the 73rd, Mornington was contriving his appointment as an aide-de-camp to the Marquess of Buckingham, who had just been appointed Lord Lieutenant of Ireland. He was anxious that his brother should not join his regiment, which was then stationed in India, and he saw the Irish post as an opening for a political career. 'My intention is,' he told the Marquess's brother, William Grenville, 'whenever I have the opportunity, to bring Arthur into Parliament for Trim and this plan would agree very well with a situation in the Lord Lieutenant's family.' His request was granted by Buckingham and, with the 'kind and anxious' assistance of the ever accommodating Grenville, Arthur was transferred to the home-based 76th, where a lieutenantcy was purchased for him. Arthur sailed for Ireland in April 1788 and was warmly welcomed by Buckingham, who gave a reception in his honour.[2]

This episode is instructive. Mornington was in no doubt that Arthur's future lay in politics and, it must be assumed, that he possessed sufficient intelligence to hold his own in the admittedly undemanding Irish House of Commons. It went without saying that Mornington was willing, as was his mother, to exert pressure on their friends to secure patronage, but this was more than normal familial duty, for the Wellesleys were not rich. Their Irish lands were mortgaged; insolvency dogged them, William's and later Arthur's careful estate management, and despite the £8,000 received in 1791 from the sale of Mornington's Dublin house; there was also the burden of the widowed Countess's £1,500 annuity, a matter about which her eldest son was often irritatingly

5

casual.[3] Small allowances also had to be given to the three brothers, whose service pay was insufficient for them to live as gentlemen. Even Arthur, who throughout his life husbanded his resources carefully, was believed to have run up debts of over £500 in eight years. No wonder Mornington was perturbed when, shortly before his brother's departure, he heard a rumour that his aide-de-camp's daily allowance of five shillings was about to be halved.[4] Memories of cheese-paring may have prompted Arthur to plead forcefully for increases in subalterns' pay during a Commons debate in 1806.

An equally strong feeling, based on experience, lay behind his views on patronage. In principle he accepted the system of string-pulling by which ministers traded pensions, administrative posts, sinecures and service promotion for political support. And yet he opposed the distribution of favours regardless of recipients' merits or needs. As Secretary for Ireland, he was confronted by an appeal from the Archbishop of Tuam for an office worth £400–£500 a year for his son-in-law.[5] Wellesley reacted strongly. Since the beneficiary stood to inherit a fortune and 'would not much like to undertake the duty of any officer' it seemed to him that 'the Archbishop might as well make a temporary provision for his son-in-law as throw him upon the Irish government'.

That same Irish government provided for him until 1796, when he resigned his post as aide-de-camp, having served three successive Lords Lieutenant: Buckingham, the Earl of Westmoreland and Lord Camden. He had been a courtier soldier attached to the staff of a civilian official and his duties were largely decorative. He was an elegant butterfly who flitted around the Lords Lieutenant on such state occasions as balls and levées and sometimes undertook small errands. Lessons in conduct learned at Angers were put to good use and he was able to polish those social graces which would, in time, serve him when he combined the roles of commander and diplomat. He changed uniforms frequently; in the course of five years he switched from the 76th to the 41st, to the 12th Light Dragoons, to the 58th and to the 18th Light Dragoons, in which last regiment he purchased a captaincy. Furthermore, and in fulfilment of his brother's plans, he took over as MP for Trim when he came of age in 1790, replacing William Wellesley-Pole, who was transferred to Westminster, where he swelled Pitt's majority as member for the pocket borough of Looe in Cornwall.

At this and later stages of his life, Wellesley owed everything to the favours of his eldest brother. Mornington influence was indispensable, but, as Wellesley recognized, an elder brother who could smooth an officer's path to promotion was a mixed blessing. Manipulations of his family's ministerial connections provoked mistrust and envy among less fortunate officers. Many years later, Wellesley recalled the strength of animosity towards him in the Horse Guards (the Commander-in-Chief's Department). There 'they looked on me with a kind of jealousy, because I was a lord's son, "a sprig of the nobility" who came into the army more for ornament than use'.[6] This was an overstatement since aristocratic blood flowed abundantly throughout the senior ranks of the army. What was resented was an officer with powerful friends in political circles who could, when required, circumvent the military hierarchy. There were also wider misgivings about the compass of Wellesley's ambition, especially after his return from India in 1805, and the pace of his promotion. For their enemies, many of whom were political adversaries and men who had been displaced or passed over, the Wellesleys were a clan of self-seekers greedy for offices and titles.

Arthur Wellesley was proof against such slurs. Throughout his life he treated his critics and their charges with patrician disdain. In July 1810 he wrote contemptuously of the great numbers of 'idle and malicious officers' who would not 'mind their business', but instead wrote dismal letters home in which his strategy was questioned and every setback exaggerated.[7] Such reports were accepted unquestioningly by newspapermen and used as ammunition against him by the government's opponents in Parliament. The 'licentiousness of the press' dismayed Wellesley, its collective incomprehension of reality enraged him. A naive press, he told his friend the Irish lawyer and MP John Croker, made the British 'the most ignorant people in the world of military and political affairs'. His countrymen would be wise to leave alone what they could never understand, and he added, revealingly, 'I act wisely and honestly towards them to do what I think is good for them, rather than what will please them.'[8]

These words lay at the heart of his philosophy. They were the statement of an aristocrat who, in youth and early manhood, had absorbed a creed based on the natural right of gentlemen to command in peace and war. It was a commonplace doctrine during Wellesley's earlier years and its principal features were outlined by the schoolmaster Lochée:[9]

> In public life gentlemen are born to assist in composing the councils of the nation, or in conducting her fleets and her armies; to be the bulwarks of the constitution; to sustain parts that require the continual execution of wisdom, fortitude, and the most highly improved talents: and, in private life, to contribute by study to intellectual and moral improvements, to be depositaries of upright principles and pure manners, illustrious examples of temperance, justice, benevolence and pity, diffusing order and happiness all around them.

All that today we most admire about eighteenth-century Britain, its architecture, music, landscape gardens, literature and scholarship, owed their creation to the patronage and taste of gentlemen. Their country houses still dominate the countryside and convey that same sense of eminence, pride and certainty about one's position in the world which distinguish the faces portrayed by Gainsborough.

Wellesley inherited this patrician self-confidence and cultivated a sense of reserved self-possession. This was founded on his unshakeable conviction that only men of his temper were fit to govern Britain. He told Croker in 1833 that 'the aristocratic influence of the landed gentry' was the only guarantee of just and honest government. Furthermore, he insisted that the Anglican clergy, who were 'the best educated gentry in the country', were the natural disseminators of 'piety, morality, good manners and civilization'.[10]

Gentlemen were a caste which shared certain unique inner qualities, of which, for Wellesley, the most important was an overwhelming confidence. This was vital for command in battle, where the slightest sign of interior doubt or nervous tension would signal irresolution to men already confused and fearful. Wellesley's self-assurance struck onlookers as close to nonchalance. Mountstuart Elphinstone, attached to Wellesley's staff during the battle of Assaye in September 1803, watched him gallop unwittingly towards the enemy's lines. 'Somebody said, "Sir, that is the enemy's line." The General said, "Is it? No, Damme so it is." (You know his manner).'[11] That manner became famous; visiting Paris soon after Waterloo, Sir Walter Scott noticed that 'All the young men pique themselves on imitating the Duke of Wellington in nonchalance and coolness of manner.'[12]

Wellesley's impassivity in the face of danger, like his patrician confidence in his own judgement, was a product of his upbringing. He grew up at the end of the Augustan age that prized calculating reason and disapproved of emotion which was labelled 'enthusiasm'. This was broadly Wellesley's view of things, although he also set much store by good sense and pragmatism. As he remarked in Spain, 'men with cool heads and strong hearts' made better generals than 'men of talent and genius', of whom past experience had made him wary.[13] He was equally disapproving of officers who let their feelings run away with them; one, whom he thought 'too rash – over brave', was told 'such boyish impetuosity would not do'.[14] Wellesley believed that no man in the public service could afford to let passion sway judgement. Nor could he permit himself the dangerous indulgence of introspection. It bred self-doubt, which undermined the outward confidence so necessary to reassure those who expected unfaltering leadership.

An Augustan by temperament and conviction, Wellesley never

allowed emotion to tamper with his judgement or to override the interests of the public service. When, in 1811, the family of a lady, said to be 'dying of love' for a major, asked permission for his transfer back to England, he responded sharply. Ladies so afflicted 'contrive in some manner, to live and look tolerably well ... and some have been known to recover so far as to be inclined to take another lover'.[15] He was most scathing towards officers who shirked their duties. 'It appears most extraordinary', he wrote at the end of operations in Mysore in 1800, 'that Lieutenant McDonnell should have been so sick as to have been obliged to quit his regiment at the moment when it was ordered into the field, and that he should have subsequently recovered so suddenly.'[16] The sarcasm here was controlled, but often such backsliders roused him to wild fury. He fell into a 'passion' whenever he disagreed with a court-martial verdict on a negligent officer or criminous soldier or a recommendation for mercy.[17]

Faced with incompetence, laziness, disobedience and backsliding his coolness evaporated, as it sometimes did when he was contradicted. 'He thinks and acts quite for himself,' noted Frederick Larpent, who served as his Judge Advocate between 1812 and 1814.[18] Everyone remarked on his short or 'hasty' temper. 'He swears like a Trooper at any thing that does not please him,' observed Lieutenant Woodberry of the 18th Hussars, and Larpent felt that officers were 'much afraid of him'.[19]

How far Wellesley's temperament and habits of mind were already formed by the time he entered manhood is impossible to say. Born an aristocrat, he had absorbed and never questioned the dogma that the inner virtues of gentlemen uniquely qualified them to govern. He remained profoundly conservative; accepting the world as it was and preferring the lessons of past experience to untested theories. His mistrusted change and those who urged it and, when inescapable circumstances forced him to become its instrument, he proceeded with caution and distaste.

The army which he had entered, more for convenience than out of any sense of vocation, reinforced his conservatism. It was a rigidly hierarchical institution, Tory at heart, which owned its first loyalty to the Crown and took the paramountcy of gentlemen for granted. In 1769, the year of Wellesley's birth, 43 of the army's 102 regiments were commanded by noblemen or their sons. During the American War of Independence (1776–83) Britain's field armies were commanded by aristocrats: Generals Gage and Howe were, like Wellesley, the sons of Anglo-Irish peers, Clinton the grandson of an earl, Burgoyne of a baronet.

The same pattern obtained on the continent. At the end of the Seven Years War in 1763, Frederick the Great purged the Prussian army of middle-class officers who had been commissioned as an emergency measure. In France, nine out of ten of Louis XVI's officers came from aristocratic families and showed a common determination to exclude the bourgeoisie from their ranks. Even the nine-year-old Napoleon Bonaparte, a scholarship boy from Corsica, had to produce a noble pedigree when he enrolled in the Royal Military Academy at Brienne-le-Château in 1779. Like Wellesley he had been born into an age which regarded waging war as an exclusively aristocratic pastime.

Wellesley never wavered from this view. In 1850, during a conversation with General Gomme, he offered his own victories as evidence that only gentlemen were fitted to command armies:[20]

> The British army is what it is because it is officered by gentlemen; men who would scorn to do a dishonourable thing and would have something more at stake before the world than a reputation for military smartness. Now the French piqued themselves on their 'esprit militaire' and their 'honneur militaire', and what was the consequence? Why, I kicked their 'honneur' and 'esprit militaire' to the devil.

He emphasized this point with a kick and toppled over. He could easily have added that many of the French marshals and generals he had defeated were not gentlemen, a deficiency for which their attachment to abstractions could not compensate.

The idea that war was the natural occupation of the gentleman derived from the Middle Ages. Although his uniform of bicorne hat, scarlet coat, white waistcoat and breeches was an adaptation of contemporary civilian dress, the young Wellesley was adorned with the trappings of chivalry. He carried a sword; around his neck hung a gilded metal gorget, which was a symbolic reminder of the armour once worn by knights; and, like them, he called his horse a charger.

Medieval patterns of thought and behaviour still permeated the lives of officers. In his everyday dealings with his colleagues, Wellesley was bound by strict rules of conduct which would have been immediately understood by the Black Prince and Sir Philip Sidney. Like them, he was expected to uphold his reputation and settle disputes by combat. Personal honour was the peculiar virtue which separated gentlemen from other men and exalted their standing in the eyes of the world. 'No man can impeach my courage in the field, my honour in the turf and my credit on the Royal Exchange,' boasted George FitzGerald, a dragoon officer and notorious duellist.[21] Every gentleman would have agreed and have admired his spirit. Duelling was attempted murder, but gentlemen set their code of honour above the law. No witnesses could be found after a fatal duel between two officers of the 61st Regiment in 1809 save the regimental surgeon. He told the court-martial of the survivor that the victim had died from a pistol shot, but neither he nor any other officer claimed to know when or by whom it had been fired.[22]

Wellesley totally accepted and lived by the code of gentlemen. In 1815, when he was Commander-in-Chief in Paris, he was snubbed by Louis XVIII. Later he rebuffed an attempt at reconciliation by telling the royal messenger, 'I am ... an English gentleman. The King has insulted me, and unless the insult be atoned for, I will never go near him except on public business.' Another insult, in 1829 when he was Prime Minister, forced him to fight his only duel. During the acri-monious debates which followed the introduction of a bill to allow Roman Catholics the vote, he was charged with deceit by the Marquess of Winchilsea, a Protestant bigot. Always proud of his reputation for honesty, Wellesley believed his honour as a gentleman had been questioned and so he challenged his traducer. When they met, he fired wide and Winchilsea apologized.

Such encounters were more than an assay of a gentleman's honour, they were tests of courage. Bravery was expected of the gentleman. It was this quality that gave him the right to command in war, for, in eighteenth-century armies, officers led from the front and encouraged their men by setting examples of fearlessness and heroism. On the battlefield soldiers closely watched the behaviour of their officers. 'The men are very proud of those who are brave in the field,' noted Rifleman Harris, and Sergeant Donaldson of the 94th remembered that, for all his foul-mouthed acerbity, the men admired General Sir Thomas Picton's 'calm intrepidity and bravery in danger'.[23] There was always respect for Wellesley's light-hearted, almost casual courage when under fire. On picket duty near Salamanca in 1812, Lieutenant John Henry Cooke of the 43rd (Monmouthshire Light Infantry) saw him and his staff inadvertently caught up in a skirmish between a crack squadron of French dragoons and a horse artillery battery. Wellesley was 'in the thick of it, and only escaped with difficulty. He also crossed the ford with his straight sword drawn, at full speed, and smiling.'[24] This was the natural behaviour of a gentleman in the face of danger and, for Wellesley, a vindication of the values and prerogatives held by all of his birth and background.

2

Gallic Breezes
1790–1793

In uniform and with enormous epaulettes, Wellesley cut an elegant figure sprawled on the government benches of the Dublin Parliament. He seldom spoke and used words sparingly when he did. During the winter of 1792/3 he suddenly became voluble, speaking three times in support of government policy. In November he backed a ban lately imposed on a body of nationalist volunteers who called themselves National Guards in the fashion of Revolutionary France and displayed the Irish harp on their banner without the loyal addition of the crown. Two months later he seconded the speech from the throne and, fittingly for a soldier, urged members to approve measures designed to raise the numbers of militiamen. The need for more soldiers was urgent, he added, 'at a time when opinions are spreading throughout Europe inimical to Kingly government'.

Those opinions were already disturbing Ireland. In February 1793 Wellesley defended the government's proposals to give the vote to Catholic property-owners by dismissing ultra-Protestant fears that the new electors would slavishly follow the instructions of their priests. Rather, he argued, they would behave like other voters who assessed the candidates' manifestos and, of course, listened to the advice of their landlords.[1] This concession was a device to smother agitation. As Buckingham cynically predicted, 'The Roman Catholics will be gratified and the rabble bullied.'[2]

The 'rabble' were the mass of Catholic crofters, sharecroppers and labourers who were showing signs of increased restlessness. Their animus towards the government was long-standing, as were their underground societies which waged guerrilla war against landlords such as the Wellesleys and the tithe collectors of the Protestant Church of

Ireland. By 1793 a new ingredient had been added to the traditional compound of Irish grievances: revolutionary political theories from France. These not only attracted the dispossessed of Irish society, but won intellectual approval among professional and business men and a few liberal-minded landowners.

Listeners to Wellesley's appeals for patriotic loyalty to George III were all too aware of the violent upheavals in France which had followed the storming of the Bastille in July 1789. Although today some historians may underestimate the French Revolution as a force for change, men of Wellesley's class and convictions were profoundly conscious of the danger it posed to their society. Events in France had moved at an astonishing pace and, like those in Eastern Europe 200 years later, left onlookers bewildered and unsure of the future. One thing was certain: between 1789 and the establishment of the French Republic in August 1792 there had been a systematic and devastating assault on the old order and the principles which sustained it.

The revolutionaries had utterly rejected the idea that the aristocracy were the natural leaders of society. Successive French governments had swept away the entire paraphernalia of noble power; out went titles, legal and enonomic privileges and finally, the keystone of aristocratic government, the monarchy. A new order emerged in which the People's Will become the sole foundation of political authority. In this new, outwardly egalitarian society the Rights of Man entitled everyone to personal liberty, justice and the choice of how and by whom they were ruled. By the summer of 1792 the left-wing Jacobin party had come to power bent on furthering what a horrified Mornington called the 'mischievous principles of ... Equality, Natural Rights of Man [and] Insurrection'.[3] Simultaneously the revolutionaries jettisoned the rights of property by using a national emergency as the excuse to confiscate the lands of the Church and of those who had fled the country or resisted the new regime.

These events were a catastrophe for men of Wellesley's rank and outlook. Speaking in the Commons in May 1793, Mornington described France as an 'odious and oppressive tyranny' which, he warned several months later, would spread anarchy and revolution across the whole of Europe. Such violent and fearful reactions were widespread. The French Revolution had exposed the fragility of the older order, the brittleness of its assumptions and the vulnerability of those, like the Wellesleys, who exercised power under it. At first, many in Britain had interpreted the events in France as the bright dawn of a new age of political enlightenment and freedom. As the scope and violence of the changes in France became clear, opinion divided. Liberal-minded Whigs hoped that the French example might encourage political reform in Britain. Those excluded from political influence saw a model for the radical reshaping of society, founded Corresponding Societies in imitation of the Jacobin Clubs, and vainly plotted a British revolution.

Conservatives rallied to the Whig MP Edmund Burke, whose prophetic *Reflections on the Revolution in France* appeared in November 1790. He fervently denounced all that was happening in France: in pursuit of abstractions, its people had made themselves slaves to fickle and destructive passions. Their collective insanity would lead to chaos and bloodshed. Behind Burke's baleful analysis lay growing fears that the revolutionary contagion would spread to Britain. This apprehension is caught in verses published in the Tory *Gentleman's Magazine* at the beginning of 1793:

> Soon may REBELLION's conflagration spread,
> Blaze fierce around, by GALLIC breezes fed,
> COMMERCE, RELIGION, and the LAWS consume,
> Expiring LIBERTY share the gen'ral doom,
> KING, LORDS, and COMMONS, in one ruin fall,
> And ANARCHY's mad reign extend at large o'er all.

These would have been Wellesley's fears. Like all conservatives of his generation he was profoundly disturbed by what had occurred in France and dreaded its repetition in Britain. The intensity of his feelings was revealed in 1830 after he had unsuccessfully attempted to block a Parliamentary Reform Bill. His defence of the old constitutional system and jeremiads about what would follow if it was tampered with were reminiscent of the arguments advanced by Burke, not least in the forcefulness of their language. For Wellesley the British constitution as it had evolved represented a perfect system of government which had made his country 'this last asylum of peace and happiness'.[3] The Glorious Revolution of 1688–9 had endowed Britain with a form of government in which power was delicately balanced between every interest in society, and so harmony, prosperity and individual freedom flourished. If, as the reformers intended, power was taken away from those whom Wellesley characterized as 'gentlemen of wealth, worth, consideration and education', then the dictatorship of the 'lowest condition of life' would follow. The selfish whims of the many would replace the wisdom of the few since, he claimed, no 'wise or just rulers were to be found among the uneducated classes'.[4] Democracy was 'the most detestable' of all sorts of government.

Wellesley's Toryism had ossified in the early 1790s. When, forty years later, he attempted to frustrate democratic forces, his arguments were much the same as those advanced by Mornington in defence of Pitt's anti-subversion policies in 1793–4. Both men's cast of mind owed much to Burke and, less consciously perhaps, to their Anglo-Irish background.

Wellesley, having been born in Dublin at Mornington House in Merrion Street, was Irish. And yet, as he once observed, birth in a stable did not make a man a horse. This was more than a stroke of wit. Neither he nor his kin ever considered themselves Irish; they were English and just happened to draw rents from property in Ireland, where some chose to live. The Anglo-Irish aristocracy had nothing in common with the indigenous, Gaelic-speaking and Catholic Irish, whom they despised and distrusted. Writing to Mornington on estate business in September 1794, Wellesley commented after a far from clear exposition of a legal problem. 'This is *Irish* but not the less true for that country of scoundrels.'[5] He knew something of the 'scoundrels' from having dealt with them while managing his brother's lands, and his animosity towards them deepened when he encountered them in the army. In June 1810 he attributed the rash of indiscipline in Portugal to the 'poor description of men' lately drafted from the Irish militia.[6] Twenty years later he was vilifying the Irish as an untrustworthy race easily misled by their priests and 'Demagogues'.[7]

This was a view from the top. For generations the Wellesleys and families like them had struggled to impose obedience and order on the Irish. They did so as conquerors – the Wellesleys had first gained land in Ireland during Elizabeth I's wars there – and they never assimilated or mixed freely with those they had subdued. Their first and deepest loyalty was always to the English monarch, who as King of Ireland gave them their lands, let them rule the natives with a free hand and rubber-stamped the laws which upheld their supremacy. The Anglo-Irish aristocracy needed all the power it could accumulate since the Irish Catholics were regarded as potential traitors, given that Britain's most persistent enemies were France and Spain, both Catholic powers. Only in 1775 were Catholics permitted to join the British army.

Extreme, uncompromising Toryism took root easily among the Anglo-Irish aristocracy, who needed little imagination to see themselves as an embattled but enlightened ruling class which held anarchy at bay. Wellesley thought along these lines, once remarking that if, as he believed, the Irish pressed for independence the best remedy was 'to keep them down by main force'.[8] Ferocious armed repression had worked a dozen years before when, in 1798, there had been a major uprising undertaken in the expectation that the French would intervene. Wellesley tenants were suspected of involvement; no rents could be collected from Trim; and William Wellesley-Pole had joined the local yeoman cavalry to help keep order. He did, however, protest to Mornington about the use of bloodthirsty German mercenaries who had slaughtered women.[9]

The French Revolution did more than stiffen Arthur Wellesley's hereditary and instinctive Toryism. It was a stroke of fate which changed the course of his life. In February 1793 the French National Convention declared war on Britain. From then until the battle of Waterloo in June 1815, Wellesley's life was devoted to waging war, first to contain the Revolution and then to uproot the order imposed on Europe by its heir-general, Napoleon. At every stage he was fighting an ideological war; the armies which opposed him in the Low Countries and in the Peninsula were filled by men who rejected everything he cherished and who imagined that their exertions would transform the world. For those who thought as he did, his victories checked and finally overcame the malignant and destructive forces released by the French Revolution. In an encomium published in July 1815, the Tory poet laureate exalted him as the general who had overthrown a 'conspiracy of the perjured, the profligate, and the lawless against the peace and order of society'.[10]

Part Two
1793–1795

1

Force and Menace,
Aided by Fraud and Corruption

The outbreak of war transformed Wellesley from a courtier–politician who happened to wear uniform into a professional soldier. He did not, however, see the change as permanent; during 1795 he was angling for a post in the Irish administration and, after his return from India in 1805, he entered the British Parliament and held the office of Secretary for Ireland. By then, through a series of victories in India, he had won himself a reputation as a general which, together with his brother's political influence, put him in the way of senior commands in the 1807 Copenhagen expedition and the Portuguese a year later.

Throughout these years and after, the direction of his career was guided by events outside his control. He was, as he often remarked, a servant of his country and bound to its government's orders. From 1793 until 1815, Britain was at war with Revolutionary and Napoleonic France and so, better to understand Wellesley's part in this conflict, it is necessary to examine its nature and outstanding features.

Britain was France's most tireless and resolute adversary. In simple terms British governments were at war to deny France unfettered control over Europe and to restore political equilibrium and stability there. At the same time the country faced the alarming possibility of invasion. Scares were common. The most serious were during 1797/8, when the Directory was considering a seaborne attack across the Channel and, with greater chances of success, a landing in Ireland, where French troops would stiffen local insurgents. Napoleon's formidable invasion force, which he mustered in 1803 on the downland behind Boulogne in full view of the Kentish coast, triggered new fears. In the event, the Grande Armée turned away to engage and decisively defeat Britain's allies, Austria and Russia, at the battles of Ulm and

Austerlitz. A few weeks before, on 25 October 1805, the navy's victory over the Franco-Spanish fleet at Trafalgar ensured that the Channel stayed a British lake across which no invasion force could sail without risk of enormous losses.

Official anxieties about an invasion receded after Trafalgar but never disappeared. During the winter of 1810/11 'alarmists' predicted a new French assault against England and Ireland, where disaffection remained strong.[1] They included George III, who was worried about a 'large proportion' of his army being tied down in Portugal and the possibility of a *coup de main* against one of his overseas dominions.[2] This flutter of nervousness irritated Wellesley, for it meant that he would be denied troops in the Peninsula. He warned ministers that 'if they don't give Boney employment here or elsewhere on the Continent, he will give them employment at home'.[3] Even at this stage in the war, and at this level in government, confidence in the paramountcy of British seapower was not absolute.

It should have been. Since 1793 the Royal Navy had enjoyed domination of the world's oceans and had decisively beaten off every challenge to its supremacy. Its victories had not only spared Britain from invasion and effectively isolated her most disturbed province, Ireland, but had enabled the economy to flourish. In 1801 Britain's exports were worth £35.4 million; by 1815 they had risen to £58.6 million. This increase is all the more remarkable since between 1807 and 1813 most of Europe's markets had been closed to British imports by Napoleon's orders. He knew next to nothing about economics and imagined, mistakenly, that his embargo would throttle British trade. Instead it did greater damage to the comparatively underdeveloped economies of France and her client states. The British survived by the exploitation of fresh markets outside Europe, an enterprise made possible because they controlled the seas.

Wellesley's political background and Indian experience gave him an understanding of commerce, and he appreciated how vital it was to Britain's survival. He was also an expansionist who saw the war as a vehicle for the extension of British trade; soon after his arrival in India in the spring of 1797, he argued enthusiastically for an attack on and annexation of Penang on the Malay peninsula. Here and in the memoranda he prepared during 1807 off the proposed invasion of the Spanish colonies of Mexico and Venezuela he heavily emphasized how their resources could be used to Britain's advantage during and after the war.[4]

He was essentially correct. It was generally accepted that Britain could only defeat France so long as her economy remained strong and expanding. At fifteen million, the population of Britain and Ireland was less than half that of France and her government was unwilling to impose universal conscription on the French model for fear of popular unrest. Britain could, however, redress the imbalance of manpower by paying other countries with larger armies to do the fighting. Between 1793 and 1815 the British government gave £65.8 million in various kinds of subsidy to continental allies, over half of which was dispensed between 1810 and 1815 to underwrite the Russian–Austrian–Prussian coalition whose mass armies finally broke Napoleon's power. More than cash and credits were involved. Industrial power had counted in Britain's favour: long before the British army secured its continental toehold in the Peninsula, hundreds of thousands of muskets, cartridges and gunpowder were shipped to Spain and Portugal. In 1813 over a million British-made muskets were distributed among the allies. The final bill, which included the expenses of Britain's own navy and army, was huge: the National Debt spiralled from £239 million in 1792 to £839 million in 1815.

And yet the burden of the war fell most heavily on the people of Europe. From the mid-1790s until 1814 a million Germans, living on either side of the Rhine, were absorbed into metropolitan France, which, during the same period, controlled Belgium (then the Austrian Netherlands) and Holland. Armies of occupation were stationed at the inhabitants' expense in Switzerland, most of Italy, the German states, Poland and, for a time, Prussia and parts of Austria.

France lacked the resources to support her war effort and so, from the beginning, was forced to extort money and goods from her defeated enemies. This stratagem was adopted by Napoleon, whose overgrown war-machine could survive only so long as cash could be extorted from tributary states. Therefore Napoleon and his satraps had to keep up a continual fiscal pressure on their subjects. The puppet Kingdom of Italy, which on its creation in 1805 had a 103 million lire budget, was, by 1812, raising 144 million, of which 46 million was swallowed up by military expenses and a further 30 million was rendered in tribute to Paris.[5] Between 1807 and 1808, 359 million francs (£15.9 million) was creamed off from the revenues of Prussia and Poland and sent to Paris.[6]

There were also exactions in kind. Grain, meat and wine were systematically requisitioned by the French authorities and, independently, soldiers plundered livestock, food and whatever they could carry. The worst offenders were at the top: in 1808, when General Junot was quartered in the Archbishop of Lisbon's palace, he stripped it of silverware, antiquities and works of art, which were shipped back to France.[7] Pillaging was not confined to the French army. With an infuriating disregard for Wellesley's orders, many British other ranks and junior officers helped themselves to whatever they could. After Vitoria, Colonel Larpent encountered an officer who had secured 'A Spanish girl, a pony, the wardrobe, monkey &c.', all the possessions of one of King Joseph's aides-de-camp.[8] For many, perhaps most, soldiers, war provided opportunities for individual profit, and taking advantage of them was seldom considered base. Wellesley disagreed, not so much on moral grounds as because the hunt for plunder distracted fighting men and undermined discipline. French commanders had no such misgivings.

Napoleon also stole men. He had no choice, since France alone could not provide all the men needed for his mass armies. The problem of the shortfall in recruitment was tackled by the extension of conscription to territories under French control. So it was that 180,000 of the 600,000-strong army which invaded Russia in 1812 were Germans, and in the same year the Kingdom of Italy was forced to disgorge 29,000 for front-line service in the east and Spain.[9] The miniature Duchy of Berg, one of Napoleon's creations, suffered appallingly from this blood tax, for none of its contingent of 10,000 appears to have returned from Russia.[10] Many pressed into French service were glad to go; the restless were happy to turn their backs on a dreary rural servitude and were easily enticed by the glamour of war. Many so inclined were found in Poland, where Baron Lejeune, a staff officer, noticed that 'The moujik [serf] bent with toil and huddled beneath his sheepskin, fastened at the waist with a rope of straw, becomes a spirited horseman as soon as he dons the plumed czapka and brandishes his lance with a floating pennon.'[11]

Victims of oppression in one country became oppressors in another; Polish lancers had a bad reputation for brutality towards Spanish civilians.[12] And yet when an Italian, taken prisoner in Spain, was asked for what was he fighting, he answered, 'My country's liberties.'[13] He clearly had faith in Napoleon's plans for his homeland, but lacked the political sophistication to query how the suppression of Spain's freedom would benefit Italians.

This Italian was probably not representative since many in his situation showed themselves lukewarm soldiers who deserted at the first opportunity. In 1810 Wellesley was astonished by the numbers of Poles, Swiss and Germans who were giving themselves up in Portugal and proposed the infiltration of the French army by 'active agents' who would encourage mass desertion.[14] Many defectors were simply hungry, unpaid and war-weary. Others belonged to an older, mercenary tra-dition and were happy to fight for anyone who would feed and pay them adequately. In 1813 a depôt was established at Lymington in

Hampshire for French POWs who had chosen to join the British army, while in Santiago a body of French, German and Italian ex-officers were waiting for permission to re-enlist as British privates.[15]

By this stage, Britain – like France – was having to cast the net wider to find enough men to meet her commitments. During 1812, 10,000 recruits were found for the British army's growing number of foreign units, which at the end of the year totalled 52,000, just under a quarter of the active army.[16] The loyalty of some of them was sometimes weak; seventeen, mainly Germans, were shot for desertion to the enemy in February 1812.[17]

Among France's soldiers there were plenty who were taken in by the deliberately gaudy uniforms or the heady talk of 'gloire', or, like the sixteen-year-old Fabrizio in *The Charterhouse of Parma*, were spellbound by the Napoleonic legend and wanted to be a small part of it. One such votary, an officer taken prisoner in the Pyrenees towards the end of 1813, asked why he thought the war was being fought, answered, 'L'Empereur le veut.' Such simple dedication counted for something on the battlefield. For an officer of the 92nd Highlanders, one of the most enduring memories of Waterloo was the incessant noise of men shouting 'Vive L'Empereur!' The words had an almost talismanic value, even in defeat, for he heard them chanted by French wounded in Brussels hospitals.[18]

The Comte de Vigny, who grew to manhood under the shadow of Napoleon, also recalled the shouts of 'Vive l'Empereur!' uttered by his classmates when their masters read aloud news of the latest victories. And yet, for all the clamour which surrounded military glory, he sensed that by 1814 'France was beginning to be cured of it.'[19] The evidence for this had been noticeable since 1805 when even the news of Ulm and Austerlitz had not stemmed the flow of draft-dodgers. The 1798 Conscription Law had let young men escape the call-up on payment of 1,900 francs, an amount which had to be raised to 3,600 by 1810. From 1806 France had to put diplomatic pressure on Spain to close its borders to the embarrassingly large number of fugitives from army service. Reluctant conscripts who stayed at home faked medical cer- tificates, usually for hernias, had their front teeth wrenched out so as to be unable to tear the paper which encased cartridges, or hacked off their trigger fingers.

Desertion and draft evasion became endemic by the winter of 1813/14, when it was obvious that Napoleon could no longer stave off total defeat. Dreams of glory evaporated as Austrian, Russian and Prussian armies crossed the Rhine and the British moved into southern France. In January 1814 an official proclamation of a *levée-en-masse* in the Upper and Lower Pyrenees was generally ignored; nevertheless

Napoleon's official mouthpiece, *Le Moniteur*, wrote that 'Fathers and sons march together giving heart to each other.'[20]

The invasion of southern France gave Wellesley a chance to explain to his soldiers that they were at war 'solely because the ruler of the French nation will not allow them to be at peace'. The war continued simply because Napoleon wanted it to. Wellesley was certain that this will for war lay behind the past ten years of conflict. Surveying the strategic and diplomatic situation at the beginning of 1810, he concluded that Napoleon had 'subsisted by conquest; and the moment it was proved the English could hold a point of the continent against all his forces, the charm was at an end'.[21]

All this was true. But when Napoleon assumed the office of First Consul in 1800 it was unthinkable that he, whose fortune had been made as a victorious general, would have relinquished what his country had conquered over the past seven years. His inner sense of destiny, vanity and determination to place France at the head of a new European order, arranged according to his will, made it impossible for him to renounce war. Once he had crowned himself emperor in 1804 he had to set about the creation of a Europe submissive to his will. To achieve this, he had, repeatedly as it turned out, to inflict signal defeats on the armies of Austria, Russia and Prussia in order to demonstrate to their rulers and the rest of the continent that resistance was futile. 'The greatest orator in the world is success,' he once remarked, but success in the form he chose, victory on the battlefield, was always chancy and expensive.

When the wars had started in 1792, the issue was stark: the survival of the Revolution. In July the National Assembly declared, 'Citoyens, la Patrie est en danger!' as an Austro-Prussian army moved into eastern France. The response from patriots was overwhelming and by February 1793 over 350,000 Frenchmen were in arms. They were fighting to survive; on one recruiting poster a father hugged his departing son and admonished him, 'This paternal embrace will be your last if you leave the army before tyranny recognizes your independence and mine … there is your property, remember that you are to defend it and never forget that a good man owes himself to his country.' Defeat would immediately wipe out all that Frenchmen had gained from the Revolution. The *ancien régime* was poised to return and wreak vengeance.

The atmosphere of panic passed when the allied armies fell back. It still remained the sacred duty of every Frenchman to fight, for having defended the Revolution he was now ready to carry its benefits to the rest of Europe. As the volunteers poured into the Low Countries and the Rhineland they sang:

> Tremble, enemies of France!
> Kings drunk with blood and pride,
> Tyrants, descend into the grave.[22]

The message of the pan-European revolution was vividly conveyed by official cartoons, often with robust scatalogical images. One showed citizen volunteers, buttocks bared, defecating on the princes of Europe and their soldiers. Another revealed these princes, including George III, recoiling from spurts of dung labelled 'Liberté ça ira!'

Whether or not uplifted by the belief that they were the advance guard of revolutionary enlightenment – and many were – French soldiers consistently beat their enemies. Between 1795 and 1799 their victories produced a crop of republics: Dutch, Venetian, Genoan, Milanese, Swiss, Roman and Neapolitan, each modelled on the French prototype.

Napoleon kept up the momentum of conquest, not just to continue the extension of revolutionary principles to Europe's downtrodden, but because he had to teach their rulers that he and his armies were irresistible. And so they seemed, for by 1807 his victories had secured him the hegemony of central Europe and a temporarily exhausted and neutral Russia. He was free to consolidate his control over the German states, whose boundaries he redrew and whose institutions he reshaped, and to turn his attention to Britain.

Neither British arms nor British gold had made much impact on the continent, where one after another subsidized coalition had fallen apart in defeat. Military incursions into the Low Countries in 1793–4 (with Austro-Prussian assistance), in 1799 (in co-operation with Russia) and in 1809 (this time alone) had ended in calamities. The lesson was clear; comparatively small expeditionary forces could never inflict more than pinpricks, even though the small-scale victory achieved at Maida in Sicily (1806) had been encouraging because it had shown that British troops could beat French veterans.

At sea it was a different story. Britain had used her command of the oceans to sequester the colonial assets of France and her sometime partners, Holland and Spain. None could defend their overseas possessions, which successively fell to British amphibious operations, although in the West Indies the cost in lives had been very high. By 1815 Britain had secured the Dutch and French sugar islands, save Sainte Dominique (Dominican Republic and Haiti), where ex-slaves had been able to hold off both a British invasion and a French attempt at reconquest. Other profitable gains included the Cape, Ceylon, Mauritius, Java and the final extinction of French influence in India.

The year 1807 saw stalemate. The situation after fourteen years of intermittent war was summed up by Napoleon, who likened the Anglo-French struggle to a duel between a whale and an elephant: one was unchallenged on land, the other on sea. So long as Britain withstood Napoleon he faced the possibility of revived resistance in Europe even though, as matters stood, the British army would remain outnumbered by the French. An economic war offered a way out of the impasse, but it only added to Napoleon's political problems. With a legion of excisemen he could try to exclude British trade from the lands under his control, but it was less easy to obtain the compliance of independent states. It was a difficulty which Napoleon intended to overcome in the only way he knew, by coercion.

In 1808 he resorted to the by now characteristic process of threats, invasion and subjugation when Portugal showed herself less than half-hearted in her enforcement of the embargo. The bullying of Portugal required a docile Spain, something which seemed well within Napoleon's grasp given her biddable, arthritic government and the presence of a body of 'Afrancesados', local quislings willing to work with a French regime. The Spanish people never figured in his calculations save as subjects for revolutionary reforms imposed from above and, of course, as future cannon fodder. Napoleon misjudged the mood of the Spaniards. On 1 May there was a popular uprising in Madrid which was brutally stamped out the following day by General Murat, an officer addicted, like so many of Napoleon's commanders, to comic-opera uniforms.

The repression, which is the subject of Goya's painting *Dos de Mayo*, triggered a spasm of spontaneous revolts across Spain. Anger against the French came from below and was universal. The original insurgents lacked cohesion, but in a few weeks regional committees, called juntas, had sprung up to direct a full-scale guerrilla war. The French armies in Spain suddenly found themselves isolated, often besieged, and dragged into a form of warfare which they had never been trained to fight: one against a whole nation in arms.

On their own, the juntas could not expel the French and so they appealed to France's only remaining adversary, Britain, for cash and weapons. These soon arrived in abundance, followed by an army under Wellesley with orders to support Portuguese resistance.

For the next four years Wellesley avoided the crushing defeats that had been suffered by Austrian, Prussian and Russian generals and that had hitherto given Napoleon the edge he needed to get his way in Europe. The war, he believed, had now entered a crucial stage. As he explained to some of his officers during the summer of 1812, Napoleon's domination of the continent 'was based upon shifting sand, essentially rotten at its foundation, and sustained by fraud, bad faith and immeasurable extortion: and ... it only required an honest understanding among the Powers of Europe, so down trodden, to put an end to the most contemptible tryanny that ever oppressed the civilized world'.[23] He never wavered from this view of Napoleon; over twenty years later he summed up the Emperor's methods of dealing with Europe as a policy of 'force and menace, aided by fraud and corruption'.[24]

Wellesley's verdict on Napoleon the man was admiration for his generalship and contempt for his morality. He was never a 'really great man' since he remained a slave to 'double dealing, equivocation, subterfuge and so forth'.[25] His dishonesty pervaded everything he set his hand to, for 'his mind was, in its details, low and ungentlemanlike ... what *we* understand by *gentlemanlike* he knew nothing at all about', Wellesley told Croker.[26] This was proved by an anecdote. In 1813 Napoleon had ordered a silver watch, with its case inlaid with a gold map of Spain, as a present for his brother Joseph, King of Spain. On hearing the news of Joseph's defeat at Vitoria, Napoleon angrily revoked the order, and the watch, unclaimed and unpaid for, remained with the Paris jeweller. Furthermore, Napoleon had bequeathed money he never possessed, including a legacy to the assassin who had tried to shoot Wellesley in Paris. 'One who could play such tricks was but a shabby fellow' was Wellesley's conclusion.

There were many thousands, perhaps millions, who thought otherwise and saw Napoleon as a truly great man destined to transform the world for the better. At the beginning of Tolstoy's *War and Peace* Pierre Bezukov spoke for them when he disturbed an aristocratic St Petersburg salon with the assertion that 'Napoleon is great because he was above the Revolution, suppressed its abuses, preserved all that was good in it – equality of citizenship and freedom of speech and of the press.' There was some truth in this and, during his lifetime and after, Napoleon was admired by Europe's liberals because he had used his victories to impose political and social reforms on the countries his armies overran. In the Rhineland and German states, for instance, French occupation had witnessed the dismantlement of feudalism and the emancipation of the Jews.

And yet, as Bezukov's critics were quick to point out, Napoleon's liberalism was skin-deep and could never have outweighed the death and destruction caused by his ambition. There was a gulf between high ideals and the reality of deceit, intimidation and bloodshed. Wellesley agreed; for him greatness required a harmony between private principles and public acts. The two could never be separated, as he forcibly remarked when writing on poets. 'I hate the whole race ... there is no believing a word they say: your professional poets I mean – there never existed a more worthless set than Byron and his friends for example – poets praise fine sentiments and never practise them.'[27] It was the same with Napoleon: for all his dreams and the martial legends so assiduously cultivated by his propaganda machine and added to by subsequent generations of admirers, there remains the image of large tracts of Europe wrecked by war and disfigured by corpses.

In human terms, the wars were a disaster for Europe. As Wellesley had seen, Portugal and Spain had suffered grievously, but they were 'mere soil', sparsely populated and therefore less vulnerable to war's destruction. He was therefore glad, he told Larpent, that he had not experienced war as it had been waged in the well-peopled and intensely cultivated provinces of Germany. What he had in mind was witnessed by Sir Walter Scott when he crossed southern Belgium and northern France a few weeks after the Waterloo campaign. 'I beheld the ocean of humanity in a most glorious storm of confusion – towns just reeking from storm and bombardment – fields of battle where the slain were hardly buried – Immense armies crossing each other in every direction – villages plundered à la mode de Prusse – soldiers of all kindred and nations and tongues. . . .' Such sights had been repeated from Moscow to Lisbon and from Antwerp to the shores of the Adriatic for over twenty years.

The movement of armies and prisoners of war accelerated the spread of epidemics, particularly typhus. It surfaced in the Low Countries in 1794–5 and followed Napoleon's armies to Italy in 1799–1800, where it killed over 14,000 in Genoa alone in six months. A more virulent epidemic followed the central European campaign of 1805, leaving over 64,000 dead in Austrian Silesia. Many who succumbed had already been weakened by shortages of food, as was always the case during sieges; fever carried off 70,000 in Saragossa during 1808. To these casualties must be added those suffered on the march and during battles. Army returns were seldom adequate, and registered losses often included deserters, while civilian deaths as a result of war were seldom counted at all. One estimate of Russian losses during the 1812–13 campaign was one and a half million, of whom as many as half a million may have been soldiers. To this may be added the half a million Frenchmen, Germans and Italians who died in battles, from wounds or from sickness, or who just disappeared.

Twenty-two years of war obviously reduced Europe's population, even though precise figures are lacking, but the demographic damage was limited. After 1800 the population of western Europe rose steadily, as it did for the rest of the century. Moreover, the period between 1800 and 1816 was one of relatively good harvests, so, while there was localized famine in some war zones such as Portugal, food resources were never seriously overstretched. In fact in Germany food prices fell during the wars.

The Europe of 1815, unlike that of 1918 or 1945, was able to recuperate from the injuries inflicted by war in a short period. Its people were predominantly countrymen (75 per cent of all Germans lived on the land) who made their livelihoods from agriculture. Such a society could more easily make good war damage than an urban one dependent on concentrations of manufacturing industry, sophisticated road and rail transport systems, and oil and coal for energy. This is not to say that the Revolutionary and Napoleonic Wars were not a wounding experience for those unlucky enough to be drawn in, either as participants or just because they happened to live in regions where the armies campaigned. What mattered in the end was that economically Europe did recover, although the political and emotional scars endured.

Recovery was Wellesley's objective. For him this meant the resuscitation of Europe's pre-Revolutionary institutions and society; the re-enthronement of historic dynasties; and laying the foundations of an honest and harmonious system of settling quarrels between nations. All required the restriction of French power and, above all, the removal from Europe of Napoleon. He thrived on war and his will for war made peace and stability impossible. Once beaten, his power evaporated and he could no longer menace. When, soon after Waterloo, the Prussian General von Müffling pressed him to have Napoleon shot, Wellesley was shocked. 'Such an act', he argued, 'would hand down our names to history stained by a crime, and posterity would say of us, that we did not deserve to be the conquerers of Napoleon; the more so as such a deed is now quite useless, and can have no object.'[28]

This incident reveals much. Wellesley spoke as an Augustan, using the voice of reason. War was a means to an end, and that end had been achieved in the form of a vanquished, discredited Napoleon. Von Müffling, whose country had been harried, mulcted and humiliated by the French, argued solely from passion. He and, for that matter his commander, Marshal von Blücher, wanted vengeance; later Wellesley had to forestall von Blücher's efforts to blow up the Jena Bridge in Paris. The twenty-two years it had taken to defeat France had generated passion throughout Europe, most of it nationalist. The Spaniards and Portuguese, both old nations, had fought for what they imagined to be the liberation of their country from an alien rule; some Poles and Italians believed that if they shed their blood for Napoleon, he would reward them with independent nationhood; and Germans, when the time had come for them to expel the French, fought as Germans rather than as Prussians or Hessians. Romantics of all nations looked on

Napoleon as a godlike individual, driven by his inner passions and sense of destiny to impose his will on history, forgetting too easily that force was always his argument.

2

The Mechanism and Power of the Individual Soldier

Two months after the outbreak of war, Wellesley paid the regulation price of £2,600 for a majority in the 33rd and, in September 1793, purchased a lieutenant-colonelcy in the same regiment for £3,500. The regiment was conveniently stationed at Cork, so he could continue his duties as an aide-de-camp. Nevertheless the steps he had taken, with help from Mornington, to secure what was effectively the command of the 33rd suggest that he was thinking in terms of active service and, with it, promotion.

This was a lean time for Wellesley. His brother's political career was stagnating; his daily allowance as a cavalry captain and aide-de-camp had been seventeen shillings and sixpence (87.5p), over and above which he enjoyed a £125 annuity from the family estates. The shortness of his purse was proving an embarrassment as he had been courting the agreeable Katherine Pakenham, a daughter of the Earl of Longford and in many ways a highly suitable match. The Pakenhams agreed, but with one reservation: engagement and marriage were out of the question so long as Wellesley lacked the wherewithal to support his wife in a manner appropriate to her station. Command of the 33rd improved his circumstances. He received thirty shillings daily (£1.50) and by cheese-paring or unscrupulousness, he was in a position to make something for himself from the regiment's War Office allowance.

Wellesley was an upright officer. Short-changing his men was unthinkable and, from the beginning, he was determined to approach every aspect of his regimental duties with dedication and thoroughness. He totally immersed himself in humdrum administrative tasks, quickly grasped everything that had to be done and learned to do it properly. Only by the understanding and mastery of small matters could he tackle larger. His military education began at the bottom and was guided by the pragmatic philosophy, 'Know your tools and how to handle them.' So informed, Wellesley later told Croker, he was able to appreciate 'the mechanism and power of the individual soldier; then that of the company, a battalion and so on'. His victories were, he claimed, solely the result of 'the attention I always paid to the inferior part of tactics as a regimental officer'. Supported by this knowledge, he felt free to confront 'the greater considerations' of strategy and tactics 'which the presence of the enemy forces upon you'.[1]

A general unprepared by such experience floundered. Archduke Karl of Austria, whom Wellesley admired as a writer on war, failed as a commander simply because 'he forgot that men are not machines'. Similarly General Sir John Moore, for all his skill and valour, fell short of Wellesley's standards, since he 'did not know what his men could do'.[2] Wellesley's basic principles had been proved by his victories, which made him dismissive of continental staff colleges and the abstract theorizing which emerged from them. For him, the best recommendation a staff officer could have was experience in a correctly run regiment.[3] He once claimed that his first lesson in the school of practical soldiering had been learned the day he joined the 73rd Highlanders in 1787, when he had ordered an infantryman to be weighed in full kit and carrying his musket. His memory of time and place may have been shaky, but the incident nicely illustrated his urge to discover everything he could about basic soldiering.

His keenness and enquiring mind were shared by few of his brother officers. One, recalling the army of the 1790s, remembered that 'the pleasures of the mess, or billiard table' came first and professional knowledge was despised as 'pedantry'. Such attitudes prevailed in the mess at Fort St George near Madras and were vividly recollected by Robert Blakiston, a young Irish subaltern who arrived there in 1802. After supper, when the officers had settled down to smoke their hookahs and drink themselves into oblivion with endless toasts, sergeants who intruded with orderly books were greeted by sighs and murmurs of 'Damn bores'.[4] Wellesley purged such slackness from the 33rd, where, under his strict and exacting orders, each officer gave the closest attention to routine duties.[5]

When Wellesley began his methodical study of command, the art of war was entering a period of transition. For the past thirty years any ambitious officer who wished to study war automatically turned to the Prussian army as his model of how any army should best be managed. The choice was dictated by its record of victories during the Seven Years War (1756–63), which was attributed to the principles and innovations of Frederick the Great. From the 1760s British officers with a sense of vocation made pilgrimages to Prussia, watched its annual manoeuvres and then went away thinking they had seen a perfect war-machine in action. Appearances were deceptive; past success had made the Prussian High Command complacent and the army was in terminal decline. When tested against Napoleon during the 1806–7 campaigns, the fossilized Prussian system shattered.

A regular observer at Prussian manoeuvres during the 1760s and 1780s was Colonel, later Major-General, Sir David Dundas, a Scot and something of an oddity among British officers since he had originally enlisted as a ranker. He distilled what he had witnessed of Prussian drill and, in 1788, published *Principles of Military Movements Chiefly Applied to Infantry*, which quickly became the handbook of the British army. Its initial value had been enormous since its wide circulation promoted a uniform system of battlefield drill. Previously, each regiment had had its own, peculiar commands and manoeuvres devised by its colonel.

The complex drill procedures detailed by Dundas served one purpose: soldiers had to be deployed swiftly and efficiently on the battlefield in order to use the mass firepower of their muskets to the deadliest effect. 'Battles are won by fire superiority,' Frederick the Great had written, for, 'Infantry firing more rapidly will undoubtedly defeat infantry firing more slowly.' So in accordance with its principles, and in his words, regiments became 'moving batteries' whose weight of fire depended upon how fast they could load and the speed with which they could occupy advantageous positions. To achieve precision of drill needed endless, rehearsals, the strictest discipline and automatic response to the words of command. The Marshal de Saxe, whose text on war Wellesley had read, claimed that perfect soldiers were 'machines which take on life only through the voices of their officers'.

The doctrine of firepower compelled soldiers to fight in straight, extended lines. Dundas favoured a line three men deep and in close order, that is shoulder to shoulder, which Prussian experience proved was the most effective formation. It enabled the heaviest fire to be directed at the enemy and, in case of shock attack, gave the men the confidence of 'mutual support'.[6] To bring these lines into play on the battlefield required slow, even marching and careful wheeling and turning with each man aligned with his neighbours. Only constant exercise could achieve this mechanical precision, which made many contemporaries compare soldiers to clockwork automata.

Linear tactics had been employed by both sides in the large, setpiece battles of the American War where, to Dundas's disapproval, British generals had preferred the two-deep line later chosen by Wellington in the Peninsula. The ponderous movement of close-packed lines was often impossible in the small engagements and skirmishes fought among the wooded highlands of the eastern American hinterland. A flexible approach was soon adopted by commanders. Soldiers fought in loose formations and made up the rules as they campaigned, rather than turning to the drill manual. This form of warfare favoured a new type of soldier, the light infantryman who had first appeared during the frontier campaigns against the Red Indians during the 1750s. By 1770 each British battalion contained one light infantry company chosen from recruits with quick wits and agile bodies who could shoot accurately. Continental armies, too, appreciated the usefulness of light infantrymen: the Prussians had jäger units of riflemen; the French chasseurs; and the Austrians grenzer and pandour battalions, which were commonly stationed on the Balkan frontiers of the Habsburg dominions. As the French and German names for these soldiers suggest, they were expected to possess the huntsman's skills of fieldcraft and marksmanship.

So, by the early 1790s, the novel light infantry formed a small portion of Europe's armies, although their duties remained confined to reconnaissance and manning pickets. Lessons in the value of such troops which had been learned in America were discounted as colonial conflicts were generally considered to be a separate, specialized type of warfare. Engagements fought in the New England backwoods between British regulars and American amateurs were beneath the notice of Europe's professionals. When August von Gneisenau returned from service with a jäger battalion in America and asked for a Prussian commission, Frederick the Great remarked, 'The people who came back from America imagine that they know all there is to know about war, and yet they have to start learning war all over again in Europe.'[7] Dundas concurred and set little store by light-infantry tactics. 'The showy exercise, the airy dress, the independent modes which they have adopted, have caught the minds of young officers,' he observed, but formations of light infantry would dissolve before 'the solid movements of the line'.[8]

Debate over the value of light infantry coincided with a period of speculation about the nature of the individual soldier. The Prussian system relied upon a passive creature whose Pavlovian responses had been dunned into him by the threat of physical punishment. This was so ferocious and the conditions of service so bleak that many officers felt that unless men fought in close formations they would desert in droves. The temptation to desert was greater for light infantrymen, who were dispersed across the battlefield in open formations, so something other than fear was needed to preserve cohesion and enforce discipline. Furthermore, the light infantryman's training emphasized individual initiative; he was encouraged to think for himself and act accordingly.

These differences reflected two opposing approaches to the treatment of the soldier. He was either, like his musket, a more or less inanimate instrument of war or a human being capable of thought and reason. The spirit of the age supported the second view, for the eighteenth-century intellectual enlightenment insisted that every man possessed virtue which could be released and fostered through kindness and education. If a soldier was treated with respect and honour, he would discover his own dignity and, with it, honour and patriotism.

Opinion among British officers was divided between authoritarians and humanitarians. Sir John Moore stood ahead of the latter. In 1803 he addressed new officers of the 52nd Light Infantry and urged them 'by their zeal, knowledge, and above all good temper and kind treatment of the soldier, [to] make the regiment the best in all the service'. His precepts were widely held. Lieutenant-General Floyd appealed to the 71st Highland Light Infantry on the eve of embarkation for Portugal in 1808 with the words: 'Officers! be the friends and guardians of these brave fellows committed to your charge! Soldiers! give your confidence to your officers!'[9] In the standing orders to officers of the 28th (North Gloucestershire Regiment) Colonel Paget exhorted them to encourage their men by 'a spirit of emulation, and a laudable ambition to excel' and to avoid 'any exertion of authority, or a resort to rigid discipline'.[10]

This awareness that the soldier was a sentient individual penetrated the army slowly, as Sergeant Donaldson of the 94th discovered when he questioned an officer's order. The response was abrupt, 'Damn you, sir, *you have no right to think*: there are people paid for thinking for you – do what you are ordered, sir, right or wrong.'[11] Wellesley would not have disagreed, although he would have been distressed by the officer's language. He believed that obedience was the cement of discipline and, given the nature of the men who enlisted in the army, could be upheld only by regularly and publicly flogging malefactors. And yet, as in all things, there was a balance to be maintained; in 1812 he confirmed the dismissal of a brutal martinet, Colonel Archdale of the 40th, after a court-martial had found him guilty of handing out excessive and unjustifiable punishments.[12]

Officers commanded, but they had always to conduct themselves as gentlemen and behave justly towards their men, taking special care of their physical welfare. In this he set an impressive example in the field by his tireless supervision of supplies, his investigation of hospital conditions and his hounding of negligent officers. During the retreat from Almeida in 1810 he came across a party of men, several wounded and all hungry, from the Light Division. Immediately he ordered an aide-de-camp to fetch bread, wine and carts.[13] Many years later, after reading George Gleig's memoirs of the Peninsular War, he commented, with some vexation, 'he talks too much of his personal comforts, and too little of his men'.[14] As for soldiers' moral welfare, Wellesley was unrelentingly hostile to schemes for the education of NCOs and other ranks which were being proposed in the 1840s. 'By Jove!', he once exclaimed, 'if there is a mutiny in the army – and in all probability we shall have one – you'll see that these new-fangled schoolmasters will be at the bottom of it.'[15] His ideal soldier was physically content, obedient and uncurious about the world around him.

'The principal motive for our soldiers to enlist is the propensity of the class from which we take them to drink,' wrote Wellesley in 1831. He expressed this and similar opinions on many occasions, adding once that 'discipline' was the only means by which the soldier could be 'weaned' from the vices he had embraced as a civilian.[16] His views were widespread, even among those who found the enforcement of discipline distressful. 'No one can detest corporal punishment more than I do,' remarked Lieutenant Woodberry soon after his arrival in the Peninsula, 'but subordination must be kept up or we shall soon go to the dogs.'[17]

The need for the astringents of flogging frame and gallows was dictated by the nature of the men who enlisted in the army. Soldiering during Wellesley's lifetime was commonly the last resort of men who could not earn a living or sought escape from the consequences of moral shortcomings. This was understood by the government, which, when faced with a dearth of recruits for the American war, had passed a law in 1779 to conscript 'able-bodied, idle and disorderly persons' and 'incorrigible rogues'. Wellesley had experience of coaxing such men into the army at the end of 1787 when he was securing his promotion in the 76th. The transaction required him to find some recruits for his new regiment which, in common with many others, was under-strength. Beating the drum for volunteers took time and was expensive; in 1795 a lieutenant of the 93rd Highlanders, scouring Staffordshire for men, had to pay for a bull-baiting to draw crowds.[18] Wellesley chose a simpler method to get his men and retained a crimp. Crimps lived on the margins of the underworld, and sometimes in it (a Whitechapel crimp active in 1794 was also a forger) and trawled the unemployed and destitute for recruits, whom they sold to officers. It was an unwholesome business, of which Wellesley was later ashamed.[19]

The crimps' hunting grounds were the slums, beer houses and gin shops of London and other large cities and their prey the derelict and desperate. Such men justified the general opinion that the army was manned by rogues. It was also a public nuisance, for the contemporary system of billeting meant that towns and villages had to endure the presence of soldiers with time on their hands. This created continual friction and a steady flow of complaints to the commander-in-chief's office from outraged innkeepers and publicans whose livelihoods and peace had been disturbed. In 1793 the citizens of York asked for the removal of a dragoon regiment whose men and horses took up accommodation and deterred the neighbouring gentry from visiting the city's annual races. Dragoons stationed at Stafford during the summer of 1800, when popular unrest was expected in the nearby industrial towns, monopolized every public house and inn.[20] There was much to moan about since official allowances for food and fodder were niggardly and the soldiers' behaviour was often rowdy. The 7th Dragoon Guards, who formed Gloucester's garrison in 1800, were 'the terror of all the principal [that is, richer] inhabitants', whom they robbed.[21] Present to keep civil order, these cavalrymen stirred up 'the ignorant ... and easily corrupted lower order of people' against their masters and urged them 'not to put up with the small bread'.

Not only were soldiers widely seen as social outcasts, but, as the petition from Gloucester makes clear, they were ever on hand to act as a police force, suppressing popular disturbances by firing or charging into mobs. Small detachments were also unpopularly employed to back up the revenue men in their wars against smugglers. The widespread scorn for soldiers was movingly rebuked by a corporal in the Coldstream Guards, Robert Brown, who published his diary of the 1794–5 Low Countries campaign, and was also, unusually, a poet.[22]

> Why that despis'd but useful race of men,
> Whose youth, whose manhood, even to grey old age,
> Is spent to serve their country and their kind,
> Shall meet with such contempt from every age
> And rank of men, that even a beggar's child
> Is taught to scorn a common soldier's name.

Brown was an uncommon soldier; he was literate and therefore able to record his experiences. So too did several rankers who served in the Peninsular and Waterloo campaigns, and their accounts of service life are vivid, highlighting the emotions as well as the sufferings of the common soldier. But their education made such men exceptional and therefore apart from their comrades. On enlistment in the 94th, Sergeant Donaldson found himself in a world where a man who shunned the prevailing 'ribald obscenity and nonsense' was mocked as a 'methodist' and the non-swearer a 'quaker'. 'Blackguardism bore the sway' and 'if a man ventured to speak in a style more refined than the herd around him, he was told that "Every one did not read the dictionar' like him"; or "dinna be gi'en us ony o'your grammar words na"'.[23]

The 94th was not entirely a bad lot. Donaldson found an Irishman called Denis who 'had no education: he could neither read nor write; but he had a most vigorous natural judgement which no sophistry or colouring could blind'. He also possessed 'a fund of honour that never would allow him to stoop to a mean action', which partly offset his only fault: 'in common with the generality of his countrymen ... when he got drunk he was a thorough madman'.[24] Always, as Wellesley knew, drink was the undoing of the soldier and the solvent of discipline.

Alongside and heavily outnumbering lettered men like Donaldson or Rifleman Surtees from Corbridge in Northumberland, whose tradesmen parents 'gave me such an education as was customary with people of their station of life', were misfits and criminals. They and their misdeeds glare from the pages of court-martial registers or proceedings like the man, charged with rape, who tried to defend himself from the gallows by arguing that he had fancied such behaviour would be permitted when the army reached France.[25] This creature escaped from his death-cell and made his way across to the French lines, where, presumably, he kept his views to himself. Desertion was the normal way out for such characters and, when they fled, the authorities seldom bothered to record more than their names. Occasionally an officer added some detail, usually of an abnormality, and for a moment the common soldier loses his anonymity. William Wallis of the 11th Light Dragoons deserted at Dorchester in January 1812; he was twenty-five, just below five feet eight inches and 'speaks thick ... he has a wife with him: stoops in the body a little: is much accustomed to Houses [that is, alehouses]: writes a good hand'. William Pearce deserted from the same regiment six months later. He was also twenty-five, but a good inch taller and 'hard of hearing and stoops in his walk: speaks rather effeminately'. George Clemenson of the 95th Rifles gave up soldiering at the same time; he was five feet three inches tall (below the regulation height) and 'has a pock-marked woman with him: stoops in his walk: clownish look'.[26] The physically as well as morally debilitated made their way into the army, which appears to have been happy to receive them, despite regulations which insisted that every recruit be sound of mind and limb.

The army had to take whatever it could get, as Wellesley appreciated. 'I am not very fastidious about troops,' he told the Secretary for War in 1810. 'I have them of all sorts, sizes and nations.'[27] He had studied this raw material since 1793 and, as a regimental and later field commander, he learned that they would fight well so long as they submitted to their officers' orders. He was an authoritarian of the old school, but open-minded enough to realize that an unjust or hectoring officer got less from his men that one who took pains to ensure that they were properly fed, watered and clothed. There were times when he would condone the utmost severity if he believed it would enforce discipline. He once ordered the retrial of a private found not guilty of threatening to shoot an officer. The evidence pointed clearly towards the man's murderous intent, but, more importantly for Wellesley, a principle was at stake. The demands of discipline outweighed those of justice: the slightest hesitancy in passing the death sentence for such a crime would dangerously weaken the whole fabric of the army.[28] He was equally relentless in his pursuit of negligent officers whose carelessness was often the cause of their men's misbehaviour.

Wellesley's conservatism reinforced his views of how the army should be managed. In all its parts it reflected right and proper ordering of civil society: gentleman officers, whose upbringing and temperament fitted them to govern, commanded men from the lower conditions who looked up to them for leadership. The relationship was paternalist and paralleled that which existed between the squire and his tenants and labourers. The British army of the late eighteenth century was a true mirror of the society it served.

Modern war is a contest of societies as well as armies. In 1793 the British, Austrian, Prussian and later Russian armies were to be tested to their extremes by the French, which was the product of a new kind of society. The armies of Revolutionary and Napoleonic France directly reflected a new social and political order.

The *levée-en-masse* of 1792–3 created a new kind of soldier, an ardent patriot ready to make superhuman sacrifices to protect his country. The fighting man was a figure of virtue not of contempt and, above all, he was a free man defending not just his nation, but his liberty. On the march he sang:

> A soldier of liberty
> When he is exulted by it,
> Is worth more than a hundred slaves.

The soldier of freedom looked across rather than up to his officers. All ranks were equal in rights and, significantly, the ranker was officially encouraged to end his letters to his superiors with the phrase, 'Salut en fraternité'. An Austrian emissary who visited the French HQ in Holland was shocked to see officers keep their hats on in the presence of a general.[29] (This was the practice at the British HQ in 1815, where it upset a Prussian general.)[30] And yet, as their adversaries soon found out, France's citizen soldiers were not a giddy rabble made delirious by slogans. In laying down the framework for the new armies, the National Convention never put ideology before military necessity. Officers had to show professional competence, and all above the rank of corporal had to be literate.

From the start talent rather than birth was the universal measure of an officer's fitness to command. Ex-rankers, NCOs and junior officers of the old royal army whose promotion had been blocked because of their background or lack of connections where now free to rise as fast as their abilities let them. Napoleon was an obvious example, although his career languished until 1795 when he drew attention to himself during the crushing of the uprising of the 13 Vendémaire. In the meantime, those men who provided the pool of talent on which he later drew were making names for themselves. The Armée du Nord, which Wellesley faced in the Low Countries in 1794, contained four future marshals: Captain Bernadotte of the 36ème, Lieutenant-Colonel Mortier of the staff, Lieutenant-Colonel Murat of the 21ème Chasseurs, and Lieutenant Ney of the 4ème Hussars.

France profited from this policy of promotion by merit. In a period of crisis it placed at the country's disposal a wave of mainly young, ambitious and brave officers. Mass mobilization on an unprecedented scale placed those whose enthusiasm for their cause compensated for deficiencies in training.

Improvised armies fought with improvised tactics. Every advantage was taken of superior numbers and the soldiers' readiness to sacrifice themselves for the Revolution. The Minister for War and principal architect of France's war effort, Lazare Carnot (significantly a former engineer captain) ordered every general to 'act offensively and in mass', and whenever possible to charge the enemy with the bayonet. His vague instructions were interpreted in different ways on the battlefield. During 1793 and 1794 commanders relied on loose formations of tirailleurs (sharp-shooters) which moved swiftly and elusively and harassed the enemy's line with independent fire. The old linear tactics were never abandoned completely, then or later, although, true to Carnot's injunctions, much use was made of mass columns of attack. These moved into positions behind screens of tirailleurs and then rushed their enemy's diminished lines, often singing the Marseillaise.

French generals were often living on their wits as they stumbled towards an ideal offensive combination of light infantry, artillery, cavalry and massed columns. What was vital, and this owed much to the wider philosophy of the French Revolution itself, was the willingness of commanders to adapt and experiment. Flexibility paid off: between 1795 and 1800, the French army, now with a growing core of veterans and well-trained men, was able to outmanoeuvre and overcome its opponents. Its victories were the result partly of experience, partly of tactical innovation, partly of major improvements in cavalry and artillery, and partly of a sense of moral superiority which was rooted in Revolutionary ideology and sustained by a string of successes.

This counted for a lot, as Wellesley recognized in 1808 when he told Croker, 'I suspect all the continental armies were more than half beaten before the battle was begun.'[31] He was right. Austrian, Prussian and Russian generals found it difficult to jettison old tactical shibboleths, so their response to French innovation was fumbling. The French, mesmerized by their invincibility, became accustomed to opponents who crumbled in the face of deft manoeuvre, light-infantry fire, heavy bombardment and the irresistible onrush of the infantry columns.

3

How Not to Wage War: Belgium and Holland, 1794–1795

For over a year after France declared war, Wellesley kicked his heels in Ireland waiting to know where his regiment would be posted. The 33rd was retained at Cork as part of the strategic reserve available for service in the West Indies or as part of a force earmarked to support counter-revolutionary resistance in La Vendée or Toulon. It was a frustrating time for Wellesley since there was a widespread feeling that the war would be over quickly. It seemed impossible that the French Republic could survive a combination of internal chaos and allied military and naval pressure. The Revolutionary armies, which Burke ridiculed as 'a rabble of drunkards, robbers, assassins, rioters, mutineers, and half-grown boys, under the ill-obeyed command of a theatrical, vapouring reduced captain of cavalry', would disintegrate when confronted by the trained professionals of Britain, Austria and Prussia.

Wellesley's months of marking time in Cork were a reminder that, like every officer, he was a servant of the Crown with no choice but to obey the orders of the King's ministers. They had ultimate responsibility for Britain's war effort, devised the broad outlines of strategy and allocated resources. In February 1793 Pitt and his colleagues were confident that they were about to wage a brief war and so decided to concentrate on short-term gains which would give Britain permanent commercial advantages. This policy, which Pitt called 'enlarging National Wealth and security', involved naval and military operations against the French sugar islands in the Caribbean; military and financial backing for French royalists; and substantially reinforcing the Austro-Prussian armies on France's north-eastern frontiers.

While attractively profitable, the West Indies campaign proved disastrous in terms of manpower. Three years of Caribbean warfare cost

35,000 lives, most the victims of yellow fever, dysentery, malaria, rum and general neglect. In July 1795 the garrison at Port au Prince (Haiti) was dying at a rate of between six and nine a day, although, as an officer noticed, the soldiers 'bear their hardships and great fatigue with patience and firmness'.[1] Such a colossal wastage of men led to shortfalls in recruitment by the late 1790s and early 1800s which placed constraints on Britain's war effort elsewhere.

Immediate problems of recruitment were solved by the resurrection of an expedient used in the American War. In April 1793 an agreement was signed with the Landgrave of Hesse Cassel for the hire of mercenaries; he received a £50,000 annuity, £19.5 shs (£19.25p) for each mounted cavalryman and £7.4 shs (£7.20p) for an armed and uniformed infantryman. The trawl was soon extended to Hesse Darmstadt and Baden, and by 1795 the bill had passed £1 million. It proved to be money squandered because at the end of the year the Landgrave made peace with France and recalled his men.[2] Other Germans, this time Hanoverian subjects of George III, were also mobilized. Like the Hessians they took the place of British troops sent to the West Indies, where all Germans prudently refused to serve.

Fighting the French where they were strongest was the task of an army of 28,000 British, Hessian, Hanoverian and French émigré troops under the command of Frederick Augustus, Duke of York, the second son of George III, who had been instrumental in his appointment. York was thirty and an affable, well-meaning but talentless general whose sole military experience had been on the parade ground and as an onlooker during Prussian manoeuvres. Not that any other commander could have done better, for he was shackled to an arthritic administrative machine and served by some notably hapless officers.

Bureaucratic sloth deprived York of vital artillery during the siege of Dunkirk, which ended with an inglorious withdrawal in September 1793. Co-operation between him and the Austrian Commander-in-Chief, Prince Frederick of Saxe-Coburg-Saalfeld, was fitful and mishandled since experienced staff officers were outnumbered by idlers. Wellesley was amazed to see officers on York's staff throw aside a message from Austrian HQ rather than let it interrupt the passage of the mess port. Stapleton Cotton, a young dragoon officer, noticed that General Erskine and his staff were always too drunk to handle any business which cropped up after dinner.[3]

Exposure of these failings came slowly. The 1793 campaigns against the Armée du Nord had been delusively successful despite Coburg-Saalfeld's nervousness, which left victories unexploited. By the turn of the year there were no further opportunities to be seized, since the military balance was swinging against the allies. York suspected that he was being starved of men, and there were signs that the Austrians were in serious difficulties. They had undertaken the war under the burden of a 400 million guilder debt and by January 1794 their government confessed to imminent bankruptcy. It was allowed to raise a £3 million loan on the London market which was secured by their Belgian possessions, but, since these were all but abandoned by the summer, less than a tenth of the money was subscribed. Prussia too was feeling the pinch and in November 1793 appealed to Britain for a subsidy. The following April, a monthly allowance of £150,000 was promised to meet the expenses of the 62,000 men designated for service in Holland during the summer. The Dutch government refused to pay its share and the first instalment was delayed until June, which gave the Prussian government a not unwelcome excuse to withhold the reinforcements.

By contrast the French were in good heart and ready for a fresh offensive with an army of 207,000 under the command of a capable and aggressive general, Jean-Charles Pichegru. He had secret pledges of future assistance from the pro-French Patriot party in Holland, which sympathized with Revolutionary ideals. With well-trained and enthusiastic troops he opened his offensive in May 1794, quickly took the border fortresses at Menin and Coutrai, defeated an Anglo-Austrian army at Turcoing on the 17th and 18th and drove a wedge between their two forces. The Austrians were beaten again on 26 June at Fleurus by General Jourdan. Pichegru followed up his advantage. As the Austrians retreated eastwards, he was free to thrust towards the Channel coast and Ostend. York, outmanoeuvred, isolated and outnumbered, fell back towards Antwerp by a series of forced marches during an oppressively hot June.

The scope and success of Pichegru's offensive alarmed the British government, which suspected that his occupation of the Flemish coast would facilitate an invasion of England. On 17 June the cabinet initiated immediate counter-measures. Ten thousand men, commanded by Major-General Lord Moira and being held in readiness for an expedition in support of the Vendéan revolt, were ordered to seize and hold Ostend. Moira would be reinforced by units from Ireland, including Wellesley's 33rd, recently shorn of its grenadier and light companies, which had been detached for services in the West Indies.

This was the first time Wellesley saw active service. It was also, as he remarked much later, a lesson in how not to wage war. A foretaste of the muddle and bungling which characterized the entire campaign was in store for him when he disembarked at Ostend on 26 June. There was no intelligence about what was happening inland, save that Moira with the main force of 5,000 had landed five days earlier and had then

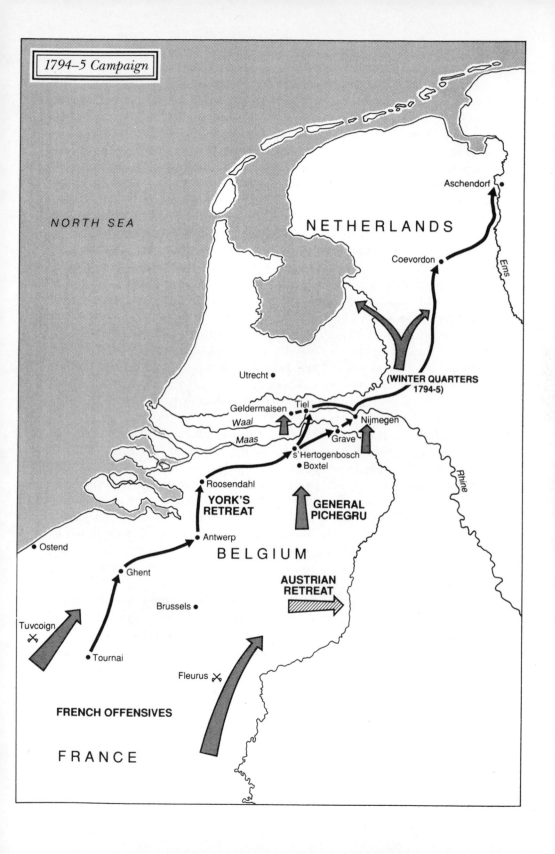

1794–5 Campaign

NORTH SEA

NETHERLANDS

Aschendorf

Coevordon

Ems

Utrecht

Geldermaisen Tiel

Waal

Nijmegen

Maas

Grave

s'Hertogenbosch

Boxtel

(WINTER QUARTERS 1794-5)

Roosendahl

YORK'S RETREAT

GENERAL PICHEGRU

Antwerp

BELGIUM

Ostend

Ghent

Brussels

AUSTRIAN RETREAT

Tuvcoign

Tournai

Fleurus

FRENCH OFFENSIVES

FRANCE

Rhine

marched off to find Field-Marshal the Count of Clarfait's Austrians and General von Wallmöden's Hanoverians, who were thought to be near Ghent.

The Ostend force of the 33rd, 44th, some light dragoons and a battery of artillery was in fact dangerously isolated. Its precarious position was revealed after a reconnaissance beyond the port. By now the Austrians had abandoned western Flanders and York was concentrating his army in Antwerp in the hope of holding the Scheldt. The Ostend brigade received orders to evacuate the port, which was undertaken during the night of 30 June/1 July under the direction of Colonel Vyse of the 44th. During this operation the 33rd, under Wellesley, were deployed among the sand dunes west of Ostend as a rearguard. At ten in the morning, French cavalry patrols were sighted, the advance guard for a larger force under orders to seize the port. Hurriedly reinforced, the 33rd prepared for action, but the French called off. There was nothing to be gained from attacking an enemy whose intention to retire was plain, so the French cavalry rode eastwards to occupy nearby villages and secure the Bruges road. Their brief appearance had upset the embarkation timetable, so stores and cannon had to be destroyed on the shore. By five in the afternoon, the Ostend contingent was aboard ship and on its way towards Antwerp.[4]

Wellesley had merely moved his regiment from one perilous position to another. York, deprived of Prussian reinforcements and unable to expect much help from the Austrians, gave up his plan to hold the Scheldt. He was forced to retreat north-east, cross the Dutch border and occupy defensive lines north of the Maas. Swollen by autumn and winter rains, the complex, interlaced rivers and estuaries of southern Holland presented a formidable obstacle which could slow down or even halt Pichegru's advance. Protected by these waterways, the Anglo-Hanoverian army could disperse and find secure winter quarters in the adjacent Dutch villages and towns.

Other considerations forced York's hand. Since the spring there had been symptoms that his troops' discipline was in tatters and morale was sagging. Although the retreat during July and August was orderly, York's shrewd and able Adjutant-General, Colonel James Craig, believed that the army owed its preservation solely to a 'complacent' enemy.[5] This was so and Pichegru's inexplicable failure to press home his advantage caused murmurings among his own troops.

By early September, Pichegru felt confident enough to plan a major offensive in overwhelming strength. With 70,000 men and 300 cannon, he intended to drive the British across the Maas in disorder, bring them and the Dutch to a decisive battle and then swing north-west towards Amsterdam where a Patriot insurrection had been planned. His intentions were uncovered on the night of 11/12 September when one of his staff officers was taken prisoner. When questioned, he admitted that 55,000 men were ready to overrun British outposts, crucial intelligence which was all but ignored, because on the 14th the French surprised and captured outposts around Boxtel and took the town. Resistance was all that could be expected from a disheartened army: two Hessian battalions broke and surrendered to French cavalry, while an émigré unit, Rohan's Hussars, scattered.[6]

Boxtel was a serious loss as it commanded the road to s'Hertogenbosch, which was one of York's lines of retreat. He ordered its immediate recapture on 15 September, but the force detailed for the task was inadequate. Wellesley and the 33rd were placed in the reserve and were able, by volley fire (companies firing in unison at their officers' command), to check a French cavalry pursuit. It was Wellesley's first action and he and his regiment were commended by York for their steadiness.[7]

York dared not risk a second attempt to recover Boxtel, and his army continued its withdrawal towards the Maas crossings. Luckily for him Pichegru's grand offensive failed to materialize. By the first week of October, and after the occupation of Nijmegen, York was free to deploy his forces, including the 33rd, in defensive positions along the north bank of the Waal. Confidence returned; the British had evaded their pursuers and were now established in safe quarters for the winter season, which, by custom, was not a time for campaigning. Wellesley shared this mood and on 19 September told Mornington that he expected to take leave soon and return to Ireland, where he would complete some legal business.[8]

During this lull, York was called to London, where, since August, a troubled Pitt had been planning his removal from the Low Countries command. After determined nudging, George III gave way and, at the end of November, York was incongruously honoured with a field-marshal's baton and designated commander-in-chief in place of the ageing Lord Amherst. Pitt hoped that by sacking York he could pave the way for a unified Anglo-Hanoverian command under the Duke of Brunswick but his candidate, a commander of slender talents, refused. It was therefore left to Lieutenant-General Sir William Harcourt, a stout-hearted cavalryman and veteran of the American War, to take command of British forces in Holland and possibly salvage something from a disastrous campaign.

It was a hopeless undertaking for, by the close of the year, circumstances beyond Harcourt's control made it impossible for his army to offer more than a token resistance against an unlooked-for French offensive.

The British army was already politically isolated. Inside Holland the pro-French faction grew in strength thanks to reports of Anglo-Hanoverian reverses. The defeat at Boxtèl helped convince Dutchmen that the British could never beat the French, whose final victory was just a matter of time.[9] Moreover the Dutch were enraged by the rapacity of British troops. Soldiers, who were starving because their commissariat had collapsed and whose officers were too lazy or indifferent to control them, lived off the countryside and its inhabitants. Firewood, food, fodder and much else was stolen from towns and villages along the army's route. The rot had set in in April when the army had left Ghent and two women had been murdered, and the sack of Nijmegen and Utrecht by departing troops showed that York had done nothing to stop it.[10] Not surprisingly, the angry Dutch turned on their tormentors, robbing and murdering stragglers.

What finally settled the British army's fate was an extraordinary hard, biting winter. On 3 December, Holland suffered 17 degrees of frost, which froze every river and dyke. The cold persisted and the French were quick to take advantage of it. The Waal was now a lake of ice and, in the final week of December, Pichegru ordered a general advance across it. Despite some spirited resistance, the British lines were soon fractured and Harcourt had to pull back his men to defensive positions on the banks of the Ems. As his adversaries abandoned Holland and dragged eastwards across the tundra-like landscape, Piche-egru gave his full attention to the wavering Dutch. Utrecht fell on 17 January 1795 and a week later the entire country was in French hands. The momentum of the British retreat was kept up by limited pressure on their rearguard and, by the spring, the detritus of the army had embarked at Bremen for England.

Wellesley was a marginal figure in this débâcle, learning how to handle his regiment in a series of skirmishes and holding actions. Once the great frost had set in, he and many others felt sure that the French could never fight in such conditions. On 7 December he sought home leave for himself and one of his officers. But the armies of the Republic ignored the old rules of war and for the next few weeks he and the 33rd were on continual standby to repel sallies across the frozen river. On 27 December, the 33rd and other battalions of Brigadier-General Sir William Cathcart's brigade were engaged in fighting around Tiel and Wardenburg in an action which temporarily stemmed the French advance. Just over a week later, on 4 January, five companies of the 33rd were among the pickets taken unaware by a French sortie against the outpost at Meteren. 'Hard pressed by a large body of the Enemy's Hussars that galloped along the road with great vivacity,' the 33rd's companies fell back two miles to Geldermaisen. Here they were joined by the rest of the regiment, the Black Watch and the 78th Highlanders, backed by two howitzers. After an hour's exchange of largely ineffective fire, the French retired.[11]

The 33rd was winning a good reputation and was selected for further outpost duty during the retreat to the Emms. In the first week of February, it was attached to Major-General Fox's division and billeted around Coevordon. On the 7th the General inspected what he called their 'forlorn and unprovided situation' and found it dangerously exposed. The soil had frozen so deep that no trenches could be dug or ramparts thrown up; the 33rd and the Black Watch were supported by an émigré unit 'which was unarmed and indisciplined, composed of deserters of all nations'; and the French were less than six miles off and closing in. Fox decided to withdraw this motley rearguard.[12]

Ten days later Wellesley was in another perilous and dismal situation, this time at Aschendorf on the banks of the Emms. He described his post in a terse report to his brigade commander, Lieutenant-Colonel McKenzie.[13]

The village in which the 42nd [Black Watch] is quartered is very small and very bad, the men and officers are very much scattered: that in which the 33rd is much better, although from the overflowing of that water, the men in some places cannot come out of their houses. With the assistance of Davis the Jew, we have been able in both places to get bread and forage. No communications with Lord Cathcart's brigade on the other side of the river: bridge at Rheide broken: dyke on this side broke and the country flooded.

Floods did not hinder the French and, on 22 February, Wellesley heard from his outposts that between 1,500 and 2,000 were at Groningen and an advance guard of 700 were within six miles of his own position.[14]

Wellesley was learning the hard way, carrying out his duties as best he could in adverse conditions. The entire army had been out-manoeuvred by an opponent with larger numbers, better generals and the goodwill of the local population. No help could be expected from the allies. The Prussians had pulled out of the campaign and the Austrians were beyond recall. They had been herded southwards by Jourdan's Armée de Sambre et Meuse and during the first week of October were regrouping along the east bank of the Rhine to engage the French advance into western Germany.

At the beginning of 1795 the allies were overstretched, outfought and weak everywhere. It is impossible to know whether events would have turned out differently if there had been a unified command and an overall strategy. Certainly political mismanagement and poor liaison

(York disliked the Dutch and treated them tactlessly) added to the difficulties of the British army. The care and patience with which Wellesley later conducted his dealings with the Spanish and Portuguese governments may have owed much to his first-hand experience of what could go awry when such matters were neglected.

Of equal importance as a lesson in the management of an army was Wellesley's unhappy experience of the army's ancillary services in this campaign. These were of a scandalously low standard: an 'infamous Disorder and irregularity' were universal and defied reform, complained General Harcourt in February 1795.[15] The view from beneath was the same and the suffering more intense. 'Perhaps never did a British army experience such distress as ours does at this time,' wrote Corporal Brown of the Coldstream Guards. 'Not a village nor house but that bears witness to our misery, in containing the dead and dying.'[16] Such distress, the inevitable product of official bungling, was not new, but in the sharp cold of the snow-covered plains of northern Germany it was most keenly felt. Wellesley slept in his overcoat as much to keep out the cold as to be ready for an emergency.

The underlying weaknesses of the British system was embedded in the recruitment and practices of the army's medical and commissariat departments, which were just not up to the tasks imposed on them by the campaign. This was soon obvious: in October 1793 Dr Everard Home, a civilian sent out by the Surgeon and Inspector-General of Hospital's department to investigate the treatment of the sick and wounded, was horrified. Ignorant staff mismanaged inadequate hospitals and there were shortages of food, bedding, medicines and transport. York was unmoved and felt that his men were not suffering unduly.[17] Nothing changed. A year later, Harcourt confessed that it was more humane to leave the wounded to the French rather than expose them to the 'pestilential air' of hospitals staffed by medical ignoramuses.[18]

The 33rd suffered along with the rest of the army from mismanagement. On 1 August 1794 it mustered 985 men, of whom 113 were sick; two months later the number had fallen to 849; and during January 1795 a further fifty men died. Losses in action had been slight – one man was killed and eleven wounded at Geldermaisen – and so the bulk of the regiment's casualties must have been the result of sickness or unhealed wounds.[19] The extremes of summer and winter temperatures, exhaustion and distempers for which there were no cures all helped to cull eighteenth-century armies, but perhaps the largest numbers died from bad nursing and illnesses contracted during convalescence.

Wellesley distrusted army doctors. In July when he had been afflicted by 'an aguish sickness caused by fatigue and damp', he wrote to his physician in England for advice. The reply diagnosed the bowels as the source of his ailment and prescribed a purgative.[20] Wellesley recovered from sickness and treatment with his faith in civilian medicine intact, for in February he asked leave of absence for Captain Elliot of the 33rd, who had been wounded in the leg and needed immediate treatment in England to avoid an amputation.[21]

A slovenly medical department added to what was the greatest problem which faced eighteenth-century generals, wastage of manpower. Invalids from the 33rd were refused permission to keep their muskets when they were carried on medical wagons, so the lucky survivors who returned to their regiments were unarmed and thus useless as soldiers. Furthermore new weapons were an additional charge on the regimental account, which angered Wellesley.

Unable to remedy the red tape and sloth of the medical departments, Wellesley undertook to have his men properly clothed.[22] Other soldiers, whose colonels were less diligent, suffered. 'I am confident that this is the worst provided British army with respect to clothing that ever was in the field,' Craig told the Commander-in-Chief in August 1794.[23] Not much was done to correct this in London, and so, by the end of the year, the army was relying on blankets and overcoats paid for by civilians who subscribed to a private relief fund.

Other factors contributed to the army's paralysis. Plunder was commonplace and went unreprimanded, which is not surprising since many officers knew nothing of their responsibilities. After the 1,100-strong garrison of s'Hertogenbosch surrendered in October it was revealed that some of its officers had no idea how to defend a fortified position and that the soldiers' will to fight had quickly evaporated.[24] Taylor White observed that captains in the 7th Light Dragoons shirked picket duties and, after the fight at Boxtel, several officers were charged with cowardice.[25] Such misconduct was a symptom of the defeatism which permeated all ranks during the closing stages of the campaign. The general despondency was described by one officer in a letter to Lord Cornwallis. The army faced disaster, 'Despised by our enemies, without discipline, confidence, or exertion among ourselves, hated and more dreaded than the enemy, even by the well-disposed inhabitants of the country'.[27]

A great calamity was somehow avoided, for the soldiers still managed to fight bravely. In March 1794, when Wellesley was back on the benches of the Dublin Commons, he rebuked a member who had mocked the militia by recalling what he had seen in the Low Countries, where 'They were not the objects of contempt to the enemies of the country.'[27] Memories of the campaign lingered; over thirty years later he blamed the 'system' which had deprived men of the chance to show their mettle. Faulty planning, an inexperienced commander and callow officers (commissions were purchased for boys of ten and eleven – even, it was rumoured, for a woman) had as much to blame for the débâcle as the system. Still, the check was salutary and even the most diehard conservatives realized that reform was needed.

What was important, and as a conservative Wellesley appreciated this, was that changes should be introduced from the top. York, with all the authority of a royal prince, was the instrument of the army's regeneration. This process cut out much dead wood and tightened up administrative practices, but left untouched its essentially patrician structure and outlook. To have tampered with these would have been politically unthinkable both for York and for successive governments, for whom army promotion was a valuable source of patronage.

Wellesley was in India during the period of most intensive reform, but he saw its results during the 1806 Danish and 1808 Portuguese campaigns and was impressed. His reactions were contained in his evidence to a Parliamentary Committee of Enquiry set up at the beginning of 1809 to investigate charges of graft made against York after his mistress had been accused of trafficking in commissions. Wellesley spoke for York and listed the differences he had noticed between the army he had known in 1794–5 and that which he had recently commanded. 'Officers are improved in knowledge,' and the staff and cavalry were transformed for the better. Furthermore, and this was of vital importance for him in the Peninsula, 'the system of subordination among officers ... is better than it was, and the whole system of management of Cloathing of the Army, the interior economy of the Regiments, and every thing that relates to the Military discipline of the Soldiers, and the Military efficiency of the army has been greatly improved'.[28] All this was indeed true, although it must be remembered that Wellesley was also defending the honour of a brother officer from the traducements of Whigs and radicals, many of whom wanted the army to adopt the French system of promotion by merit.[29]

Part Three
1795–1805

1

A Certain Fortune:
1795–1798

In September 1796, Lieutenant-Colonel Wellesley, an officer with limited means and extensive debts, sailed for India; he returned nine years later, knighted, a major-general and solvent.

On his return from north Germany in the spring of 1795, Wellesley faced a year of inactivity, illness and setbacks. His efforts to pick up the threads of his political career and find preferment in the Irish government came to nothing. In the autumn the 33rd was ordered to join the reinforcements for the West Indies which were being mustered at Southampton. Wellesley was unwell at the time and so service in the febriferous Caribbean must have been a sombre prospect. He was spared; at the end of December the West Indies convoy was scattered and forced back to port by heavy storms. In April 1796 the 33rd received fresh orders to embark for India. Wellesley, after making a good recovery, followed in June, having resigned his seat for Trim.

There was no way of knowing how long he would remain in India. The 71st Highland Light Infantry and the 73rd and 74th Highlanders had been in the country for between eight and eleven years – then as later the army believed that sturdy Highlanders were more durable in tropical climes than soldiers recruited elsewhere. All three regiments, like the 33rd, were on loan to the East India Company, which paid their costs.

In professional terms, Indian service was sniffed at in the Horse Guards, where campaign experience against what, by European standards, were 'savage' armies was discounted. Shortly before there had been murmurings among British officers stationed there who felt undervalued to the point where inexperienced newcomers were promoted over their heads. Like Major Thorn of the 21st Light Dragoons, the

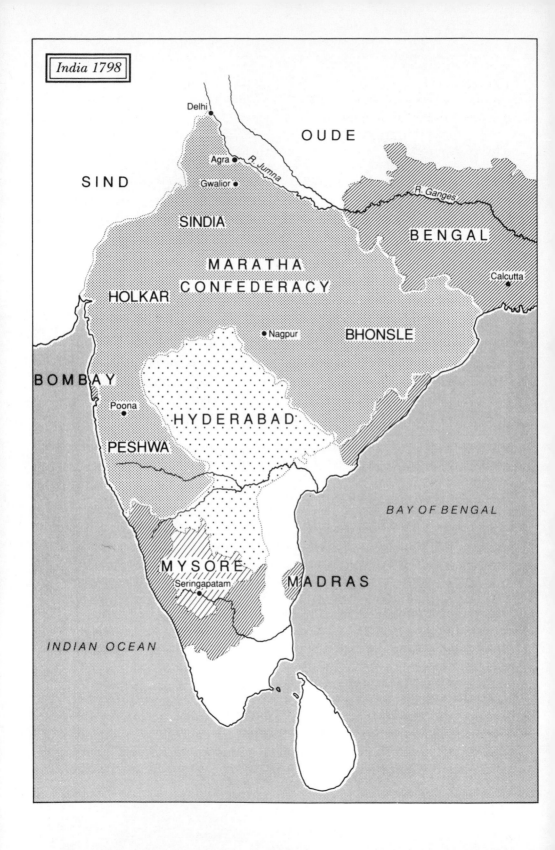

India 1798

SIND

OUDE

Delhi

Agra R. Jumna

Gwalior

SINDIA

R. Ganges

BENGAL

MARATHA
CONFEDERACY

Calcutta

HOLKAR

Nagpur

BHONSLE

BOMBAY

Poona

HYDERABAD

PESHWA

BAY OF BENGAL

MYSORE

MADRAS

Seringapatam

INDIAN OCEAN

disgruntled believed that fighting in India 'affords the widest scope and most momentous opportunities for the application of military science in the combined energies of genius and valour'. Campaigns against native armies taught an officer to be 'vigilant by necessity and sagacious by experience'.[1] Wellesley concurred. He found India an ideal training ground and, recalling his departure in 1805, admitted, 'I understood as much of military matters as I have ever done since or do now.'[2]

For those with a lesser sense of vocation, India was a treasure house whose doors could be easily forced. Waging war there was inextricably linked with making profit. 'A command in Bengal is a certain fortune,' Stapleton Cotton assured his family. Soon after his arrival of 1802, he noted enviously that Major-General Floyd was receiving between £14,000 and £16,000 a year from his combined incomes as a regimental officer and staff general and from Company allowances.[3] There were also additional payments made to officers on campaign and shares in the prize money accumulated from the spoils seized from the camps of defeated armies or loot taken from captured cities.

This practice seemed perfectly justifiable to Wellesley. Soon after his disembarkation, he confessed to Mornington that India was 'a miserable country to live in, and I now begin to think that a man well deserves some of the wealth which is sometimes brought home, for having spent his life there'.[4] His own profits were considerable and soon wiped out his debts. After the fall of Seringapatam in 1799, the total value of gold, silver and jewels found there was 2.5 million pagodas (£835,000: one pagoda equalled about 35 pence). As a lieutenant-colonel, Wellesley received a portion of 6,480 pagodas (£2,300), although he protested that he was entitled to four times that amount since he had served in the capacity of a general officer during the campaign.[5] There was some compensation later when he was granted 10,000 pagodas (£3,500) by the Company for the destruction of Daundia Wagh and his army in 1800.

Having flourished himself in India, he later helped others to do so for he worked tirelessly on the Deccan Commission, which divided the £2.2 million that had been collected during the 1817–19 Mahratha war. In 1827, when the business was finally settled, he felt pleased that he had helped 'the brave officers and soldiers entitled to the booty'.[6] And yet there was in his mind a clear division between spoils legitimately obtained and parcelled out and plunder taken indiscriminately by individuals. This was not so obvious to those whose share of the official loot was restricted because of their lower rank. Their drive for profit was as strong as their superiors': Robert Blakiston was horrified by the violence of pillagers he encountered at Gawilghur in 1803. When he reminded them that Wellesley, their commander, had forbidden such behaviour, he was told to 'get about my business for a meddling rascal, or they would put their bayonets into me' for they had a right to steal.[7]

Wellesley abhorred such conduct, which he punished vigorously. He hanged looters and harried officers and administrators whose greed drove them to cheat the government. After the court-martial of three such creatures, charged with embezzlement and theft of stores, Wellesley confessed that he had witnessed 'a scene of dirt and villainy such as never before disgraced the character of an officer, or shocked the feelings of those who were obliged to investigate it'.[8] Private profit was permissible so long as it was never gained at the expense of duty. Early in 1800, when offered what his brother promised would be a rewarding command in an expedition planned for Java, Wellesley demurred. He could accept the post, he argued, only when he had pacified western Mysore and defeated Daundia Wagh.[8]

Such high-mindedness was uncommon in a country where most were out for what they could get and moral codes were lax. In 1795 Sir John Shore, the Governor-General, regretted a universal decadence among his countrymen. Horse-racing was preferred to Sunday church attendance, the local clergy were 'not very respectable characters', and 'The Climate of Bengal (ridiculous as the assertion may seem) is not favourable to religion.'[9] This 'climate of Calcutta' encouraged the sexual drive of Mornington, who soon after his arrival there as Governor-General confessed to his wife that his passions would need an outlet. With remarkable tolerance, she agreed to let him find fulfilment, but warned him to be circumspect.[10]

Wellesley allowed his own men their native mistresses: in standing orders issued for the 33rd, he approved their presence in barracks so long as they were attached to 'well behaved men' who had their company officer's permission. Every woman had to be medically examined for symptoms of venereal diseases and the 'disordered' were banned.[11] Wellesley helped junior officers in their affairs and enjoyed flirting, particularly with officers' wives. He was notably generous towards one, Mrs Shore, who had once worked in 'a house much resorted to by men of fashion' in London and had followed her husband to India, where she arrived penniless. Hearing of her embarrassment, Wellesley sent her £400.[12]

He also showed a good-natured benevolence towards drinking. He always went to pains to see that his men were well supplied with arrack, a local liquor distilled from either rice or coconut oil. Arrack's importance, at least in Wellesley's mind, can be measured by the seventy-six carts and 304 bullocks he set aside to carry nearly 5,000 gallons of it during the advance on Poona in March 1803.[13] This was for 1,500 British soldiers, which gives each man's ration as three gallons over two or three months. While he punished drunken soldiers ferociously, Wellesley was prepared to offer dispensations to officers who drank too heavily. 'The most correct and cautious men were liable to be led astray by convivial society, and no blame ought to attach to a cursory debauch,' he remarked to the 33rd's chaplain after the latter had run around a troopship stark naked, singing lewd songs. On another occasion when a junior officer had exchanged angry words with a senior he observed, 'A drunken quarrel is very bad,' but, 'the less of it is inquired the better'. He avoided such excesses and their uncomfortable consequences. At dinner he took four or five glasses of wine and afterwards a pint of claret, which was considered abstemious by the standards of the time and place.[14]

In his conversation and bearing, Wellesley struck observers as a man of easy patrician charm and animation. 'Colonel Wellesley makes it agreeable where he commands,' commented Lieutenant John Brown after a two-month campaign in western Mysore early in 1802. Whenever possible, Wellesley dined with his staff and subordinate officers in his huge marquee, which was carried by an elephant and needed thirty lascars to set up. Wherever possible he drank and ate well, liking best a roast saddle of lamb with green salad. Not only did he entertain like an English country squire, he regularly hunted. As commander at Seringapatam he hunted antelope in the local manner, using cheetahs and leopards, and on campaign he occasionally pursued foxes with greyhounds – imported English foxhounds did not thrive in the Indian climate.[15]

At the dinner table or during the chase, Wellesley relished lively conversation, speaking quickly with a trace of a lisp and pursing his mouth when he was pleased. He stood about five feet seven inches and had 'a long, pale face, a remarkably large aquiline nose, a clear blue eye and the blackest beard I ever saw'. This, Colonel Elers added, forced its owner to shave twice daily. Wellesley's hair was unfashionably short-cropped and he never wore powder, claiming that it encouraged sweating, which was unhealthy in the tropics. (A miniature of 1794/5 shows him with conventional, white-powdered hair tied with a bow.) On formal occasions in India he wore the long scarlet coat of the 33rd, loose white pantaloons, Hessian boots and a cocked hat and carried a long sabre with gilt mountings.[16]

If fragmentary anecdotes have any substance, the diffident young man on the fringes of Irish politics had grown into a confident, good-humoured and tolerant aristocrat. By temperament he was well suited to contemporary Anglo-Indian society, where before his arrival his standing had been enhanced by the announcement that his brother

Mornington had been appointed Governor of Madras. It rose higher at the end of the 1797 when the news reached Calcutta that Mornington had been named as the new Governor-General, ruler of all the Company's possessions.

Although Mornington pledged himself 'to govern without favour or affection', this proved impossible.[17] He quickly appointed his younger brother Henry as his secretary, came to lean heavily on Arthur for military advice and facilitated his promotion, often in the face of intense opposition from more senior officers. This was more than nepotism. Mornington needed trustworthy accomplices in a country where fractiousness, jealousy and backbiting were a way of life. Moreover, he needed men at his side who shared his vision of India's future.

Since 1793, when he had joined the India Board, Mornington had taken a close interest in the country's affairs. His strongly held views on India's political and commercial value to Britain coincided with those of the Board's president, Henry Dundas, who had helped to engineer his appointment as Governor-General.

Mornington imagined that if he distinguished himself in India, he could return to Britain and at last grasp the political prizes which had so far eluded him. On his voyage out he confided to Grenville that he intended to stay for five or six years and accomplish 'grand Financial, Political, Military, Naval, Commercial [and] judicial reforms'. Having set his stamp on India he would take Dundas's place as President of the Board of Control and so enter the cabinet.[18]

All this would be undertaken in a splendid style. Like Lord Curzon a hundred years later, Mornington was an instinctive autocrat who was easily intoxicated by the power he wielded and mesmerized by the richness and splendour of traditional Indian pageantry. When he entered Cawnpore in 1803 to meet the Nawab of Oude he rode on an elephant 'in the true style of Eastern pomp' and 'distributed his rupees with a liberal hand'. He built two new palaces, embellished one with an aviary, the other with a menagerie; he dressed elegantly; and he treated those beneath him with disdain. 'The society of my subjects [a revealing word]', he told Grenville in November 1798, 'is so vulgar, ignorant, rude, familiar, and stupid as to be disgusting and intolerable, especially the ladies, not one of whom, by the bye, is ever decently well-looking.'[19]

Mornington's addiction to magnificence and dreams of transforming India were at odds with the reality of his position. He served both the King and the directors of the East India Company, a commercial enterprise that wanted him to keep down costs and provide good dividends for its shareholders. Its interests were represented on the

Board of Control in London which, theoretically, supervised the Governor-General, whom it could recall. Distance diluted the Board's authority, leaving Mornington free to take crucial decisions on his own. An urgent letter from London, if it travelled by the fastest route through the Mediterranean, across the Suez isthmus and down the Red Sea, took between eight and ten weeks to reach Calcutta. Furthermore, the Board relied heavily on the Governor-General and his staff for its information on Indian affairs, and Mornington, when he considered it personally advantageous, delayed or withheld vital information. In the event of criticism or efforts to recall him, Mornington relied on political friends in Britain to take his part. Nevertheless, in 1800, he took the precaution of sending his brother Henry home to lobby on his behalf and even suggested that Arthur might do the same.[20]

One matter occupied Mornington's mind during his six-month voyage to India, the overthrow of Tipu (the Tiger) Sultan of Mysore. Tipu wanted to recover power and territory lost to the Company in two wars and saw Britain's conflict with France as the means to this end. His ambition was symbolized by the famous mechanical tiger which he had had made and which is now in the Victoria and Albert Museum. It stands astride an automaton in the dress of a Company officer who lets out terrified shrieks. Tipu also had a menagerie of real tigers which, sadly, Wellesley ordered to be shot after the fall of Seringapatam because there was no food for them.[21]

Mornington learned about the Tiger Sultan's ambitions during his two-month stay at Cape Town at the beginning of 1798 when he read reports from India, including memoranda written by Arthur. He also discussed the state of the country with homebound officials and soldiers. The Cape was the centre of the Company's intelligence-gathering in the Indian Ocean, where for the past year attention had been focused on the French colony of Mauritius, which was the base for subversion in India. Information from this source indicated that efforts were in hand to draw the Nizam of Hyderabad into France's orbit and offer Tipu an alliance and military assistance if he made war on the Company. This and what he heard from India convinced Mornington that plans were in readiness for a revival of French influence in India and he would therefore be entering a war zone.

This was certainly the feeling inside India. For some time the major source of disquiet had been developments in Hyderabad, which were revealed to Mornington by Major Kirkpatrick, who until recently had been the resident at the Nizam's court and whose findings were passed on to Dundas in a letter of 28 February 1798.[22] The French officers who trained and commanded the 14,000-strong Hyderabad army were becoming increasingly insolent; they embraced the 'most virulent and notorious principles of Jacobinism', flew the tricolour and, most ominously, were enticing sepoys to desert from the Company's army. All this suggest that some 'adventurers' were preparing to 'see a new order of things' inside the state, turning an ally into an adversary.

What Mornington heard at Cape Town confirmed what he had already been told by Arthur, who had been writing to him on Indian business since the previous May. His letters were incisive and showed for the first time his remarkable ability to penetrate to the centre of any problem or issue. Everything in India revolved around one question – 'are we or are the French to have superiority in the Deccan?' He had been aware of the recent influx of French 'aristocrats, democrats, modérés &c. &c.' into India, all peddling their services as military advisers to native rulers. 'All Frenchmen in such situations are equally dangerous,' Wellesley insisted, for they drilled and trained Indian soldiers 'in the new mode', that is in the European style of warfare. If this continued unchecked, the military balance would swing against the Company's army, which always relied on its modern techniques to maintain superiority.[23]

This dangerous process had to be stopped, so an excuse would have to be contrived, Wellesley suggested, to provoke a showdown with Hyderabad and Mysore. This would have to be done without arousing the suspicion that the Company was fearful. A few months in India had taught him that prestige was vital for the preservation of British rule; the Company had always to appear unruffled, unflinching and omniscient.

Advice of this tenor continued to flow from Wellesley during the months which followed his brother's arrival in Calcutta in July 1798. Drawing heavily on intelligence reports from Captain Malcolm in Hyderabad, he pressed for swift action to neutralize its army, now commanded by 'a violent democrat', General Perron. Once the threat from this quarter had been removed, the Company was free to invade Mysore.[24]

Wellesley's approach was always that of a soldier; for him India's problems were essentially military. British expansion there rested on force alone; earlier victories in the field had been followed by annexations and contributed to a widespread belief that the Company's armies were invincible. Consequently native rulers were anxious to reach an accommodation with the Company, placing themselves under its protection and, in some cases, accepting Company garrisons in their provinces. The process was not inexorable. For the past twenty years independent princes had been adopting measures designed to change their armies and bring their training and equipment in line with the Company's.

Military reforms were most advanced in central India, where two Mahratha rulers, Raghuji II Bhonsle of Nagpur and Daulat Rao Sindia of Gwalior, had retained a corps of Western advisers who were creating new, formidable regiments of infantry. What was more, native rulers were desperately anxious to secure European technology; there was a foundry producing cannon at Hyderabad and craftsmen there were making flintlock muskets that were more reliable than the traditional matchlock, a weapon which had been abandoned by European armies a century before. At Agra too, Mahratha gunsmiths were manufacturing flintlocks, and modern powder mills had been established.

The rearmament and modernization of native armies invited pre-emptive campaigns to reassert the Company's military reputation. As matters stood in 1798, and as Wellesley realized, the Company still had many advantages. Its light artillery was better handled and more mobile, although Wellesley had called for the introduction of horse artillery to supplement pieces drawn by slow-moving bullocks. Above all, the Company's resources were far greater than any available to the native princes. Its system of revenue collection was such that there were always reserves of cash and credit with which it could pay, feed and equip its armies without strain. On campaign, the Company's soldiers often had to face food shortages, but their wages were paid. Their opponents were less fortunate: reports from spies during the campaigns of 1799–1804 contained details of armies without rations or fodder and of sullen men deserting in droves for lack of money. Moreover, the Company could call on mass-produced, British-made muskets which were imported by the thousand. Despite their rulers' efforts to remedy the deficiency, India's native craftsmen could not compete with the Birmingham workshops. As testament to this, an eighteenth-century Indian chess set now in the Victoria and Albert Museum shows British pieces armed with cannon, muskets and pistols, Indian with swords, shields and spears.[25]

Nevertheless, Wellesley and other officers emphasized the need for immediate offensives to prevent the Company from being overtaken in the arms race. Furthermore, and this added considerable weight to their arguments, Britain was engaged in a global war against France, which, the Company's intelligence sources believed, was seeking ways to create mischief in India. The French had many willing accomplices, most notably Tipu Sultan, and possibly the Mahratha princes.

Although preoccupied with military problems, Wellesley found time to air his views on the long-term future of India. He appreciated its economic value and in one memorandum regretted the Company's failure to modernize and make Bengali agriculture more profitable. He rejected entirely any idea of colonization since while the Hindus 'hold every European in the greatest awe' they would surely react violently against a settler tyranny, and the colonists, like the Americans, might turn against their mother country.

Wellesley wanted as far as possible to preserve the traditional institutions and culture of India. The country's overriding need was for a firm central authority which governed justly. This, as he told his brother, could never come from within:[26]

> They [the natives] are the most mischievous, deceitful race of people I have seen or read of. I have not yet met a Hindu who had one good quality, even for the state of society in his own country and the Mussulmen [Muslims] are worse than they are. Their meekness and mildness do not exist. It is true that the feats which have been performed by Europeans have made them objects of fear; but wherever the disproportion of numbers is greater than usual, they uniformly destroy them if they can, and in their dealings and conduct among themselves they are the most atrociously cruel people I have heard of.

Wellesley's probity was offended by the discovery that 'there is no punishment for perjury' so that 'no man is safe in his person or property, let the government be ever so good'. These pessimistic judgements would be confirmed by Wellesley's experiences between 1800 and 1802, when he was in charge of the pacification of the turbulent western marches of Mysore.

There was, for Wellesley, only one long-term solution to the problems of corruption and anarchy and that was the extension of British government across the entire subcontinent. The British, like the Mughals (the Muslim dynasty which controlled India in the sixteenth and seventeenth centuries) before them, were one in a long line of conquerors of a passive people. 'As for the wishes of the people', he wrote in 1800, 'I put them out of the question: they are the only Philosophers about their governors that ever I met with, if indifference constitutes that character.'[27]

The chance to set the machinery of conquest in motion came in the summer of 1798. Mornington, already persuaded by his brother and others of like mind that a war with Tipu was both unavoidable and much to be desired, received intelligence from Mauritius that the French were planning active intervention in the affairs of Mysore. The previous January, Anne-Joseph Malamarche, the Governor of Mauritius, had responded to a Mysorean embassy with a proclamation calling for volunteers to fight in Mysore. This inept gesture was just what the war party in Calcutta had been waiting for and Mornington ordered the mobilization of the Company's army for the invasion of Mysore. He already had an assurance from Dundas that he would be free to take such a measure once he had evidence of Tipu's collusion with the French.

Back in Britain, the government was troubled by reports of the concentration of French land and sea forces at Toulon under the command of General Bonaparte. By mid-April it was clear that his sights were set on Egypt, which alerted Dundas to the possibility that India was his ultimate destination. His worst fears were confirmed in the second week of June when he received a report from the Abbé de Lisle, a British spy, who had heard from a trustworthy source in Frankfurt that 'the Directory for a long time past employed agents in Persia and India' and that 'measures have been fully concerted' with Zeman Shah, the ruler of Afghanistan, and Tipu, both of whom had been promised French troops for a war against the Company.[28]

On 18 June fresh instructions were sent to Mornington. They warned that Bonaparte had set sail from Toulon on 19 May and at least 4,000 of his men had been earmarked for a landing on the Indian coast. 'A satisfactory explanation' of his conduct must be extracted from Tipu, if necessary through force. If he mobilized, then an immediate attack was to be launched to 'carry our arms into our enemy's country'.[29] When these orders arrived in mid-September, the preparations for the invasion of Mysore were already well under way. This was a war which Wellesley and his brother wanted and the news from England gave them the satisfaction that by waging it they were striking a blow at France.

2

Light and Quick Movements: 1799

In three years, Wellesley fought three wars. The first was against Tipu Sultan; the second was a prolonged series of small-scale frontier engagements against bandits and rebels in Coorg and Malabar; and the third was a three-month pursuit of Daundia Wagh. Each gave him a variety of experience. He took charge of the logistics of the Madras army, commanded a heterogeneous brigade of British, Company and native troops during the invasion of Mysore, and led a small division against Daundia. He was also, as Military Governor of Seringapatam, involved in the everyday business of civil administration and undertook negotiations with local native princes.

He plunged himself into his duties with vigour. His professional dedication was total and no matter was too small for his detailed consideration. Looking back on this period, he felt proud of his energy and application. 'The real reason why I suceeded in my campaigns', he recalled with reference to those in Europe as well as India, 'is because I was always on the spot – I saw everything and did everything for myself.'[1] This taxing principle was learned in India, where he soon became sceptical of the talents of both superiors and subordinates. There were exceptions whom he came to cherish, like John Malcolm, a talented political officer who became his close friend. There were others, too many, of lesser calibre. Men died because of contaminated water supplied to the 33rd by a lazy officer whom Wellesley acidly rebuked, and on the road to Seringapatam he found that one Company officer was 'stupid' and another a 'rascal'. Both needed watching.

Not only did he have to put up with human failing, he had to cope with human vice. Again during the Seringapatam campaign he had to reprove a fellow colonel who had profitably contrived to combine the post of superintendent of the army bazaars with a monopoly of the arrack sold in them. He had to be lectured on the moral boundaries between self-interest and duty.

These revelations were each the result of Wellesley's determination to investigate everything in person. It was sometimes a risky habit: in 1800 Wellesley and another officer ventured into the bandit country of Cotaparamba unescorted.[2] Elers recalled another such hazardous reconnaissance, this time in the territory of a hostile rajah. 'Now, Elers, if we are taken prisoner,' Wellesley remarked, 'I shall be hanged as being brother to the Governor-General, and you will be hanged for being found in bad company.'[3]

In mundane matters Wellesley never wholly trusted the purposefulness or industry of his subordinates. Orders and initiatives were always closely followed up and letters and memoranda poured from his secretaries. Nothing seemed beneath his notice: in the middle of the Daundia campaign he issued specific instructions for the sale by auction of the Company's redundant camels, for the return of elephants loaned by the Nizam of Hyderabad and for the disposal of young, infirm and 'old male unsociable' elephants. A white one was to be retained, presumably for his own use.[4]

What Wellesley had witnessed four years before in the Netherlands had obviously convinced him that, if war was to be waged successfully, it needed methodical preparation in which nothing was left to chance. The experience of India confirmed this philosophy.

Local conditions were such that flawed planning, even in the smallest matters, could lead to disaster. The geography of southern and central India required the Company's armies to penetrate the upland regions through passes or ghats and operate on extended lines of supply and communication. These were always vulnerable to guerrilla warfare and to changes in climate. Ghats and roads became all but unusable and rivers flooded during June and July when the South-West Monsoon was most intensive.

Seasonal transport difficulties added to the problems of supplying food and fodder for men, horses and pack animals. It was impossible for an army to live off the land for while some areas produced a surplus which was exported, others survived on a subsistence agriculture. Crops could be deliberately destroyed, as they were by Tipu when Mysore was invaded, or devoured by marauders, as happened in the vicinity of Poona before Wellesley's expedition there in April 1803. Farmers unlucky to live in the path of armies hid their grain stocks in underground bunkers which could be detected by specially trained natives equipped with iron probes. The dietary prejudices of the Company's native troops further complicated the commissariat. On the eve of operations against the Mahrathas Wellesley had to make provision for men accustomed to eating rice, which was not available locally, and for cavalry chargers with digestions unused to the local variety of grain.[5]

Only with efficient and plentiful transport could these obstacles be overcome and armies survive to fight. In India, transport meant bullocks: after the Mysore campaign had ended, Wellesley concluded, 'It is impossible to carry on a war in India without bullocks.'[6] These creatures had occupied the greater part of his working hours since November 1798 when he had begun the task of arranging the Madras army's commissariat. He had some foretaste of what would be involved because during his voyage from England he had read Captain MacKenzie's exhaustive report of the 1792 Mysore campaign. MacKenzie had drawn up detailed tables of how many bullocks would be required for every department of the army in the field. A six-pounder cannon needed 35 trained draft bullocks to drag it and a further 105 to carry fodder rations and ammunition carts. A twenty-four-pounder siege piece needed 775 in all, and 1,000 cavalrymen (each with his attendant grass-cutter, who gathered fodder for his master's horse) and their horses required 6,000 bullocks. By MacKenzie's computation an army of 80,000 soldiers and camp-followers would have to be served by 1.1 million bullocks.[7]

He probably erred on the side of caution. Even so, one British infantry battalion and its servants was accompanied by 20,000 bullocks during the 1784 Mysore campaign.[8] Bullocks were the sinews of the Company's power and yet, as Wellesley discovered, it kept no stocks of them, so they had to be hired with their drivers from native entrepreneurs.

As well as trawling southern India for bullocks, Wellesley was engaged in other staff duties. In rapid succession, he turned his attention to the possible strategic options open to the invading armies; to measures for withstanding a counter-invasion of the Carnatic or Travancore; and to the resources which would have to be mobilized before the Madras army marched. One of his most important responsibilities was the preparation of summaries of intelligence reports from Company political officers attached to native courts and analyses of climate, topography and the availability of food and fodder along projected invasion routes. He usually confined himself to the reproduction of facts, but sometimes his own ideas intruded: considering how best to resist an attack by Tipu, he proposed organizing local natives into partisan units which could harass the enemy's lines of communication. Indian warfare encouraged a flexibility of tactical thinking which would have been rare in Europe.

Neither the novelty nor the bulk of this work troubled Wellesley and when it was completed in February 1799 he was congratulated by Lieutenant-General Sir George Harris when he took command of the Madras army. When war had first been contemplated the previous July, Harris, a fussy middle-aged officer, had first favoured appeasement and repeatedly cautioned Mornington that mobilisation would take at least six months. He had been right and Wellesley, who had undertaken so much of the donkey work, concluded that the Company would need to overhaul radically its military machine. 'In the wars which we may expect in India in the future, we must look to light and quick movements; and we ought always to be in that state to be able to strike a blow as soon as a war might become evidently necessary.'[9]

The apparatus for delivering the hammer-blow against Tipu had been assembled by the end of January 1799. A swift offensive would be launched by two armies against Tipu's island capital and stronghold, Seringapatam. The larger army of 20,000 under Harris would advance from Vellore, and a smaller of 6,400 under General Stuart would move inland and eastwards from Cannanore. Rapid movement was essential because the first rains of the monsoon, which began in the last week of May, would flood the Cauvery, and Seringapatam would be unapproachable.

The diplomatic preparations, like the military ones, had been successful. In September the Company's agents, playing on the Nizam of Hyderabad's fears of the Mahrathas on his northern frontier, had persuaded him to accept an alliance. The price was the dissolution of his French-officered regiments and a garrison of Company troops in Hyderabad. The coup was brilliantly stage-managed and the French were expelled along with many of the men they had trained. Some found their way into Mahratha service and, still carrying their tricolours, were fighting against the British four years later.

Inside Mysore, Tipu tried to prevaricate in the hope that by diplomacy he could delay the invasion until the onset of the monsoon. A Muslim ruler over a predominantly Hindu state, he was uneasy about the loyalty of those closer to him, and with good reason. One of his cavalry generals, Kumraddan Khan, deserted with a detachment of horse during one engagement and the Company expected others to follow suit. On 27 January Wellesley was among the officers ordered to deal with turncoats who offered their services to the company.[10]

This was his first experience of an Indian campaign. It was conducted on the general principle, rooted in past experience, that success on the battlefield depended ultimately upon the prowess and courage of European troops. They were what Cornwallis had once described as 'the pith and essence' of the Company's army: if there were enough of

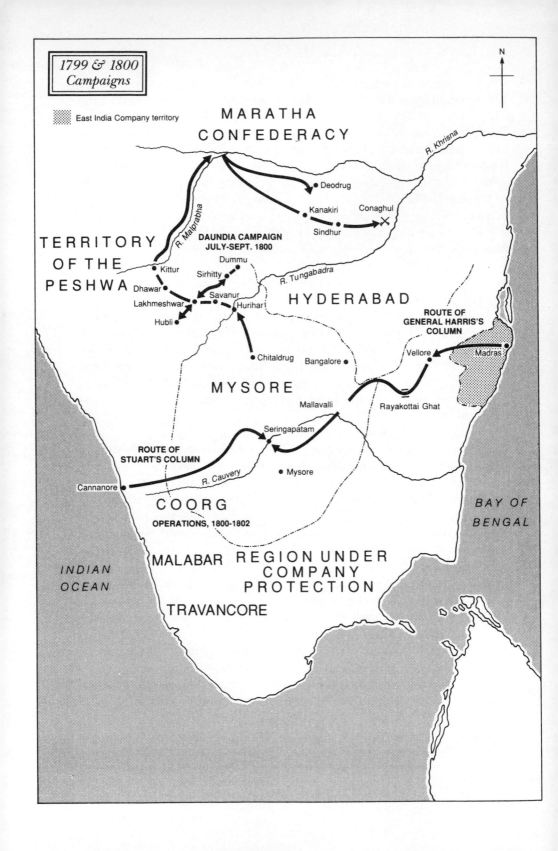

1799 & 1800
Campaigns

░ East India Company territory

MARATHA
CONFEDERACY

R. Khrisna

• Deodrug

Kanakiri   Conaghul
                              ✗
     Sindhur

R. Malprabha

DAUNDIA CAMPAIGN
JULY–SEPT. 1800

TERRITORY
OF THE
PESHWA

• Kittur   Dummu
          Sirhitty
Dhawar•   R. Tungabadra
Lakhmeshwar•   Savanur
                Hurihar   HYDERABAD
Hubli •

                                        ROUTE OF
                                    GENERAL HARRIS'S
                                        COLUMN
• Chitaldrug   • Bangalore   Vellore   Madras

MYSORE

          Mallavalli
                          Rayakottai Ghat
ROUTE OF
STUART'S COLUMN   Seringapatam

Cannanore •   R. Cauvery   • Mysore

                                        BAY OF
COORG   BENGAL
OPERATIONS, 1800–1802

INDIAN
OCEAN   MALABAR   REGION UNDER
                        COMPANY
                        PROTECTION

TRAVANCORE

N

them, fresh and in good health, then victory was certain. Equally important were the British officers who commanded the sepoy battalions. 'The exertions of the Native Corps depend almost entirely upon their officers,' Wellesley observed after a year's campaigning.[11]

European soldiers of all kinds were always in short supply. In 1800 the Company's European regiments were 2,200 men under strength and this deficiency was most acutely felt in that vital arm, artillery, where 700 additional gunners were required.[12] This was in part the consequence of Company policy, which in 1770 forbade natives from entering the artillery, a ban which was extended in 1795 to include Eurasians – many of whom took their skills to the Mahrathas. To this shortfall in recruitment was added the natural wastage of men from heat, fatigue and sickness. It was once estimated that at any given time one in four Europeans in India was unwell or unfit for duty despite the elaborate measures taken to preserve their health.[13]

The rigours of active service, even in the cool season, forced up the numbers of invalids. The muster of the 65th (North Riding Regiment) while serving on the northern front in the 1803/4 Mahratha war fell from 700 to 100 in a few months. As this campaign progressed, the numbers of Europeans fit for action dropped and commanders were forced to depend on the tougher sepoys. Alone they had to bear the brunt of the assault on Agra in October 1803, for as General Lake admitted, 'I cannot spare Europeans.'[14] Nevertheless the hardy came through. Veterans of the Scotch Brigade, whose regiments had seen up to ten years' service in India and fought under Wellesley against the Mahrathas, struck one officer as 'hard as iron, being proof against sun without and arrack within'.[15] They were present when Wellesley entered Poona in April 1803, at which time Colonel Malcolm believed their 'Gaelic addresses will produce an excellent effect', since he believed it was vital that the natives saw 'the essential article of the Feringhees [Europeans]', in other words their fighting men.[16]

There was widespread appreciation of 'Jack Sepoy', as the Company's native soldier was called. The sepoys were drilled by their British officers in the European manner and, on the battlefield, their discipline, weaponry and firepower made them irresistible. At least one of their officers thought them more than a match for European regulars, which was proved in 1811 when they fought the Dutch during the invasion of Java.[17] And yet he qualified this praise by the observation that the sepoys' performance depended solely on the leadership of their officers.

The Europeans, upon whom everything rested, were always vulnerable. No one escaped local distempers. Wellesley suffered a bowel disorder which 'teased me much' on the march to Seringapatam and, in 1801, fell victim to 'Malabar Itch', caused by a parasite which buried itself under the victim's skin. It was cured by bathing in dilute nitric acid. So potent was the solution that Wellesley recalled how it burned his towels.[18] He was physically tough and, even when he contracted the unavoidable campaign infections, he was able, by superhuman willpower, to keep going. As an old man he boasted that he had never missed a day's service in the field through illness and only once had he taken to a sickbed and then as a child with measles.[19]

Given the climate, prevalence of disease (especially forms of diarrhoea or, as it was then known, 'camp fever') and contemporary hit-or-miss cures, Europeans went to great lengths to take care of themselves on campaign. Mountstuart Elphinstone, one of Wellesley's staff during the Mahratha campaign, travelled in a dhoolie (shaded palanquin) carried by native bearers.[20] Like every officer he had plenty of servants; subalterns got by with ten or so and field officers, like Wellesley, had thirty or more. As well as their ménages of cooks, grooms, grass-cutters, sweepers and laundrymen (Elphinstone had a dozen suits of clothing), officers were accompanied by their own flocks of sheep and goats which provided a supply of fresh meat. European rankers were provided with the customary salted beef and biscuit, but fresh meat was also available: over 11,000 sheep followed the army which marched to Poona in March 1803.[21]

Servants were plentiful and cheap in India. Campaign service was attractive since the Company paid good wages and, like the soldiers, servants got their share of the prize money. Servants therefore proliferated on campaigns, as did hordes of camp followers such as prostitutes, arrack pedlars and cookshop proprietors. There were also brinjarries, self-employed, low-caste Hindu rice and grain merchants who served as an unofficial commissariat. Armed against bandits, they were accompanied by their families and possessed their own bullock transport. With their unequalled knowledge of local food markets, they were vital for any army's survival and Wellesley soon learned to put a high value on their goodwill and services.

The swarms of servants, camp followers, drivers and brinjarries gave an Indian campaign a distinctive flavour and atmosphere. For every soldier there were at least ten supernumeraries; when Wellesley's column of the 33rd, ten native battalions and 10,000 horse marched towards Seringapatam it covered eighteen square miles. The movement of such a mass was ponderous and restricted by the heat. The army decamped before dawn and marched from six until midday, covering as much as ten miles if the going was good. Public war attracted private enterprise and it was customary for every column to have its own officially licensed bazaar with stalls selling arrack, dal, chappatis and rice.

The Mysore invasion began on 11 February when Harris's army trundled westwards from Vellore towards the Ryakotta ghat and its entry into the interior highlands. Wellesley commanded the 33rd, which with 869 men was the strongest European regiment.[22]

A week into the campaign, Harris placed him in charge of a brigade which comprised six sepoy battalions and 3,000 Company cavalry, all of whom he rated 'excellent'; four 'rapscallion' battalions from Hyderabad; 10,000 horsemen 'of all nations, some good and some bad'; and fifty cannon. The command had originally been intended for Colonel Aston of the 12th, who had died after a duel, and Wellesley's appointment stirred up some resentment among other officers who felt they had been passed over. Most chagrined was Major-General David Baird, a Scots careerist, who like many others attributed Wellesley's preferment to his brother's influence. What really lay behind this bickering was the knowledge that the higher an officer's field rank the greater was his portion of the prize money. Long after, Wellesley characterized Baird as a courageous but prickly officer who mishandled the natives and was handicapped by a lack of gentlemanly qualities.[23] Also unsuited for command was Mornington, who had lately arrived in Madras with the intention of joining the army. Wellesley warned him off. His vanity and an urge to dominate would have impelled him to meddle and so make Harris's position unbearable.

Tipu's response to the invasion was hesitant and his strategy was confused. His numerous light cavalry burned the countryside through which Harris's and Stuart's columns marched in the hope that they would be delayed for lack of food and fodder. He also proposed to ambush Stuart's smaller detachment as it passed through the Coorg ghats, but missed his opportunity.[24] When he did intercept Stuart at Sedaseer, the half-hearted attack was beaten off.

A similar lack of determination marked attempts to hinder Harris's advance by sudden cavalry attacks. On 9 March Wellesley's contingent came under attack by 2,000 horse, who tried to cut out his baggage train but quickly withdrew under six-pounder and musket fire. Tipu himself took the field at Mallavalli, six miles short of Seringapatam, but his ill-coordinated attack was thrown back without difficulty. Again firepower was decisive: the 33rd displayed its mettle by swiftly deploying into line, unnerving the enemy with steady volley fire and then pressing home the advantage with a bayonet charge. There were only two casualties. As Wellesley noticed, Tipu's offensive was feeble and he neglected to exploit either tactical advantages or the reckless bravery of some of his men.[25] As he dragged his cannon back to Seringapatam he was already beaten in spirit.

On 5 April Harris's army approached Seringapatam. No contact had been made with Stuart's column since 9 March and it was only reopened on 6 April when it was within a day's march of the city.[26] It was imperative to establish siege lines since the monsoon was eight weeks away and Harris had rations in hand only for a further thirty-three days.[27]

Before trenches could be dug and earthworks thrown up for the siege batteries, the area on the south bank of the Cauvery immediately opposite Seringapatam had to be cleared of enemy. On the night of 5/6 April, Wellesley and the 33rd were engaged in these operations. Vague orders, a vaguer reconnaissance of the ground to be fought over and an unfamiliarity with night fighting led to a reverse. Wellesley and some of his men became entangled in a tope (covert) and after confused fighting fell back, losing a dozen men who were taken prisoner and later hideously murdered by Tipu. Wellesley, lightly wounded in the knee, became hopelessly lost and finally made his way back to Harris's tent, where he fell asleep.

His misfortune fuelled some unpleasant gossip, but, exonerating him from any suspicion of dereliction of duty, Baird observed, 'Colonel Wellesley has failed not through want of skill or bravery, but from circumstances.'[28] The following morning a fresh and successful assault in which Wellesley and the 33rd took part was made on the enemy's position.

With the Mysoreans driven back across the Cauvery into Seringapatam, the siege began. As always the besieger's objective was to edge their earthworks closer and closer to the ramparts until the larger cannon could fire at a range of 400 yards, at which distance it was easy to smash open breaches for storming. This stage was reached by 26/27 April after a sustained onslaught in which Wellesley and the 33rd were engaged.

The pressure of time forced Harris to order a massive escalade on 4 May. Baird commanded the assault troops and Wellesley was given charge of the twelve reserve battalions, including eight of Swiss in the Company's service. After several hours of intensive bombardment, two columns, led by sappers with scaling ladders, waded the shallows and rushed the breach. They then fanned out and cleared the ramparts on either side.

The storming parties carried all before them, but there were nervous moments when it was realized that at least 15,000 of Tipu's men were in the inner city. Their presence prompted fears that a street-to-street battle would follow, accompanied by looting and rape. (The ancient customs of war sanctioned such behaviour if a city had fallen to storm, as Henry V had reminded the Governor of Harfleur.) As it was, the remnants of Tipu's army showed no fight and either gave themselves up or fled. By this time Wellesley and his reserve had entered the city to enforce order and assist in the search for Tipu's corpse. It was Baird who discovered the body of the short, plump prince, who in his final moments had taken pot shots at his enemies with a succession of sporting guns.

Forty or so years later, Baird commissioned the Scottish artist Sir David Wilkie to reproduce the scene on a huge canvas which now hangs in the National Gallery of Scotland. It is a splendid piece with Baird, the conqueror of Seringapatam, at the centre of the picture, a rather comely Tipu at his feet, and Wellesley, immediately recognizable by his hooked nose, in the background.

This magnificent painting was belated compensation for Baird. The morning after Seringapatam fell, Wellesley was appointed its military governor. He took up his duties in a characteristically brisk manner which must have vexed Baird, whom he found taking breakfast with his staff. 'General Baird,' he announced, 'I am appointed to the command of Seringapatam, and here is the order of General Harris.' Baird stood and turned to his officers: 'Come, gentlemen, we no longer have any business here.' 'Oh, pray finish your breakfast,' replied Wellesley.

The overthrow of Tipu delighted Mornington. He had added a province to the Company's possession and believed that he had raised its prestige, since he imagined that the Sultan's 'Dreadful fate' would prove a salutary lesson to other princes. For his part he was elevated to the British peerage as Marquess Wellesley and the Company granted him a £5,000 annuity. The French had been confounded and many present during the campaign would have echoed Major Alexander Walker's view that their exertions would 'make a strong impression on the political occurrences in Europe'.[29]

3

Something More Than a Fighting Machine: 1799–1802

Mornington delivered the government of Mysore into the hands of a commission headed by Wellesley. Wellesley was assisted by two experienced and hard-working political officers, Colonels Barry Close and James Kirkpatrick, and two equally dedicated secretaries, Captains John Malcolm and Thomas Munro. Wellesley quickly came to trust their judgement and appreciate their talents; Close in particular he prized as 'the only man I have seen yet who manages the natives properly'. Colleagues and subordinates who fell short of his standards suffered accordingly. Faced with an idle and inefficient engineer officer Wellesley 'badgered him and annoyed him so much' that he resigned.[1]

The commissioners faced an almost overwhelming task. On the civil side, they had to build an administration that would both impose order on Mysore and manage its resources to the Company's profit. On the military side, they were faced with large tracts of western Mysore where the inhabitants rejected any form of outside control and were ready to resist the encroachments of the Company's officials.

Native resistance was probably the greatest of Wellesley's problems and certainly the one which consumed most of his time and energy for the next three years. Throughout this period punitive columns were sent into inaccessible regions to chastise and coerce in what were, in many respects, the forerunners of the small campaigns of pacification waged in every part of the British Empire for the next 150 years. The battle-lines were always the same. On one side stood warrior proconsuls, like Wellesley, who believed themselves the agents of a just, incorruptible government which offered peace and stability. Against them were local rulers who cherished their independence and natives who refused to bow to new laws and jettison traditions such as feuding.

Wellesley, with his powerful faith in an authoritarian but fair system of government, was repelled by what he witnessed during a tour of the troublesome districts of Malabar and Wynad early in 1800. Their inhabitants were 'savage, cruel, and everything that is bad' and their rulers were capricious tyrants. The countryside was overrun by brigands who, like other evildoers, flourished because of the region's remoteness.[2] This, together with a landscape of rugged hills, rivers and often inpenetratable jungle, had hitherto given its inhabitants a sense of immunity from punishment.

What he saw and read in the reports of local political officers convinced Wellesley that these districts needed taming. His methods were those of the Romans and, in time, they became the routine British imperial response to areas of chronic instability. Roads were cut through the wilderness and small forts erected, garrisoned by soldiers who would, at the first sign of restlessness, deliver swift and condign retribution. It was a slow, gruelling and uphill struggle, for resistance was dogged.

Many of those who fought back did so because of an instinctive dislike of all government. One official observed that many who refused to submit to the Company had been its allies during the war against Tipu, but had chosen sides so as to 'establish their independence and not merely for the sake of changing masters'.[3] Others feared that the Company would uproot their customs. During 1800 there were reports that 'ignorant or designing Hindus' were spreading rumours that the Company would soon 'extirpate the castes of the Moplahs'.[4] Tipu, once a resented overlord, was transformed into a hero. Tales circulated that he was still alive and would reappear at the head of a huge army to expel the Company.[5] The story of how, after his death, British officers had clipped his moustaches so incensed some Moplahs that they disinterred and abused the corpse of a British general.

For Wellesley this was clear evidence that he was dealing with wild, credulous races who would come to their senses only after the most severe chastisement. Fear alone was the key to their psyche. He therefore encouraged his subordinates to deal ruthlessly with those whom he considered rebels. In May 1800 he told Colonel Montresor, the commander of a Malabar punitive column, 'The more deserted villages and forage you burn and the more cattle and other property that are carried off the better; and you will find by these little expeditions the confidence of our Native Troops will be increased and that of their opponents' diminished.'[16] Displays of superior strength enforced obedience. 'The people of Malabar are not to be coaxed into submission,' he wrote in January 1802; 'terror, however, will induce them ... to give up their arms.'[7]

However repugnant such sentiments may seem today, Wellesley's assumption that the Company's authority rested on fear alone was essentially correct. Any slackening of its resolve or a setback in the field encouraged resistance and shook the faith of its allies. Native chiefs who had expressed 'the greatest cheerfulness to die in the Company's service' during an expedition against the rebel Rajah of Pyece in August 1802 suddenly lost heart after a detachment had been ambushed and lost 100 dead.[8] Disconsolate, they refused to carry on until sepoy reinforcements arrived.

In his own campaigns against insurgents Wellesley used intimidation freely. When the rebels Daundia's fortress at Dummul was taken in July 1800 he ordered the immediate execution of its governor. A few days later, the garrisons of two smaller forts were massacred after they refused a demand to surrender.[9] At the conclusion of an extended pursuit of the contumacious Rajah of Bullum in February 1802, he and six of his leading adherents were hanged the day following their capture. John Brown of the 2nd Madras Native Infantry, who witnessed the proceedings, excused Wellesley's omission of a trial on the ground that the insurgents had treated British prisoners in the same manner.[10]

By far the most serious challenge to the Company's still fragile authority came from Daundia Wagh, a bold and resourceful Pathan soldier of fortune who had escaped from Tipu's gaol when Seringapatam had fallen. He shifted northwards across the border into Mahratha territory, collecting fugitives from Tipu's army as he went. He survived by plunder and, assuming the title 'King of the Two Worlds' (Heaven and Earth), aimed to establish himself in an impregnable position in the marches between Mysore, Hyderabad and the Mahratha states. Their titular overlord, the Peshwa Baji Rao, lacked the powers to expel him and probably the inclination too, since he was suspected of having given him covert encouragement.

The Company distrusted Daundia and feared his local influence. He tempted its sepoys to desert to his army, was believed to be the mainspring behind the subversion of its new subjects and was seeking the co-operation of its enemies in Malabar.[11] So long as he flourished, he was not only a source of mischief, but evidence of the Company's impotence.

For these reasons, Wellesley sought his brother's permission to enter Mahratha territory and destroy Daundia and his army before they could do any further harm. Even before the campaign had been sanctioned, Wellesley, true to his doctrine of the rapid offensive, began gathering forces at Chitaldrug in northern Mysore. He was travelling there to take up his command when, on 6 June, he received permission to proceed; Daundia was, in Marquess Wellesley's words, to be hunted down, taken and publicly hanged as 'a murderer and robber'.

The expedition to eliminate Daundia was Wellesley's first independent command and he had made the preliminary arrangements with his usual thoroughness. Nevertheless he was taking a gamble since he planned to begin operations during the monsoon season. His cavalry advance guard had an awkward time crossing the Tungabadra and twice his movements were delayed because food supplies had been held up.[12] Still he was full of confidence about the campaign's outcome, telling Munro on 1 July that he need no longer fear Daundia's machinations in Malabar.[13]

The war against Daundia provided an ideal opportunity for Wellesley to test his theory that success in such operations depended on swift movement. In the year since his appointment as military governor of Seringapatam, he had masterminded the transformation of the city into a military base that could equip and supply the field forces needed for short campaigns of pacification. Above all, he had obtained a permanent and reliable source of transport animals, having appropriated Tipu's stock of trained artillery bullocks. With herds of these sturdy white beasts at his disposal Wellesley was released from dependence upon what he once described as 'the corruption, the knavery, and robbery in all native governments'. He also achieved self-sufficiency in transport wagons through the creation of a manufactory managed by an engineer officer. Its activities were closely supervised by Wellesley and it was soon producing twenty carts a month and proved a great saving to the Company, which was no longer forced to pay often excessive hire charges.[14]

Backed by an efficient supply system, Wellesley was free to experiment with tactics of rapid movement. When it was over, he summarized the campaign against Daundia as an exercise in survival rather than a trial of arms. 'The success of military operations in India depends upon supplies; there is no difficulty in fighting, and in finding the means of beating your enemy without or with loss.'[15] In this vindication of his system and foresight, Wellesley was less than generous to his men, whose stamina matched the demands he had made of them. He had under his command two brigades of cavalry, including the 19th and 25th Light Dragoons, three infantry brigades comprising the seasoned 73rd Highland and 77th Regiments and six sepoy battalions, each accompanied by an artillery brigade. As the campaign progressed Wellesley was joined by detachments of Mahratha light horse, who proved a nuisance since they soon reverted to their customary brigandage. On 14 September he complained, 'My Mahratha troops are plundering in all parts of the country and I don't believe there is now a party of five collected in one place.'[16]

The campaign against Daundia was in two stages. The first started on 24 June with the crossing of the swollen Tungabadra, after which Wellesley moved north towards Savanur, where Daundia was reported to have concentrated his forces. Always conscious that his adversary, who was well supplied with light cavalry, could easily have harried his lines of communication, Wellesley systematically occupied every enemy fort along his line of march. On 12 July his army entered a deserted Savanur, where intelligence was received that Daundia was contemplating an offensive. In fact he had just overcome a Mahratha force and, in a mood of elation, made a brief reconnaissance of Wellesley's camp near Savanur. What he saw unnerved him and he hurriedly withdrew to Hubli.[17]

Immediately Wellesley abandoned his baggage and gave chase. By the time he reached Hubli, Daundia was retreating towards the Malprabha. A further rapid march was out of the question as the army was running short of rations and bullocks. Wellesley prudently decided to fall back on Savanur to await the supply convoys. Heavy monsoon rains between 19 and 22 July further delayed him and it was only on the 26th, when the additional bullocks had arrived, that he felt confident enough to continue the hunt.[18]

The second and last phase of the campaign began on 29 July when definite intelligence was received of Daundia's whereabouts. He was at Sondetti and his baggage train was in the process of fording the Malprabha. Wellesley snatched at the chance and ordered a rapid twenty-six-mile dash to cut out Daundia's transport. It took nine hours and the cavalry advance guard swept Daundia's forces into the river, where many were drowned. Large numbers of camels, bullocks and two elephants were captured along with six cannon.

Deprived of much of his baggage, Daundia moved into the open countryside between the Krishna and Tungabadra rivers. By 7 August, Wellesley was proceeding north-eastwards, following the course of the Malprabha. His road was littered with dead and dying people and pack animals and he met a steady stream of deserters, all evidence of Daundia's panic and his army's disintegration.[19] Daundia's destination remained uncertain and Wellesley feared he could turn around, strike at Savanur and 'play the devil' with his lines of communication. To forestall this he sent Colonel James Stevenson with a detachment to Deodrug with orders to block any move that Daundia might take to the north. With the rest of his army, Wellesley swung south through Kanakiri by a series of forced marches. On 8 September he heard that Daundia was close and, it appears, unaware of his latest movements.[20]

Again Wellesley risked a sudden dash. Leaving the infantry to follow at its own pace, he pressed ahead with his cavalry. The following day he heard that Daundia was moving across his line of march, but he was forced to postpone the attack because 'the night was so bad, and my horses so much fatigued'. The next morning, with his infantry and artillery fifteen miles behind, he led his cavalry towards the enemy. Despite desertions, Daundia still had 5,000 horsemen and outnumbered his attackers, but Wellesley had the element of surprise. He deployed his horse into an extended line to prevent their being outflanked and, trusting to 'the determined valour and discipline' of his regulars, he ordered a charge. Daundia's men broke before the moment of impact and scattered, closely pursued by their assailants.[21] Between 600 and 700 were cut down, including Daundia, whose body was later found covered with wounds.

In political and military terms, Daundia's overthrow considerably enhanced the Company's local prestige. And yet elsewhere resistance refused to die down and fresh offensives had to be mounted along Mysore's western frontiers. Wellesley continued to be hard pressed and in August he had confided to Munro his fear that 'the extension of our territory has been greater than our means'.

The preservation of order was only one of Wellesley's responsibilities. He had to give continual attention to a mass of routine administrative matters such as the laying of roads, the repair and construction of barracks, the quality of cloth supplied for tents, and the misconduct of subordinates. He had also to devote time to negotiations with local rulers and to settling the local legal system. Here his conservatism showed itself in his preservation of existing institutions and customs; Company assessors in Muslim courts were instructed to take advice from cadis and in Hindu from pundits. His justice was absolute. When asked whether a rebellious chief should be brought to trial as well as his followers, he replied that it 'would be the worst kind of tyranny and injustice' to allow his immunity from prosecution for offences for which lesser men had been hanged.[22]

Significantly for his own career and the future of the British army, his experience in Mysore persuaded him that army officers made the best imperial administrators. He urged his brother to employ more of them as Collectors (senior revenue officers) in disturbed districts. Thirty years later he argued that every officer should receive an education which prepared him for colonial government. 'An officer must be more than a fighting machine, and should therefore acquire such knowledge and habits of thought as shall qualify him to fill a post with credit to himself and benefit to the public such as governor of a colony ... or magistrate'.[23] This was in keeping with his wider view of the army as a public service and had been the practice in India during his time there. Company officers with ability and vocation learned local languages and, like the excellent Close, gained some insight into the native mind. (Their education in these subjects was commonly assisted by native mistresses.)

Circumstances had forced Wellesley to spend three years as a military administrator. It was time well spent. In the future, he would understand, better than most generals, the vital but tenuous connection between such apparently trifling matters as wagon axles and keeping an army in the field. He mastered the rudiments of routine staff work and realized that precision and diligence in small matters produced success in great.

He had also acted as a colonial policeman, a frontier commander imposing order on chaos. Here experience strengthened convictions already held; he saw at first hand how men deprived of authority reverted to a Hobbesian state of nature and preyed on each other. Without any natural instinct for order or sense of what ultimately was to their advantage, they had to be coerced into submission by a superior force often pitilessly applied. Like most conservatives of his generation he accepted that man was indelibly tainted by original sin and that in consequence his capacity for evil was unlimited. What he witnessed in the lawless regions of India confirmed this view and deepened Wellesley's pessimism about human nature.

4

Wellesley Badahur:
1803–1805

In the field against Daundia, Wellesley had yearned for a chance to strike a crushing blow against the Mahrathas. Their fissile confederation of states was a permanent danger to the Company, providing a refuge for brigands like Daundia and a breeding ground for French-inspired subversion.[1] A collision between the Mahrathas and the Company had been inevitable for several years and for Wellesley it was highly desirable.

The impetus behind the Mahratha war which began in August 1803 was the Marquess Wellesley, who had long hoped for the opportunity to bring the Deccan and the land between the Ganges and the Jumna under the Company's sway. The strategic and political benefits of such a war were obvious: secure overland communications between Calcutta and Bombay; stability in central India; and the emasculation of the Mahratha states, where, the Marquess Wellesley believed, there was still much sympathy for the French.[2]

A crisis inside the Mahratha confederacy gave the Marquess Wellesley the chance he had been seeking. In October 1802 its nominal overlord, the Peshwa Baji Rao, was forced to flee his capital, Poona, after his army and that of his ally Sindia had been beaten by Jaswant Rao Holkar. The Peshwa threw himself on the Company and agreed to submit to its control in return for an army which would retake Poona and restore his authority. Acting in the name of the Peshwa, the Company could legally demand concessions and obedience from even the strongest Mahratha prince.

This same stratagem of turning an impotent figurehead with decayed powers into an instrument of Company authority was adopted towards the Mughal Emperor. He lived in faded state in Sindia's city of Delhi,

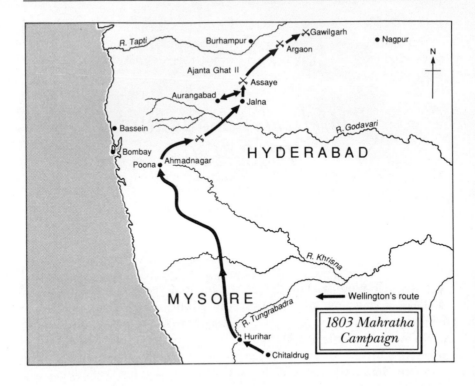

from where the Marquess Wellesley planned to abduct him once the war was under way.[3]

Hijacking the Peshwa's authority was a means to one overriding end, the dissolution of the European-officered and trained armies which had been built up over the past thirty years by Sindia and Bhonsle. Sindia's array was the most menacing: he could muster 26,000 infantry and 199 guns as well as thousands of irregular, sabre-armed light horsemen in quilted tunics who customarily augmented their pay with loot. Wellesley had come across these brigands during the Daundia campaign and thought poorly of them. He also discounted the Mahratha infantry, about which he knew very little. Sindia's included four brigades (campos), each of 4,000 men who had been instructed in European tactics by French, German, Portuguese, American and British officers under the direction of General Perron, who had commanded the Hyderabadi army. Four out of five men in these detachments were armed with flintlock muskets and, unlike the usual Indian matchlockmen, were trained to use the bayonet. Bhonsle had far fewer modern soldiers, about 11,000 out of an army of 25,000 infantry and about 28,000 regular and irregular horse.[4]

On paper these armies represented a continual threat to the Company. As war approached, the Marquess Wellesley insisted that there could be no negotiations until all their white officers had been dismissed and expelled.[5] There were just over 100, of whom the twenty-three Frenchmen were the most feared. It was commonly imagined that they were secret agents of outstanding ability who had been sent out by their government to make mischief. Once the fighting had commenced, proclamations were issued asking them to give themselves up and on 1 November 1803 all those of British birth who had not done so were declared traitors.[6]

The impressive roll-call of the Mahrathas' European-style battalions was misleading. While ignorant of their fighting qualities, Wellesley felt certain that they were serving princes whose resources were unequal to supporting a long war effort. In the end economic power and logistic support systems would tell and the Mahrathas were deficient in both. After three months of fighting, Sindia and Bhonsle were close to exhaustion, the latter on the verge of bankrupcy. Neither had the means to feed and pay his men and the result was a steady flow of desertions, and some soldiers were forced to sell their clothes and weapons to buy food from the army bazaars. To stay alive, soldiers were driven to live off the land, so their army's movements were dictated by the need to find food rather than by the search for strategic advantage. The plundering advance guard of light horse avoided villages which offered protection money, with the result that Mahratha armies often followed serpentine lines of march.[7]

Command of the army which was destined to restore the Peshwa and, if it proved necessary, expel the rebel Holkar from his territories had been given to Wellesley. He enjoyed the rank of major-general and the advancement was welcome after three years during which he had been rejected for a variety of other senior posts. There had always been the pressure of his duties in Mysore and strident objections from older men with longer service (Wellesley was thirty-four in 1803) who insinuated that his brother's influence rather than merit would lie behind his preferment. Baird made a particular fuss in 1801 when Wellesley was in line for command of an expeditionary force being collected for Egypt, where it was to assist in the expulsion of the rump of Bonaparte's army. Baird, who enjoyed some sympathy in the army, got the job and Wellesley, believing himself more talented, felt piqued.[8]

His knowledge of Mahratha politics made Wellesley confident that their decrepit states would collapse swiftly. Like the British, the Mahrathas had grown in power as a consequence of the implosion of the old Mughal Empire. By 1700 they had made themselves supreme over large areas of central and northern India, but now their decline was rapid and terminal, its progress marked by a sequence of civil wars and palace revolutions. The ultimate losers had been the Peshwas, hereditary overlords of the Mahratha sub-states; by 1802 the Peshwa Baji Rao was a cipher, his authority a sham and his treasury empty.

Real power was jealously shared by Sindia, Bhonsle and Holkar. As Wellesley appreciated, their states were politically insecure and sustained by disproportionately strong armies. 'In India ... governments are all weak, and their instruments generally comparatively powerful,' he observed in July 1803, contrasting the gulf between the Mahrathas' military muscle and their ramshackle administrations.[9] Smash the armies and what passed for governments would dissolve. After his victory at Assaye the following September, he interpreted the efforts of Sindia and Bhonsle to recuperate as evidence that their states were dying. 'Their exertions,' he told Munro, 'I fear, cannot last, and yet if they are relaxed, such is the total absence of government and means of defence in this country, that it must fall.'[10]

This prospect worried him. As a soldier he was subject to the Government-General's orders and served as the instrument of policies he devised. He was also, thanks to his day-to-day experience, in an excellent position to assess how far these policies were practical. He had come to believe that they were not and that his brother, far from settling India, was creating conditions which would lead to further instability and conflict. His judgements were those of a soldier who gauged power in straightforward terms of an ability to use force or the threat of it to get one's way. Using this scale, the Marquess had added little to the overall influence of the Company. Instead he had burdened it with a sheaf of treaties and alliances which were hard to enforce and of no real value.

Such agreements as those with Hyderabad, Oude and most recently the Peshwa made the Company an 'object of suspicion to rajahs themselves and odious to their servants'.[11] Moreover, as he discovered during the Mahratha campaign, the Company's stooges were uncooperative. The government of Hyderabad encouraged Holkar's defiance of the Company and its servants obstructed attempts to use forts near Assaye as hospitals for the wounded.[12] Another outwardly friendly state, Jaipur, offered no impediment at all to Holkar when he entered its territory.

Promises meant nothing in a country where, as Wellesley had already noticed, perjury was no crime. Only superior strength counted for anything politically. As Malcolm warned during the negotiations with the Peshwa, the Company was dealing 'with wily scoundrels who do not possess respect even for the most solemn engagements, when they

'A sprig of the nobility': a diffident Arthur Wellesley in the uniform of the 33rd Regiment, *c.* 1795.

Opposite Upstaged at Seringapatam: Sir David Wilkie was commissioned by General Baird to paint his version of the discovery of Tipu Sultan's body in which the General is unmistakably the victor of the siege; Arthur Wellesley is behind and to his right.

Right 'Jack Sepoy': The East India Company's native infantry practise the drill that made them so formidable.

'At them with the bayonet!': Wellesley leads the charge at Assaye.

Above left Richard, Marquess Wellesley, Arthur's wayward but politically influential elder brother.

Above right Viscount Castlereagh: an ally of the Wellesleys who was responsible for Arthur's appointment to the Peninsular in 1808.

Above Lord Liverpool: as Secretary for War and Prime Minister, Liverpool did all in his power to help Wellesley and defend him from his critics.

Right Lieutenant-General Sir George Murray: a brilliant administrative officer who helped mastermind Wellington's intelligence in the Peninsular.

British infantrymen *c.* 1814: an ensign and a colour-sergeant of the 9th (Norfolk) Regiment lead the attack.

British riflemen *c.* 1808: their excellent shooting and fieldcraft made these riflemen more than a match for French light infantry.

British cavalry *c.* 1814: a skirmish between French Hussars and light dragoons; the new dark blue uniforms and shakos sometimes led to these horsemen being mistaken for French cavalry.

Opposite page, top Supply lines: a column of mules moving across country; such trains kept Wellington's armies in the field.

Opposite page, bottom Behind the lines: bivouac in Portugal 1813/14; thanks to Wellington the soldiers had bell tents for their winter quarters.

Busaco 1810: French columns face British volley fire.

Salamanca 1812: Wellington consults with his staff; ADCs hover around ready to deliver orders.

Right Intelligence-gathering *c.* 1810:
British Hussars scouting in the
Peninsular; their fur busbies were
mocked as 'ladies' muffs' and were
extraordinarily uncomfortable when
they became wet.

Above This etching by
Goya, taken from life
during Wellington's stay at
Madrid in the summer of
1812, shows a tired and
strained general.

A Spanish general and his
staff: the appearance and
behaviour of the Spanish
officers amused their
British counterparts who
felt convinced that few
were gentlemen.

conceive that they operate against their interests'. In the end all rested on 'the able application of our forces'.[13] This was exactly Wellesley's position: he warned the government that it was foolhardy to withdraw troops once victory had been secured since their departure would always trigger an upsurge in resistance.[14] His brother's network of semi-independent native states whose rulers accepted Company garrisons and subsidies gave the illusion of power.

There were other, more trenchant criticisms of the Marquess Welles-ley's policies. In March 1802 an Anglo-French peace had been signed at Amiens, although it soon proved no more than a truce for both nations were on a collision course within six months. This was lucky for the Marquess, who was coming under censure at home, where the Company's directors were horrified by the vast debts he had incurred to pay for his expansionist policies. By 1805, when he was recalled, the Company owed £28.5 million, of which two-thirds had been borrowed to pay for the wars of the past six years. Viscount Castlereagh, who had succeeded Dundas as President of the Board of Control in 1802, was also alarmed by the runaway spending, but as the situation in Europe deteriorated, he swung behind the Governor-General.

For the Marquess Wellesley, India's security came before the moans of penny-pinching businessmen in London and the demands of the equally myopic Horse Guards, which wanted to withdraw British troops from the country.[15] He pressed ahead with costly treaties designed to isolate the Mahrathas and unilaterally turned back French troopships which, in accordance with the Treaty of Amiens, were carrying gar-risons for France's tiny outposts on the west coast. Moreover he delib-erately fudged details of his war preparations in the reports he sent back to London. The risk paid off. On 11 September 1803 a four-month-old despatch was received from London informing him that war with France was imminent; it had in fact been declared on 16 May. By the time this news was received, the Mahratha war was a month old and Wellesley was about to close with the combined armies of Sindia and Bhonsle.

Wellesley and his army had left Hurihar for Poona at the beginning of March. His first task was to rally the local chiefs behind the Peshwa and in some cases restore the dispossessed to their property. This required patience and good humour; on one formal occasion, Blakiston was appalled when 'a fat fellow of a chieftain' belched in Wellesley's face. Such 'a savoury eructation' was a mark of goodwill and respect.[16]

The Peshwa needed all the support he could get, so Wellesley had to be careful not to upset local susceptibilities. He expected that the appearance of the Company's army on the road to Poona would force

Holkar into an alliance with Sindia.[17] In fact, Holkar showed no inclination to resist. As Wellesley approached Poona, he withdrew northwards towards the Godavari, taking his loot with him. By late May there were reports that his army was falling apart and being harried in its retreat by partisans from villages which had been ravaged.[18] On 12 July he heard that 4,000 Pathan mercenaries had deserted and a month later Holkar was across the Narmada in his own country.[19]

Wellesley had been in possession of Poona since 20 April, when he had entered the city with an advance guard of cavalry to forestall its destruction by the commander of Holkar's rearguard. Having listened to local chiefs and after meeting the Peshwa, who arrived from Bombay on 13 May, Wellesley realized that the Company had shackled itself to a corpse. Baji Rao was universally detested and his state in ruins.

Nevertheless, Wellesley had been instructed to place the Company's forces behind its puppet and, acting in his name, secure the submission of his overmighty subjects. Holkar had departed, unwilling to challenge the Company, while Sindia and Bhonsle remained with substantial forces near Burhampur and close to Hyderabad's borders. There they heard the Company's terms, laid down by the Marquess Wellesley and delivered on his brother's behalf by Colonel Collins, the Company's resident at Sindia's court. Sindia was asked to submit to the Peshwa's sovereignty, accept the Company's new dominant role in Mahratha affairs, relinquish his European-trained troops and surrender the lands he held between the Jumna and the Ganges. Bhonsle too had to swallow the new order and hand over his province of Orissa. This was effectively an ultimatum, although negotiations dragged on until the first week in August.

In the meantime, Wellesley was deploying his forces for war, even though he felt certain that Sindia would cave in. On 4 June he ordered the army to leave its camp near Poona and move to a position within striking range of Sindia's fortress of Ahmadnagar on the Hyderabad frontier. The troops passed through a region which had successively suffered drought, famine and the ravages of war. Fodder was soon in short supply and thatch had to be dragged from peasants' houses to feed bullocks and horses. The price of conventional fodder spiralled and one junior officer with a personal train of ten bullocks feared he would soon run out of cash.[20] The monsoon was still in full spate; guns sank to their axles in mud and had to be extricated by elephants; and movement was restricted to two or three miles a day.[21]

There was no immediate hurry since Sindia was still prevaricating. If he refused concessions, Wellesley was confident that he had enough men to beat him outright. He commanded the veteran 19th Light

Dragoons and three regiments of Company cavalry together with 5,400 Mysore and Mahratha irregular horse. He was also well provided with infantry: the seasoned 74th and 78th Regiments, six battalions of Company infantry and 16,000 Hyderabad foot. Aware that he might have to launch an offensive before the end of the monsoon, Wellesley had provided the army with light boats made of leather stretched over wickerwork for river crossings and had ordered the construction of a pontoon bridge at the Company's naval dockyard at Bombay.[22]

Negotiations collapsed at the end of July and, having sent Sindia a message in which he blamed his obstinacy for the war, Wellesley moved on Ahmadnagar on 3 August. After a three-day delay caused by heavy rains, the fortress was invested and taken on the 11th, despite fierce resistance by its mercenary garrison. Ahmadnagar cost 160 casualties, but was a valuable gain: its loss deprived Sindia of his only base in the southern Deccan, and it was a district which yielded 634,000 rupees annually (£63,000). It was immediately transformed by Wellesley into a rear base for his operations.

It was unclear at this stage what form these operations would take. His was one of three armies which the Marquess had ordered into the field against the Mahrathas. The largest, commanded by the Commander-in-Chief in India, General Sir Gerard Lake, a hearty sixty-year-old foxhunter, undertook the invasion of the region between the Jumna and Ganges which commenced in the first week of August. A smaller force overran Cuttack and another, of which Wellesley was nominally in command, moved from Bombay into Gujerat.

He and the army in the southern Deccan remained largely in ignorance of events on these other fronts, and his was, to all intents and purposes, an independent command. As his offensive moved into northern Hyderabad, Wellesley became isolated from the rest of India despite the Company's swift postal service. It took ten days for news from Gujerat to reach him, and his messages to Calcutta took a month. A temporary breakdown in cross-country communications prevented him from receiving any intelligence or orders from his brother between 12 September and 3 October.[23]

In the broadest terms, Wellesley's objective was to find Sindia's army and engage it. He therefore moved cautiously northwards towards Aurangabad, rightly anticipating that Sindia would eventually invade Hyderabad. Given that the Mahratha army survived on plunder and would collapse without it, Sindia had no choice but to move into a region which offered rich pickings. This is exactly what happened: in the last week of August Wellesley began to receive reports that Mahratha light horse had passed through the Ajanta ghat and had fanned out towards Jalna, looting as they went.

Intelligence was vital at this and later stages of the campaign. Most of the raw material of Wellesley's intelligence was provided by hurcarras, professional messengers and spies who travelled on resilient and fast camels. One, riding from Holkar's camp where he had seen starving cavalry mounts eating mango leaves, covered over 100 miles in five days.[24] There were drawbacks in relying too much on hurcarras. Company hurcurras, trained to gather military intelligence, could not mingle anonymously among the crowds in a Mahratha camp because they were natives of the Karnatic and stuck out as plainly as Europeans would have done.[25] There was also a tendency for hurcarras to miscalculate numbers and present false reports.

Wellesley's remedy was to fashion a system which was proof against collusion and lying. Three intelligence departments, each directly answerable to him, were created, with their own staff of about twenty hurcarras. Each departmental head cross-questioned his hurcarras and passed on reports to Wellesley, who compared and assessed. Verifiable intelligence which proved accurate earned the hurcarra a generous reward, while the fabricator of bogus information was punished and sacked.[26] There were also amateurs willing to sell information to the highest bidder like 'a fellow by name Mahtab Khan who was formerly in Tipu's service' and afterwards raised horse for Raghuji Bhonsle and who had informed Wellesley about starvation in his master's camp.[27] Wellesley, who spoke some native language, relied on Mountstuart Elphinstone, one of his intelligence department heads, as a translator. On 16 August, the first day of the new system, he ran into difficulties, not knowing the word for shell or being able to translate 'mahtaubel' (blue light) into English.[28]

There was much intelligence about the Mahratha army from Collins, whom Wellesley met at Aurangabad on 29 August. Known mockingly as 'King' Collins, his appearance was droll; he wore a scarlet coat, white breeches, sky-blue hose and 'a highly powdered wig, from which depended a pig-tail of no ordinary dimensions, surmounted by a small round black silk hat, ornamented with a single black ostrich feather'. In all, Blakiston thought, he resembled 'a monkey dressed up for Bartholomew Fair'. Collins had, however, seen the Mahratha army at first hand and warned Wellesley, 'As to their cavalry, you may ride over them wherever you meet them; but their infantry and guns will astonish you.'[29] Wellesley knew the first and dismissed the second, and rode away from the meeting, sharing his staff's amusement at Collins's expense.

By the time of the discussion with Collins, Wellesley had enough intelligence of his enemy's movements to prepare a general strategy. Since 24 August large bodies of light horse had passed through the

Ajanta ghat and were making incursions southwards towards the Godavari. This suggested that a full-scale invasion of Hyderabad was in the
offing and would get underway once Sindia's infantry followed. Moving
across the almost dried up Godavari, Wellesley intended to intercept
this force, sweeping aside the parties of light horse he encountered. This
would require swift marches since he predicted that Sindia would seek
to avoid an engagement. He told Elphinstone that he intended to
abandon his baggage at the end of August, and the young officer
expected a regime of 'hard marching Daundia style'. It was a wretched
prospect for one suffering from diarrhoea and with eyes inflamed by
the dust and hot winds.[30] Wellesley was prepared to push his men to
the extremes of endurance to procure the battle, which, he felt sure,
would conclude the campaign. He set an example of energy by, according to his recollection thirty years later, riding up to fifty miles a day.[31]

For the first fortnight in September he kept his forces in the vicinity of
the Godavari, expecting to meet Sindia's advance. By the 14th, he had
intelligence that Sindia, having heard of his approach, had abandoned
his offensive and was falling back on Ajanta. After waiting for supplies,
Wellesley gave chase on the 21st, moving northwards. Two days later
he proposed to split his army, sending Colonel Stevenson and his
Hyderabad contingent along a parallel route to avoid a blockage at a
pass which lay between him and Sindia's last reported position. Stevenson would use another pass and the two forces would unite on 23
September.[32] The risk seemed minimal. Wellesley kept in close contact
with Stevenson, who was never less than a dozen miles off. Moreover,
he believed that Sindia was thirty miles distant at Bokerdun and
underestimated both the number and quality of the campos present.[33]
As Elphinstone later remarked, 'we knew nothing of the nature of
Sindia's troops'.[34]

Having heard on the 22nd that Sindia had broken camp and was
moving north again, Wellesley pressed ahead. Reliable information
was in short supply: the hurcarras had been unable to penetrate Sindia's
camp and the presence of numerous enemy light horse ruled out a
forward reconnaissance by a British officer. At about eleven on the
morning of 23 September, when he was about to halt and make camp,
Wellesley heard from some brinjarries that sizeable enemy forces were
six miles distant at Assaye. No one seemed clear about their intention:
one report suggested they were retiring, another that their light horse
was about to attack Stevenson. Wellesley decided to see for himself.
Dismounting, he and his staff loaded their pistols, remounted and then
rode to within two miles of Sindia's camp, which Wellesley surveyed
through his telescope.

What he saw was open ground sloping away to a triangle of land within the fork of a river and a tributary stream. Inside this space was the camp of Sindia's army of upwards of 40,000 men, including two campos of 10,000 infantry commanded by a Hessian and a French colonel which were grouped with the artillery nearest to the confluence of the stream and river. Although Sindia's cavalry pickets had already made contact with Wellesley's forces, his army does not appear to have been deployed for action. Mahratha command was irresolute and there was no cohesion between Sindia and Bhonsle. Their army, which hitherto had shunned combat, was in retreat but strong enough not to expect an attack by an outnumbered and outgunned force.

Perhaps for this reason, Wellesley decided on an immediate attack. If he fell back, his baggage would be cut out by the enemy's cavalry and a retreat would severely damage Company prestige. Speed was essential for he still had an element of surprise. He decided to hit the enemy where they were strongest and go for the position on his right where the guns and infantry were concentrated. If these were thrown back, the masses of light horse would flee. Moreover, given his inferiority in cannon, he had to neutralize as many of his adversary's guns as possible in the shortest time.

Leaving his cavalry to screen his front, Wellesley rode back and brought up the infantry and artillery. In the meantime large numbers of Mahratha horse crossed the river to their front and approached the cavalry screen. Then and later they behaved half-heartedly, refusing to charge. With his flank covered, Wellesley deployed his 5,000 infantry (the 74th and 78th and four sepoy battalions), which he led in column towards a ford; later he insisted that 'common sense' dictated the existence of a crossing point close to the village. His instinct was correct but, leaving nothing to chance, he sent out one of his intelligence officers, Captain Johnson of the Bombay Engineers, to investigate. He returned with details of a crossing which would allow the passage of artillery.[35]

As the infantry approached the ford, the Mahratha gunners found their mark and the bombardment intensified; an orderly dragoon trooper riding close to Wellesley was decapitated by one ball, splattering the staff with brains. With 'nerves ... wound up to the proper pitch', the men continued their advance despite awkward delays as the cannon were manhandled across the ford.[36] Once over, Wellesley deployed his infantry and guns in two lines, facing their opponents' flank. Their own were protected by the river and stream.

Such a manoeuvre under fire might have been enough to unnerve a conventional native army, but the Mahratha campos, who knew their drill, swung round to meet the threat and their gunners realigned their pieces. This display astonished Wellesley and those of his staff who had mocked Collins's assessment of the Mahratha army. Worse followed; the Mahrathas opened at close range with grape and chain shot, cutting down artillery bullocks and gun crews. Rather than fight and probably lose an unequal artillery duel, Wellesley, by now 'very impatient', ordered a general advance.

What followed was described by Elphinstone as a 'suicidal' frontal attack against 'the Divil's own cannonade'.[37] Outgunned, Wellesley's only hope lay in the discipline and courage of his men, who would have to cut their way through the enemy with bayonet and sabre. Volley fire, which traditionally won battles against native armies, was valueless against larger numbers who could respond in kind, so the head-on charge was the only answer. Colin Campbell of the 78th was amazed that his men pushed on 'without firing two rounds'.[38]

Such an attack depended on momentum and this was sustained by Wellesley himself. Of equal, perhaps greater, importance was his ability to recognize and instantly exploit whatever advantages came his way. At first the attack succeeded and, after hard fighting, the Mahratha first line was overrun. At this stage things began to go wrong. The remnants of the 74th, on the flank next to the village of Assaye and heavily depleted by cannon fire, were in peril of being ridden down by Mahratha horse. They were saved in the nick of time by the 19th Light Dragoons whom Wellesley had placed close by, ready for such an emergency. His foresight and the dragoons' courage saved the day, although, as many troopers discovered, their sabres were blunt from repeated drawing and sheathing on the parade ground.

The cavalry had averted disaster on Wellesley's right, but the 74th, now down to half their strength, could not continue unaided. Matters were healthier on the left, where the Mahrathas were crumbling, so Wellesley took charge of the 78th and led them to the right. Despite the tenacity of some Mahratha gunners who, having feigned death, sprang to life and turned their cannon on the backs of the British, the reinforcements tipped the balance. Severely mauled in the hand-to-hand fighting, the Mahratha infantry retired across the stream. This was a signal for the masses of Mahratha cavalry to withdraw; it appears that Sindia and Bhonsle had departed somewhat earlier.

Wellesley's leadership rather than his tactics won Assaye. 'I never saw a man so cool and collected as he was the whole time,' wrote Campbell. 'No man could have shown a better example to the troops than he did.' His personal courage certainly inspired: leading from the front he once nearly blundered into the enemy line and he had been unhorsed twice. Immediately after the battle, he believed that his favourite charger Diomed had been 'piked', but somehow it survived and was later recovered 'in a sad condition' from Sindia's camp.[39]

On one level, Assaye had been a triumph for Wellesley. He had shown he could command in action and by his quickness of mind had snatched victory from defeat. Previously, as he admitted on several occasions, his generalship had been distinguished only by his prudent husbanding of resources. And yet, as the details of the action became known, there was some criticism of his offering battle in such adverse conditions. His decision to fight had undoubtedly been taken in ignorance of the sort of army he was about to engage, but had he backed off, the political consequences would have been disastrous. It was axiomatic that the Company always held the initiative and never flinched in the face of its native enemies. The cost of prestige was high. Just over 2,000 men, a third of Wellesley's force, were killed or wounded during three hours of fighting. Casualties among officers were very high, evidence of how faithfully they followed their general's example of personal leadership; of the 74th's 135 dead, eleven were officers.

Assaye was decisive. Mahratha losses were not totalled, but they had abandoned just under 100 cannon, and the bulk of their ammunition and powder had been destroyed by retreating gunners. The detritus of Sindia's and Bhonsle's forces fled northwards, following their leaders, towards the Ajanta ghat, and Wellesley commanded Stevenson and the Hyderabad contingent to harry them. On 16 October Stevenson took Burhampur and then besieged Asirghar, the last of Sindia's Deccan strongholds. Here nine European mercenaries and four professional gunners gave themselves up.[40] By now news was reaching this region from the north, where Lake had been winning spectacular victories. In eight weeks he had taken Aligarh, Delhi and Agra and had defeated a Mahratha army at Laswari. Early in the campaign, General Perron had thrown in the sponge and his example was being followed by more and more of his fellow mercenaries.[41]

The need to take care of the wounded restricted Wellesley's movements for several days after Assaye. There was also a fear that Sindia, who still possessed substantial forces, could turn southwards and use his horse to play havoc with British communications, so during the first week of October Wellesley fell back to cover Aurangabad. This caution was unnecessary; Sindia was beaten and his only wish was to salvage something from the wreckage of his defeats. On 10 November his vakils (ambassadors) asked for an armistice, which was arranged on the 24th.

With Sindia out of the contest, Wellesley felt free to delivery a hammerblow against his accomplice, Bhonsle, who was retreating north-eastwards towards his own territories. He turned at bay on 28

November and deployed his army in battle array on open ground six miles from Argaon. Wellesley observed the position from a village watchtower three miles off and immediately decided to attack, even though it was mid-afternoon.

It took a further three hours for the Company's army to form up. Again it was outnumbered and forced to advance into heavy fire from forty well-handled cannon. The battalions in the centre faltered and fell back and would not be rallied by Wellesley – memories of the cannonade at Assaye were still vivid. Undismayed, he rode after the retreating battalions and ordered their officers to herd them to a nearby village, where under cover they could reform. When the offensive restarted, Wellesley instructed his men to lie down to avoid cannon fire.

As the attack was pressed home, the Mahratha cavalry broke and their example was followed by the infantry. Fortunately for Wellesley, the will to fight was even weaker in Bhonsle's army, which had been drained by desertions. Elphinstone, keen to get to grips with a foe, joined the Company's horse, but when he reached the enemy lines he found no one to fight. 'I saw nobody afterwards but people on foot, whom I did not think it proper to touch. Indeed there is nothing very gallant in attacking routed and terrified horse, who had not the presence of mind either to run or to fight.' Undistracted by the enemy, 'I was at pains to see how the people looked, and every gentleman seemed at ease as much as if he was riding a-hunting.' Wellesley would have approved, even though the day's sport ended with cries of 'Gone away!' since the quarry was in pell-mell retreat.

The chase was kept up until 6 December, when Wellesley invested Bhonsle's fortress of Gawilgarh, held by a garrison of 8,000. Twelve-pounders made no impression on the walls, so the besiegers had to wait for Stevenson, who brought up four eighteen-pounders and a howitzer. This arrived on 12 December and three days later a breach was made and the fortress was stormed. Nearly all the defenders were killed, including two of Bhonsle's generals, who had ordered their wives and daughters to be put to death rather than suffer ravishment. This was a local custom of war which was justified on this occasion since the city was ferociously plundered and its inhabitants abused in defiance of Wellesley's orders.[42]

By now Sindia and Bhonsle were desperate to submit; both were facing bankruptcy and their armies were hungry, unpaid and mutinous. Bhonsle asked for terms on 16 December and a fortnight later Sindia signed a peace treaty. Each surrendered his political independence, agreed to be guided by British political residents, dissolved the campos and signed alliances with the Company. There were also territorial concessions, the most considerable being Cuttack, which deprived Bhonsle of nearly half his annual income.

The Marquess was jubilant at 'the glorious (I must say magnificent and noble) result of operations' and praised his brother's skill as a negotiator.[43] Two powerful princes had been reduced to ciphers and the balance of power in India swung decisively in the Company's favour. Annexations in the north gave it control over a broad strip of land which connected Bengal to Bombay, and possession of Cuttack linked Bengal to Madras. The landlocked rulers of central India were now held in an iron grip and bound to the Company by unequal treaties.

Unlike his brother, Wellesley was in sombre mood. Malcolm, well supplied with beer and wine from Bombay, joined him towards the end of December and found his normally convivial table rather subdued.[44] The treaties he had imposed at gunpoint had, in his view, given the Company the phantom of power and were bound, in the future, to engender further strife. Moreover, Wellesley was soon aware that his brother's grandiose schemes were the subject of sharp criticism in Parliament, where the Directors' spokesmen were asking whether the political gains were really worth the enormous outlay of borrowed money. There were also well-founded suspicions that the Governor-General was behaving as if he was his own master and deliberately misleading the Directors and the government. As a result Marquess Wellesley's political support at home was withering. News of these developments reached Arthur in January 1804 in a letter from his brother Henry which reported a conversation between him and the new Prime Minister, Henry Addington. Addington, who had formerly been counted an ally, suggested that it would be prudent for the Marquess to resign and return home. Wellesley agreed and tried to persuade his brother to follow this course rather than face dismissal and disgrace.[45]

The Marquess, intoxicated by his success and hungry for more, ignored this advice and went ahead with fresh plans for expansion. He pressed Malcolm, now attached to Sindia's court as resident, to demand the surrender of the fortress city of Gwalior. Malcolm, backed by Wellesley, refused. Such a request could not be justified legally and would blemish the Company's reputation for fair-dealing. Wellesley regarded the business with distaste and feared that his brother had fallen victim to 'the demon of ambition'.[46] Worse still, the governors of India were succumbing to the amorality of those they ruled. 'I would', he wrote,' sacrifice Gwalior or every frontier in India ten times over, in order to preserve our credit for scrupulous good faith; and the advantages and honour we gained by the late war and the peace.'[47]

The matter was settled with Sindia keeping Gwalior, but not without a tantrum from the Marquess. 'Mr Malcolm's duty is to obey my orders,' he insisted. '*I* will look after the *public's* interest.'[48]

Wellesley was now keenly aware of his brother's flaws. His purblind arrogance and rashness threatened not only his own but his family's reputation. Discredited in India, the Wellesleys would find the path to advancement at home blocked. Hitherto relations between the two brothers had been cordial. When, after the division of the Mysore spoils, Arthur had offered to repay the sum he had been advanced by pay for his lieutenant-colonelcy, his brother generously refused. He now had enough money for his present and future needs and advised Arthur to put his cash in the Company's 8 per cent Loan Stock.[49] A coolness followed after the Marquess had given way to pressure and chosen Baird for the Egypt command rather than Arthur. By the beginning of 1804, familial loyalty was stretched almost to breaking point when it seemed obvious that the Marquess was riding for a fall.

The Marquess Wellesley finally overreached himself in April 1804 when he declared war on Holkar, the Mahratha prince who had so far stayed neutral. The subsequent war went badly for the Company: Colonel Monson's column, which attempted to penetrate Holkar's territory during the monsoon, was roughly handled and forced to retire on Agra. Holkar then took the offensive against Delhi, which was unsuccessfully besieged. In January 1805 an attempt to restore the Company's prestige ran into difficulties when Lake found himself bogged down in the siege of Bharatpur and suffering heavy losses. Reports of these disasters convinced Pitt that the Marquess would have to be recalled and replaced by the veteran Cornwallis.

Wellesley played a passive role in this war. He remained in Mysore, keeping a watchful eye on the Company's new and unwilling allies, Sindia and Bhonsle. Since April 1804 he had been contemplating a return to England, where he imagined he would find an outlet for his talents. Moreover he had every reason to expect preferment since his Indian campaigns had established his reputation as a commander. News of Assaye had been published on 30 March 1804 when *The Times* proclaimed it a victory equal in importance to Plassey. His despatches and further details of Assaye and Argaon were announced over the next three weeks, and drawing on these, *The Times* noted that Wellesley's 'active spirit was conspicuously displayed wherever the battle raged'.[50] Official recognition of his generalship and diplomacy came at the end of August when he was made a Knight of the Bath – the announcement reached him in February 1805. A month later he sailed from Calcutta.

After Assaye the Indian soldiers had called him Wellesley Bahadur (Wellesley the Champion).[51] He had won the title by his resolution and courage on the battlefield, although in his correspondence he attributed his victories to the painstaking supervision of transport rather than tactical genius or charisma. And yet his leadership, in particular his clear-headedness and calm, deeply impressed his subordinate officers. Versions of his conduct at Assaye and Argaon circulated in Britain and did much to enhance his standing. In September 1806, Grenville wrote that he held a 'very high opinion of his talents and military knowledge and particularly of his prowess in exciting spirit and confidence in his troops which I have heard so very strongly stated by indifferent persons'.[52] Such admiration was never universal; three years later General Lord Moira dismissed Wellesley as 'a very gallant and gentlemanlike fellow, but very limited in talents'.[53] Such remarks were tinged with jealousy and coloured by wider animosity towards the Wellesleys.

For Wellesley the lessons he learned in India were invaluable. He admitted leaving the country knowing all that he needed to know about the waging of war and his Indian experience guided him throughout the Peninsular campaigns, especially in matters of transport and intelligence. Of equal, perhaps greater, importance was his intimate understanding of the ways in which geographical, economic and political considerations affected the conduct of war. He had been soldier, administrator and diplomat, and in the last capacity, had earned himself a somewhat dubious reputation, at least on the continent. In 1815, General von Gneisenau warned Count von Müffling to be wary when dealing with him since 'by his transactions with the deceitful Nabobs, this distinguished general had so accustomed himself to duplicity, that he had at last become such a master in the art as even to outwit the Nabobs themselves'.[54] So much for Wellesley's lofty view of himself as a paragon of probity and honour!

Wellesley the man had his inner misgivings about human nature confirmed in India. Although full of admiration for the sepoys, he had little but contempt for their countrymen. Everywhere he saw moral depravity and chaos, which could be checked only by superior physical force; 'It would not do to carry liberal principles to India,' he once insisted.[55] On the boundaries of Mysore and elsewhere he had seen the melancholy consequences of the collapse of an ordered society. The powerful basic and natural human impulses of greed and destructiveness took control and the result was chaos. As he saw it this law of nature was ever present and, in his imagination, he detected its primeval forces just below the surface of British society. 'The people are rotten to the Core,' he wrote in 1831, when Parliamentary reform was impending. 'They are not bloodthirsty, but they are desirous of Plunder. They will plunder, destroy and annihilate all Property in the Country. The majority of them will then starve. ...'[56] This was the chilling sequence of events he had seen for himself during the winter of 1802/3 after the Mahratha civil war.

While he was repelled by such explosions of instinct, he believed that little could ever be done to change or eradicate them beyond constant coercion. In fact he did everything he could to preserve Indian society and its customs, for his conservatism was too deep-rooted for him ever to contemplate the wholesale reforms needed for regeneration. In this he differed from his brother, who, prompted by humanitarianism, had attempted to suppress suttee (the Hindu ritual of burning widows on their husbands' funeral pyres), and from the next generation of warrior proconsuls who arrived in India full of liberal ideas and with a burning desire to remodel the country's institutions along British lines. And yet, like them, he believed that it was Britain's destiny to conquer and rule the entire subcontinent. This conviction, acquired during his eight years' service in India, remained strong throughout his life. It meant that after 1818, when he re-entered British politics, officials who adopted forward, annexationalist policies and generals anxious to impose order on restless frontiers would never lack an influential ally and protector in London.

Part Four
1805–1808

1

An End to the Old World: 1805–1808

Wellesley returned to England in the spring of 1805. He was thirty-six and now able to settle his old debts including £14 2s 1d (£14.12) owed to a Dublin tailor since 1795.[1] His future prosperity and advancement were by no means assured; he had distinguished himself in what was commonly regarded as an Indian sideshow, but there were a further 146 major-generals on the army list, most of them senior to him, and, since the government was waging war by subsidizing continental allies, there was no immediate prospect of an active command.

Faced with a period of inactivity, Wellesley re-entered politics. Assisted by Lord Grenville, who had become Prime Minister on Pitt's death in January 1806, he secured the handful of votes needed to become MP for Rye. Nine months later he switched to the tiny Cornish borough of Mitchell, for which he paid its owner £4,000. In the general election of April 1807 he was returned for Newport on the Isle of Wight, where the two dozen electors were bought off for less than £1,000.[2]

His family's rather than his own interests were served by these transactions. Once in the Commons, Arthur joined his brother William in defending the Marquess against charges of irresponsibility and dishonesty during his period as Governor-General of India. Criticism of the Marquess had first been voiced publicly in 1804 and, by the beginning of 1805, it had reached such a pitch that Pitt was forced to demand his recall.

When the Marquess returned home early in 1806 he was brimming with confidence and unshakeable in his conviction that everything he had done in India had been in the national interest. He told Grenville that the clamour of his accusers was 'quite tedious to me' and, suffering another bout of ill-health, he left his brothers to silence his traducers. The most persistent was James Paull, a former Bengal merchant, who charged the Marquess with corruption. He was backed by a number of Whigs and Radicals who were keen to disgrace the Wellesleys and discredit their political allies. As it was, the Wellesley clan survived unscathed because their friends stayed loyal, although the suspicion generated by Paull's charges was strong enough to keep the Marquess out of the cabinet for some time.

Arthur had been quick to defend his brother's integrity and policies, despite his inner misgivings about their effectiveness. He had canvassed Pitt three times and found him sympathetic. Their conversations extended to the conduct of the war and Pitt was much impressed by the young General's grasp of the complexities of political and military affairs. After one encounter he predicted that Wellesley would be the general 'on whom the preservation of Europe would depend'.[3] At that time Britain's and ultimately Europe's survival depended on Lord Nelson, whom Wellesley briefly met at 10 Downing Street in September 1805. He recalled that the Admiral talked effusively 'all about himself' in 'a style so vain and so silly as to surprise and disgust'. On discovering his listener's identity, Nelson shifted his tack and reviewed the current state of Europe 'like an officer and a statesman'.[4]

During the winter of 1805/6 Wellesley took time off from politics and renewed his courtship of Kitty Pakenham. They married on 10 April 1806 in St George's church, Dublin, and settled in an elegant town house in Harley Street, Marylebone, then an expanding and fashionable London suburb.

It was a wretched marriage which Wellesley later repented. He recalled its circumstances and melancholy aftermath to his confidante Mrs Arbuthnot in June 1822. In India he had all but forgotten Kitty Pakenham, although there can be little doubt that his self-esteem had been bruised by her father's rejection of him as unfit to marry his daughter. Relations were reopened by a self-appointed and forceful matchmaker, Lady Sparrow. Her line of attack was aimed at Wellesley's conscience, since she told him that Kitty had spurned all suitors since his departure.

Wellesley remained lukewarm about the marriage, but once back in England he succumbed to intensive persuasion. Sixteen years later he was still bewildered by what he had done. 'Would you believe', he asked Mrs Arbuthnot, 'that anyone could have been such a damned fool? I was not the least in love with her. I married her because they asked me to do it and I did not know myself. I thought that I should never care for anybody again, and that I should be in the army and, in short, I was a fool.'

The extent of his folly soon became painfully evident. Ten years in India had transformed the hesitant, impoverished major into an industrious professional soldier with a commanding knowledge of and passionate interest in public affairs. His bride was unchanged and never attempted to accommodate herself to what her former lover had become. According to Mrs Arbuthnot he complained, 'She did not understand him, and she could not enter with him into consideration of all the important concerns which are continually occupying his mind, and that he might as well talk to a child.'

What made matters worse was that she entertained an exalted view of her own intelligence and was indifferent to her husband's. The intellectual gulf between them was so great and her conversation so trying that whenever possible Wellesley avoided her and looked else-where for congenial female company.[5] Two sons were born before 1809 and for the next five years Wellesley remained in Portugal and Spain. He never invited his wife to join him nor – and this would have seemed to him a gross dereliction of duty in any case – did he contemplate home leave.

Kitty Pakenham died in 1831, aged fifty-three, and Wellesley never remarried. To compensate for an unappreciative wife and a house which she made 'so dull', he deliberately cultivated a circle of intelligent women, often safely married like Mrs Arbuthnot. He regretted this banishment for, as he confessed to Mrs Arbuthnot, 'his tastes were domestic' and he had expected 'a home where he could find comfort'.

The denial of private pleasures and relaxation affected the per-formance of Wellesley's public duties. Without domestic distractions he could allow national and international affairs to become the focus of his life. As the details of his unhappy private life became known, they added to the public image of an austere, lonely man wholly dedicated to his country's service.

Ambition and the realization that he would not enjoy a satisfying or comfortable family life encouraged Wellesley to seek a foreign command during 1806/7, although few were available.

It was a period during which Napoleon enjoyed a monopoly of both initiative and success. When Wellesley had returned home in 1805, the threat of invasion was still strong and remained so until August, when the Grande Armée abandoned its Boulogne camp and marched into Germany. The battle of Trafalgar in October confirmed British naval supremacy and fears of invasion faded. French supremacy on land was spectacularly proved by victories over the Austrians, Russians and

Prussians at Ulm, Austerlitz, Jena-Auerstadt and Friedland. This last battle, in June 1807, convinced Czar Alexander I to withdraw from the conflict and a few days later he signed a peace treaty with Napoleon at Tilsit. The French Emperor was now master of Europe.

Britain had been the allies' paymaster throughout this period, underwriting their armies' wage bills and supplying them with weaponry. This had been Pitt's policy and it rested on the assumption that Napoleon could be overcome only by the mass armies of the continental powers. Russian, Austrian and Prussian manpower, which was far greater than Britain's, could be conscripted and armed by British gold. The trouble was, as Napoleon demonstrated, that size alone was not the measure of an army's effectiveness: French speed of concentration, organization, leadership and tactics were infinitely superior to their adversaries'.

The campaigns of 1805–7 gave Napoleon the political power to wage economic war against Britain by throttling all commerce between her and Europe. The prospect of the embargo was chilling; after hearing of Jena-Auerstadt, Lord Fitzwilliam concluded, 'There is an end to the Old World, we must look to the New.' This was Wellesley's view and he enthusiastically joined an influential lobby of businessmen, soldiers and sailors who pressed for the conquest of Spanish America, where Britain would find markets which would more than compensate for those lost in Europe.

At first the outlook had seemed promising. In June 1806 a small-scale amphibious operation by forces from the Cape had secured Buenos Aires and triggered spasms of excitement among London's merchants, who expected quick fortunes, easily made. The bubble soon burst: despite reinforcements from the Cape and Britain, the army was in severe difficulties and suffered reverses at the hands of local nationalist insurgents who did not want Spanish colonial government replaced by British. Final collapse came in July 1807 when the criminally incompetent General Whitelock was trounced at Buenos Aires.

Wellesley had been gripped by the general enthusiasm for a South American empire. In September 1806 he had been proposed as commander of forces earmarked for the River Plate, but William Windham, the Secretary for War, warned Grenville that the appointment, while 'proper' in that Wellesley was well qualified, would arouse the jealousy of other generals.[6] Hopeful that he might secure command of an army in another American theatre, Wellesley set about producing sheafs of memoranda in which he detailed plans for the invasions of Mexico and Venezuela.[7] He stressed opportunities for profit, but argued against any co-operation with local patriots who were, of course, in arms against their legitimate king, Ferdinand VII. Most significantly, Wellesley suggested ways in which existing colonies' assets could be exploited in these operations: Indian troops could reinforce the Mexican expeditionary force having been shipped across the Pacific by way of the new Australian settlement at Botany Bay. Additional native units, vital in a climate where Europeans perished in large numbers, would be recruited from the West Indies sugar plantations. If insufficient Negro free men volunteered, then slaves, purchased at £80 a head from their owners, would make up the shortfall.[8]

All these schemes came to nothing. By the summer of 1808, after setbacks on the River Plate and in response to developments in Europe, the government shed all plans for conquest in South America. This was a disappointment to Wellesley since Grenville had been inclined to offer him command of the Indian contingent destined for Mexico.[9] Nevertheless his carefully prepared and well-argued operational plans had impressed ministers and enhanced his reputation as an energetic and capable general.

Deprived of an operational command, Wellesley decided in April 1807 to concentrate on his political career. He accepted an offer from the new Prime Minister, the Duke of Portland, to join his ministry as Secretary for Ireland. Wellesley was guided by friendship and a sense of public duty. 'I am no party man,' he told General Sir John Moore over a year later, 'but have long been connected in friendship with many of those persons who are now at the head of affairs in England.'[10] Among these were two close confidants of similar age and outlook, Robert Stewart, Viscount Castlereagh, another young son of an Anglo-Irish aristocrat, and Robert Jenkinson, Lord Hawkesbury, who is better known as Lord Liverpool, the title he assumed in 1808. The trust and goodwill of both men were invaluable to Wellesley. Castlereagh, who had served as Secretary for War in 1805/6 and again from March 1807, respected his judgement in strategic matters and had confidence in him as a commander.

And yet, as Wellesley was well aware, such connections were not without drawbacks. Shortly before taking office, he had approached the Commander-in-Chief and asked whether acceptance would jeopardize his army career. York was reassuring and told him that 'instead of being a prejudice to my profession, it will be considered as giving me extra claims to employment'.[11]

This was polite, but misleading. As Wellesley knew, there was a substantial and durable body of envious and ageing senior officers who, in conjunction with his political enemies, raised continual objections to his advancement. His success never purged their malice. When his promotion was under consideration soon after his spectacular victory at Salamanca in 1812, Colonel Sir Henry Torrens, York's Military

Secretary, found that old rancour was still strong. After extensive enquiries he discovered, much to his dismay since he admired Wellesley, that promotion 'would serve to embarrass him ... by reviving the jealousy which certainly had been felt by Senior Officers upon his advancement to command disproportionate to his standing'. There was, he noted, counter-pressure from Lord Liverpool, then Prime Minister, and the Wellesley family.[12] A further handicap for Wellesley was George III, who regularly meddled in army matters, on which he fancied himself an expert, measuring fitness for command according to age rather than proven ability.[13]

It was Castlereagh's influence which secured Wellesley's appointment to command a brigade in the Copenhagen expedition that was being mustered at the end of July 1807. The campaign had been forced on the government by a clause in the Tilsit agreement by which Alexander I undertook to sponsor an anti-British Baltic League that had been formed as part of Napoleon's trade war. Denmark, directed by its pro-French Crown Prince, joined this association, and the cabinet, alarmed that the Danish fleet might slip into French hands, demanded the ships' surrender. If negotiations failed, which they did, a *coup de main* was to be launched against Copenhagen.

In today's language the Copenhagen campaign was a surgical operation which required meticulous planning and swift movement. Neither were much in evidence during the four weeks of fighting. On 14 August, when Lord Cathcart, the commander of the land forces, joined the flotilla of transport and men-of-war which been gathering off Helsingör (Elsinore) for the past week, he knew next to nothing about the Danes' strength or intentions.[14] One fact soon became clear: the Danes would fight rather than relinquish their fleet and for some time had been mobilizing their militia. 'Bloody work' was predicted by Captain Alexander Gordon of General Baird's staff.[15]

Wellesley, whose transport HMS *Prometheus* had been one of the first ships to heave to off the Zealand coast, was almost immediately conscious of Danish anger. 'We are very unpopular in this country,' he told Lord Hawkesbury. Local resentment added to the problems of the campaign: it was hard for commissaries to buy provisions, and cavalry patrols found villagers deaf to requests for information.[16] The enemy benefited for, after one skirmish, two Danish prisoners were found in possession of full and detailed accounts of British positions, intelligence that could have come only from local spies.[17] The situation around Copenhagen was the reverse of that which Wellesley encountered a year later in Portugal, where a friendly population swamped him with intelligence about the French.

Cathcart's battle-plans were simple and largely forced on him by political circumstances. His engineer officers had warned him that Copenhagen's landward defences could not be breached without a siege train, which the British lacked, and were too strong to be stormed. The only option open was a close-range, intimidatory bombardment by cannon, mortars and Congreve rockets supported by broadsides from Admiral Gambier's battleships. Shattered buildings and fires started by the rockets' incendiary warheads (which had proved highly effective at Boulogne a year before) would, it was believed, force the Danes to submit.

The 16,000-strong army disembarked at Vedboek on 16 August. Wellesley's brigade was first ashore and secured the beachhead by occupying the rising ground beyond the small port. By mid-morning the entire force had landed and was marching towards Lyngby, which was taken in the afternoon. Five days later Copenhagen's suburbs had been captured and the city was invested. During this time, Wellesley's brigade had been detailed to guard lines of communications northwards to Helsingör and fill a gap in the besieging lines caused by the delayed arrival of the King's German Legion.[18]

From 22 August Wellesley's brigade was solely concerned with the defence of British lines from surprise attack from the rear, the breaking up of concentrations of Danish forces inland and the interception of supply convoys on their way to Copenhagen. It was a force well suited to its task. Wellesley commanded three battalions of light infantry, the 43rd, 52nd (Oxfordshire Light Infantry) and 95th Rifles together with the 92nd Highlanders, a Royal Horse Artillery battery, some light foot batteries and some squadrons of Hanoverian Hussars. All were well-trained, excellent troops and, in the case of the cavalry and light-infantrymen, highly mobile and accustomed to operate in small units.

Their skills and their general's were well tested during the next fortnight since the Danes, lacking the numbers needed to dislodge the invaders, were determined to hamper their operations by lightning raids. Keeping the enemy at arm's length needed an efficient cavalry screen and fast counter-movements by light infantry backed by artillery. The same flexibility and rapid cross-country marches which had been the keys to Wellesley's survival in India served him well in the country-side beyond Copenhagen.

On 26 August, after hearing from his cavalry patrols that 4,000 or so Danish regulars and militiamen were collecting at Roskilde, he fell upon the town. The Danes retired south to Kiöge. Wellesley, determined to give them no respite, followed up with a two-pronged offensive against the town on the 29th. He intended to take the bulk of his brigade along the coast road while General von Linsingen with a smaller force would shift south from Roskilde and take up positions south-east of Kiöge to cut off the Danish retreat.

Co-ordination proved impossible, much to Wellesley's annoyance. Von Linsingen was harried by Danish cavalry, which had to be driven off by cannon fire, and he failed to find a vital river crossing near Lellinge. Meanwhile Wellesley's advance had proceeded smoothly thanks to his light infantryman, who swept the countryside clear of Danish sharpshooters. At Kiöge he found the Danes occupying an entrenched position west of the town which, deploying his men in an extended line, he immediately attacked and overran. The Danes, many of them militiamen and armed peasants, flinched and scattered. Some of the fugitives were chased by von Linsingen's cavalry, which had just arrived, and by the end of the day 1,700 prisoners had been taken.[19]

For the next week Wellesley pushed his outposts westwards to Ringsted and patrols under von Linsingen probed inland, occasionally skirmishing with small enemy formations. By 3 September Wellesley assured Cathcart that he had dispersed nearly all the Danish forces on Zealand. He had done so for the loss of six dead and 115 wounded.[20] One incident, the first of many which would consume his time and temper over the next seven years, marred the small campaign. A few riflemen stole some silver plate from a convent but, thanks to Wellesley's intervention, it was retrieved and the culprits punished.[21]

On 8 September the Danes capitulated rather than endure further devastation of their capital (Sir William Congreve believed that his rockets alone had caused one million pounds' worth of damage) and arrangements were made to tow the Danish fleet to British ports.[22] For those taking part, and Wellesley was probably no exception, this had been a distasteful campaign. 'Poor Danes!', commented young James Napier. 'A soldier cannot fight an enemy he pities.'[23] Wellesley returned home and back to the Irish Office, where he settled down again to the thankless tasks of holding the lid down on local unrest and dispensing offices to the needy and greedy.

2

I Am Not Afraid of Them: Portugal, 1808

Responsibility for the Peninsular War lay solely with Napoleon. During the winter and spring of 1807/8 his arrogant, hamfisted diplomacy threw France into a war that was unexpected and ultimately unwinnable. His miscalculations were understandable. For several years he and his satraps had become accustomed to the prostration of Spain's royal family and had mistakenly assumed that Spanish society was stagnant. This error was discovered in the spring of 1808, when it was too late for Napoleon to revise his policy, not that he was a man for second thoughts.

In November 1807 Napoleon had set about tightening his grip on the Iberian Peninsula. A Franco-Spanish army invaded Portugal at the same time as French reinforcements entered northern Spain in readiness for a coup in Madrid designed to replace Carlos V by Napoleon's nominee. In March the Spanish royal family was kidnapped and hustled over the border to Bayonne. Carlos was deposed and his son Ferdinand VII proclaimed king. As supine as his father, Ferdinand was easily persuaded to abdicate, leaving the way clear for Napoleon to declare his own brother Joseph King of Spain.

Resistance had been expected but its animus surprised Napoleon, who imagined that 100,000 men and their military reputation alone would be enough to cow the Spaniards. Madrid was the centre of unrest: on 2 May insurgents took to the streets and attacked French soldiers, and the next day order was ruthlessly restored by Marshal Murat. The spirit of the two events was portrayed by Goya's *Dos de Mayos* and *Tres de Mayos*, but it was utterly misunderstood by Murat, who merely blamed British agents for the disturbances.

Within days Madrid's example had inflamed Spaniards elsewhere.

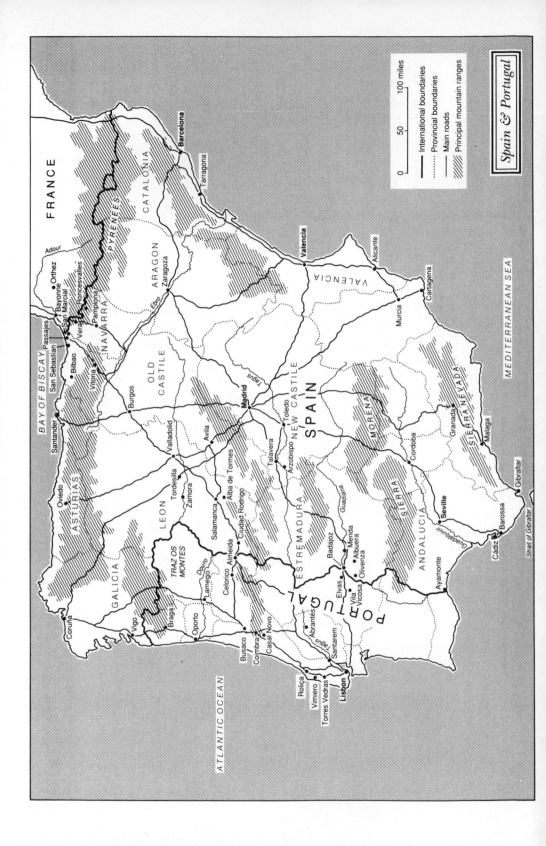

Spain & Portugal

The north-western provinces, notably Asturias, led the way in a sequence of popular uprisings. From the start, resistance was generated from the bottom upwards and churchmen were in the forefront; they had much to lose from the inevitable French policies of secularization. Leadership, when it emerged, tended to come from local mayors, bishops and landowners, those men to whom the masses traditionally looked for guidance. Emotions were patriotic, in that the Spaniards did not want French government or revolutionary innovations, but the strongest bonds were provincial pride and loyalties. These proved a powerful adhesive but created many future snags for tidy-minded legalists like Wellesley, who were desperate to find someone who represented the whole of Spain rather than spokesmen for the provincial juntas. These juntas, organized during the first days of the uprising, were committees that directed local resistance, often haphazardly and independently of each other.

As these events unfolded, the French were temporarily bewildered, although they never lost faith in their ability to stifle the unrest. Murat's troops were concentrated on the major routes between Madrid and the frontier and, on paper, were adequate to handle the provincial revolts one by one. A 50,000-strong corps under Marshal Jean-Baptiste Bessières, based in the southern Pyrenees, made good headway in north-western and north-eastern Spain. Barcelona was secured, which deprived the Spanish of a port through which assistance from the British garrison in Sicily could be summoned.

It was a different story in the south, in Andalucía, where on 20 July General Xavier Castaños trapped an exhausted and hungry French army at Bailén and took 18,000 prisoners. This blow to French prestige enraged Napoleon and shook the all but universal assumption that his soldiers were invincible. The Spanish were exultant and their confidence soared to the point where they became convinced that, unaided, they could overcome any French army. This elation was premature and dangerous; for the next five years Spanish armies were consistently beaten in battle. Nevertheless, Bailén mesmerized generals and juntas and made them alternately stubborn and cocksure whenever the question of British military assistance was raised.

Once the Spanish independence movement was under way and the provincial juntas had assembled, British help was sought. The juntas of Asturias, Galicia and Andalucía were first off the mark and, by early June, their representatives were in London with requests for cash and arms. News of the insurrections and French reverses, much of it fanciful, had aroused great excitement in Britain, where optimism ran wild. At last one oppressed nation had turned and it was widely believed that, if the Spanish were encouraged, others would do likewise. This was the opinion of George Canning, the Foreign Secretary, who on 15 June told the Commons 'that any nation of Europe that starts up with a determination to oppose the power which ... is the common enemy of all nations ... becomes instantly our essential ally'. Ample subsidies of cash and arms were pledged for the juntas, which by the end of the year had received £1.1 million and 200,000 muskets.[1]

Soldiers followed money and arms. On 14 June Wellesley, who had been promoted lieutenant-general six weeks before, was appointed to take command of 12,000 men being mustered for an expedition to Portugal. His orders, prepared by Castlereagh on the 30th, reflected the immediate preoccupation of the cabinet, which was to secure Lisbon as a naval base. Beyond this, Wellesley was to give the Portuguese 'every possible aid in throwing off the yoke of France'.[2]

Events in Portugal had followed a similar pattern to those in Spain. Faced with the Franco-Spanish invasion in November 1807, the Regent Don João had surrendered the Portuguese fleet to Britain, and fled with the government to Brazil, which he promised to open to British commerce. Inspired by the Spanish example and encouraged by mutinous Spanish soldiers, the Portuguese peasantry rose in arms during June. They were helped by Vice-Admiral Sir Charles Cotton's Tagus squadron, whose officers and ships gave every support to insurgents in coastal towns, in one of which, Oporto, the local bishop had placed himself at the head of the Supreme Junta of Portugal.

Cotton also sent a stream of intelligence reports to the Admiralty, most based on hearsay, which included a wildly inaccurate assessment of French strength as 4,000 men. Soon after, he added that they had lost 3,000 in a battle south of Lisbon![3] Like every other Englishman on the spot, Cotton was carried away by local enthusiasm and swallowed any tale of a French reverse. Moreover, since the Spanish and Portuguese were desperate for money and weapons, they deliberately exaggerated their successes. The cabinet sensed that it was being fed inaccurate information, so Castlereagh instructed Wellesley to call in at Coruña on his way to Lisbon and enquire about the situation in Galicia and further south.[4]

The decision to entrust Wellesley with the liberation of Portugal had been taken early in June on the assumption that operations would be on a small scale and over quickly – for this reason he was allowed to keep his ministerial post. The troops available to him (just under 7,000 from Irish garrisons and a further 5,000 from Gibraltar under his second-in-command, Major-General Sir Brent Spencer) were considered sufficient to defeat what was imagined to be a smaller French force. On this matter the cabinet had been misled and by 15 July, when the error had been detected, reinforcements of a further three additional brigades were ordered to Portugal and were followed by 10,000 men under General Sir John Moore's command who had been just withdrawn from Sweden.

At the same time as rushing extra men to Portugal, the cabinet decided to change the command structure of an army which would eventually total 40,000. The new commander-in-chief was Lieutenant-General Sir Hew Dalrymple, a fifty-three-year-old sedentary officer with little fighting experience, and his second-in-command was Lieutenant-General Sir Harry Burrard, another ageing warhorse similarly under-qualified. They had been foisted on a reluctant Castlereagh by the Duke of York at the prompting of his royal father, for whom length of service mattered more than talent. Wellesley, who guessed that York's dead hand lay behind the business, was bitterly dismayed.[5] He heard the news on 1 August as his forces were coming ashore at Mondego Bay and his public reaction was resigned. 'Whether I am to command the army or not, or I am to quit it,' he told Castlereagh, 'I will do my best to ensure its success.' He added that he would not seek the credit of victory by seeking a battle rashly before his new superiors arrived.[6]

Wellesley left Cork on 12 July and his ship HMS *Crocodile* reached Coruña eight days later. Once ashore he had to feel his way blindly since there was no reliable intelligence as to what was happening anywhere in the Peninsula. In Coruña he listened to the Galician junta's highly coloured reports which claimed the French had all but lost control of the country. Uncomfortable details such as the defeat just suffered by the junta's forces at Median de Rio Seco were glossed over. He also heard that the junta had over 2,000 men to put at his disposal to meet a French army in Portugal now believed to be at least 14,000 strong. There was a further pledge of assistance at Oporto, this time from 5,000 Portuguese regulars who were at Coimbra together with about 12,000 unarmed but enthusiastic peasants. Off Fort Figueira, where he met Cotton's squadron, Wellesley heard for the first time that 20,000 Frenchmen under General Androche Junot, nearly all close to Lisbon, were preparing for his arrival. This estimate, forwarded from Spencer at Cádiz, was the first accurate assessment he had been given of his enemy's strength.

Cotton advised Wellesley to put his men ashore at Mondego Bay, where they would be safe from a sudden French attack. The local roads were impassable to artillery and cavalry and the nearby Fort Figueira had been in the hands of bluejackets from HMS *Alfred* for three weeks.[7] The landings in boats guided through the breakers by sailors took four days.

From the beginning, Wellesley took full personal control over every detail of the army's life. From his headquarters poured a steady stream of orders that regulated everything from surgeons' mules to the allocation of rations to those women and children who had elected to follow their husbands into battle. Much to his annoyance there were areas of indolence made impenetrable by red tape and antique administrative custom. He had already been frustrated in his endeavours to get additional artillery horses and drivers, who were subject to the chronically inert Ordnance Department, and, once in Portugal, he discovered inadequacies in the commissariat, which was the responsibility of the Treasury. Nonetheless he persevered, sacking the most slovenly commissaries and complaining to Castlereagh about the rest. On 8 August he told him that Spencer's artillery had had to be abandoned for lack of horses and the commissary's department was hopelessly out of its depth. 'The existence of the army depends upon it and yet the people who manage it are incapable of managing anything out of a counting house.'[8] It was all disturbingly reminiscent of Flanders.

By 14 August the army, now joined by Spencer, set out southwards, marching at the 'regular steady' pace Wellesley insisted on and which it managed 'tolerably well'. Everyone, he reported, was in 'high spirits' despite an absence of tents, which had been delayed. He now commanded 13,500 men, including 1,800 Portuguese under an eccentric British officer, Colonel Nicholas Trant. Efforts to secure the service of the larger force at Coimbra had foundered; the commissariat could not provide rations for them and their general, Bernadino Freire, was sulky and obstructive. (His lukewarm nationalism cost him his life in March 1809 when he was lynched by a mob in Braga.)[9] Spanish reinforcements, promised in Coruña, never materialized.

This half-hearted co-operation did not trouble Wellesley unduly. He placed his faith in British troops under his leadership. 'My die is cast,' he had told Croker on 14 June; 'they may overwhelm me but I don't think they will outmanoeuvre me. First, because I am not afraid of them, as everyone else seems to be; and secondly, because if what I hear of their system of manoeuvres be true, I think it a false one, as against steady troops. I suspect all the continental armies were more than half beaten before the battle was begun. I, at least, will not be frightened beforehand.'[10] What he had in mind was the French habit of attacking in mass columns preceded by skirmishers. In Denmark he had witnessed the skill and effectiveness of British light infantrymen and rightly judged them more than a match for their French counterparts. If, and this in fact proved to be the case in the Peninsula, they could drive off the French tirailleurs, then the columns were vulnerable since their narrow front allowed only a few men to fire their muskets.

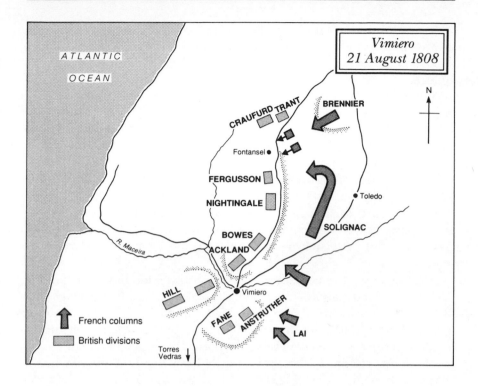

By contrast, a British battalion formed in a two-deep line could concentrate its entire firepower on the enemy at close ranges. Wellesley had decided that in theory firepower rather than mobility and the moral force of the bayonet charge would be decisive.

His first two battles, at Rolica and Vimiero, justified this theory. They were fought as his army moved slowly southwards towards Lisbon. Transport and supply shortages, uncertainty about the intentions and whereabouts of the French, and the danger of putting too much distance between the army and its vital seaborne reinforcements compelled Wellesley to keep close to the coast. He was also constrained by the lack of horses, because his one cavalry regiment, the 20th Light Dragoons, mustered only 240 mounted men and was barely adequate for scouting.

The French too moved cautiously. Junot had sent General Henri Delaborde north with 5,000 men to make a reconnaissance in force supported by 8,200 under General Louis Loison, who had just been released from counter-insurgency operations in the south. Unable to combine with Loison at Leiria, Delaborde fell back, closely followed by Wellesley's advance guard of light troops. The pursuers got the bit between their teeth at Obidos and, after scattering a French tirailleur rearguard, collided with larger forces and had to be rescued in the nick of time by a battalion under Spencer. 'Unpleasant because it was quite useless' was Wellesley's summary of a skirmish caused by over-impulsive officers.

There was more serious fighting two days later on 17 August when the army confronted Delaborde holding high ground above the village of Rolica. Wellesley directed two brigades to outflank the French, who fell back to an equally formidable position on a ridge behind the village of Columbeira. Again Wellesley ordered flanking movements, but through a series of misunderstandings the co-ordination of the assualt went awry and one section attacked prematurely. Impetuousness again played its part; the 29th (Worcestershire Regiment) rushed forward, unsupported, and was roughly handled. The French extricated themselves and fell back southwards, full of respect for their adversaries' courage but unimpressed by their generalship.[11]

After Rolica, Junot decided to concentrate his forces, including Delaborde's and Loison's divisions, at Torres Vedras. Forewarned that British reinforcements were coming by sea and conscious that a hostile population inside Lisbon made his position precarious, he decided to launch an offensive. Wellesley expected as much and had begun to take precautions. He placed his army, now raised to 17,000 thanks to the arrival of two additional brigades, on high ground around Vimiero and sent small cavalry patrols probing south-east. During the night of 20/21 August the dragoons detected signs that a substantial French army was moving towards Vimiero from Torres Vedras. The news, carried by a dragoon sergeant, did not surprise Wellesley, whose men had been in their positions and standing by since sunset. Speaking calmly and cheerfully he gave his instructions to his brigade commanders: 'Now, gentlemen, go to your stations: but let there be no noise made – no sounding of bugles or beating of drums. Get your men quietly under arms, and desire all the outposts to be on the alert.'[12]

This composure was deceptive; for the past day Wellesley had been wrangling with Burrard, who had just arrived off Maçeira Bay in the sloop *Brazen*. The vinegary exchanges had opened with Wellesley's candid assessment of the situation, in which he stressed the present difficulties of feeding the army. The pernickety and faint-hearted Burrard was disturbed by what he heard, which confirmed his view, based on garbled accounts of Rolica, that Wellesley was an impatient and irresponsible young officer. No more risks were to be taken; the army would remain where it was and Moore's reinforcements were to be immediately diverted from Mondego Bay to join it. Wellesley's suggestion that Moore press inland to occupy Santarém in readiness to cut off the French retreat from Lisbon was brushed aside. Only with

massive strength would Burrard move against the French. The conference over, he shifted his quarters to a cabin on HMS *Alfred* and
Wellesley returned to the army.

As it was, the row had been purely academic; Junot had taken the
initiative and soon after sunrise opened his attack on the British.
Wellesley, true to the principles he had outlined to Croker, had decided
to rely on firepower and so posted his brigades in extended lines on
rising ground. Junot, after a brief inspection of his position, decided to
concentrate his column attacks against the centre, which lay in front
of Vimiero, and the far left, where he hoped to turn the British flank.
From the high ground his movements, carried out in bright morning
sunlight, were perfectly plain and Wellesley accordingly shifted men
from the right to the left. Although this manoeuvre had been carried out
in dead ground (where the lie of the land prevented observation and
his men were out of the enemy's sight), Junot guessed that Wellesley was
strengthening his left. Without a thought for the consequences, he
hurriedly withdrew General Solignac's brigade from the centre and
sent it northwards to stiffen the force earmarked for the flank attack. His
depleted centre then threw themselves in columns towards Wellesley's
centre.

The fighting was over by half-past ten, having lasted just over two
hours. The collision between the columns of attack and the line ended
as Wellesley had predicted, with the French suffering heavy losses from
steady volley fire. The effect was most marked on the left flank where
the uncoordinated attacks of Brennier's and Solignac's brigades ended
in disaster. The hammer-blows fell heaviest on the centre, which was
held by the brigades of Brigadier-Generals Harry Fane and Robert
Anstruther. Here the tenacity of the French provoked admiration,
Rifleman Harris being particularly struck by their grenadiers, who
'were all fine-looking young men, wearing red shoulder-knots and
tremendous-looking moustaches'. Whenever one fell a cry went up:
'There goes another of Boney's Invincibles.'[13] There was praise too for
the marksmanship of the British riflemen, whose dark-green uniforms
made one French officer liken them to 'grasshoppers'.

Less easily measurable than the weight and regularity of musketry
were the inner moral qualities that contributed to the steadiness of the
British infantryman and made him stand his ground against French
onrushes. An unknown nineteen-year-old private in the 38th (Staffordshire Regiment) who had been an ardent chapel-goer before enlistment,
recalled that at Rolica he had feared eternity more than the French
and made 'a resolution to amend my life'.[14] Fear, whether of death or
the enemy, was reduced by the careless bravery of officers, who inspired
confidence. William Warre, an ADC to Brigadier-General Ronald

Ferguson, observed that his whole brigade worshipped Ferguson 'for his bravery and skill and coolness in fire like hail about him'.[15]

Words of encouragement, uttered at the right moment, could be talismanic. At Vimiero General Fane rode among his men and shouted, 'Well done 95th!, well done 43rd, 52nd, and well done all. I shall not forget, if I live to report your conduct to-day. They shall hear of it in England, my lads!' One listener, a rifleman, handed him a green feather torn from the cap of a French tirailleur he had just shot and cried, 'God bless you, general! Wear this for the sake of the 95th.' He did and shortly after ordered a counter-charge against the wavering French columns. 'We sprang to our feet, gave one hearty cheer, and charged along with them ... The enemy turned and fled, the cavalry dashing upon them as they went off.' So ended the battle of Vimiero for Rifleman Harris. All that he had seen fulfilled his commander's prophecy: the French mass attacks had withered before the superior firepower of unbroken, self-confident and well-officered troops.

At Vimiero the odds had been in Wellesley's favour. His numbers equalled his adversary's; Junot's planning had been slapdash; and the French offensive had been poorly synchronized. As it became clear that the French, who had suffered about 2,000 casualties, were falling back, Wellesley realized that an immediate bold counter-attack would shatter their army. He prepared to hurl his three fresh and undamaged brigades towards Torres Vedras, where they would occupy the high ground which crossed the Lisbon road and so cut off Junot. The rest of the army, which was still in good shape (losses had been about 700), would harass Junot, who, denied Lisbon, would be driven inland and probably forced to surrender.

Wellesley's plan was stillborn. Burrard, who had come ashore and joined him during the later stages of the battle, forbade an advance. Wellesley was furious and 'remonstrated' with his superior, without success. 'The French army would have been entirely destroyed if I had been allowed my blow as I wished', he told Admiral Cotton.[16] This was the conclusion of the rest of the army; Sir John Moore, who arrived soon after, wrote, 'from everything I have heard ... the French would never have reached Lisbon'.[17]

Extreme caution coupled with an underlying fear that Wellesley was at heart a gambler explains Burrard's behaviour. While praising Wellesley's dispositions at Vimiero, he was convinced that precipitate action, even against a temporarily disorganized enemy, might end in disaster. His misgivings were shared by Dalrymple, who arrived the next day, 21 August, to take full command of the army. Quite what strategy he would adopt nobody could tell, although he seems to have shared Burrard's extreme prudence. Not that he was given the chance to formulate a plan of campaign for, during the early afternoon of the 22nd, General François Kellerman rode up to the pickets outside Vimiero under a flag of truce with a request for an armistice.

On the surface his terms, which included an offer to withdraw all French troops from Portugal, were an admission of the perilousness of Junot's position. And yet at the same time it was more likely that the French were thinking in terms of getting a breathing-space in which to cobble together a defence of Lisbon. Junot was pinning his hopes on the co-operation of a Russian squadron of nine battleships which had been anchored in the Tagus since November under the command of Admiral Siniavin. Russia was technically at war with Britain, and the government feared that Siniavin would, if requested, disembark some of his 10,000 sailors to help the French.[18] On 24 August, two days after the armistice had been signed, Kellerman asked Siniavin for assistance in the defence of Lisbon, but was firmly refused.[19] Faced with Russian neutrality, the French had no choice but to confirm the armistice and evacuate Portugal.

The proposals made by Kellerman were extremely tempting. A ceasefire would be followed by a convention which would settle the details of the French withdrawal and the surrender of all Portuguese fortresses. For Dalrymple the arrangement represented the fulfilment of the government's instructions and he was prepared to overlook the demand that the French with all 'their military baggage and equipments' should be shipped home in British vessels. Wellesley objected, arguing that only a forty-eight-hour truce should be conceded. He was overruled by Dalrymple and the preliminary agreement was signed that evening.

An eyewitness to the negotiations, Major-General Sir John Hope, told his brother-in-law Dundas that 'the eagerness of his temper' had impelled Wellesley to play a prominent role in the discussions. The arguments in favour of the arrangement appeared to be strong: the army was unprepared for a winter siege of Lisbon and, if the French were permitted to pull back to Spain, they would add to the Spaniards' difficulties. Most importantly, at least for Dalrymple and Burrard, 'Any want of brilliancy in regard to the Issue of Military Operations was thought to be counterbalanced by the advantage of getting the French out of Portugal without further mischief to the country or the capital.'[20] Hope believed that the armistice was unavoidable, although, like the rest of the army, he imagined its terms would be reviled in Britain.[21]

This consideration weighed heavily with Dalrymple, Burrard and Wellesley and explains the curious charade which marked the formal signing. What passed was recorded by an officer present. 'Sir Hew was going up to the table to sign the convention, but Kellerman observed that as he himself was only a General of Division, Sir Hew Dalrymple better let some inferior officer sign it, upon which Sir Arthur, without even being asked, or without the slightest appearance of reluctance went up to the table and signed.'[22] If this was so, then Wellesley had very successfully disguised his feelings. The following day he wrote to Castlereagh, 'Although my name is affixed to this instrument, I beg that you will not believe that I negotiated it, that I approved of it, or that I had any hand in wording it.'[23] As to signing the paper, he later admitted to having acted against his better judgement. 'I thought it my duty to comply with the wishes of the Commander in Chief from the wish which I have always felt, according to which I have always acted, to carry into effect the orders and objects of those placed in command over me, however I might differ in opinion with them.'[24]

In short the agreement, known in its final form as the Convention of Cintra, was a flawed settlement that was prejudicial to British interests and, some argued, dissipated the advantages which had been gained at Vimiero. It permitted the French to return with their considerable loot, contained no provisions which forbade the redeployment of the evacuated army elsewhere in the Peninsula and took no account of the interests of the Portuguese. Ultimate responsibility rested with Dalrymple, and Wellesley had done as he had been told impassively despite his inner misgivings which were to a large extent based on the knowledge that the Convention of Cintra would provoke a violent outcry at home.

He was also aware that by obeying his commander he had made himself vulnerable to public censure and he took steps to deflect it. On 23 August he pleaded with Castlereagh to be recalled, adding 'if you wish me to stay, I will: I only beg that you will not blame me if things do not go on as you and my friends in London wish they should'.[25] He became increasingly angry and depressed. He found Dalrymple, who was contemptuously nicknamed 'Dowager' by the army, unbearable and was insulted by his suggestion that he travel through Asturias and draw up plans for operations there. Wellesley protested that he was not a 'topographical engineer' and that a duty which involved the planning rather than execution of strategy 'would bring disgrace upon me'.[26] On 5 September he privately appealed to Castlereagh for permission to return home; his predicament was intolerable and the fault lay with York. 'It is better for him, for the Army and me that I should go away; and the sooner I go the better.'[27]

Motives of expediency mingled with Wellesley's private wish to escape from a painful situation. As he had guessed, the news of Cintra, which broke on 15/16 September (just a fortnight after the public celebration of Vimiero) plunged the country into a mood of sullen gloom. Public opinion condemned the treaty as a humiliating sell-out and quickly cast about for scapegoats. Wellesley's letters to Castlereagh had already outlined the extent of the concessions and they were followed by others to his friends in which he distanced himself from the agreement and stressed that had he not been overruled by Burrard, the remnant of Junot's army would have been easily destroyed and Lisbon taken.

It was essential that Wellesley's version of events should be made known to his friends, who in turn would broadcast it to their own political and social circles. He proceeded with delicacy and discretion, emphasizing that the matters in dispute occurred after he had been superseded by Dalrymple. He did not seek any scrutiny of the events leading up to Vimiero or of the battle itself, for which he had gained considerable public acclaim. In particular he wanted as little reference as possible to Burrard's battlefield decision to call off an advance, although it was by now well known. Even though his adherents were making much of Burrard's irresolution, he assured the General's family that he had no desire to become embroiled in 'unpleasant discussions' of what had occurred at Vimiero.[28]

It was inevitable that the charges against Wellesley would become a party matter; he was a minister and Castlereagh was anxious for the vindication of a general he had chosen and in whom he had enormous faith. The government press rallied to his cause. The *Morning Post* and the *Courier* were sympathetic, while the *Sun* of 29 September claimed that he had been forced to sign the armistice under the threat of court-martial and death.[29] The Grenvilles and their circle supported Wellesley, and the Marquess of Buckingham reported that the Prince of Wales was favourably inclined.

Cintra provided an opportunity for enemies of the Wellesley family who had been denied their prey in April when allegations of corruption against the Marquess had been dropped after the suicide of James Paull, his accuser. Family presumption and influence as much as patriotic indignation over Cintra united Wellesley's detractors. William Cobbett, the radical journalist, denounced the 'arrogance of that damned infernal family' and Samuel Whitbread, the brewer and radical MP, saw a fresh chance to humble the Wellesleys. In the end political allies counted; at a public meeting in Westminster Hall called to censure Wellesley one speaker predicted that no punishment would fall on those 'great delinquents who had the advantage of Parliamentary influence'.[30]

The government's eventual answer to the debate was to convene a public court of enquiry which opened at Chelsea Barracks (now the Royal Hospital) on 15 November. Chaired by General Dundas, of drill-book fame, the commission of seven senior officers heard evidence from Wellesley, who had been in England for some weeks, Burrard and Dalrymple, who had been recently recalled from Portugal. Although the investigations were officially confined to events after Dalrymple took command, references to Vimiero were unavoidable and assisted Wellesley's case. Dalrymple's clumsy attempt to make him solely responsible for the terms of the armistice also helped Wellesley, who felt himself morally free to criticize his commanding officer.[31]

The verdict of the court, delivered on 22 December, was a fudge, with majority votes in favour of the Cintra agreement and its terms. No specific blame was allocated, but Wellesley's successes in the field were singled out for praise. In effect he had been publicly exonerated and his career was no longer imperilled. Dalrymple and Burrard received no further active commands, returning to the obscurity from which they should not have been plucked.

The public outcry and the enquiry were both distasteful experiences for Wellesley, although he was characteristically contemptuous of popular and press criticism. What was most disturbing was public intrusion into what, for him, were purely military matters that were best left to those who understood them. When the uproar had been at its most strident he had written, 'I think it fatal to the public service to expose officers to the treatment which I have received, and to punishment for acting upon their own military opinions.'[32]

Nevertheless, on 27 January 1809, when he replied to the Commons' vote of thanks for Vimiero he confessed to being deeply honoured by 'a distinction which it is in the power of the representatives of a free people alone to bestow, and which it is the peculiar advantage of officers and soldiers in the service of His Majesty to have held out to them as the object of their ambition and to receive as the reward of their service'.[33] And yet some of these 'free people' had been clamouring for his blood a few months before in the belief that he had betrayed the army and the country. The experience had been salutary and would haunt him for several years; the British had the highest and often most completely unrealistic expectations of their generals and paid the closest attention to how and with what success they waged war. Whatever else emerged from the 1808 campaign and its rancorous aftermath, it was clear that the public entertained a strong belief that their army, properly led, could beat the French in the Peninsula and that victory there would be a prelude to the final downfall of Napoleon. It was also equally clear that, if the public was disappointed by the army's performance, its anger would be directed against generals rather than politicians.

Part Five

1809–1812

1

Acute and Decisive Talents for Command: The Road to Talavera, 1809

In the first week of August 1809 Wellesley resigned his post as Irish Secretary and accepted command of the British army in Portugal. On the 14th he boarded the frigate *Surveillante* and eight days later disembarked at Lisbon having narrowly escaped shipwreck off the Isle of Wight.

The events of the past four months had favoured his appointment. He had survived the Cintra recriminations, continued to enjoy the trust of Castlereagh and no longer had to fear the meddling of York, who was now embroiled in a scandal that involved the sale of commissions which would cost him his post as commander-in-chief. The victory at Vimiero had not been forgotten: Walter Scott, an admiring fellow Tory, spoke for many when he praised Wellesley's 'acute and decisive talents for command'.[1] Moreover the only other general whose talents matched Wellesley's, Sir John Moore, had died from wounds near Coruña in January.

In the seven months after Wellesley's departure from Portugal, the overall strategic situation had swung in France's favour. In November 1808 Sir John Moore, under orders to combine with the Spanish, led a British army into northern Spain, where he encountered insurmountable problems. It was soon clear that the cabinet had overestimated the resources and abilities of the Spaniards and he found himself isolated and in danger of being overrun by vastly superior French forces commanded by Napoleon in person. Catastrophe was averted by a retreat to Coruña which was marked by a series of hard-fought rearguard actions. The residue of Moore's army took ship from Coruña and deprived Napoleon of the signal victory that, he had hoped, would end the Iberian campaign and overawe the rest of

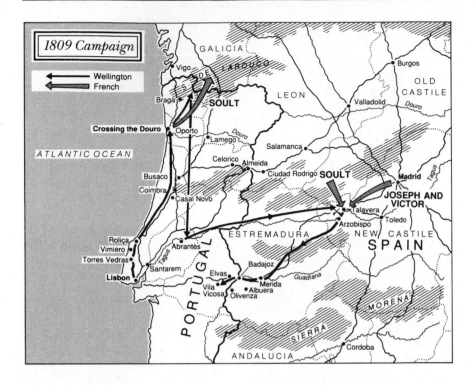

Europe, especially the restless Austrians. He never returned to the peninsula, leaving operations there in the hands of subordinates whom he showered with detailed orders that often showed a total ignorance of the realities of warfare there.

Elsewhere in Spain the tide flowed in France's direction. In the east, Marshal Gauvion de St Cyr beat down resistance in Aragon and Catalonia, where he captured Saragossa, relieved Barcelona and scattered the local Spanish field armies. There was success too for Marshal Nicolas Soult's 2nd Corps, which overran Galicia and, by 29 March 1809, had occupied Portugal as far south as Oporto. In the same week General Horace Sebastiani's 4th Corps won a victory at Cuidad Real and Marshal Claude Victor's 1st Corps defeated General Don Gregorio Garçia de la Cuesta's army at Medellin. These two battles gave the French a temporary ascendancy in Estremadura and opened the way to an invasion of Portugal from the east. Confidence soared. One of the first reports read by Wellesley when he disembarked was an intercepted letter of 23 March from General Solignac to his brother in which he asked him to address his reply to Lisbon.[2]

All this was bleak news for the British. Writing from Lisbon, Colonel

George Bingham of the 53rd told his mother that the army would remain in Portugal 'as long as the French allow us', and Major George Scovell noted in his diary that the army was 'much dispirited'.[3]

Yet the omniscience of the French was illusory. Despite the deployment of 324,000 men in Spain, their armies were overstretched. They had won and would win victories over poorly led and trained Spanish troops but they were not up to the vital task of pacification. The guerrilla war, which had been under way since the summer of 1808, quickly had an impact, forcing generals to detach troops in penny packets to garrison lines of communications, guard supply convoys and escort messengers. Matters steadily got worse as the war dragged on: intelligence reports which reached Wellesley in October 1811 revealed that Marshal Soult needed the protection of a squadron of dragoons, fifty hussars and two battalions of infantry when the crossed Andalucía.[4] Such precautions were of limited value. 'We were the masters of all the towns and villages upon the road,' one French officer recalled, 'but not of the environs at the distance of one hundred paces.' The enemy was 'everywhere and nowhere'.[5]

Guerrilla, or as French generals designated it 'bandit', warfare played havoc with their sorely pressed supply system. Even without the guerrilla bands, it was hard for an army to subsist in a country which grew barely enough for its inhabitants. From the start Wellesley had understood this. Early in September 1808 he had assured Castlereagh that 'from what I have heard of the state of the resources in the country' an army of 40,000 would find survival difficult.[6] The French discovered this fact of life painfully; at the end of March 1809 St Cyr had to abandon his hitherto successful Catalan campaign when his army faced starvation near Tarragona.[7]

These factors were barely discernible when Wellesley landed in Lisbon. His arrival revived the morale of the army, which now felt that 'something decisive' would follow.[8] The Portuguese, remembering Vimiero, hailed him as a saviour and a fortnight later the ladies of Coimbra showered him with roses and sugar plums as he rode through the town.[9]

His instructions, prepared by Castlereagh, offered no chance for a decisive stroke. He was to expel Soult's corps from Oporto and secure Portugal from further invasion. As for operations in Spain, Wellesley was advised to proceed carefully, use his own judgement and seek Spanish co-operation only if it was to Portugal's advantage. No Spanish campaign was to be undertaken without cabinet approval. To achieve his objective, he was allocated 19,000 infantry and 4,400 cavalry, of whom a quarter were being embarked at English and Irish ports.

As Wellesley fully appreciated, Portugal could not be held by British troops alone. During the winter and spring of 1808/9 a series of arrangements had been negotiated under which the Portuguese Council of Regency placed their country's manpower at Britain's disposal in return for material and cash subsidies. By April 13,000 Portuguese militiamen had been drafted into the British forces as auxiliaries and a new Portuguese army was being created under the command of Wellesley's friend William Carr Beresford, whom he had recommended for the post. Beresford, backed by a cadre of British officers, supervised the organization and training of what, by 1810, had become a branch of the British army. To ensure that Britain's interests were paramount, a British representative was admitted to the Council of Regency. Politically and militarily emasculated, Portugal was transformed into a British dependency for the next five years.

As well as securing the submission of Portugal, the government was anxious to open up a new front in Germany in 1809 where hopes were pinned on a renewal of the alliance with Austria, whose declaration of war against France would be accompanied by a nationalist uprising in Prussia. As usual Britain was the paymaster, but the cabinet decided to offer the Austrians further assistance in the form of a diversionary attack on Antwerp. The amphibious assault on the Belgian coast followed the baleful pattern of similar operations in the past. Once ashore, the British became stuck on Walcheren Island, where thousands were soon infected with fever, and, by September, the detritus of the army was pulled out. The whole affair, which starved Wellesley of men, was a feckless squandering of resources and had no impact on events on the Danube, where, after a victory at Aspern-Essling, the Austrians were decisively beaten at Wagram in July.

The priority given to the Walcheren expedition was a reminder that in terms of broad strategy the campaign in Portugal was still a sideshow. No one in London or Lisbon was sure how it would turn out and, after Coruña, soldiers and politicians were deeply divided over whether operations in the Peninsula would ever achieve much. Within the army there was widespread disenchantment with the Spanish which soon became contempt. For one officer, Spain was the 'abode of ignorance, cruelty and indomitable pride', and another told his sister that the government had been a 'parcel of fools' to set any store by the Spanish since 'no activity, no spirit is to be found in them'.[10] Such views were transmitted to Britain, where they added to the groundswell of opinion which dismissed the war as a wasteful adventure doomed to failure. Throughout 1809 and 1810 events in the Peninsula provided a focal point for Opposition criticism of the government and there were plenty of armchair generals who questioned Wellesley's strategy.[11]

The interaction between what happened at the front and domestic politics made life extremely difficult for Wellesley, who also had to contend with discontented officers whose letters home found their way into the press. His reaction was the same as it had been during the Cintra controversy; in June 1809, after a staff surgeon had publicly exposed the mismanagement of hospitals in Coimbra, Wellesley protested, 'If we are fit to be trusted with the charge with which we are invested, our characters are not to be injured by defamatory reports of this description.'[12] For him complex military affairs were no concern of amateurs, particularly journalists. No machinery existed to muzzle the press and so, much to his irritation, he had to wage war in the knowledge that his judgement would always be open to public scrutiny and that any subordinate with a grievance could have it vented in Britain. Only his 'friends' in the government could defend him, and their arguments would rest ultimately on his success.

Success in 1809 depended on Wellesley's ability to outmanoeuvre and bring to battle the armies of Soult and Victor which were threatening Portugal. Intelligence reports, delivered to Wellesley at the end of April and including French despatches taken by guerrillas, indicated that Soult's 25,000-strong corps at Oporto would advance on Lisbon once he had been joined by 10,000 reinforcements from Salamanca. The intentions of Victor were not known: his 44,000 men were concentrated between Badajoz and Merida and might either combine with Soult or march on Lisbon independently.

Wellesley therefore planned a campaign in two stages. First he would eject Soult from Oporto, drive his corps back across the border into Galicia and then engage Victor. On 29 April, he assured Cuesta that he would join him on the Tagus as soon as Soult had been seen off.[13] For their part, the Spanish promised to do all in their power, short of a general engagement, to hinder Victor if he moved on Lisbon. Also ready to harass Victor was an Anglo-Portuguese force that Wellesley had detached with orders to defend the passes through which the French would advance.

Everything hung on a swift offensive against Soult. On 2 May Wellesley ordered his 18,000-strong army to advance northwards from Coimbra while Beresford's Portuguese headed north-east towards Lamego in readiness to cut off Soult if he retreated. The campaign began smoothly thanks to French negligence. Deserters' reports that the French were casual in their posting of pickets and sentries were confirmed by a sequence of surprise attacks which overwhelmed outposts south of Oporto.[14]

By the morning of 12 May, Wellesley reached the heights on the southern bank of the Douro overlooking Oporto. As organized by Soult, the defence of the city rested on the belief that the Douro was an impassable barrier. His soldiers had destroyed the pontoon bridge, towed all the local river craft to the north bank and broken the ferry at Avintas four miles upstream. A quarter of the French army had been placed in positions beyond the city, stretching as far as Amarante on the River Tramega, as an insurance against attacks from bodies of Spanish and Portuguese and to facilitate an unimpeded retreat. As a precaution against seaborne attack, French units had been placed between Oporto and the coast.

Wellesley directed Major-General John Murray to take a division to Avintas, repair the ferry and establish himself on the north bank. At this stage he had a stroke of good luck which he instantly exploited. An Oporto hairdresser, who had rowed across the river, revealed the wherabouts of four unguarded barges which could be untied and brought across. This was done with the help of Colonel Waters, who spoke Portuguese, and some local boatmen.

Speaking in that 'simple and distinct manner' to which his officers were still unaccustomed, Wellesley gave the order, 'Well, let the men cross!'[15] First over were a platoon of the Buffs (3rd East Kent Regiment) who were instructed to occupy a stoutly walled theological seminary by the river's edge. The building, close to the city walls, was an obvious strongpoint and its approaches were within the range of an eighteen-gun battery which Wellesley had placed on high ground opposite.

Astonishingly, since it was a bright, sunlit morning, the passage of the soldiers went undetected for nearly an hour, by which time the seminary was held by 600 men. Once alerted to what had happened, the French attempted to retake the building by storm and bombardment. Neither succeeded since the defenders were supported by heavy fire from the battery on the opposite bank, which, using the novel Shrapnel shell, silenced the French artillery. Efforts by the French to bring more cannon to bear were frustrated by local men and women who closed the city gates to a horse artillery battery.

Unable to hold the city, Soult ordered a general withdrawal. What began as a helter-skelter rush towards Amarante would have become a rout if Murray, whose division had by now crossed at Avintas, had acted boldly. As it was he stood by and within a few days the French had recovered their cohesion.

Wellesley had had extraordinary good luck and had shown amazing temerity. Thanks to the torpor of the French, his gamble paid off, but circumstances combined to prevent him from exploiting his *coup de main*. Although Anglo-Portuguese forces chivvied Soult's army as it fell back towards Galicia, no opportunity presented itself for a battle. Never-theless the pace of the pursuit forced Soult to abandon or destroy large quantities of baggage, transport and artillery. Although he regretted having missed the chance to secure a total victory, Wellesley was satisfied that he had rendered Soult's corps ineffective. Relying on Soult's letters, intercepted on 29 June, he felt sure that his corps no longer posed a threat to Portugal since it was in a 'miserable state' without artillery, ammunition or stores.[16]

The British army too was suffering from shortages. Twenty days of campaigning had stretched the commissariat to breaking point, and by the end of May Wellesley was facing a crisis of supply which threatened to bring operations to a halt.

Money was the first problem. On 5 May Wellesley had protested to William Huskisson, the Secretary to the Treasury, that he had received only a quarter of £400,000 due to him to meet operational costs, adding, 'You may depend upon it that I shall keep the expense as low as possible.' By 30 May the situation was desperate and he demanded £300,000 immediately. The following day he repeated this plea to Castlereagh alongside an urgent request for one-and-a-half million pounds of biscuit, three million pounds each of hay and oats. In private, he was furious that delays and muddle were wrecking his plans. 'I suspect', he told John Charles Villiers, the British Minister in Lisbon, 'Ministers in England are very indifferent to our operations in this country.'[17] A fortnight later, after hearing that reinforcements had landed, he nudged the government's conscience. 'The ball is now at my foot, and I hope I shall now have strength enough to give it a good kick: I should begin immediately, but I cannot venture to stir without money.'[18] He would not, he added, advance without first having paid the army's debts. On 28 June matters had still not improved and he wrote ruefully, 'It will be better for the Government, in every view of the subject, to relinquish their operations in Portugal and Spain, if the country cannot afford to carry them on.'[19]

Government inertia threatened the fabric of the army. Operations in northern Portugal during the last two weeks of May had taken it into a barren region of subsistence farming where the retreating French had destroyed crops, stores and farm implements to create an artificial famine. Soldiers' rations were reduced on 17 and 19 May and attempts, largely unsuccessful, were made to feed horses on local fodder, which they found indigestible. Much blame fell on the commissariat, although Wellesley was prepared to excuse it on the ground that many of its officers were inexperienced.[20] Others were less generous. After explaining his difficulties to Major-General William Payne, Commissary Auguste Schaumann was told, 'I forgive you; but in that case allow me to shit and spit on your Commissary-General who is squatting comfortably in Oporto.'[21]

Hungry soldiers fended for themselves. On 30 May Wellesley wrote that his men 'have plundered the country most terribly' and, not having been paid for two months, some had stolen bullocks and resold them to the Portuguese. Discipline began to dissolve, as George Bingham noticed during the march to Abrantès early in June. 'The excessive long marches, frequently by night, narrow roads, want of bread and other causes occasioned straggling and plunder, and having the example of the French before their eyes, they [British soldiers] have signalized themselves to the great annoyance of the inhabitants we came to protect.'[22]

There were other signs that discipline was disintegrating, in particular a spate of assaults on officers and NCOs which alarmed Wellesley. Condign punishment was his cure for the malaise that was infecting his men: four looters from the 42nd (Black Watch) were given 500 lashes each at Abrantès in June and a month later a murderer from the 97th was hanged. These punishments did not deter effectively and so, by the spring of 1810, plunderers were regularly executed.[23] For Wellesley the enforcement of discipline was ultimately the responsibility of regimental officers and his General Orders repeatedly remind them of this. Not all officers responded. When Major-General Robert Craufurd entered Viza on the night of 12/13 July he encountered a disorderly company of the 43rd whose officers had vanished. Craufurd stilled the men and ordered the arrest of their company commander. It was necessary, he claimed during the consequent court-martial for negligence, because of 'the great relaxation of Discipline which I had myself witnessed in the army at the end of the last campaign [Coruña] and the general tenor of the orders which I found the present commander of the army had been giving.'[24] Such compliance was not universal: on 16 June Wellesley had reprimanded two colonels for their 'irregularities' in the enforcement of regimental discipline.[25]

An empty war-chest, shortages of victuals and a spate of indiscipline were unwelcome distractions at a time when Wellesley was anxious to implement the second stage of his plan and open operations against Victor. The French marshal had just taken Alcantara, a bridging point on the Tagus, and appeared on the verge of a drive towards Lisbon. This development came at just the right moment for Wellesley for on 11 June he had received cabinet permission to take his army into Spain and negotiations were already under way with General Cuesta for a combined manoeuvre which would trap Victor. They came to nothing thanks to Wellesley's lack of cash and Cuesta's curmudgeonliness.

With the arrival of money at Abrantès on 27 June (it had taken ten days to carry from Lisbon) Wellesley, now short of time, began his offensive. A gruelling sequence of forced marches in suffocating heat brought the army to Plascencia on 8 July and two days later Wellesley met Cuesta at Almaraz. Their conversations were carried on through an interpreter, Colonel O'Donohue, for Wellesley knew no Spanish and Cuesta refused to speak French.[26]

At the end of this exchange, Wellesley admitted that it was 'impossible for me to say what plans General Cuesta entertains'. It had been a trying encounter during which Wellesley had found it hard to contain his impatience with a lethargic, seventy-six-year-old pantaloon who concealed his ignorance of war behind a mask of arrogance. Cuesta, who travelled everywhere in a coach pulled by six mules, was soon reviled throughout the British army; Rifleman Costello, who saw him at Talavera, remembered him as a 'deformed-looking lump of pride and ignorance'.[27] His officers were worse. Lord FitzClarence of the staff was horrified at their appearance for 'not only did they not look like soldiers, but not even like gentlemen'. Their 'mean and abject appearance' made it 'impossible to know what class of society they came from'. 'Few troops', he added revealingly, 'will behave well if those of whom they ought to look up are undeserving of respect.'[28] As for the Spanish rank and file, they were marked by their slovenliness ('Falstaff's ragged regiment') and indolence. Every prejudice was confirmed during the next fortnight, during which cravenness was added to the list of Spanish shortcomings. Even Wellesley eventually succumbed to the general feeling of contempt for the Spanish army, which was no more than an armed mob in a permanent state of disobedience and deliquescence.

For their part, the Spanish distrusted the British and Wellesley in particular. It was well known that Frere, the British representative to the Supreme Junta, had been demanding Cuesta's replacement and Wellesley's appointment as commander-in-chief of all Spain's armies. This was part of a broader policy which seemed directed towards reducing Spain to the same condition of abjectness as Portugal. These fears were never fully understood by the British, who thought the Spanish obstructive. Only with much forbearance on Wellesley's part was a joint plan devised.

The Anglo-Spanish army's aim was the elimination of Victor, now close to Talavera with 20,000 men. To keep him isolated, Anglo-Portuguese forces, distributed in northern Portugal and on roads leading south from Old Castile, were ordered to hinder Soult or Ney if they chose to intervene. General Venegas' army in Estremadura was instructed to distract Sebastiani's 22,000-strong corps by a feint towards

Madrid. Unfortunately this order was countermanded by the Supreme Junta on account of fears that Cuesta was becoming over-ambitious, and so Sebastiani was free to reinforce Victor.

Victor's destruction was left to Wellesley and Cuesta with an Anglo-Spanish army of 53,000 which advanced eastwards along the Tagus from Oropesa on 21 July. Within two days it was within striking distance of the French, thanks to Victor's dilatory intelligence service. This piece of good luck was thrown away when Cuesta refused to bring up his forces for a surprise attack. Victor made good his escape and was able to amalgamate with Sebastiani and a further 12,000 men rushed from Madrid by King Joseph. The blame for this and other blunders rested with Cuesta. 'It is impossible to do business with him,' complained Wellesley, exasperated by what he called 'the whimsical perverseness of his disposition'. This was displayed when, on hearing of Victor's departure, he hurried after him along the Madrid road where Wellesley feared 'he will get into a scrape'. He nearly did; faced by a now formidable French army, Cuesta narrowly escaped back to Talavera and the protection of the British.

As a result of Cuesta's waywardness, which many British officers believed was treachery, all Wellesley's earlier advantages had been thrown away. He was now forced to fight a battle on terms that he had hoped to avoid in concert with a slothful incompetent whose troops were unproven. Moreover, as the Spanish poured back towards Talavera, Wellesley had to detach forces to cover their retreat. In a sharp rear-guard action on the 27th, a British division was badly mauled, losing several hundred casualties.

Having extricated the Spaniards, Wellesley deployed his forces in a-mile-and-a-half line which stretched northwards from the bank of the Tagus and was anchored on rising ground. The Spanish were concentrated nearest the river in front of Talavera, where they were protected by the remains of the town wall and makeshift ramparts thrown up during the day. British and Hanoverian troops occupied the rest of the line and detachments of Anglo-Spanish cavalry were placed beyond the rising ground to block any outflanking movement.

Faced with this position, the French command was divided as to whether or not to attack. Joseph was nominally in overall command, but Victor, by force of his personality, was able to get his own way. He urged an immediate advance and predicted a pushover; the experience of beating them many times before had convinced him that the Spanish would fall apart and what he had seen of the British during the engagement on the 27th indicated that they were not to be feared. The prudent advised postponing the battle on the ground that the army would soon be reinforced by Soult, Ney and Marshal Edouard Mortier,

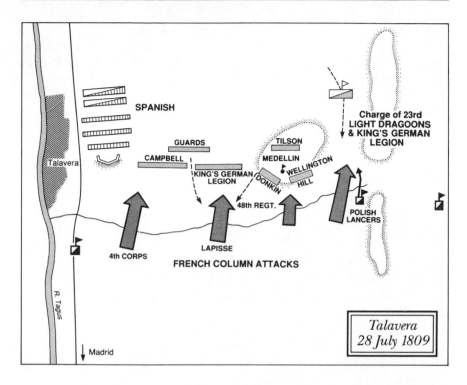

SPANISH

GUARDS

CAMPBELL

Talavera

KING'S GERMAN LEGION

TILSON

MEDELLIN

DONKIN

WELLINGTON

HILL

48th REGT.

4th CORPS

LAPISSE

FRENCH COLUMN ATTACKS

Charge of 23rd LIGHT DRAGOONS & KING'S GERMAN LEGION

POLISH LANCERS

R. Tagus

Madrid

Talavera 28 July 1809

who were hurrying south. When they arrived, and Soult was expected at Plascencia on 28 July, Joseph would have an overwhelming superiority of men and the British would be cut off from their bases in Portugal. Impetuosity prevailed and Joseph, not altogether willingly, approved a frontal attack on allied lines.

The battle of Talavera began with an alarming night attack by three French columns. One got lost, another withdrew after a desultory exchange of fire and the third surprised the King's German Legion troops on the Medellin hill, which commanded Wellesley's northern flank. The thrust failed, thanks to Major-General Rowland Hill, who recognized the danger and improvised a counter-attack in which, once again, a column dissolved under the firepower of the line.

The following morning Wellesley and his staff took up positions on the Medellin, from where they had an overview of the battlefield. It was an oppressively hot day: one Guards officer lately arrived from 'the shady side of Pall Mall' was conspicuous 'reposing in the shade of a green silk umbrella'.[29] During the several lulls in the fighting, French and British soldiers rushed from their lines to drink from the narrow Portina stream which lay just in front of the allied position. Onlookers noticed that neither showed any animosity and men from both armies mingled freely.

The battle opened just after seven with a cannonade and skirmishes between light infantry. Victor had correctly identified the Medellin as the key to the allied position and it was the target of his first mass attack. Perhaps in consequence of the lesson learned at Vimiero and during Moore's campaign, the French had slightly altered the formation of their columns by doubling the width to sixty men and reducing the depth to twenty-four. These adjustments made no difference to the outcome of the assault, which was thrown back by musketry.

After a brief armistice in which the wounded were recovered and thirsts slaked, a second, heavier offensive began. Thirty thousand French advanced across a wide front towards the centre of the allied line. The columns nearest the Tagus soon came to grief and were repulsed from a large stone farmhouse which marked the boundary between the British and Spanish. Further north, the defenders had similar success, but as the forward French columns fell back, they were chased by men from the Guards and the King's German Legion. Lord FitzClarence, watching from the Medellin, noticed how in all these engagements once the French had been shaken by musketry it needed only a British shout of 'Huzza!' and an advance with the bayonet to make them run off. There was virtually no resistance and FitzClarence later observed that very few men from either side suffered bayonet wounds.

This was so, but as the Guardsmen and Hanoverians rushed after the scattering French, they collided with the formed supporting columns. It was now their turn to run and in hurrying back they masked the fire from their own line. Wellesley saw what was happening and immediately grasped its significance. He ordered the 48th (Northamptonshire Regiment) to leave its position on the Medellin and engage the French columns who were converging on the gap left by the Guards and the Hanoverians. Its volley fire broke the momentum of the French advance and gave time for the fugitives to rally. The line held and, as the French retired, they were harried by Major-General Cotton's light dragoons. He too had seen the danger and was about to sound a charge off his own bat when Wellesley's order arrived.

A simultaneous offensive was under way beyond the northern flank where nine French battalions were cautiously edging forward. Again Wellesley foresaw the threat and ordered the 23rd Light Dragoons and the King's German Legion Hussars to charge, supported by artillery. The dragoons galloped forward pell-mell and, before they knew it, were plunging into an unseen gully. Nearly 200 men were killed or wounded in the ditch, but the survivors, rallied by Major Frederick Ponsonby, rushed on and became entangled with a larger body of Chasseurs à

Cheval. In all 207 men were casualties out of 480 and losses of horses were higher, making this a worse cavalry disaster than the Charge of the Light Brigade. The Hanoverians were luckier and avoided the hazard, but they could make no impression on the French infantry, which by now had formed defensive squares. Crowded together in a protective mass, the French made excellent artillery targets and their losses were heavy enough to force a withdrawal.

By the late afternoon the French had failed either to fracture or to outflank the allied line. Exhausted and having suffered 7,000 casualties, a sixth of their strength, the French withdrew during the night. The cost to the allies had been proportionally greater: the British had lost about 3,800 dead and 1,500 wounded, a quarter of the army, and the Spanish assessed their casualties at 1,500, a figure which was treated sceptically by British officers. Nevertheless, Talavera was counted a victory and secured Wellesley the title Viscount Wellington, although, as he was the first to admit, the advantages gained from the battle were few and questionable.

2

No Brilliant Event:
Spain and Portugal, August 1809–
September 1810

'We wish the battle of Talavera had never taken place,' wrote Lieutenant Andrew Leith Hay of the 29th a day after the battle.[1] It was an understandable and common reaction from a soldier in an army which had been on half-rations since 22 July and was about to face starvation. Its commander spent the night in the open on the battlefield; he probably slept fitfully since the air was crowded with the harrowing cries of the wounded, many of them burned in the fire that had swept the Medellin during the closing stage of the battle.

The sombre aftermath of Talavera began the most onerous period of Wellington's life. The next fourteen months were a time of uncertainty and setbacks during which he was continuously under intense pressure. His stamina, nerves and capacity for decisive judgement were tested to extremes. The survival of the army depended upon his patience, steadfastness of purpose and those almost superhuman powers of concentration which he applied to every aspect of the army's life as well as vital matters of strategy. He showed qualities which were little short of genius; certainly without Wellington the course of the war would have been very different, probably ending in disaster. Just how vital he had become was already apparent to a handful of officers. One, George Bingham, had told his mother on the eve of Talavera, 'We are badly off for Generals. After the commander of the Forces you must descend low before you meet with such talent.'[2]

All Wellington's talents were needed in the weeks after Talavera. Without adequate transport and perilously short of provender the army could not be risked in a pursuit of Victor, even though, as Wellington knew, his decision not to press his advantage would be criticized at home. Furthermore it was soon obvious that the junta of Estremadura could not fulfil its obligations to make good the shortfall in supplies. Not only was the army threatened by famine, its strategic position was precarious.

On 2 August intelligence was received that Soult and Ney with 25,000 men, after brushing aside a Spanish force detailed to hold the pass at Baños, had reached Novalmoral and were poised to sever the vital Lisbon road. Marching northwards to deflect them, Wellington heard that early reports had miscalculated Soult's numbers; 40,000–50,000 French troops, including Mortier's corps, were converging on his lines of communication. In danger of being trapped between Soult in the west and Victor in the east, Wellington hurriedly pulled the army back to El Puente del Arzobispo where, on the night of 4/5 August, it crossed to the south bank of the Tagus and safety. As a precaution against pursuit the newly arrived Light Division destroyed the bridge downstream at Almaraz.

The changing strategic situation scared Cuesta, who precipitately left Talavera on 3/4 August, callously abandoning 1,500 wounded British soldiers. They were, as Wellington guessed, humanely treated by the French and in some cases were given a share of French loot. After a quarrel in which Wellington refused to split his army for an Anglo-Spanish offensive, Cuesta departed full of boasts that he would attack single-handed. His forces were broken and not long after he suffered a stroke.

Wellington now faced a choice of retirement into Portugal or staying put to offer whatever assistance he could to the Spanish. On 8 August he estimated that there were about 70,000 French troops in western Spain, which was about right. For the moment these forces were concerned with mopping up Spanish resistance. On 11 August Venegas was decisively beaten by Sebastiani and three months later the Duke del Paque, having briefly occupied Salamanca, was defeated at Alba de Tormes. The piecemeal extinction of the Spanish field armies continued with the invasion of Andalucía in November, which culminated in the occupation of Seville on 1 February 1810. The Supreme Junta fled to Cádiz, which, for the next year or so, was all that remained of 'free' Spain.

Despite the Supreme Junta's pleas for assistance, there was nothing which Wellington could do to intervene, let alone reverse the tide of defeats. His army was on the verge of disintegration. 'A starving army', he told his brother Richard on 8 August, 'is worse than none. The soldiers lose their discipline and their spirit. They plunder even in the presence of their officers. The officers are discontented, and are almost as bad as the men; and with the army which a fortnight ago beat double their numbers, I should hesitate to meet a French corps of half their numbers.'[3] Unfed men were highly susceptible to distempers and during the second week of August up to 100 men were dying daily from various illnesses, including dysentery. On 13 August and with a day's rations in hand, he decided to fall back to the Portuguese border and leave Spain to its fate.

By the first week in September, Wellington had established his HQ at Badajoz and his army was distributed along forty miles of the Guadiana valley, straddling the Portuguese–Spanish border. If, and this was unlikely as winter pressed on, the French moved on Portugal by the Madrid road, he could reach Lisbon before them. The dismal Spanish episode was over and from now on all his efforts would be concentrated on the defence of Lisbon.

Wellington was convinced that Spanish generals and politicians had made his strategy unworkable and had squandered the fruits of his victory at Talavera. He openly railed against Spanish 'imbecility' and his correspondence with the Supreme Junta was crammed with expressions of barely concealed contempt and recrimination.[4] He made his position plain to the junta of Estremadura in October. 'Spain is either unable or unwilling to furnish supplies of Provisions and Forage for the Armies necessary for her defence, and in either case it is imposs-ible for me to risk the existence of His Majesty's army in a country so situated.'[5] Early in August he had left publication of his Talavera despatch to Castlereagh's discretion, but expressed the hope that his brothers Henry and William and his friend the Duke of Richmond would be provided with full details of his predicament so that they could publicly defend him from charges of having shown too much accommodation to Cuesta.[6]

The hitches during the Talavera campaign, like those that marked Moore's operations, revealed the need for a new Anglo-Spanish accord by which British forces could secure free access to the agricultural, human and financial resources of Spain. In August negotiations for such an arrangement were placed in the hands of the Marquess Wellesley. In particular he was to act as go-between in relations between his brother and the Supreme Junta and calm the former's temper.

On arrival in Seville the Marquess was horrified by what he found. On 19 September after extended and futile discussions he told Arthur that the 'country is on the verge of ruin'. He added, and this must have pleased his brother since it was an exact reflection of his own view, that he had told the junta's Foreign Minister, Don Martín de Garay, 'I would not trust the protection of a favourite dog to the whole Spanish army.'[7] And yet, as the Marquess realized, Britain could not beat the French in the Peninsula without Spanish help. He therefore proposed a series of measures designed to regenerate Spain's system of government which would give it more effective authority.

For all his emollient manner, the Marquess Wellesley found it hard to overcome Spanish suspicions about Britain's hidden motives. Neither country shared any common interest beyond an urge to defeat the French. For nearly 200 years the two countries had been colonial rivals; before the May 1808 uprising Britain had been seeking to conquer Spain's New World empire and afterwards objected strongly to Spanish plans to suppress the uprisings there. Furthermore, from the moment Spain had asked for aid, the British government had strongly pressed for commercial concessions throughout the Spanish empire. In short, the Spanish suspected with good reason that Britain would demand a heavy price for its help; at one point there were rumours that Cádiz and Havana would be surrendered.

What the British regarded as Spanish 'pride' was in fact a combination of misgivings and the fear that concessions would reduce Spain to the same condition of dependency as Portugal. Nevertheless, French successes in Andalucía and Wellesley's persuasiveness concentrated the minds of Spain's politicians. The Spanish Cortes (Parliament) was recalled and by the spring of 1810 had vested power in the Council of Regency. Relations between it and Wellington were conducted through Henry Wellesley, whose appointment as minister to Cádiz was one of the first acts of the Marquess after he had entered the cabinet as Foreign Secretary the previous November. Until his resignation in 1812, Anglo-Spanish affairs were exclusively in the hands of the Wellesley family.

Wellington was not impressed by subsequent efforts to regenerate Spain's government. As late as August 1813 he regretted that 'there exists no authority whatever in this country' and, distrusting the strong liberal presence within the Cortes, he was contemptuous of the 'Democracy' of Cádiz.[8] Unlike his elder brother, who was keen to foster it, he placed little faith in Spanish nationalism or 'enthusiasm' as he disdainfully called it. Remembering what he had witnessed during the summer, he wrote in October 1809 that 'enthusiasm ... creates confusion where order ought to prevail and disobedience of orders and indiscipline among the troops'. He rejected the prevailing view that it had been 'enthusiasm' which had inspired the French army; rather, he argued, it had been political leaders and factions within France which had channelled popular energies and afterwards kept them under tight control.[9]

However much he despised popular nationalism, it was vital for Wellington's war effort; Spanish guerrillas disrupted French communications and forced French generals to detach troops for endless small campaigns of pacification. Most importantly perhaps, the Spanish resistance movement provided Wellington with the basis for an intelligence-gathering network which covered every part of the country and gave him regular reports of his enemies' movements and often details of their strategy, even during 1810 and 1811 when no British army was active in Spain. For this reason alone it was necessary for the Spanish to be cultivated and assisted.

Such help was never undervalued, either by Wellington or by his officers. It was however a means to an end which, for Wellington, had little to do with national emancipation. Thirty years after the end of the war he wrote, 'My object was to maintain in Spain ... the ancient organization of the powers of the state ... notwithstanding the existence of a democratical constitution.' This demanded his defence of 'conservative interests' within a country where ideally 'men of property' served as the focal points for popular emotions.[10] How far these sentiments were understood by the Spanish is not known; their strained alliance with Britain was purely one of convenience. That it eventually worked owed much to Henry Wellesley's persistence and tact and his elder brother's willingness to suppress his true feelings.

While Anglo-Spanish relations were being slowly rebuilt, Wellington's first priority was the preservation of his army and the defence of Portugal. The events of the summer and autumn of 1809 had damaged the morale of the army, which by and large shared his view that their exertions and suffering had been purposeless. The feelings of the rank and file were expressed by John Bald of the 91st Highlanders, who wrote to his parents in November: 'Give William [his brother] my advice not to go for with soldiers ... No man knows what a soldier goes through, only those that endure the hardship of an expedition. I have been sixteen months without a bed and most of the time in the open fields lying in my clothes. I was eight days without provisions being served out to me, only what I could forage for myself.'[11] Self-help on campaign was plundering and was severely punished at Wellington's orders, even though he sympathized with the hungry.

The mood of disillusion and discontent was shared by officers. Many looked forward to a general peace, including Surgeon Boutflower of the 40th (Somersetshire Regiment), who in October was keen to return to England.[12] Leith Hay was sour and wrote home, 'The army which in the day of Battle made up for all the Deficiencies of generalship (and that those deficiencies did exist is notorious) bore with privations of food and fatigue, extricated him from one of the most precarious situations a General was ever placed in, and now we seem to have been forgotten.'[13] This final reproach may have been a reaction to the fact that three weeks earlier Wellington had spent some time shooting deer on the Duke of Braganza's estate, where he had enjoyed 'pretty good sport'.[14] Certainly the flow of grumbling letters from Portugal which reached Britain during the winter of 1809/10 gave the impression of a sullen army dissatisfied with its commander. 'Lord Wellington is unpopular with his army, equally in all ranks, in the great degree possible,' observed Major-General Lord Moira, presumably drawing on news from correspondents in the army.[15] There were even rumours that Wellington was about to return home.

In fact he had been busy since October with preparations for the defence of Lisbon. This involved throwing up a series of earthworks across the twenty-nine-mile-wide neck of land north of the city which would be known as the lines of Torres Vedras. Preliminary investigation of the area had already been undertaken by a Portuguese officer, Major José Neves Costa. Using his report as a guide and accompanied by Lieutenant-Colonel Richard Fletcher, RE, Wellington toured the district and, on 20 October, completed a memorandum in which he outlined his future plans for the defence of Lisbon.[16] The system of ramparts, ditches, gun-emplacements and redoubts represented a final stronghold. To reach it, the invading French army would have to cross a landscape in which every possible obstacle was defended and from which everything, including transport vehicles, livestock, food and fodder, had been stripped. In short, the French army would march through a desert and at the end face a siege. For its part, Wellington's army would retire on Lisbon, from where it would be supplied by British merchantmen protected by men-of-war. Seapower would underwrite landpower.

Wellington's plan was an answer to Castlereagh's demand that, if all else failed, Lisbon was to be held as a base for future operations against the French. It went without saying that so long as the city stayed in British hands it remained a challenge to French continental paramountcy. Both Castlereagh and Wellington assumed, rightly as it turned out, that once the French had consolidated their position in Spain they would mount a full-scale invasion of Portugal, probably in the spring of 1810. In this event it would be highly likely the French would attack in overwhelming numbers and the British have no choice but to wage a defensive, Fabian campaign of delay and attrition. As Wellington explained in a letter of 28 November to Castlereagh's successor, Liverpool, the position in Portugal was 'by no means hopeless', but 'no brilliant events' could be expected from the forthcoming campaign. On a personal note, he added that if he failed 'I shall be most confoundedly abused and … lose the character I have gained.'[17]

Since October there had been a new government in Britain formed after a squabble between Canning and Castlereagh which had ended in a duel, news which disturbed Wellington.[18] The new ministry was led by Spencer Perceval, who had ability as a party manager and little else, and included two of Wellington's closest allies, his brother Richard, who took over the Foreign Office, and Liverpool as Secretary for War. This suited Wellington, who, in his letter of congratulation, looked forward to all the 'fair support, protection and assistance ... to which an officer is entitled when he acts fairly by the Publick and all the friendship and kindness which I have been accustomed to receive from you'.[19] All this Liverpool gave in abundance, even adding, in some of his correspondence, details about the welfare of Wellington's wife and children, whom he occasionally visited.

Such loyalty would be needed throughout 1810. Wellington had never tried to conceal the fact that his army in Portugal was still insecure, despite the measures in hand for the defence of Lisbon. By the end of December he had drawn up a plan in readiness for an emergency evacuation of Lisbon which might be necessary to save the army if it was opposed by an irresistible French force. On 3 January 1810 Liverpool approved the scheme and, by May, the Admiralty had directed 45,000 tons of shipping to the Tagus, which was the amount Wellington thought he would need.[20] After embarkation, 6,000 British troops would be shipped to Gibraltar and the rest to Cádiz, from where, with Spanish approval, they could open a new front in southern Spain. The best-trained Portuguese would be sent to Brazil.

These preparations for a smooth abandonment of Portugal reflected the nervousness both of Wellington and of the cabinet. There was no way of knowing the outcome of the French offensive and the government was anxious to avoid repeating the Coruña and Walcheren débâcles. Both had provided ammunition for critics in Parliament and beyond and, during the winter and spring of 1809/10, there was additional censure of Wellington which focused on the outcome of the battle of Talavera. According to Lord Grey, who spoke in opposition to the Lords' vote of thanks to Wellington, this had 'all the consequences of defeat' and he demanded the full publication of every relevant despatch.

A week later, on 1 February, there was an opposition attempt to divert the Commons into a wide-ranging debate over strategy. Several charges were laid against Wellington: he 'had imprudently brought his army into a critical situation'; 'he seemed to have fought merely for a peerage'; and through his 'vainglorious, partial and incorrect' despatches he had deceived his countrymen.[21] His allies, including Castlereagh, successfully defended the vote of thanks and squashed demands for a public enquiry of the kind which was being conducted into the Walcheren affair. Wellington also had champions outside

Parliament, like an anonymous Cheltenham poetaster, who wrote to the *Gentleman's Magazine*:[22]

> But not a true-born Briton can be found
> Who does not rapturously hail the sound
> Of WELLINGTON's heroic, glorious name,
> Who is not proud of TALAVERA's fame
> Then let not party spirit e'er debase
> A noble mind....

The acrimony which followed Talavera was a further reminder to Wellington that he had continually to look over his shoulder to see how his actions were being received in Britain. 'Alehouse politicians' scrutinized his strategy and offered their own versions of how the war might be waged and, whenever he was faulted, his detractors were always ready to remind listeners that he was a political creature who had been advanced by his intimates in the government[23]. And yet, in March 1810, he secured one valuable ally. George III read his assessment of the situation in Portugal and was profoundly impressed by its clarity and the wisdom of its author. He accordingly advised his ministers to permit Wellington 'to proceed according to his judgement ... unfettered by any particular instructions which might embarrass him in the execution of his general plan of operations'.[24] This piece of good sense was one of the King's last decisions; by the end of the year his mind had finally passed into desuetude.

Wellington's plan of campaign for 1810 offered few chances of spectacular gains. The best he could hope for was a stalemate which would hurt the French more than their enemies. In Paris, Napoleon was demanding a decisive victory which would drive the British into the sea and deliver Portugal into his hands. The invasion was committed to the hands of the fifty-five-year-old Marshal André Masséna whose reputation alone would make his enemies lose heart, or so the Emperor believed.

Masséna's real strength lay in the numbers of men he could deploy against Wellington. There were, in all, 325,000 French troops in Spain and up to 85,000 were available for the invasion of Portugal, the rest being deployed in besieging Cádiz and crushing resistance elsewhere in Spain. Wellington had just over 40,000 Anglo-Portuguese and, in the event of Masséna crossing the border, a third of a million Portuguese civilians of the ordenança, an armed home guard, many of whom were busy constructing the lines of Torres Vedras.

With the advantage of numbers, Masséna could afford to take his time and his campaign proceeded in a ponderous, almost leisurely fashion. Its tone was characterized by the presence of his mistress, who dressed in the heavily braided uniform of a hussar and accompanied her lugubrious lover everywhere, much to the annoyance of some of his staff. It was shared by the Duchess of Abrantès, formerly Mme Junot, who felt demeaned. Since making himself Emperor, Napoleon had scattered titles among his generals and marshals, so transforming them into courtiers and they soon embraced all the traditional courtiers' vices of envy, snobbery and prickliness. Masséna was Prince of Essling and Soult Duke of Dalmatia, which British soldiers rendered as 'Duke of Damnation'.

The Prince of Essling opened his campaign in June by detaching 26,000 men under Ney to besiege the Spanish frontier fortress of Cuidad Rodrigo. It lay across the Salamanca–Coimbra–Lisbon road along which Masséna intended to mount his invasion. By 13 June Ney had completely surrounded the stronghold, confident that he could call on over 30,000 men held in reserve if Wellington chose to raise the siege. Wellington's offensive options were further reduced by the presence near Talavera of a smaller force under General Reynier which could move either northwards to assist Ney or westwards towards Lisbon.

There was little that Wellington could have done to hinder the French, let alone offer them battle. Throughout the spring and summer of 1810 he was like a chess-player who dared not hazard his few remaining strong pieces. Moreover many of his men were still in poor shape: recent reinforcements were suffering the symptoms of Walcheren fever and many veterans had not shaken off the sicknesses contracted the previous year in the Guadiana valley. Last year's diffi- culties over cash allowances reappeared and supply continued to cause headaches. In July the Commissary-General complained that his lack of transport had reduced the army in eastern Portugal to 'living from hand to mouth'.[25] Nevertheless the army remained in good heart and keen to get to grips with the French. Captain Carss of the 53rd expected a battle as hard as Talavera, but dreaded a defeat because of the disparity in numbers between the British and French.[26]

This was Wellington's fear. On 30 June he admitted that he lacked the men to save Ciudad Rodrigo, which fell, after a stubborn defence, on 10 July. Almeida was Masséna's next objective and, as his forces probed westwards towards the Portuguese frontier, Wellington pru- dently withdrew his outposts from beyond the Coa. For the previous three months this area had been held by Craufurd's Light Division, which had been successfully engaged in the collection of intelligence about the enemy's movements and checking his reconnaissance patrols. As this division fell back, Ney chanced his hand and drove his corps forwards to catch it with its back against the deep-banked and fast-flowing Coa, where it should not have been if Craufurd had kept to his orders. His heavily outnumbered division narrowly escaped destruction after a sharp engagement, thanks to luck and a French blunder in the shape of a headlong infantry rush across a well-defended bridge.

This and an earlier skirmish in which some dragoons had been badly cut up when they had ambushed a French patrol angered Wellington because they were 'foolish affairs' that wasted lives to no purpose. And yet he forgave and stayed well disposed towards Craufurd. 'I cannot accuse a man who I believe had meant well,' he told his brother William, 'and whose error is one of judgement, and not of intention.'[27] There was in fact much to recommend Craufurd. He had been a pupil of Moore, he had a high sense of professionalism, he maintained tight discipline (when he saw a man break ranks to avoid a puddle, he would shout 'Sit down in it, Sir!'), and he was popular among his light infantrymen, whom he kept fit and healthy. He was, however, cantankerous, temperamental and thought he knew better than his commander, whose orders he often disregarded. In time Wellington became exasperated and many years later he characterized Craufurd as an able general but 'a dissatisfied, troublesome man' with the disconcerting habit of begging forgiveness for his mistakes 'in a way which one has read in romances'.[28]

Craufurd's misconduct on the Coa occurred at a moment when, in Wellington's words, 'Affairs have begun to take a serious turn in this country.' In an emergency he could field an army of 50,000, of which half were untried Portuguese, against an enemy who mustered 74,000 with a further 13,000 in close reserve.[29] Rather than risk an engagement on such unequal terms, Wellington decided to abandon the Portuguese hinterland and pull back all his forces to Lisbon. By 31 July arrangements for the retreat were complete; his only hope lay in the Portuguese garrison at Almeida, who might be able to detain the French until the autumnal rains began.

Ill-luck dogged the stout-hearted Portuguese defenders of Almeida, who were forced to surrender on 28 August after a howitzer shell detonated the powder magazine. Reinforced by the 17,000-strong division of General Reynier, which had marched from Sabugal, Masséna was free to begin the conquest of Portugal. As Wellington correctly predicted, he took the road which ran south-westwards towards Coimbra. This and Masséna's decision to follow the road which passed through Viseu gave Wellington a chance to block his path at Busaco, where he could fight a delaying action on favourable terms. To this end he summoned Lieutenant-General Rowland Hill, whose division had been guarding the Madrid–Lisbon road, and Beresford, whose Portuguese had been based at Abrantès, to join him on the north bank of the Mondego.

3

Lions at Bay: Portugal, September 1810–December 1811

Among those gathered on the Mondego was Captain Neil Douglas of the 79th Highlanders, who, accompanied by his gundogs, spent the morning of 25 September shooting quail. A bugle call interrupted his sport and he returned to his regiment, which had been ordered, along with the rest of the 1st Division, to take up a position on the Serra de Busaco.[1] After fourteen months of shadow-boxing, Wellington had decided to fight a major action, a decision which pleased many who had become sick of endless retreats. A victory might also dull the edge of domestic criticism which, he knew, would follow the news that he had refused to save Ciudad Rodrigo.

In the event it was Masséna's ignorance of local topography which forced Wellington's hand. Ill-served by his intelligence staff and dependent on an atlas with thirty-year-old maps, Masséna had chosen the worst possible route to Lisbon along stony roads which played havoc with his wheeled transport, shattering axles and gun-carriages. It needed six days for the army to recover at Viseu, a delay which gave Wellington the opportunity to deploy his forces on a defensive position unequalled in Portugal.

The Serra de Busaco was a ten-mile-long hog's back that stretched northwards from the Mondego astride the Viseu-to-Coimbra road, rising in places to between 1,200 and 1,500 feet. It was a perfect defensive position, since its flattish crest enabled a commander to dispose his men out of sight of the enemy and safe from artillery fire. There was, and here Wellington was taking a calculated risk, the possibility that such an experienced commander as Masséna would shy away from assaulting so formidable a position and instead would shift his army around its northern flank by way of Boialva. Nevertheless the

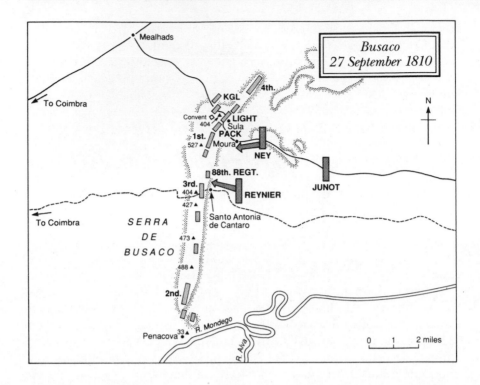

temptation to fight here proved irresistible; Wellington set up his HQ in the Carmelite Convent at Busaco, where, no doubt all too aware of local vermin, he insisted on his bedroom being cleaned and white-washed, and waited for Masséna's arrival.

Ney, who arrived with his corps on the evening of the 25th, was first to survey the hill and he felt uneasy about attacking blindly. It would be better, he argued, to return to Viseu and outflank Wellington by a march on Oporto. His fellow corps commanders, Reynier and Junot, shared his apprehension, but all were overruled by Masséna, who doubted the quality of Wellington's Portuguese and was unwilling to allow an unbeaten army to occupy a position close to his communications. Moreover, he felt confident that he faced no more than a rearguard and that the main British army lay nearer Coimbra, where he had originally planned to bring it to battle. In fact he was opposed by an army of 51,000, just under half of them Portuguese. Why, despite the cavalry available to him, Masséna attempted no serious reconnaissance of the Serra de Busaco remains a mystery.

In placing his men, Wellington had imagined that Masséna would throw his heaviest assault against the northern spur of the ridge, using the Coimbra road that ran beside the convent. He therefore concentrated 12,000–14,000 men here, including an untested Portuguese division, and spread the remainder out southwards for seven or eight miles. Just before he retired to bed, his Quartermaster-General, Colonel George Murray, warned him to move additional forces to cover a small track which ran through the village of Santo António do Cantara, parallel with the main Coimbra road. Earlier in the day Murray had noticed Masséna and his staff, conspicuous in their gorgeous uniforms, making a detailed examination of this route. He correctly assumed that at least one of the French columns would follow this track and Wellington adjusted his dispositions accordingly.[2] It was a judicious move which paid dividends the following day.

Masséna's attack began shortly before six on the morning of 27 September and was in two phases. The first involved Reynier's corps, which, as Murray had foreseen, advanced through Santo António. An early-morning mist gave the French some cover, which must have been reassuring since none of the French commanders had any exact knowledge of where their opponents were deployed or how many there were. Nevertheless the French advance was brisk and determined; after the haze had cleared, Major Scovell reckoned that the columns had covered two and a half miles in forty-five minutes.[3] The British too were buoyant. Leith Hay watched Wellington ride along the lines 'in the highest spirits' and he sensed that there was 'not a man present ... that did not burn with ardour to face the foe'.[4]

Quick thinking as well as ardour were needed once the columns of Reynier's corps came over the crest. One division collided with the 74th Highlanders and two Portuguese battalions and a fire-fight began. Another, by chance, came upon a gap in the line which was hurriedly plugged by the 88th (Connaught Rangers), a notoriously undisciplined regiment known as the 'ragged rascals'. Urged on in splendid style by their colonel, Alexander Wallace, they met the French with volley fire and pressed home the advantage with the bayonet. Wellington had been an onlooker and afterwards offered his congratulations. 'Wallace, I have never witnessed a more gallant charge.' A third division, under General Maximilien Foy, also escaped detection and its presence at the top of the ridge was first revealed by a Frenchman on a rock waving his hat in exultation. Major-General Sir James Leith, still weakened from Walcheren fever, immediately led his division forward into the undefended area with his ADC and nephew, Leith Hay, in the vanguard alongside the colours of the 9th (East Norfolk Regiment). Once again sustained volley fire broke the attackers, who, their nerve broken, fell back under the threat of a bayonet charge. As they scattered down the hill, Leith Hay noticed how the men of the 9th took 'deliberate aim' at their disappearing backs.[5]

The disaster which overtook Reynier's corps above Santo António was repeated to the north, where Ney's corps delivered its attack. Here the Portuguese showed their mettle, throwing back a French division, and, as they charged, the sportsman Neil Douglas cheered heartily; a few moments later he was struck by a ball in the shoulder.

After the repulse of Ney's corps, Masséna realized he had miscalculated his adversary's strength and was beaten. The French had lost 4,000–5,000 casualties against the British 1,250, but without cavalry Wellington could not exploit his success. On 29 September his army withdrew from the Serra de Busaco and the retreat to Lisbon continued.

Wellington had fought and won a battle which would later be acclaimed as one of his classic defensive actions. Busaco had further vindicated his faith in the efficacy of the line over the column and the terrible power of volley fire. A French staff officer, who had seen the effects of such fire at fifteen paces, described it as 'murderous' and was deeply impressed by Wellington's use of concealed infantry.[6] Leith Hay, who had been in the thick of the fight above Santo António, believed that the bayonet also played a vital part. 'A Frenchman will stand at a distance and fire as long as you choose, but the moment a British bayonet gets within twenty yards of him he soon shows his back.'[7] Surgeon Boutflower went further and claimed that the British bayonet charge was a token of national moral superiority, an ideal which was later embraced by Victorian military writers, who were unhappy about letting technology take all the credit for British victories.[8]

As the Anglo-Portuguse army drew closer to Lisbon, closely pursued by French cavalry patrols, it was joined by swarms of Portuguese refugees, whose fortitude and patience were both pitied and admired. Everywhere the countryside and towns were stripped of everything which might help the French. Deep in the hinterland, the partisans of the ordenança became increasingly audacious. Led by the enthusiastic, heavy-drinking Colonel Trant they attacked French supply columns, harried stragglers and took hideous revenge on any Frenchman they caught. More than once Masséna complained to Wellington about their torture and murder of prisoners. This was humbug from a man who had condoned the wholesale looting of Coimbra and had himself stolen scientific instruments, but Wellington attempted to save captured Frenchmen by offering bounty money for any whom the ordenança surrendered to British patrols.

By 14 October Masséna's army reached the outer lines of the Torres Vedras. So poor was French intelligence that neither he nor any of his staff knew of their existence. Two days of mounted inspection of the defences convinced Masséna that they were impregnable and he would not attack them. The lessons learned during the headlong assault on the Serra de Busaco were still fresh and the entire French siege train was at Almeida. Bringing it to Lisbon was impossible; winter had started, and the bad roads were all but impassable and were infested with roving bands of ordenança.

Masséna was effectively checkmated. Behind the Torres Vedras was a well-supplied and healthy British army ready to engage any French units that broke through the outer earthworks, which were held by 249 cannon and 30,000 Portuguese militia. By contrast the French army was short of food and losing men from sickness; the number of men available for service plummeted from 55,000 on 1 October to 44,800 on 15 November.[9] There was nothing that Masséna could do but retire thirty miles to positions around Santarém and live off the land until supplies arrived from Spain. They never appeared and so, on 6 March, Masséna ordered a retreat to his bases on the Portuguese border.

All this vindicated the strategy Wellington had devised over a year before and he was delighted that events had followed the course he had predicted. When Major-General Miles Nightingall disembarked in February 1811 and dined with Wellington, he found him 'very sanguine' and his army in high spirits. There was 'excellent beef and bread' and it was rumoured that the French were eating cats and donkeys. Although critical voices had not been stilled, there was a growing faith in Wellington's generalship which increased as it became clear that Masséna's army was in a state of deliquescence and beyond the control of its commanders. Captain Carss spoke for many when, using John Bullish language, he recounted the reversal of fortune during the winter of 1810/11.

> Mr Massina gave chase in full cry from Coimbra, thinking he would be in at the death before his lordship and his lions could get covered by the wooden walls of old England! Early in the morning of 10th October Mr Massina was greatly astonished when he found his lordship and his lions at bay in full view, where neither he nor his bloodhounds dared even venture to step to smell, hungry as they were.[10]

And yet residual doubts remained about Wellington's conception of how the war in Portugal and Spain would be won. On hearing the news of Masséna's flight, the rheumaticky and malcontented Nightingall remarked, 'How fortunate for Lord Wellington!! but he is always lucky.' There was much in the same vein from armchair generals in Britain, many of whom were still bitter about the speed of Wellington's promotion.[11] More harmful, since they could hamper his operations, were the criticisms levelled against him within the Portuguese council of Regency. These were based upon well-founded fears that Wellington's scorched-earth policy was causing tremendous suffering and would leave Portugal a blasted and penniless country.

Wellington attempted to alleviate some of the privation which, in fairness, owed much to French rapacity. In June 1811 he had appealed to the Council for building materials and seed corn for the peasantry of the bare uplands around Thomar and Leiria, where a famine was impending.[12] At the same time he was anxious that the Portuguese pulled their weight in the war effort and so he and Charles Stuart, the British representative on the Council, continually pressed for greater efficiency and commitment. Their severest censure was directed towards the Junta de Viveres, which handled the collection and distribution of transport and supplies and was suspected of lassitude and corruption. Why else were only 600 of the 26,000 two-wheeled carts demanded by the Commissary-General delivered in July 1810?[13] Overwhelmed by similar cases of incompetence, Wellington concluded in January 1811 that the entire Junta de Viveres should be placed under British direction.

While Stuart and Wellington forcefully demanded administrative reform, a faction on the Council, led by Don José António de Menenzes e Sousa, evaded the issue and called for the revision of a strategy which was destroying their country. This was undeniable: so too was the fact that a country without resources could not be taxed and had therefore to rely on Britain's annual subsidy of £2 million. This was the stick which, when persuasion had failed, Wellington wielded to bring the Council to heel. In August 1811 Stuart, backed by Wellington, threatened the subsidy's suspension and the Council agreed that in future all allowances would be paid into a Military Chest under British control. During the winter of 1811/12 the Council made another concession and accepted part of the subsidy in military stores, although Wellington mistakenly told them that such supplies were an extra. In the end the Portuguese efforts to achieve efficiency were half-hearted and more and more of the burden of equipping and feeding their army fell on the British commissariat.[14]

Portuguese cussedness was a distraction for Wellington at a time when he was evolving a new strategy in the light of Masséna's rebuff. The failure of the second invasion of Portugal had again demonstrated the limits of Napoleon's military power and had given encouragement not only to the Spaniards, but to others in Europe who were growing weary of military dictatorship. In January 1811 heartening intelligence was received from Cádiz that the situation in Portugal had forced King

Joseph to withdraw forces from anti-guerrilla operations in Catalonia and Valencia and concentrate them in Madrid. There were further reports that French soldiers 'fear the brave Lord Wellington and his Trenches'.[15] Agents in Paris described how the news of Masséna's setbacks had caused considerable consternation.[16]

How Wellington might exploit his advantages depended on the numbers of men available to him. The more the government allowed him the more he could achieve. This view was obvious enough in Lisbon, but less so in London, where the government was having a rough passage and briefly seemed in danger of falling. At the end of December 1810 it was clear that George III's equilibrium was irrecoverable and that the regency arrangements would have to be extended, a bleak prospect for Perceval's ministry since the Prince of Wales, who would permanently act as regent, favoured the Opposition. If he chose a new cabinet it would certainly be dominated by supporters of peace. Wellington, fearing the worst, urged his brother Henry to stay put in Cádiz if the government changed, for his appointment was professional rather than political, and added that he would do likewise.[17] A month later in January 1811 he heard from a gloomy Liverpool that the Prince was surrounded by 'jacobins'.[18] His fears were premature, for the Prince Regent did not embrace the Opposition and the ministry survived.

Aware of its vulnerability, the government was extremely hesitant about any increased commitment to the Portuguese campaign. Throughout the winter of 1810/11 it fought a running battle with Wellington over reinforcements and was very reluctant to maintain, let alone increase, the allowances available to him. Part of the problem was the shortage of men: between June 1808 and June 1809 13,200 men had been enlisted into the army and the following years the number rose to 15,000. At this rate of recruitment the army was barely making good the losses from death, disease and desertion in the Peninsula not to mention the yearly wastage from these causes in home garrisons, which stood at about 8,000.[19] Between April 1809 and December 1811 22,000 reinforcements had been shipped to Portugal and Cádiz, during which months losses had been 16,200.

What troubled Wellington most were the fluctuations caused by sickness, which often left him dangerously short of men. Out of the 33,000 men under his command when Masséna first approached the Torres Vedras, 9,000 were convalescents. Matters had looked up by January 1811 when his monthly returns listed 47,600 British and 45,000 Portuguese, but at any given time he could expect at least 30 per cent of his strength to be either sick or travelling to or from a hospital. The government, while sympathetic, was unwilling to deplete reserves from

British and colonial garrisons for a number of reasons. First, there was the residual suspicion that the Portuguese front was a sideshow which would never add up to much or contribute substantially to Napoleon's overthrow. In addition there remained the possibility that, as in the past, British forces might be deployed in northern Europe in support of a new anti-French coalition.

Wellington rejected both arguments. Nowhere but in Portugal and Spain could Britain 'keep in check so large a proportion of Bonaparte's army' so cheaply and, whatever else happened on the continent, 'no seat of operations holds out such prospects of success'.[20] His view on cheapness was not one shared by the cabinet, which was disturbed by the spiralling costs of his campaign. These had risen from £2.63 million in 1809 to £6.60 million in 1810, making it, in Liverpool's words, 'absolutely impossible' for Wellington to wage war as he had done previously. Rather he should pursue a strategy of 'steady and continued exertion on a moderate scale'. A fortnight later, at the very end of February 1811, he reminded Wellington that the option of complete withdrawal from Portugal was still open.[21] These arguments for restraint did not convince Wellington, who believed that had he been allowed an extra 10,000 men in the summer of 1810 the outcome of that campaign would have been more favourable. Furthermore he suggested that the official figures were false because the government would have had to pay out money for his soldiers and their supplies, irrespective of whether they were in Portugal or Britain. The real cost of operations had been, he reckoned, about £1.5 million.[22]

By April, when the news of Masséna's retreat was known in Britain, the tenor of the debate over cash and reinforcements changed. Those who had opposed Wellingon's strategy in Parliament were, for the moment, silenced and a few like Sir Banastre Tarleton, the Liverpool MP and veteran of the American War of Independence, were complimentary. As Liverpool wrote on 11 April, 'the eyes of the world are now completely open to the wisdom of the system which you have been acting'. 'You know', he added, 'our means, both financial and military are limited; but such as they are, we are determined not to be diverted from the Peninsula to other objects. If we can strike a blow, we will strike it there.'[23]

It was up to Wellington to decide how and where the blow was to be struck. He chose to launch three blows against the border fortresses of Almeida, Ciudad Rodrigo and Badajoz, which had fallen to Soult early in January 1811 after a brief offensive from Andalucía. This was a surprisingly ambitious strategy given that Wellington lacked the necessary siege train, which had to be shipped from Britain and reached

Almeida only in December. Unable to knock down walls, he chose instead to blockade the strongholds with extended cordons of troops in the hope that the garrisons would be starved into surrender. Inevitably his activities invited intervention from Soult's army in Andalucía and Victor's in Old Castile, both of whom could and did call on reinforcements from elsewhere in Spain. The greatest danger lay in a concerted effort by two or more French armies, although this was lessened by the uncooperative attitudes of their commanders.

In the spring, Beresford's Anglo-Portuguese forces established themselves in front of Badajoz, where their antiquated artillery, borrowed from the Portuguese arsenal at Elvas, made little impression. Wellington took his main army eastwards into the uplands near Almeida and Ciudad Rodrigo. His presence there was a magnet to Victor, who despite previous setbacks was still full of fight and anxious to refurbish his reputation. Having, in Wellington's words, 'collected every vagabond they had in Castile', the French advanced to break the blockade of Almeida, which, so long as it was held, was a vital springboard for any future invasion of Portugal.

Wellington had expected such a response and planned to offer battle on a defensive position of his choice, a six-mile ridge that ran north from the village of Fuentes de Oñoro, a village between Almeida and Masséna's base at Ciudad Rodrigo. It was a decision which pleased many of his officers, who felt that the 'dignity', that is morale, of the army would be bruised by another tactical withdrawal.[24]

Over half of Wellington's 48,000-strong army (including three out of six divisions) was concentrated on the high ground above Fuentes. It was an imbalance which he regretted as the battle developed, but he lacked the men to be strong everywhere. As it was his deployment seemed justified when, on the morning of 3 May, Masséna launched his first offensive against the village. It was stubbornly held and Wellington, watching from high ground, was able to throw in reinforcements when the French appeared to get the upper hand. These included the 71st Highlanders, whose colonel spurred his men on with the promise of food. 'My lads, you have had no provision for these two days; there is plenty in the hollow in front, let us down and divide it.' As they advanced at the double the Highlanders were mocked by light-company men who were falling back: 'Seventy-first, you will come back quicker than you advance.' Undismayed, the 71st attacked: 'Thrice we waved our bonnets, and thrice we cheered; brought our firelocks to the charge, and forced them back through the town.'[25] After several hours of street-fighting in which his men came off worse, Masséna was forced to abandon the offensive.

The following day was an armistice during which Masséna, brought to his senses by the failure of his first attack and remembering the lessons of Busaco, carefully reconnoitred the British position. Wellington too reconsidered his position and shifted his 7th Division two miles south of Fuentes, where, as he later realized, it was perilously exposed.[26] It was this unit which bore the brunt of Masséna's second offensive, which began shortly after dawn on 5 May.

Masséna launched two simultaneous, large-scale assaults: the first against Fuentes and the second, an outflanking sweep, to the south. Here the cutting edge of the attack was a force of 3,500 cavalry supported by three infantry divisions. Vastly outnumbered, the 7th Division was soon in trouble. Seeing its difficulties, Wellington ordered Craufurd's Light Division to cover its retreat and at the same time swung his line round to meet the northwards thrust of the French attack. The manoeuvre worked and in the meantime the 7th and Light Divisions fought a heroic retirement action, repeatedly throwing back their pursuers. They were helped by a Royal Horse Artillery battery, which in the teeth of French cavalry charges unlimbered, fired a few rounds and then galloped back. The French horsemen attacked with 'great impetuosity', which made Lieutenant Edward Cocks think them all 'picked men and drunk'.[27] The British light dragoons showed 'courage' in plenty but little 'conduct', that is discipline. This was the opinion of Major Scovell of the staff, who joined in the hacking match with French dragoons; he later observed, 'our sabres are not sharp enough and there can be no doubt of the thrust being superior to the cut. I saw several men receive 5 or 6 cuts in the arms and shoulders without any impression.'[28] Despite this handicap, the British cavalrymen did their bit to stem the French onslaught and help the infantry fall back. But it was the sustained fire of the infantry which finally settled the matter by showing the French that further advance was futile.

The second French attack on Fuentes like the first made no headway. Again there was savage street-fighting with Highlanders and Irishmen of the 88th playing a major part. The 79th had been raised from the Cameron clan and when its colonel, Philips Cameron, was shot the cry was raised, 'Thuit an Comsbronach' (Cameron has fallen). It was taken up by the Gaelic-speakers of the 71st and 88th, who rushed to join the Camerons as they avenged the death of their chieftain's son. This was the stuff of Highland legend and it stirred the heart of Scott, who included the incident in his epic poem 'The vision of Don Rodrigo' which appeared the following year:

> And what avails thee that for Cameron slain,
> Wild from the plaided ranks the yell was given?
> Vengeance and grief gave mountain rage the rein,

And, at the bloody spear-point headlong driven,
Thy despot's giant guards fled like the rack of heaven.

With Fuentes still in British hands, Masséna abandoned his attack and retreated; he had lost 2,200 men, 700 more that his opponents. During the night of 5/6 May Wellington ordered trenches to be dug which effectively ruled out a third French offensive. A day later, and after a display of bravado in the form of a review in full view of the British, Masséna retreated to Almeida. Within a week he had received a letter from Napoleon ordering his recall to Paris and naming his successor as the thirty-seven-year-old Marshal Auguste Frédéric Marmont.

The victory of Fuentes convinced General Anthoine Brennier that he could no longer hold Almeida. Showing considerable skill he foxed the troops surrounding the fortress and slipped away with 1,400 men on the night of 10/11 May. Wellington was enraged and blamed the escape on the negligence of the the divisional commanders. He was also much dissatisfied with his performance at Fuentes, in particular the overstretching of his line. Afterwards he commented, 'If Boney had been there, we would have been damnably licked,' and suggested to Liverpool that the public announcement of the battle should not be followed by the customary celebrations.

Within a few days, as he hurried south with detachments to reinforce Beresford, he heard news of the battle of Albuera, which had been fought on 7 May. It was less than reassuring. Beresford's Anglo-Portuguese and Castaños's Spaniards had narrowly escaped destruction in an extraordinarily bloody battle in which over half the allied army were casualties. In private, Wellington was horrified by the 'loss and dis-organization' suffered by Beresford's army and he prudently censored official Spanish accounts of the action, for 'a whining report ... would have driven the people of England mad'.[29]

Short of engineers and without proper artillery, the besiegers of Badajoz made little progress and, not long after, when threatened by a combination of Marmont's and Soult's corps, Wellington withdrew northwards to concentrate on Ciudad Rodrigo. A period of static warfare followed and in July one general expected the army to spend an inactive summer in cantonments.[30] This was not Wellington's view for, on 2 July, he told his brother William that now Soult and Masséna had parted, 'I am waiting to see whether I can give one of them a knock.'[31] Neither offered him the opportunity and so, until late autumn, the army hovered around Ciudad Rodrigo.

There was some consolation for Wellington during this period. The government relaxed its restrictions on reinforcements and between June and October drafts of 16,000 were sent to Portugal. Their immediate value was limited since a high proportion were infected with the recurrent Walcheren fever picked up two years before.[32] Most needed were cavalry: at Fuentes British riders had been outnumbered four to one and at Albuera French horsemen, in particular a regiment of Polish lancers, had wreaked terrible havoc. York, who had been recalled as commander-in-chief in May, pledged Wellington substantial reinforcements of heavy dragoons.[33]

Nevertheless in September, when Marmont edged his army of 50,000 forward in what turned out to be a half-hearted probe towards British lines, Wellington was forced to withdraw for lack of numbers. He took up a strong defensive position on high ground near Fuenteguinaldo which Marmont, whose forces had been sharply resisted by a small rearguard at El Bodon, decided not to attack. Further south, Beresford's army, which had been guarding the Tagus from any sudden push by Soult, inflicted a salutary defeat on a French force at Arroyo Molinos on 22 October. These minor actions, although not contributing greatly to the outcome of the war, confirmed that man for man and in conditions where the imbalance of numbers could be redressed the Anglo-Portuguese army was more than a match for the French. The French still fought well, but one of King Joseph's staff noticed towards the end of 1811 the growth of disillusionment with a war which offered no more than 'a series of dangers without glory'.[34]

As the year closed, forces which were beyond Wellington's control began to assert themselves, changing completely the circumstances under which he waged war. In September Napoleon ordered an intensive effort to crush resistance in Valencia and Catalonia, and so Marmont had to transfer 10,000 men to Marshal Louis Suchet's army. This sudden reduction of Marmont's army ruled out a third invasion of Portugal, which had anyway been made more difficult by the recapture of Almeida. Moreover, as Marmont's troops took up their winter quarters in Salamanca, Wellington had a slight numerical superiority on the Portuguese frontier. Of greater importance was the intelligence received in January 1812 which confirmed nine-month-old rumours that Napoleon's relations with Russia were deteriorating to the point where war appeared unavoidable.[35] For the first time since the summer of 1809 France might face war on two fronts.

Part Six

The Iron Duke

1

Lord Wellington Don't Know How to Lose a Battle: The Commander and His Men

January 1812 was a turning point in the Peninsular War and Wellington's career. With his Anglo-Portuguese army he had shown the rest of Europe that Napoleon no longer had a monopoly of victory. Vimiero, Talavera, Masséna's refusal to risk battle before the lines of Torres Vedras, Fuentes de Oñoro and Albuera reversed the trend of a dozen years. The results were clear and ominous for a dictator who relied solely upon force of arms to enforce his will; Portugal was unconquered and his hold over Spain looked increasingly fragile. It was now possible, Wellington believed, for his army to begin the liberation of Spain and, when this had been accomplished, to invade southern France. And yet, seen from the perspective of British camps around Almeida, such an outcome to the war still appeared unlikely. There were at least 200,000 French soldiers in Spain and no way of telling how Napoleon's Russian adventure would end.

Nevertheless the achievement of the Anglo-Portuguese army had been enormous and the credit was Wellington's. He had made his army the instrument of his will and, against the odds, had led it to victory against forces of equal courage and greater numbers. His leadership may not have been charismatic, like Napoleon's, but it was certainly talismanic. 'Glorious news, Nosey has got the command, won't we give them a drubbing' was the reaction of soldiers of the 51st (West Riding Regiment) to the news that Wellington had taken charge of the allied armies in Belgium in May 1815.[1] This confidence was unshaken, even during the darkest moments at Waterloo, when a rifleman of the 95th was overheard to say, 'Lord Wellington don't know how to lose a battle.'[2]

How then did Wellington know how to win? Answers have been

provided at many levels by experts who subsequently dissected and analysed his campaigns and battles. The task was not easy and the results sometimes unconvincing. Indeed Wellington thought the exercise not worth undertaking. 'Write the history of a battle?' he once asked. 'As well write the history of a ball.' He liked the analogy, which suggested events far beyond the control of one individual and following no preordained pattern. A battle, he once told guests at a dinner party, was 'like a ball' for 'one remembered one's own partner, but knew very little what other couples might be about; nor, if one did, might it be quite decorous to tell all he saw'.[3] This was the modesty of a man who was then widely considered the greatest living general.

He was less shy among his fellow professionals in the Peninsula, where dinner was often accompanied by detailed discussion of past, present and future strategy. At these and other times he would comment, often unfavourably, on his past battlefield decisions.[4] And yet he was right when he remarked how difficult it was to produce a complete picture of a battle. 'A person may see much fighting, and yet know very little about a battle in which he is taking part,' concluded one of his staff after Waterloo.[5] The confusion of men and animals; the lie of the land; the size of the area which was being fought over; and the fact that every soldier's mind was concentrated on survival and what was happening close to him made it impossible for one man to discern an overall picture. When the battle was over most men came away with a series of striking images, often quite trivial. The sight of French unhorsed cuirassiers who 'lay sprawling and kicking like so many *turned* turtles' around the squares at Waterloo remained with Wellington for over ten years.[6]

Not surprisingly, survivors were keen to scan their commander's official despatches to find out what had happened and, of course, to discover whether they or their unit merited special mention. Anecdotes were shared by officers and men and these, together with personal experiences, were set down in diaries or letters home. One result then and later was endless wrangling among participants and military historians over such matters as what a regiment did or did not do. Furthermore, and this exerted a peculiar fascination, much energy was devoted to uncovering when and how the 'decisive' moment of a battle occurred. Such investigations often ended in the sterile world of subjunctive history in which the question 'What if?' was asked and hypothetical answers provided, tailored to fit the author's theory. In public and after 1815 Wellington distanced himself from the close scrutiny of his battles, although in the 1830s he permitted the publication of his despatches, which provided the world with an insight into his strategic thinking and the day-to-day management of his campaigns.

What emerged was how effectively he stamped his own will on his army; at every level his influence was felt, and invariably his views prevailed. Less obvious from his despatches, but clear enough in the writings of his officers and men, was the way in which his personality pervaded every activity of the army. His leadership was omniscient, his judgement final and his authority absolute. And yet he was not, he insisted, an authoritarian. Once, in 1812, he reprimanded his Adjutant-General, Charles Stewart (Castlereagh's brother and later Marquess of Londonderry), who had stuck rigidly to army custom and had not allowed other officers to interrogate French POWs. Stewart, whom Wellington identified as a 'mischief-maker', showed his pique by letting prisoners go. Again Wellington confronted him for, in his own words, 'I like to convince people rather than stand on mere authority.' The force of his argument was so great that Stewart 'burst out crying, and begged my pardon, and hoped I would excuse his intemperance'.[7] Soon after, Stewart returned to Britain, much to Wellington's satisfaction.

This episode is instructive. Wellington led an army in which he was the only source of authority; disobedience in even the smallest matter would never be tolerated from any officer under his command. At the same time, and this is clear from his correspondence and General Orders, he went to considerable lengths to give the reasons for his decisions, especially when they might be unpopular or misunderstood. For instance in 1811 he issued an order that banned meetings of Free Masonic lodges in the army (they seem to have been very popular) on the ground that they upset the ultra-orthodox Portuguese Catholic hierarchy and it was necessary to sustain the goodwill of an ally.[8]

Wellington's leadership could never have rested solely on the passive obedience of his officers, a quality which did not come naturally to the late-eighteenth-century aristocracy and gentry. Many, the young in particular, showed an alarming cussedness. This was spectacularly revealed by a series of public school rebellions during this period, which included a 'mutinous conspiracy' at the new Royal Military College at High Wycombe in 1804 and the appearance of a 'dangerous spirit of Jacobinism' among the officer cadets six years later.[9] A wild anarchic streak infected many officers in the Peninsula, especially when off duty, and gave Wellington much trouble. In October 1809 he was shocked by the 'riots and outrages' committed by officers who in uniform hovered around backstage in the Lisbon theatres and even appeared on the stage. Such conduct, he claimed, would be intolerable to the British public and he insisted that 'officers who are absent from their duty on account of sickness, might as well not go to the Play House, or at all events upon the stage and behind the scenes'.[10]

The court-martial records which he examined daily provided abundant evidence of officers who malingered, ignored their duties or were temperamentally unfit to carry them out. What example could their men take from Lieutenants Lyne and Poe of the 47th (Lancashire Regiment)? One called the other 'coward', 'scoundrel' and 'Damned Rascal' after he had thrown his sash from their tent and had told him he was no better than 'the bloody old rogue his uncle', who happened to be the regimental paymaster.[11] And then there were the lazy and backsliding. 'How can you expect a Court to find an officer guilty of neglect of duty', Wellington asked, 'when it is composed of members who are all more or less guilty of the same?' Again, after being inundated with applications for leave during the wet, cold winter of 1813/14, he observed, 'A pretty army I have here! They all want to go home: but no more shall go except the sick.'[12] The stream of requests for home leave was particularly galling since it was evidence of a half-hearted commitment, and had the requests been granted companies would have lost their officers for months on end. Frequently Wellington's patience snapped: in May 1813 he angrily demanded that an exacting enquiry be made into why Lieutenant Lewis of the recently arrived Life Guards wished to return to England 'on the point of taking the field'.[13]

Somehow, and it was often an uphill struggle, Wellington had to instil into such men a sense of public duty as strong as his own and at the same time give them an equally firm sense of common purpose. On the surface at least cohesion came from the bonds of outlook and behaviour shared by all gentlemen. For Wellington the words 'officer' and 'gentleman' were synonymous, although, as he was aware, there were gentlemen who could never make good officers. Two who could, his brother-in-law Captain Edward Pakenham of the 95th and Captain Lloyd of the 43rd, were recommended by him to the Commander-in-Chief for promotion in August 1810. Included in the letter was an outline of his own preference in such matters.[14]

I have never been able to understand the principle on which the claims of gentlemen of family, fortune, and influence in the country, to promotion in the army, founded on their military conduct, and character, and services be rejected, while the claims of others, not better founded on military pretensions, were invariably attended to. It would be desirable, certainly, that the only claim to promotion should be military merit; but this is a degree of perfection to which the disposal of military patronage has never been and cannot be, I believe, brought in any military establishment ...

Wellington concluded by wishing it might be otherwise, adding that the system forbade him from even making a corporal. Dundas, like his successor York, was unwilling to allow Wellington an overriding say in who received advancement, although both paid serious attention to his suggestions. In defence of this monopoly of army patronage, Wellington's friend, former ADC and the Commander-in-Chief's Military Secretary, Colonel Torrens, reminded him that 'the mischievous clamour' of the Opposition might be provoked by the promotion of those whom Wellington favoured, irrespective of their qualifications.[15]

Lack of control over promotion and the appointment of brigade and divisional generals was a handicap for Wellington which he regretted but finally came to terms with. It meant, for instance, that he had to accept as his Deputy Adjutant-General Colonel Duncan Darroch, a nominee of General Sir Harry Calvert, one of the Commander-in-Chief's staff, even though he proved himself 'notoriously incompetent'.[16] At the end of 1812 he pleaded with the government, 'I hope I have no new Generals; they really do us but little good, and they take the place of officers who we could use.'[17] In three years he had learned the strengths and weaknesses of his senior staff and had done what he could to put them in positions where those with talent might prosper and those without do little harm. Nevertheless, the enthusiastic and gallant General Sir William Stewart had to command a division, even though Wellington knew he 'cannot obey an order'. There were others beyond redemption; in a letter of 2 December 1812 he listed three whom he wished recalled, including one who, despite being a 'friend', 'spends the greatest part of his time in England, and is not very energetic when he is here'.[18]

Torrens agreed and characterized one candidate for dismissal, Major-General Edward Long, as an officer notorious for 'his indifferences to his profession'.[19] His shortcomings had been known to Wellington for at least eighteen months; in June 1811 he had disregarded orders and endangered his men by his ignorance of basic cavalry routine.[19] To balance men like Long were excellent senior officers such as Beresford, whom Wellington counted the best, Cotton, Hill, Sir Thomas Picton, Sir Lowry Cole and even the headstrong Craufurd. Nevertheless, and perhaps because of their endeavours, some of his best generals were wounded or suffered illnesses which meant absences from the front. Picton and Leith were away for several months, and Wellington, knowing how thin his talents were spread, was extremely impatient about the time it took one of his best brigade commanders, Major-General James Kempt, to convalesce.

Much of Wellington's raw material among the officer corps was unpromising, but, he believed, it was the backbone of the army. He had therefore to bond his officers together and impose a common standard of behaviour which would promote efficiency and provide that vital ingredient of personal leadership which inspired men on the battlefield. To this end he quite deliberately appealed to his officers as gentlemen and, in his own public and private behaviour, set an example of how a man of birth should conduct himself. As in India, the tenor of his campaigns was patrician.

He entertained frequently and in style. By 1814 he was allowed £5,000 annually in table money, employed three cooks under a Spanish and an English chef who produced dinners on alternate days, and maintained a good cellar of local wines and brandy.[20] Once, soon after the first occupation of Madrid, Francisco Longa, a Spanish guerrilla general, presented him with 1,000 bottles of fine claret which had been captured on their way from Napoleon to King Joseph, or 'Napoleon el Chico' as his subjects called him.[21] Dinners for his generals, staff and any officer whom he might casually invite were held regularly and there were special parties on the anniversaries of his victories and on occasions such as the Prince Regent's birthday. These were more than diversions since they gave Wellington the chance to meet, hear and assess his officers, and for this reason he took special care to draw new arrivals to his table whenever possible.

Not only did Wellington entertain in the fashion of an English grandee, he rode to hounds as often as he could. Hunting was the natural pastime of the aristocrat; twenty years later he remarked: 'Nothing the people of this country like so much as to see their great men take part in their amusements. The aristocracy will commit a great error if ever they fail to mix freely with their neighbours.'[22] He had sixteen couples of hounds, nicknamed the Peers, but he had no huntsman, so the pack straggled, which allowed foxes to escape easily; only one was killed during January 1813, despite the efforts of a staff officer who blocked their holes.[23] This did not trouble Wellington who, it was suspected, knew little of the finer points of hunting. What he wanted was 'a good gallop', and one onlooker noticed that he 'enjoys the fun uncommonly'.[24]

Army affairs were not allowed to intrude upon Wellington's sport. Generals who interrupted the chase with army matters were fobbed off with 'Oh damn them! I won't speak to them again when we are hunting.' His fellow huntsmen were usually his staff and other officers who shared his passion, but in January 1814 a Spanish general was invited to join in.[25] What he thought of the proceedings or of Wellington in the sky-blue colours of the Hatfield Hunt is not recorded; nor are Wellington's views on the bull fight he attended in Madrid, although many of his countrymen thought the show needlessly cruel.[26]

Hunting had psychological and practical value. The sight of their commander-in-chief in full cry was a reminder to his officers that he shared the traditional sporting tastes of an English gentleman and was one of them. These tastes were widely indulged throughout the army: officers shot game; one kept 'an old poacher' as a servant who managed his ferrets and terriers; and a cricket match was played in 1810 at Almeida, not far from the French lines.[27] For Wellington, riding to hounds was more than a display of his patrician enthusiasms: it was a valuable exercise.

He was a remarkable horseman who, having learned the art of riding long distances in India, could cover up to seventy miles a day in the Peninsula. This was exceptional, but the nature of Wellington's generalship demanded that he move swiftly to wherever he thought his presence and judgement were needed. He owned seven chargers, of which the most famous was Copenhagen, a fifteen-hand chestnut mare foaled in 1808, and seven hunters. A good horse had enabled him to escape a cavalry mêlée at Fuentes and he was always determined to be well mounted; in 1813 he paid 400 guineas each for two horses.[28] Inevitably, given how far he had to ride, he had many falls and once, near Freineda in February 1813, he and one of his staff officers, Colonel William de Lancey, were thrown and hurled into a river. As usual the bruised Wellington remounted and rode on.[29]

As well as setting an example of how a gentleman ought to behave, Wellington had to deal with those officers who had lost sight of or never fully appreciated the rules of proper conduct. His General Orders for publication throughout the army listed offenders and their offences; during April 1811 officers were castigated for skulking in hospitals, failing to control stragglers and leaving forage parties to their own devices, which led to random looting.[30] It was a trying business and, at times, Wellington injected a shot of his own indignation into the official prose. For instance, in November 1812, after the public reprimand of one regiment's officers, he added his regrets 'that the time of other officers of the army should be taken up in inquiring into and passing sentence upon the improprieties of behaviour of a set of men whose neglect of duty must be obvious to every person who sees the establishment under their charge'.[31] A sharp call to duty was appended to the rejection of a staff officer's application for leave in November 1813. 'The Marquess of Wellington expects the Staff ... to sacrifice their natural inclinations to visit home for the performance of the essential duties attached to their employments.'[32]

The underlying philosophy was always the same. The officer had public duties towards the army and his men which he could not shirk or undertake casually. There were, as the frequency of exhortations and public humiliations suggest, plenty of officers who refused to allow that a gentleman had to accept his responsibilities. Others, however, were moved by Wellington's appeals to their sense of honour. In consequence of their plundering after the battle of Vitoria, the 18th Hussars were rebuked by Wellington, who warned that similar conduct in the future would force him to have the regiment dismounted and sent home in disgrace. A month or so before, he had praised the newly arrived hussars as 'the finest body of Cavalry I ever saw' and Lieutenant Woodberry was bitterly ashamed at this fall from grace. 'O God,' he wrote, 'is it come to this? I want language to express the grief I feel on this occasion, to think I should have come out with a Regiment who have contrary to all expectation, acted so differently.'[33]

Dishonour mattered greatly to Woodberry. By his own admission he had been 'much intoxicated with Foppery' and hoped that, on return to his modish friends at Brighton, 'I shall not be the puppy I was.'[34] Wellington knew the power of such vanity and manipulated it. Once, when praising the 'gentlemanly' spirit, he gave as an example its effect on officers of the Guards who never 'misbehaved when there was any duty to be done. *White's window* [a self-appointed court of honour among the fashionable] *would not permit it.*'[35] He could, when necessary, act as his own 'White's window' and deliver caustic reproaches. In November 1811 he encountered Craufurd the day after he had ignored orders to move his Light Division by night. 'I am glad to see you safe, Craufurd.' 'Oh I was in no danger, I assure you,' the General answered. 'But I was, from your conduct,' riposted Wellington. Unchastened, Craufurd later complained, 'He is damned crusty to-day.'[36]

Wellington's acerbity became famous. But his hastiness of temper disappeared when the moment came for dispassionate judgement and he never lost a sense of humour, even when furious. After hearing a plea on behalf of a negligent officer, he said the man 'might go to hell' as far as he was concerned. 'I'll go, Sir, to the Quarter-Master-General for a route' was the petitioner's reply, which delighted Wellington.[37]

Observers commonly noted Wellington's animation and 'high spirits' even on occasions when he could have excused their absence. To have appeared otherwise in public or, more importantly, on the battlefield would have been fatal. As commander he had always to maintain a façade of jauntiness and confidence; they were inspirational qualities which had to flow downwards and enthuse all ranks. A powerful inner faith, not only in the justice of his country's cause, but in the rightness of his decisions, was vital. Moreover he knew that there were many officers who doubted his judgement and believed the campaign doomed to eventual failure. Behind them, and sometimes in correspondence with them, were politicians who distrusted his and his family's ambitions and looked for their downfall.

Conversion of the army to his view of how the war should be waged was slow and uneven. Alexander Gordon of his staff was one of the few who was convinced early. In November 1810 he told his sister, 'the termination of this Campaign will be a signal for the gradual diminution of Bonaparte's power and will end in his ruin', which echoed his commander's opinion.[38] An officer of the 92nd Highlanders praised his 'consummate prudence' in 1811, and Charles Napier of the 50th wrote, 'Take Lord Wellington away and we are *general-less*,' a view common in other quarters which said, unfairly perhaps, little for his subordinate generals.[39] Captain Carss of the 53rd considered him 'A good soldier and very much beloved by the army. He gives no unnecessary trouble if people will conduct themselves as they ought, but otherwise is very severe.'[40] Nevertheless, his colonel, George Bingham, remained doubtful about the war's outcome until as late as March 1813, when he wrote, 'unless the Russians gain ground, I am not very sanguine as to our success'. In the same month Lieutenant Woodberry dined with an officer of the 52nd, who refused to raise his glass to Wellington and observed from other contacts that 'he is much disliked by all officers who have come from the army'.[41] Success dissipated such misgivings, but only gradually.

For the common soldier, Wellington was a remote figure. He was, as some knew to their cost, a relentless disciplinarian, although he could unbend. One story, which may be apocryphal, had him discover a looter with a beehive. Asked where he had obtained it, the man said over a nearby hill and advised him to hurry if he wanted one for there were only a few left. This saucy answer amused Wellington who apparently took no action against the soldier. On another occasion, according to Gunner Whitman of the Royal Horse Artillery, he encountered soldiers stripping the roof of his billet for firewood and 'begged them to go away to some other places, and for God's sake to let him have a roof for one night'.[42] Perhaps, but such a reaction is hard to square with his regular injunctions against such vandalism.

The point was that the ordinary soldiers prized such displays of comradeship from their generals. Seeing Sir William Stewart, lately returned from convalescence, fellow Scots of the 92nd called out, 'Oh General, ye maun drink wi'us.' 'With all my heart, men' was his reply and he shared their wine. Private Gunn of the 42nd Highlanders recalled to his grandson how he and other men were approached by Major-General Denis Pack as they were boiling potatoes in their kettles. Untroubled by hearing that these had been looted, he asked the Highlanders to fetch him some, and added with a smile, 'Take care of the provosts.'[43] Finishing his tale the old soldier concluded, 'Such indeed appears to be the character of a, or most of British generals as to gain, and deservedly, the love and esteem and obedience of the troops they command.' This is a view from the bottom and one worth heeding since Gunn had kept in his mind the details of this small incident for over forty years. Acts of generosity and kindness counted for much: men of the 95th Rifles noticed how Pakenham would always wait his place in the queue for rations and Captain Lloyd of the 43rd carried the knapsacks of weary men on his horse.[44] Both were officers for whom Wellington had the highest regard.

They were also light-infantrymen, beneficiaries of Sir John Moore's training, which emphasized the humanity of officers towards their men. Captain Cooke, another officer trained by Moore, was impressed by the manner in which officers were introduced to their duties. He had to 'drill with a squad, composed of peasants from the plough *trail* and other raw recruits', and with them learned all the light-infantryman's craft. He also learned charity, for during the Peninsular campaign he regretted how officers went 'rambling about' while their tired men were kept under arms and in full pack. Such indifference, Cooke believed, destroyed '*esprit*' and created 'feelings of dislike in the breasts of soldiers'.[45]

Cooke also noticed how men who were well treated responded in kind, for 'when a young officer fell in action the old soldiers professed their services with parental care'. The death in battle of a popular officer often aroused men to a fury of vengeance. Reports, not strictly accurate as it turned out, of the cowardly killing of Colonel Sir Frederick Ponsonby by French lancers at Waterloo angered men from his regiment, the 12th Light Dragoons, and 'made lions of them, instead of men'.[46]

On the battlefield, it was every officer's task to make lions of his men by words of inspiration and by example. Just how this was done was vividly recalled by an unknown private of the 38th in his account of Salamanca:[47]

> In a few seconds General Leith came up waving his Hatt as crouching men waited for an attack order. 'Now my lads! Is the day for England, thay would play at long Ball with us from Morning untill Night. But we will soon give them something else'. So as soon as he got to the right of the line, the Bugle sounded to our Harm and to Charge. Then Immediately as soon we rose up: there was 3 Cannon firing upon us which we took.

This was no Crispin's Day speech; it was down to earth, to the point and very similar to many others remembered by listeners. What mattered was that the General was seen to be at the head of his troops and sharing the dangers of battle.

The style of such leadership varied. Sir William Stewart gave his orders with a lisp, nonchalantly switching his chestnut with a white cane, oblivious of fire. Picton commanded through sheer force of character. He was a figure who might have been drawn by Smollett, a rumbustious Welsh squire who carried an umbrella to shade his weak eyes and with which he once hit Wellington's butler after the Commander's baggage train had got in his way. Picton harangued his men into battle – 'Come on ye rascals! Come on ye fighting villains!' Abuse was ever his common currency. 'You are a disgrace to your moral country, Scotland,' he told the 94th Highlanders after they had looted a wine shop and killed some sheep (following the example of an Irish officer!). He finally became apoplectic and one present picked from his 'torrent of abuse' the words 'Damned Scotch', 'brutes', 'dirty', 'barbarous'.[48]

And yet he retained much affection, for he was brave and knew his business as a soldier. This mattered more to the men he commanded than his explosions of rage and was why Wellington cherished him. Inept, muddle-headed officers hazarded men's lives, but they had to be obeyed. One sent Lieutenant James Gairdner of the 95th Rifles to occupy, unsupported, a ridge in the lower Pyrenees during operations there in December 1813. 'Too well aware of the useless danger', Gairdner said he would not go forward 'without an order', which he got.[49] In the subsequent engagement cannonfire killed an officer and two sergeants.

Only discipline and a sense of duty could impel men on in such circumstances. 'I was bound by my Duty as A Soldier,' thought the unknown private of the 38th as he advanced at Salamanca, and this knowledge dispelled doubts raised by his memory of the text which promised death by the sword to those who lived by it.[50] This young man had been much addicted to the evangelism of the meeting houses and so would have understood the nature of the oath he had taken to the King. For others, less conscious of their moral obligations, discipline was a vital ingredient of their fighting spirit.

Wellington set the highest store by discipline and he spent much time and energy on its enforcement at every level of the army. His concern was understandable since his battlefield tactics relied heavily on his men's steadiness and their unhesitating obedience to orders. He required his infantrymen to fire their volleys at exactly the right range so as to inflict the heaviest casualties and force the French columns to flinch, halt and disintegrate. This needed great nerve, for the soldiers had to wait patiently, often under fire, until their opponents were within less than a hundred, sometimes even thirty or twenty yards. The tension must have been enormous, as was the temptation to open fire early or, when faced with massed columns of thousands of shouting Frenchmen, to fall back. 'Why don't we give the rascals a volley?' anxious men from the 94th Highlanders shouted to Picton during one rearguard action. 'Steady, my lads, steady,' he answered, 'don't throw away your fire until I give the word of command.'

As potentially dangerous as the mistimed volley was the impetuous advance, although it was natural enough for men to break ranks and rush a faltering or fleeing foe. This had occurred at Talavera and the consequence had been near disaster. Again it was discipline and obedience to their officers' commands which restrained eager men, although this control was never easy; there was always a natural urge to get at the enemy and finish the battle.

In his formal speech to newly enlisted men of the 95th, Colonel Beckwith claimed that it was 'disciplined valour' which made the British soldier invincible. This quality, he told them, was nourished by the regimental spirit. Every officer appreciated the value of this spirit and encouraged it. When Wellington cancelled the death sentence passed on three men from the 57th, which had fought valiantly at Albuera, he explained that he had done so 'in order that the regiment might avoid the disgrace of their public execution'. Picton, who had with some justice labelled the 88th the worst 'blackguards' in the army, congratulated its survivors after Fuentes with 'Well done the brave 88th!' A voice from the ranks answered, 'Are we the greatest blackguards in the army now?' 'No, you are brave and gallant soldiers, this day has redeemed your character.'[51] A regiment's sense of honour was deeply felt by officers and men; it was perhaps the most potent and binding of the emotions which made up regimental spirit.

A regiment's honour was inextricably bound up with its fighting reputation. Commanding officers believed that appeals to both would enkindle courage. They were taken for granted in the simple but effective address given to the 10th Hussars by Major-General Sir Richard Vivian at Waterloo. 'Tenth, you know what you are going to do, and you also know what is to be done: I shall therefore say no more, only to wish you success.' When they returned from the charge, he spoke to them again, 'Now, Tenth, you have not disappointed me, you were just what I thought you were,' and he added that they had given ample proof of their 'bravery and good discipline'.[52]

These words were part of a recital of the hussars' actions set down by Private John Marshall in a letter intended for publication after he had been angered by newspaper reports which had ignored his regiment's part in the battle. Such oversights offended regimental pride and were deeply resented. There was much grumbling after Busaco when officers of the 9th discovered that Wellington had understated their role in the battle in his official despatch. There was also annoyance when his Badajoz despatch passed over the work undertaken by the Royal Engineers.[53]

The regiment was more than just a convenient fighting unit. Its members were conscious of an inherited reputation which they had to preserve and embellish if the regiment were to maintain its honour. The shared hardships of the campaign, the dangers of battle in which men looked to each other for support and example, and devotion to brave and considerate officers also played vital parts in the generation of a regimental spirit. When he first joined the 43rd in Portugal Captain Cooke noticed that 'early discipline had not only been maintained amidst privations, battles and camps but had been matured by experience'.[54]

Patriotism stirred the rank and file less than loyalty to their regiments and officers. There were exhortations to fight for 'Old England', appeals to Scottish pride, and Irish regiments celebrated St Patrick's Day, but the letters, diaries and memoirs of individual soldiers contain few references to distinctly national pride. According to an unknown private of the 71st Highlanders 'true spirit' enabled him and his companions to counter-attack and throw back the French at Fuentes, and Private Whitman of the Royal Horse Artillery noted in his diary that 'British courage is not easily daunted'.[55] When a French prisoner told Private Gunn that war 'is natural for man as to beast', he replied that 'it was neither of our faults but of our grandees'. For many, the motives for fighting were simple and selfish, like those overheard in a bivouac during the retreat from Madrid in October 1812.[56]

> The conversation among the men is interspersed with the most horrid oaths declaring what they will do with the fellow they lay hands on. What they intend to plunder, hoping they will stand a chance that they may split two at once. Then someone more expert at low wit than his companions draws a ludicrous picture of a Frenchman with a bayonet stuck in him or something of the kind, which raised a loud and general laugh. ... They marched off and forgot the evening and for amusement by the way commenced their wit upon each other with grossness and sometimes point hardly to be exceeded. As they grow tired they begin to swear at the country and the inhabitants ... at soldiering and at the commissaries.

Although Wellington repeatedly informed his army through General

Orders that it was fighting for the liberation of Portugal and Spain, most soldiers were contemptuous of the Portuguese and Spaniards. Private Wheeler of the 51st spoke for all when he set down his first impressions of Lisbon. 'What an ignorant superstitious, priest-ridden, dirty, lousy set of poor Devils are the Portuguese. Without seeing them it is impossible to conceive there exists a people in Europe so debased.'[57] Similar vehement opinions were expressed about the Spanish, to whom the adjectives 'idle', 'proud' and 'cowardly' were usually attached. Of course many British officers and soldiers were the heirs to generations of anti-Catholic propaganda which contrasted the sturdy individual freedom and prosperity which flourished under Protestantism with the poverty and servitude which were the natural consequences of 'Popery'. The condition of the Iberian peasantry seemed to confirm these stereo-types. By and large the British showed a marked preference for the French, with whom they often mixed freely and cordially, much to the hurt of the Spanish and Portuguese, who found such behaviour inexplicable.

Officers, who were usually better informed about the broader issues behind the war, were more prone to express patriotic sentiments. On leaving for Portugal, William Warre looked forward to fighting 'the would-be Tyrant of the world'.[58] After Vitoria, in which he had had a narrow escape, Lieutenant Woodberry prayed, 'God dispose my heart to return thanks for thy goodness for withholding the sword that was pointed at my existence from having the effect it was intended. Oh Lord send this Glorious Victory may lead to General Peace, and give happiness to the troubled world, but more particular England.'[59]

There were many in Wellington's army for whom the war offered a chance of private gain in the form of plunder, which they took to be their right. After Fuentes, the unknown private of the 71st took a gold watch and crucifix from the body of a Frenchman, 'as I had as good a right to these as another'. Two guardsmen plundering the corpses after Waterloo similarly justified themselves – 'we fought hard enough yesterday to allow us the right to share what no one claims'. Another survivor from a hard fight, this time an officer, proudly displayed 'two or three massy chalices as his share of the spoil' after the sack of Badajoz.[60] All this was legitimate although the guardsmen had deserted their regiment to go plundering.

For Wellington their abandonment of duty was unforgivable and he would have punished them, possibly with death. He rarely tolerated any lapse of discipline in an army where it was the greatest single source of cohesion. The British army was not homogeneous; it was the sum of many parts bound together by discipline, regimental spirit and the force of its commander's personality. And yet there was an attachment between the leader and led even though Wellington never courted the affections of his soldiers. 'We anxiously longed for the return of Lord Wellington,' wrote Captain John Kincaid of the 95th shortly before Fuentes, 'as we would rather see his long nose in the fight than a reinforcement of ten thousand men.' At Albuera one soldier, probably a North Countryman, asked, 'Whor's ar Arthur?' When told he was not there he remarked ruefully, 'Aw wish he wor here.'[61] Wellington sensed such feelings and valued them; he told Larpent that his soldiers 'would do for me what perhaps no man else can make them do'.[62]

2

Laborious Attention: Wellington's Logistics

From the moment he landed in Portugal Wellington had been compelled to fight a war of attrition. In sum the French army was vastly superior to his own, the Portuguese and the Spanish, yet decisive victories eluded its High Command. Even in 1810/11, when the British were penned in at Lisbon and the Spaniards besieged in Cádiz, the French were not masters of the Peninsula. Far from it: the British army survived intact; guerrillas forced French troops into fortified positions; and whenever the French beat a Spanish field army the defeated soldiers slipped away to their homes to reassemble later.

Wellington understood these facts and shaped his strategy accordingly. Depending on the strength of the French armies and where they were positioned, he snatched the opportunity for an offensive, as he did before Talavera, or fell back and adopted a defensive position, as he did at the end of 1810. His purpose was always the same, the preservation of his own army and the piecemeal exhaustion of the French. None of his victories between 1808 and 1812 was decisive, but each weakened the French and demonstrated their vulnerability. With good reason Napoleon likened the Peninsular War to an 'ulcer', a fatal growth which debilitates its victim by stages.

Wars of attrition wore down both sides and, given that Wellington's army was the smaller, it could easily have succumbed first. Justifying his refusal to invade southern France in the summer of 1813, Wellington reminded the government that even successful campaigns like the one he was fighting had damaging side-effects. Ammunition was expended, shoes wore out and men became dispersed.[1] He was also aware that no battle was ever a foregone conclusion and so he had, wherever possible, to reduce the odds or, if they looked unfavourable, to refuse an engagement. This deliberate calculation of risks aroused criticism among fire-eaters in his army and the public at home. His riposte was crushing. 'There is', he told Croker in 1810, 'a great deal of difference (particularly in the blood to be spilt) between fighting in a position which I choose or in one which the enemy chooses to fight.' After the war, he remembered how, during the battle of Toulouse in 1814, Picton had disregarded his orders and gone bald-headed at a French position and lost 500 men. 'Bonaparte would have approved of it, because he did not care for the lives of his men; we were obliged to husband them.'[2]

Every attention had to be given to measures which kept the army alive. When, in 1815, a selection of Wellington's General Orders was published as a guidebook for officers, the author identified the 'very laborious attention paid by him to the preservation of his forces' as the key to his success. By and large this was so and, given his Indian experience, there was no officer better qualified for the task. Moreover, Wellington's pessimistic view of the sense of vocation of many of his subordinates made him insist on control over every department of his army. 'The real reason why I succeeded in my campaigns is because I was always on the spot,' he later told Stanhope, 'I saw everything and did everything for myself.'[3]

Nothing escaped his eye and no one his censure. On the march in June 1812, he noticed an artillery brigade accompanied by three bullock carts rather than the regulation one and immediately upbraided its commander.[4] Torrens, who had briefly worked alongside him, summed up his attitude to those beneath him as 'I care not who I have, provided he can write for I do everything for myself.'[5] Life was always uncomfortable for those beneath him, who often interpreted his interference as criticism, which in fact it usually was. He was always acerbic with the maladroit or those who failed to conform to his ideals of public service.

Getting things done his way and seeing them done needed enormous intellectual energy and stamina. One day in March 1813, having completed official business, he rode seventeen miles in two hours for the celebrations of General Lowry Cole's knighthood. He relished such occasions and believed it proper that such an honour to an officer should be lavishly commemorated. On arrival he dined for two hours, danced at the ball and ate supper. At 3.30 the next morning he rode back to HQ by moonlight, was in bed by 6.00 and up at midday attending to his papers. He could survive on as little as four or five hours' sleep, thanks to a knack of being able to drop off for an hour or so whenever the chance occurred.

Off duty he relaxed completely. 'When I take off my clothes I throw off my cares,' he once remarked, 'and when I turn on my bed it is time to turn out.' When dining he would ignore the war and direct conversation towards British politics or local gossip. Rumours, largely spread by his enemies, suggested that he kept a mistress who, like Masséna's, accompanied him on campaign. She was spotted by Lieutenant Sullivan in his company at a British Embassy ball in December 1813 at Lisbon and he heard how she 'not only goes to public parties with his Lordship but attends him on all his peregrination'. Given that he named her as Madame Grassini, a singer with whom Wellington was intimate in Paris a year later, his remarks may be fanciful or his memory shaky. What is strange is that this woman's presence at camp was ignored by the overwhelming mass of officers who wrote letters or kept diaries. If this was discretion then it was most unusual since there was little prudery about sexual adventures at this time. One officer confided to Commissary Schaumann that he had seduced a married woman, her daughter and her maidservant in one of his billets.[6]

Celibate or not, Wellington kept himself remarkably fit throughout the campaign. He recovered quickly from riding falls and from being bruised or grazed by spent musket balls, and only once, in August 1813, was he forced to keep his bed, with a bout of lumbago, a misfortune he clearly forgot since he would later claim never to have missed a day's active service through illness.[7] He recovered within a week, but appeared 'pale and worn' and there are distinct marks of stress stamped on his features in the famous Goya portrait for which he sat during August 1812.

Wellington needed all his mental and physical powers for he was fighting a war shackled to an infirm military system. The administrative machinery that regulated the British army had evolved during the eighteenth century in a form designed not for efficiency but to forestall any one man from getting complete control over the armed forces. Memories of Cromwell were still evergreen and frightening. As a result many officials directed the army's business and operated within autonomous and often mutually jealous departments of state. The Treasury managed transport and supplies; the Board of Ordnance took care of gunners, engineers and their equipment; the Commander-in-Chief controlled promotion and uneasily shared responsibility for certain supplies and hospitals with the Secretary of State for War, who answered to Parliament on all army matters. Inter-departmental co-operation was fitful and established procedures slow.

Wellington was extraordinarily lucky that two successive Secretaries of State, Castlereagh and Liverpool, were close friends, political allies and broadly sympathetic to his ends. Torrens, Military Secretary to Dundas and the envious York, was an admiring well-wisher who did

Infantry in a square: French lancers shy away from the massed bayonets of the 28th Regiment, steadied by their mounted officer.

Prince William of Orange: young, brave and inexperienced, his orders at Quatre Bras and Waterloo led to the destruction of two battalions.

Standing firm: Waterloo was a
favourite subject for Victorian genre
painters; in this spirited picture by
R. A. Hillingford, Wellington
steadies an already battered
regiment while, in the distance,
French cavalry begin their charge.

After the battle: drawn from life this watercolour of the field of Waterloo clearly shows the fields of maize; in the foreground a peasant strips the body of a cuirassier whose equipment he will no doubt sell to tourists like Sir Walter Scott.

Conquering hero: a popular print of 1815 shows Wellington crowned by victory while Britannia looks on; at his feet lies a captured French eagle, and Blucher stands discreetly back.

'The highest incarnation of English character': a thoughtful but alert
Wellington from a daguerrotype taken in 1844.

The giant of his age: M. C. W. Wyatt's statue of Wellington is admired before it is raised to its position of honour on Constitution Arch; below Wellington discusses the work with the sculptor, 1846.

'Bury the great Duke': Wellington's catafalque passes through Constitution Arch, November 1852.

whatever he could to accommodate Wellington in matters of promotion and appointments. Relations with the Ordnance Board were frosty and Wellington concurred with Torrens's view of it as a 'mélange of jealousy, intrigue and stupid prejudice'.[8] After hearing that the Board had ignored his specific instructions for siege equipment and had neglected to send desperately needed ammunition in August 1813, Wellington wrote of its officials, 'Whenever they are left to themselves they blunder.'[9]

The Treasury, a persistently negative force in British history, also failed to measure up to the tasks imposed on it by war. Twice, in 1809 and 1812, Wellington had to delay offensives because the Treasury had failed to send funds. On the last occasion he complained about the embarrassment of a debt of five million Spanish dollars (about £1.15 million) that made life awkward for commissaries seeking to buy food on credit. Furthermore British and Portuguese troops were owed two months' back pay and Wellington warned that his straitened circumstances would force him to start the disbandment of some Portuguese units.[10]

However imperfect, the Treasury controlled two of Wellington's most vital resources, victuals and transport. In a war of attrition the army which was better fed and equipped would fight better and survive the longest, a truth that Wellington had learned in India. It took the French four painful years to discover it, by which time they were facing general defeat. Only in 1812, and then somewhat half-heartedly, did they begin the establishment of magazines in the British manner. Hitherto they had lived off the land, which, as Wellington drily observed, was 'a system of making war a resource and advantageous to a state instead of being expensive and burdensome'.[11] But it failed utterly in the Peninsula, as Wellington had predicted, and for that matter in Russia, where resources were sparse. Furthermore, feeding an army by what Wellington called 'the bayonet' generated resentment and drove men and women into the underground resistance.

Wellington was convinced that the British army survived because of its superior logistics. The Peninsular logistical system was the joint creation of Wellington and Sir Robert Kennedy, his highly cherished and extremely industrious Commissary-General, who served intermittently between 1808 and 1814. Kennedy placed in Wellington's hands the wherewithal to wage a defensive or offensive war, although his commissariat was always fragile when overstretched. What Wellington sought was a network of magazines spread across Portugal where supplies could be stored and from which regular mule-trains could fan out to deliver food and fodder to troops on various fronts. There were twelve of these magazines in operation by 1809 and thirty-seven at the end of 1812, all staffed by British commissaries, often men with commercial experience, local clerks and locally hired muleteers.

According to Wellington's calculations, one mule could carry a 200-pound load twelve miles in one day, so the magazines could conveniently sustain troops up to fifty miles away. Beyond that distance hitches occurred: in 1811/12 troops operating near Badajoz, sixty or more miles from the nearest magazine, were on short commons. Again, in September 1812, over-extended lines of communication led to ammunition shortages among forces around Burgos.[12] The forces of attrition worked both ways and on each occasion Wellington was forced to modify his plans. Problems of supply and delivery were continually uppermost in his mind. The future shape of a campaign was dictated as much by the needs of his troops or whether a region's economy could support them as by the manoeuvres of the French.

The margin between subsistence and starvation was always fine, despite Wellington's planning and the efforts of Kennedy and his commissaries, whose labours were often made heavier by the recriminations of hungry soldiers. Picton, who in March 1811 had had to call off his division's pursuit of Masséna because he had outrun his lines of supply, once threatened to hang a commissary if he did not bring provender within a day. The frightened man complained to Wellington, who coldly assured him, 'Well, sir, if he said so, believe me he *means* to do it and you have no remedy but to provide the rations.'[13] He did provide them.

The amounts needed to support the Anglo-Portuguese army were huge. In March 1810 twelve magazines were stocked with 1.49 million pounds of biscuit (an army staple rather like today's dog biscuit, the brand imported from America reputedly being able to stop a musket ball), 2.7 million pounds of flour, 1.52 million pounds of salted meat and 72,000 gallons of spirits, mostly West Indies rum. For horses and mules there were 750,000 pounds of oats, 900,000 of barley and one million of wheat. Such stores needed continual replenishment. By the middle of the year four-fifths of the oats had been consumed and Kennedy was pleading for a further 2.5 million pounds of oats and barley.[14]

This produce was imported by sea. 'It is', Wellington remarked in January 1814, 'our maritime superiority that enables me to maintain my army.'[15] At the time the army was being supplied by a fleet of 265 transports, most between 200 and 400 tons, of which just over a half solely carried food and fodder.[16] The sea was a vital lifeline and when, during the winter of 1812/13, French privateers stepped up raids on shipping, Wellington became nervous and demanded an increase in Royal Navy activity off the Spanish coast. 'The loss of one vessel only', he warned in April 1813, 'may create delay and inconvenience which may be of the utmost consequence.' No doubt he had in mind the recent capture of a vessel carrying 20,000 pairs of army shoes.[17] The Admiralty's answer was send ships in convoy under the protection of men-of-war.

The Navy helped Wellington in other ways. In 1811 sailors superintended the building of a pontoon bridge over the Guadiana near Badajoz and guided bullock-hauled barges up the Tagus to Abrantès and beyond.[18] Equally useful were stocks of eighteen- and twenty-four-pounder shot which were delivered from the Channel Fleet to forces besieging San Sebastián after it became clear that the Board of Ordnance could not provide them.[19]

Sea-power gave Wellington an advantage over the French which was recognized by General Foy when he looked back on the war. 'On vu', he wrote, 'des chevaux anglais en Portugal nourris avec foin coupé dans les praires de Yorkshire, et les hommes avec farines apportées d'Amerique.'[20] This was perhaps an overstatement. The outbreak of war between Britain and the United States in 1812 cut off that source of grain, although by early 1813 it was being imported from Egypt. Moreover, the volume of imports was never constant since it depended on such wayward factors as sailing conditions in the Bay of Biscay, privateers and bureaucratic energy at home.

Imports supplemented food and fodder bought by commissaries from contractors. As in India, British regiments marched to war trailed by herds of cattle which, when they had outstripped the mule-trains, provided the soldiers' main form of sustenance. In April 1813 a commissary informed Wellington that his men had eaten nearly every ox in Portugal. 'Well then,' he answered, 'we must now set about eating all the sheep, and when they are gone I suppose we must go home.'

Wellington seldom joked about such matters. Behind his obsessive concern with the conservation of his army was the knowledge that his supply of fit soldiers was being continuously eroded. Flanders and India had shown him the sombre facts of how natural wastage, unconnected with enemy action, drained an army of soldiers. Debilitating and fatal diseases together with desertion worked with terrifying effect on Wellington's soldiers, as he knew from the monthly returns of his army's strength. The fortunes of one regiment, the 11th (North Devon Regiment), may stand for many others as a measure of how natural wastage consumed men. The 11th, which disembarked at Lisbon 1,200 strong in April 1809, lost 207 men by the end of December 1811 without ever having been in action. Between January and September 1812 the dead totalled 198, of whom 96 were killed in the battles of Sorauen and Salamanca. In November 1812, after six months' active service, the regiment mustered 508 fit men, 351 invalids and a draft of 150 drawn from the reserve battalion at Barnstaple. Interestingly the 11th's traditional West Country recruiting grounds were all but exhausted by early 1814, when most of the newly enlisted men were Irish.[21]

It was a worse story for the 5th Dragoon Guards, mainly Irishmen, which landed in May 1811 and lost seventy-six men in twelve months, only thirty-five as a result of action. During 1813 and the early months of 1814 this regiment, which usually numbered between 450 and 500 troopers, lost three men in battle and seventy-one from other causes. So in any year and without ever fighting an engagement, a regiment might confidently expect to lose at least a tenth of its strength, possibly more, from natural causes. Horses and pack animals also suffered grievously. Of the 756 possessed by two small cavalry units and an artillery battery stationed near Tarragona in February 1813, 333 died within two months. The losses were made good, largely with animals taken from the French, for which a grateful army paid £25 apiece to their captors.[22]

This unending process of dilapidation was a nightmare for Wellington. Unlike his adversaries, who could draw on a reservoir of conscripts from France, Italy and the German states, he had to beg the government for reinforcements, all of whom were volunteers and often unfit for service. He had correctly identified the principal cause of wastage as the sickness and fatigue suffered by freshly drafted men who were unacclimatized and unfit for a regime of hard, gruelling marches. He pleaded for veterans with at least one campaign under their belts and, during the winter of 1812/13, ordered regimental officers to ensure that their men undertook ten- to twelve-mile marches twice weekly when the weather was fair.[23]

When seasoned regiments dropped below strength and were due for replacement, he proposed their merger into temporary battalions. York, who had a high regard for regimental traditions, was unhappy about this and less than pleased with another of Wellington's stop-gap measures, the recruitment of Spaniards and their dispersal among undermanned regiments.[24] Both expedients were a response to the knowledge that home recruitment figures were dropping; at the end of 1813 the annual shortfall had risen to 9,000 and was set to go higher.[25] Wellington and York believed the trend could be reversed if more generous allowances were offered for the upkeep of soldiers' families, but a cost-conscious government prevaricated.

In such circumstances, Wellington had to rely on self-help. He was convinced that in the Peninsula, as in India, he could minimize wastage by persistent and careful supervision of his army's logistics. Much of what he achieved in this field was through the application of common sense. The men were provided with wholesome bivouacs; overcoats were issued in winter; and a supply of sprung wagons was made available for the wounded, who would otherwise have had their sufferings exacerbated by journeys along stony tracks in fixed-wheeled carts. Memoranda were drafted on such humdrum matters as the right balance of Indian oats and corn for a cavalry charger's diet, and, as in Mysore, Wellington set up a manufactory for four-wheeled carts made to his own specification.[26]

The results were uneven. After Talavera and during the retreat from Burgos in October 1812 his supply lines snapped and the army fragmented as bodies of men scoured the countryside for food. This occurred again during the summer of 1813 when over 4,000 British and Portuguese troops temporarily vanished. In desperation Wellington instructed his provost-marshals to hang without trial looters caught red-handed. Desertion was treated with equal severity. In March 1813 he ordered a court-martial to reassemble and reverse its verdict on one deserter because of the 'disgraceful prevalency' of the crime. Quite simply Wellington wanted the man executed publicly for 'examples of the consequences of their enormous offences ... operate on the minds of soldiers'.[27] They did, but not always as he imagined; in 1812 Gunner Whitman witnessed the hanging of three Irishmen and, like other members of the audience, was more interested in how long it took the men to die than in the reason for their execution.[28]

Another source of wastage which he had to stem was straggling. Stragglers were walking wounded on the way to or from hospitals or men who fell behind their units, often in order to plunder. Straggling made it impossible for a commander ever to gauge the effective strength of his army and hindered its swift concentration. It was, Wellington always insisted in his General Orders, an officer's responsibility to keep his men together and chivvy those who wandered off unsupervised.

There was little he could do to raise standards of surgery or treatment in hospitals and it was a cold fact of life that diseases carried by contaminated water and vermin were incurable. Nevertheless, ward hygiene could be improved, extra surgeons could be procured and officers placed in charge of convalescents could be forced to perform their duty. Harry Smith of the 95th remembered with horror how, in accordance with Wellington's wishes, he had been ordered to convey 600 newly recovered men back to their regiments. None was willing to obey a stranger and so he kept discipline by bellowing at them and riding down the obstreperous. Wellington would have approved; he needed every one of the 600 men and was always pleased when an officer carried out a routine but necessary duty well.

He did not overcome completely the problems of wastage, but he did keep it within manageable bounds. This counted in a war of attrition, as the French belatedly realized. In January 1812, Victor complained to Soult of his recent setbacks in southern Spain: 'Il était devenu impossible à nos convois d'arriver, et il y avait déjà cinq jours que nos soldats éprouvaient le plus affreuse disette; leurs besoins étaient tels, que ne pouvant faire de feu, et mourant de faim, ils mangent de la viande cru. Cette circonstance seule justifierait la lévée du siége de Tarifa ...' To the north, Marmont admitted in March that his Army of Portugal had lost the war of attrition. 'L'armée de Portugal', he wrote, 'est assez bien forte pour battre l'armée anglaise, mais elle est inférieure à celle opérer, par suite de la pénurie de moyens. L'armée anglaise, qu'a d'avance de grands magasins et de moyens de transport suffisants, vit partout également bien. L'armée de Portugal, sans magasins, avec très-peu de transports et sans argent, ne peut vivre qu'en se disséminant.'[29] Both letters were captured, deciphered and read by Wellington, who must have found them deeply satisfying. They were admissions that he had been right in his judgement of the nature of the Peninsular War and justified all his careful husbandry of men and resources.

3

The Other Side of the Hill: Intelligence and Weapons

An uninterrupted flow of accurate intelligence was vital for Wellington. He needed tactical intelligence of his opponent's manoeuvres before a battle, which offered clues about his intentions, and strategic information, which gave an insight into the long-term plans of the French High Command. Until the middle of 1813 he constantly ran the risk of being trapped and outnumbered by a combination of two or more of the French armies in the Peninsula. This had almost occured in August 1809 and in the summer of 1811 when Marmont came to Soult's assistance. On both occasions catastrophe had been averted thanks to the forewarning provided by various intelligence sources. They also gave him invaluable details about Marmont's strength and movements which made him decide to abandon the blockade of Ciudad Rodrigo in 1811 and attack it at the year's end.

By this time Wellington was convinced that he had achieved intelligence superiority over the French. He confidently asserted, 'The French armies have no communication and one army no knowledge of the position and circumstances in which the other is placed; whereas I have a knowledge of all that passes on all sides.' Much later he concluded, 'All the business of war, and indeed all the business of life, is to endeavour to find out what you don't know by what you do; that's what I called "guessing what was on the other side of the hill".'[1] On campaign he gave the reassuring impression of omniscience. In the spring of 1813, after a two-hour interview on what he had seen of the French army during his time as a POW, Leith Hay left feeling that Wellington had exact information about every French soldier in Spain.[2] Experience had taught him that the French rarely changed their order of battle, so he instructed all those concerned with observing the activities of French forces always to discover the names of units and officers. Once these were known it was possible to identify divisions and army corps.[3]

Wellington was his own Director of Intelligence. When, in May 1811, he briefly mislaid the keys to his secret boxes the army's intelligence service all but ground to a halt.[4] Its machinery was largely his own creation, based upon the principles and methods he had learned in India. In 1808 there was no British secret service in the modern sense; each department of state had its own specially hired agents who reported to ministers personally, while commanders in the field were expected to improvise intelligence-gathering agencies. It was usual to put such work in the hands of quartermaster and adjutant-generals (who supervised the interrogation of POWs), but Wellington ignored this custom. He did however make an exception in the case of his Quarter-Master-General, Colonel George Murray, the son of a Perthshire laird and an officer of outstanding industry and administrative talent, who handled all the army's topographical intelligence.

Wellington always liked to cross-check reports and, when on campaign, see for himself what was happening, testing the observations and judgements of even his most able and trusted officers. One, Leith Hay, spotted French columns hastening towards a ford over the Tormes near Huerta during the final phase of the battle of Salamanca and immediately carried the news to Wellington, who rode off to take a look for himself.[5] As always he examined the enemy through his glass. Telescopes were essential campaign equipment habitually carried by British officers, whereas the French, he later noted, seldom used them and suffered accordingly.[6]

At his HQ Wellington sifted through all the other kinds of intelligence which the army received: topographical surveys; miscellaneous reports of French movements made by 'scouting officers' in no-man's land; and material provided by 'confidential correspondents' (spies) who operated inside enemy-occupied territory. Detached commanders, British and Spanish, and the Cádiz Embassy also had their own intelligence networks and passed information on to Wellington.

There were obvious parallels in methods of collection and collation between Wellington's intelligence services and today's infinitely larger intelligence agencies. But there was one major difference: the time which it took for information to reach army HQ. Delays were unavoidable; a Spanish agent active in the Seville area during 1810/11 sent his material to British HQ at Cádiz 'upon a Mule which is old but equal to the task' which covered the 100 or so miles in fifteen days![7] As the war proceeded, measures were taken to expedite the transmission of intelligence. News of Soult's preparations to march north from the Cádiz siege lines on 23/24 March 1812 was received by Wellington at Badajoz five days later. Accounts of King Joseph's activities in Madrid during March 1813 were carried 150 miles to HQ at Freineda in six days.[8] Such messages were delivered by mounted couriers who were well paid for the risks they took in French-occupied territory; one, who rode from Alicante in eastern Spain to Wellington's HQ before San Sebastián in August 1813, received 120 dollars (£27.60p).[9]

Slowness in the passage of intelligence was to some extent offset by the fact that contemporary armies moved ponderously and that details of a French corps' mobilization or concentration retained some value even when it was a fortnight old. Nevertheless Wellington appreciated that the fresher the intelligence the greater its value. When the Torres Vedras lines were constructed, he had a series of mechanical telegraphs placed on high points along and behind the defences and linked to HQ. So, once signs of a French attack on one sector were observed, a report could be quickly passed to HQ and reinforcements moved. A similar telegraph chain connected Lisbon to Badajoz. A telegraph was assembled from three tent-poles, one of which was an extended arm from which coloured flags and balls were hung. Various combinations of flags and balls corresponded with numbers, which were translated into words through a code-book. This form of communication depended on clear visibility and each post being manned by officers with telescopes and steady hands. The system and code-books used in 1810/11 were hurriedly borrowed from the Navy ('2026' stood for 'I shall leave off action'), but within a year HQ staff had devised their own ciphers using the same form of word/number substitution.[10]

Tactical intelligence obtained in the no-man's land which separated armies on campaign was provided by cavalry patrols and sent by galloper either to divisional or general HQ. Here speed was vital. During early June 1811, when Wellington was anxious to deliver a 'knock' against either Soult's or Marmont's army as they drew apart, he needed a continual flow of precise information about enemy movements. From his lines north-west of Badajoz, a stream of cavalry patrols fanned out and penetrated twenty-five to thirty miles inside French-held districts. One, from the 23rd Light Dragoons and commanded by Lieutenant Cocks, a gifted officer already experienced in such duties, probed the villages north of the Mérida–Talavera road, questioning local peasants about French activity. Cocks finished his reports by five each afternoon and had them delivered by galloper to his divisional commander, Stapleton Cotton, at Campo Maior for transmission to Wellington's HQ at Quinta de Santa João ten miles away. One urgent message, written at two in the afternoon, was carried by a sergeant who covered the twenty miles to Campo Maior in eight hours so that it could reach Wellington the next morning.[11]

Officers whose abilities had aroused Wellington's interest were picked for this work. 'Vigilance and intelligence' were essential, General Leith told Lieutenant Gomme, 'to guard against the vague and unsatisfactory style of intelligence which is common'.[12] It was exciting, challenging work with plenty of risks, which attacted the younger, more raffish officers. When Leith Hay departed for an extended reconnaissance behind French lines early in 1813, he was accompanied by Lord Tweed-dale, a fox-hunting officer with his own pack and a taste for what he called 'amusement'. Leith Hay, one of Wellington's most resourceful and daring scouting officers, admired the gameness of one who was 'in every respect an honour to the Scotch peerage'.[13]

Both officers would have worn their uniforms on such missions so that if they were captured they would have been treated as POWs rather than tortured and shot as spies. Leith Hay took his sword and officer's crimson sash with him when he entered Piedrabuena to rescue one of his informers, 'the wife of a Spanish colonel who I had promised not to leave to the mercy of the French'.[14]

Local spies were recruited by all scouting officers. Cocks placed a high value on what he heard from Spanish villagers, who watched the everyday activities of French soldiers. 'A great deal may be done in this country', he told Cotton in July 1811, 'through the peasants than by patrols. I get almost hourly intelligence from the direction of Montijo through this source.' There were snags because 'Spanish peasants are always telling some story about artillery' which was often false.[15] On his perambulations during early 1813 Leith Hay established networks of peasants who scanned the roads near Ciudad Real for troop movements.[16] Many were probably guerrillas, but Leith Hay always found that a supply of cash lubricated the flow of intelligence. Elsewhere money was always useful; between 87 and 144 dollars (£18–£33) were dispensed monthly by General Sir William Clinton to his spymaster Antonia Roco in eastern Spain during the second half of 1813, as well as smaller 'secret service' payments to anonymous informants.[17]

Infiltration of no-man's land and French-held districts by British officers and patrols ultimately depended on the goodwill of the inhabitants. This was universal and of immense value; hundreds, probably thousands of Spaniards were prepared to risk their lives to assist scouting officers. Some of Leith Hay's road-watchers were taken by the local French commander, Jean-Pierre Marazin, during March and April 1813 and presumably executed. None betrayed him even though a French spy offered a 100 dollar reward for his capture and French soldiers threatened to murder a peasant suspected of knowing his whereabouts.[18]

The mood and activities of Spanish patriots severely restricted French intelligence-gathering. In March 1812 Marmont complained that the entire area between his and Wellington's advance posts were infested with guerrillas, whose numbers made it impossible for him to send out reconnaissance patrols.[19] Guerrillas were always a valuable source of intelligence to the British; in June 1813, when information about crossing points on the Ebro were urgently needed, a scouting officer was ordered to collect it from Longa's HQ at Medina de Torma. Spaniards were generally helpful. Major-General John Byng discovered 'a smart young Spaniard who has been six weeks with General Abbé's Baggage' at Roncesvalles in July 1813 and learned from him details of French artillery and numbers. In the same month a picket encountered Jean de la Rosa, a Frenchman who claimed to be 'employed by Lord Wellington in pursing Intelligence' and who had come the day before from Bayonne with an extensive report of Soult's forces and their plans. This was immediately conveyed to HQ. There were also Spaniards who feigned friendship for the French and wheedled information from them. One Spanish spy, who had shadowed Soult's advance to Badajoz at the end of 1811, asked that the property of a colleague 'be respected because it is widely felt that he is pro-French'. Another who simulated such sympathies was a Spanish lady admired by Victor 'but not for any bad purpose' who sent reports of his confidences to British army HQ in Cádiz.[20]

The usefulness of intelligence from sources close to the French varied enormously. Two reports, forwarded from Cádiz early in 1811, gave Wellington's HQ physical descriptions of two enemy agents. One was a rubicund French engineer who masqueraded as a Royal Artillery officer and another a bow-legged Spaniard with a squint. During the winter of 1811/12 reports from an agent who had somehow penetrated the French High Command and eavesdropped on its conferences provided vivid evidence of backbiting by disgruntled marshals. So did the lady to whom Victor offered his attentions, and to whom he confessed his anger at the division of command in Spain and his fear that he would never capture Cádiz.[21]

Quarrels and recriminations among senior French officers were confirmed from their correspondence. One letter received at HQ in April 1812 revealed that a disheartened Marmont was overwhelmed by his problems, imagined himself abandoned by Napoleon and felt starved of resources.[22] There was little sensational here, but it added to the general picture of disharmony between the marshals and the effects of Napoleon's distant interference in their campaigns. Such intelligence gave Wellington an insight into the minds and preoccupations of his opponents and he could plan his future moves knowing the difficulties which they had to contend with. The ultimate value of such knowledge is not easy to assess precisely, but the efforts Wellington made to acquire it are a mark of how highly he regarded it.

Much captured enemy correspondence was in cipher. Code-breaking was first undertaken by Wellington and anyone on his staff willing to have a go, but by the end of 1811 most was being undertaken by Major Scovell, the Assistant Quartermaster-General, who had discovered a talent for it. French ciphers relied on a system in which a staggered sequence of numbers stood for words and phrases, for example '678' = 'Badajoz', '1370' = 'brigade'.[23] One of these systems had been unravelled by October 1812 when secret messages between Soult and Suchet were being read.[24] Another which substituted symbols for words had been broken by Scovell early in 1812.[25] Joseph's code had been partly revealed by June 1812, but that used by Napoleon's War Ministry proved harder to crack and examples of it had to be sent to the War Office for decipherment by experts there. They succeeded and a key was despatched to Wellington in April 1813.[26] British messages, whether by telegraph or courier, also used codes based on irregular number sequences, for example (from the 1813/14 code-book), '503' = '1st Division', '4' = '2nd Division' and '504' = '3rd Division'.

At all times high priority was given to the accumulation of topographical information, first about Portugal and then about Spain. There was virtually nothing of any military value obtainable locally. The defects of the López maps which landed Masséna in so much trouble during his 1810 advance to Lisbon were soon realized by British HQ. It was also discovered that Portugal had never been accurately mapped, an oversight that was blamed on Jesuit prejudice against scientific enquiry, and so during 1808 and much of 1809 the British army waged war in what was an unknown country. Steps were first taken to survey Portugal in November 1808 when an officer of engineers, Captain Landemann, began a preliminary investigation of the region around Abrantès.[27] He classified roads according to their ability to support artillery and wheeled transports, assessed local crop yields and calculated how many men could be billeted in towns and cities.

This work progressed under George Murray's supervision and by December 1810 his survey teams had produced a reliable four-inch-to-the-mile map of central Portugal. Additional topographical information was accumulated at HQ from data collected by diligent officers as they travelled to and fro. One set of such notes, made by a cavalryman, included an inn-guide ('right strong vino', 'horrid rot-gut stuff') which delighted Wellington.[28]

Murray's co-ordination of all topographical intelligence was essential for the performance of his other major duty, the planning and direction of the army's routes of march. The widths and surfaces of Iberian roads rendered impossible the easy movement of masses of men, animals, vehicles and guns, so the army moved in sections by more or less parallel and convergent routes. Many had to be charted and evaluated before a march began. Early in 1813 Murray commissioned parties of officers to examine roads and river-crossings in hitherto uncharted northern Portugal in preparation for Wellington's spring offensive. They did their work well; 50,000 men marched round the flank of the unsuspecting French, who were caught off-balance.[29]

This was a coup, admittedly for the less glamorous area of intelligence work. There were however occasions when Wellington wondered whether such elaborate planning and efforts were worth while. He was making war in a completely open society which possessed no machinery for military censorship. Full, frank and often revealing details of his campaigns were freely published in British newspapers, which, much to his annoyance, were smuggled across the Channel and read in France. In November 1809 he protested to Liverpool about newspapers which printed 'paragraphs describing the position, the number, the objects and the means of attacking possessed by the armies in Spain and Portugal' and demanded their suppression since their revelations 'will increase materially the difficulty of all operations'.[30] The government dared not meddle with press freedom, but Liverpool suggested that Wellington might copy Moore and impose censorship over soldiers' letters, the main source of such harmful material.[31]

Wellington chose not to take such an unpopular and distasteful measure; gentlemen did not read other gentlemen's correspondence. The matter lapsed for a time and the reports continued. For instance on 18 January 1811 *The Times* listed reinforcements due to be disembarked at Lisbon and in March gave the total number of men laid up sick. The more widely read provincial newspapers followed suit: in March 1811 the *Aberdeen Chronicle* specified all the units which had just been shipped to Algeçiras in support of the Cádiz front. As there were no war correspondents, all this came from soldiers' letters.

Much of what was written was based solely on hearsay. 'As soon as an accident happens,' Wellington complained after a skirmish in July 1810 in which British cavalry had been roughly handled, 'every man who can write sits down to write to another of what he does not know.'[32] And yet he did not object when, in June 1812, his new Adjutant-General Colonel James Gordon proposed to send campaign reports to the Opposition leaders, Grey and Whitbread. His patience dissolved when it was discovered that Gordon had abused his position to examine official despatches and had leaked their contents before official publication. Soon after and thanks to Wellington's agitation, Gordon was sacked.[33]

Some officers heeded Wellington's warnings and forbade publication of their letters, but most did not and grudgingly he had to accept that he could neither filter the information which flowed from the front nor prevent its publication. Nevertheless, he remained convinced that 'the contents of all newspapers are intelligence to the enemy, upon which I know that plans of operation have been formed'.[34] He was correct; his own despatches appeared, suitably doctored, in *Le Moniteur* and were referred to by Napoleon in his orders to King Joseph. The Emperor also relied on the British press for information on the course of the war in Spain during the late summer of 1812 when he was in Russia.[35] Likewise Wellington's men scanned newspapers from home to gain an overall picture of their predicament and the war's progress.[36] The harm done, notwithstanding Wellington's protests, was probably slight. There is no direct evidence that intelligence that was at least a month old when it reached Paris was of much value in Madrid four weeks later.

Wellington's intelligence and logistical services were vastly superior to those of the French, which was fortunate given their numerical superiority and the parity of weapons available to both sides. This was a period of stagnation in military technology during which all European armies relied on armaments that had been in use for the past fifty years, even longer in the case of the basic infantry firearm, the smoothbore musket.

There were continual modifications, mostly minor, to existing weapons but very little serious research and innovation. What there was was confined to the British army, which introduced the Shrapnel shell, the Congreve rocket and the Baker rifle. The French were conservative; in 1800 Napoleon abandoned balloon observation (a novelty of the Revolutionary armies) and seven years later withdrew rifles from his light infantry.

British inventiveness was an offshoot of the Industrial Revolution, which was gaining momentum during the wars. By their end, the output of hundreds of small foundries and workshops had made Britain the arsenal of Europe. Even the small manufactory at Woolwich which fabricated warheads for Congreve rockets turned them out at a rate of 900/1,000 a month.[37] As demand rose, efficiency became paramount and forced the Board of Ordnance to impose control over all the workshops making musket parts and set up one of its own for casting barrels at Enfield. Such measures were also dictated by the venality of contractors and their tendency to supply shoddy goods.

The flintlock (sometimes called a 'firelock'), muzzle-loading musket was the universal infantry weapon, although quality varied from country to country, with the Russian being the worst. The British version, known as 'Brown Bess', had a .75 bore and fired a soft lead ball which fitted loosely for ease and speed of loading. A trained, well-drilled soldier, who kept his lock and trigger mechanism greased with pig fat, could fire three or four rounds a minute, although mechanical breakdowns, fouled barrels and the pressure of combat quickly reduced this rate. The black powder charge gave a vicious kick (greater than that of a modern twelve-bore) and one soldier recalled his shoulder black with brusing after Fuentes.[38] The most effective killing range of a musket was 100 yards, beyond which the ball rapidly lost impetus, which is why so many soldiers, including Wellington, were struck by spent balls that seldom caused more than minor contusions.

The smoothbore musket was notoriously inaccurate. In 1842, when it was obsolescent, firing tests revealed that three out of four shots struck a twenty by six foot target (presumably equivalent to the front of an advancing infantry column) at 100 yards.

A breakdown of the British army's shooting at Vitoria showed that 3.5 million balls were fired and that it needed 450 to cause a casualty.[39] Relying on his own observation, Rifleman Surtees estimated that 1 in 200 musket balls found a target.[40] So, for firepower to have an impact, it had to be intense and at close range. For this reason Wellington insisted that all his men were drilled regularly in order to manoeuvre with 'celerity and accuracy' so that infantry lines could move easily into the best possible firing positions on the battlefield.[41] Shooting practice against wooden targets in the form of painted Frenchmen occupied less time.[42] Nevertheless it was generally admitted that the British volleys were more deadly than those of the French, who commonly fired high.

The 60th and 95th Rifles, the Portuguese Caçadores and some Hanoverian light infantry were equipped with the Baker rifle, which had a slower rate of fire than the musket but a range of up to 250 yards and greater accuracy. A crack shot from the 95th examined his cartridge box after Waterloo and remarked, 'Well, I did not know I had one left, there's three more Frenchmen standing than there should have been, had I known of these three rounds of ammunition.' An eyewitness to a skirmish in October 1812 later commented, 'The rifleman brought the enemy down as if they had been partridges.'[43] Such men were the forerunners of the modern infantrymen; they wore dark-green uniforms, chestnut brown for the Caçadores, used cover and aimed carefully, often lying down and resting their rifles on their shakos. Their accurate shooting at longer ranges meant that they invariably got the better of the French tirailleurs.

While the firepower of British infantrymen was superior to that of the French, British cavalry excelled in enthusiasm rather than skill at arms. This was Wellington's judgement and one that upset cavalrymen, which explains why he was fulsome when he praised them publicly at reviews.[44] In private he was full of censure, particularly for senior cavalry officers unaccustomed to commanding large bodies of horsemen. After an engagement in 1812 in which British heavy dragoons had gone pell-mell at the French and lost 48 casualties, 116 prisoners and a larger number of valuable chargers, he wrote angrily about 'the trick our officers of cavalry have acquired of galloping at everything, and their galloping back as fast as they gallop at the enemy'. The root of the problem was inexperience. 'Our cavalry', he wrote in a cooler mood, 'is the most delicate instrument in our whole machine. Well managed it can perform wonders, and will always be of use, but it is easily put out of order on the field.'[45] A British cavalry charge had something of the wild quality of a hunt in full chase and it was observed that cavalrymen deliberately adopted the short stirrup of the 'hunting seat' when they rode at the enemy. There were, however, a few exceptional officers who balanced courage with field discipline such as Cotton and Lord Henry Paget (later Marquess of Anglesey), whom Wellington cherished. He was also well disposed towards his best horsemen, the dragoons and hussars of the King's German Legion, who were noted for the great care they took of their horses.[46]

There was a disparity too between British and French artillery. The latter always had more guns and, thanks to a high proportion of eight- and twelve- pounders, fired a heavier weight of solid shot. This preponderance was to some extent offset by Wellington's frequent deployment of men on the reverse slopes of hills where they were sheltered from the long-range bombardment which was always a prelude to a French offensive. The British did possess the Shrapnel shell, a time-fused shell which exploded in mid-air and scattered small balls. Wellington appreciated its value, although once, after an interview with an injured French general, he noticed that it inflicted only superficial wounds.

He had little time for the Congreve rocket, one of the might-have-beens of military technology. It had been developed in the early 1800s by the opinionated Sir William Congreve (he thought Wellington an inferior strategist) with the backing of Pitt. The Congreve rocket was a sophisticated version of the crude devices which Wellington had seen employed by the princely armies of India. Fired either from tripods or along the ground, the rockets consisted of a stick to which was attached the cast-iron warhead that contained a propellent and 'bursting powder'. Enthusiastically patronized by the Prince Regent, Congreve batteries had been employed on various fronts since 1806, including Cádiz, and in the winter of 1813/14 one was sent to Wellington despite his preference for nine-pounders.

In January 1814 he and his staff watched a demonstration of rockets. It was a spectacular show; one onlooker was astonished by the 'most tremendous noise' of the 'formidable spitfires', but some rockets were easily blown off course and others exploded prematurely. Without means of stabilization their flight was often erratic, but they had an enormous psychological impact. After they had been used during the crossing of the Adour, a French veteran confessed to having been scared stiff when he first saw them. So too were some British troops because some of the rockets turned round in mid-flight and returned to their firers.[47] Wellington was unimpressed; their principal value was as incendiaries which set fire to buildings, and in France, as in Spain, he was waging war to liberate rather than terrorize and destroy.

Part Seven

1812–1815

1

The Most Successful Campaign:
Spain, 1812

At the end of 1811, Wellington believed that the strategic balance had swung in his favour and that the moment was right to strike a decisive blow in Spain. 'I was the only person in the Peninsula', he later wrote, 'who really commanded an army' and therefore in a position to inflict lasting damage on the French.[1] A victory in Spain would encourage the Spanish to redouble their efforts and inspire 'general resistance throughout Europe to the fraudulent and disgusting tyranny of Bonaparte'.[2] He wrote this on 24 December when there was no way of knowing the outcome of France's quarrel with Russia or even whether it would end in war, since Napoleon still clung to the hope that Czar Alexander would bow to the threat of invasion by the 600,000-strong army that was gathering in eastern Europe. Russian resolve might be stiffened by the knowledge that resistance was flourishing in Spain.

With all his energies directed towards a settlement in the east, Napoleon ordered his commanders in Spain to mark time until after he had dealt with Russia and was free to take command in person. His chief worry was the proliferation of guerrilla warfare, especially in coastal regions where he rightly feared that the insurgents would be sustained by British seaborne assistance. Accordingly he instructed his marshals to concentrate on campaigns of pacification that were to be waged most vigorously in Valencia and Asturias, where the French were in danger of losing control completely. Continued reverses here imperilled that strategically vital road which ran northwards from Burgos to the major French base at Bayonne and carried men and traffic from Salamanca and Madrid. At the same time the scale of proposed operations in Russia demanded the depletion of armies in

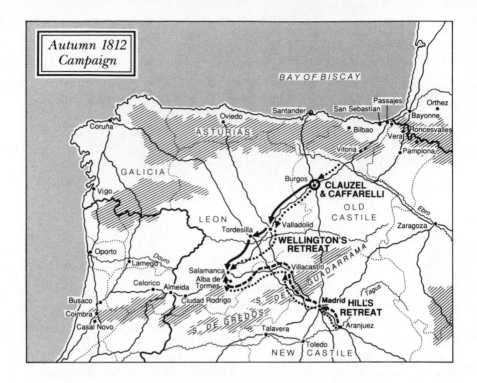

Spain, although, where possible, the losses were made good with conscripts from France and Italy.

Intelligence of French withdrawals, particularly that received on 25
December, which described units transferred from Marmont's army to
Suchet's, alerted Wellington to the possibility of a coup against Ciudad
Rodrigo.[3] Before he embarked on an offensive in Spain he had to secure
the frontier strongholds of Ciudad Rodrigo and Badajoz, which would
keep open the roads to Salamanca and Madrid and forestall further
invasions of Portugal. There were tremendous risks involved in attacking these fortresses; as he soon discovered, his siege artillery lacked the
weight of shot and shell necessary to reduce their defences quickly and
once news of the sieges reached Soult and Marmont they would be
compelled to intervene, singly or in tandem.

Time or the lack of it dictated Wellington's actions. He advanced
swiftly towards Ciudad Rodrigo, where, after a four-day delay caused
by snow storms, his siege lines were established on 8 January. A week
later Marmont heard news of the attack at Valladolid and immediately
began to collect troops for a relief force. Unknown to Wellington, he
was woefully ill-prepared for such an operation; his men were living

from hand to mouth and lacked transport. Nevertheless, Marmont calculated that he would be ready to march on 29 January. Wellington had anticipated a faster response; fearful that he might be trapped or forced to abandon the siege he decided to launch an infantry attack on the fortress's well-defended breaches on 19 January. It was a desperate gamble since his own guns had not stopped the garrison from throwing up makeshift defences across the breaches that would have to be stormed head-on in the teeth of heavy musket fire and grape shot.

Ciudad Rodrigo fell, but at a cost of 1,300 casualties, including Craufurd, who was fatally wounded. The following day an intercepted message from Marmont's HQ indicated that the French could not have moved for another nine days.[4] Even with the extra time it is unlikely that Wellington could have avoided a frontal attack. The preliminary bombardment had revealed the inadequacy of his artillery and measures were in hand to supplement it with naval cannon from Lisbon. All that the sailors could offer were twenty Russian eighteen-pounders, which were useless since their barrels were too narrow to take British shot.[5] The French too had problems in this quarter for by a stroke of good luck Ciudad Rodrigo contained Marmont's siege artillery park, which included thirty-two mortars and sixty twelve- and sixteen-pounders, mostly without carriages.[6]

Wellington's next objective was Badajoz, a more formidable stronghold that was well supplied with a determined garrison of 5,000. On 28 January he made his first move; Hill's corps was detached and sent to Almaraz to block any attempt at relief by Joseph's Madrid-based Army of the Centre. On 16 February, when it was clear that Marmont had returned to Valladolid after hearing of the loss of Ciudad Rodrigo, Wellington began his detailed plans for the new siege.[7]

Again he was taking risks. Badajoz lay beyond the reach of the nearest Portuguese magazines, so the army would have to survive on provender purchased locally, which was no easy matter given the commissariat's temporary shortage of hard cash.[8] As with the operations before Ciudad Rodrigo, Wellington's timetable would be set by the French. Napoleon felt sure that Wellington would never dare to attack Badajoz so long as Soult and Marmont were capable of lifting the siege.

To reduce this likelihood, Wellington asked the Spanish to intensify guerrilla activity in southern Andalucía where intelligence reports indicated that Soult was already in difficulties.[9] Measures were taken to mislead the French about Wellington's intentions and his army moved with as much secrecy as possible. As a result Soult, after a false alarm at the beginning of February, remained unaware of the threat to Badajoz until 23 March, seven days after the siege had begun.[10] He immediately collected a relief army which he expected to reach Albuera on 7 April. He kept to schedule for he reached Zafra on the 6th, and two days later his cavalry patrols had penetrated to within ten miles of Badajoz.[11]

There was also pressure from the north. On 30 March, and in accordance with Napoleon's wishes, Marmont launched a destructive raid on the thinly defended region between Ciudad Rodrigo and Almeida. Without siege artillery he could do no more than blockade the fortresses, but at Wellington's HQ there were doubts about the reliability of Ciudad Rodrigo's Spanish garrison. This demonstration and the closeness of Soult forced Wellington's hand. He could either withdraw inside Portugal or adopt the bloody expedient of throwing men against stone walls.

He chose to attack Badajoz after nightfall on 6 April. It was a decision which pained him; during the day and throughout the two hours of the assault he appeared tense and desperately anxious. He knew that losses would be unbearably heavy and had been forced to suspend his principle of never offering battle save in favourable circumstances. Within the troops picked for the onrushes a sense of fatality mingled with one of determination. As at Ciudad Rodrigo, the heaviest attacks were made over ditches against partially demolished sections of the walls, which the defenders had barricaded. As well as the hazards of musketry and grape shot, there were *cheveux de frise*, barriers bristling with sabre blades.

The assault was successful; over 4,000 casualties were suffered, mostly victims of the defenders' ferocious fire. The losses among officers were strikingly high but not unexpected, since at every stage they had to lead and urge on the storming parties. Six generals, including the gouty Picton, were wounded and the 95th Rifles lost twenty-two officers. The approaches to the walls were a hideous sight. The next morning Gunner Whitman found 'killed and wounded laying in all manner of postures and forms, some crying out with their wounds, others crying for water, and some crawling the best way they could, some praying instant death to put them out of their pain.'[12]

Wellington wept when he saw all this. He admitted later that when Picton, whom he called 'as hard as iron', came to congratulate him, 'I actually could not help crying. I bit my lips, did everything I could to stop it for I was ashamed he should see it; and he so little entered into my feelings that he said, "Good God, what is the trouble?" and I was obliged to begin swearing and cursing the Government for giving us no Sappers and miners as an excuse for my agitation.'[13] Callousness was in fact the order of the day, for once Badajoz had fallen its captors succumbed to what one called that 'uncontrolled licentiousness which is regarded as the just reward of successful victors'.[14] For the men and women of the town this meant murder, rape and pillage. Rifleman Costello imagined himself 'in the regions of the damned' as he listened to 'The shouts of drunken soldiers in quest of more liquor, the report of firearms and crashing in of doors, together with the appalling shrieks of hapless women'. The next morning as Wellington rode through the streets he was confronted with some drunkards who called out, 'Old boy! will you drink? The town's our own – hurrah!'[15] Within a few hours gallows and lash restored order.

In the breathing-space which followed the taking of Badajoz, Wellington examined his strategic position and the options open to him. Portugal was safe and he was free either to strike at Soult, who had scurried back to Cádiz once he heard of Badajoz's fall, or at Marmont, who was still threatening Ciudad Rodrigo. While an offensive against Soult was attractive in so far as his defeat would knock away the main buttress of French power in southern Spain, Wellington could not allow Marmont to rampage unchallenged in central Portugal. Moreover since the Spanish Governor of Ciudad Rodrigo, General Carlos de España, had been neglectful there was a danger that it could be retaken by a *coup de main*. Wellington was therefore forced to rush to its assistance.

Having concentrated his forces on the border between Spain and Portugal, Wellington decided to throw his main weight against Marmont, who had withdrawn to Salamanca. Its capture and the elimination of the Army of Portugal offered valuable strategic and political dividends. An Anglo-Portuguese army would be in a position to straddle the road to Bayonne, which would effectively strand Soult in Andalucía and Joseph in Madrid, and additional assistance could be delivered to the guerrillas in the Asturias. With north-western Spain liberated, the French High Command would be faced with two equally bleak alternatives. Joseph could either deplete his armies in the south, east and centre for a counter-offensive or else cling to these areas with the prospect of severely reduced help from France.

To execute this ambitious strategy Wellington, for the first time, could count on superior numbers. He commanded 43,000 Anglo-Portuguese troops and, for what it was worth, had the promise of Spanish help. Marmont was thought to have less than half that number although, once Wellington's intentions became clear, he could summon reinforcements from other fronts. This was a slow business and he had no assurance of co-operation from his fellow commanders.

To alleviate the problems of bickering and muddle which had for the past years bedevilled French efforts to create a united strategy, Napoleon had appointed Joseph commander-in-chief shortly before his departure to Warsaw in May. But, as intercepted messages revealed, the old difficulties remained. Joseph enjoyed no respect; his interference was resented or ignored; and subordinate marshals remained as curmudgeonly as ever in their response to orders for the transfer of their men. Matters were made worse by the deterioration in French communications; by mid-June guerrilla bands had all but isolated Marmont and from August Soult was cut off from contact with France. The constant loss of reports and orders made it impossible to co-ordinate strategy effectively and commanders suffered periodic blackouts of intelligence about their enemies' movements. All this was known to Wellington.

His campaign opened with a sequence of diversionary actions designed to make French commanders reluctant to send help to Marmont. During May, Hill's 22,000 British, Portuguese and Spanish occupied Almaraz and destroyed the bridge over the Tagus. If Soult chose to march north he would have to drag his army along a circuitous route over the uplands of southern Spain to Madrid. He was further discouraged from undertaking such a move since he was busy enough fending off attacks by General Francisco Ballasteros's demonstrations in southern Andulacía and the game of hide-and-seek played in Estremadura by Hill against General Jean-Baptiste D'Erlon's corps. For a time at least Soult feared that this was the first stage of a full-scale offensive by Wellington. Around Madrid, the guerrilla leader El Empecinado ('the pitch seller') carried out a series of audacious raids, and insurgent activities were stepped up in Asturias, a region from which Marmont hoped to draw reinforcements.

Wellington's hammer-blow against Salamanca was delivered on 13 June when his army advanced from Ciudad Rodrigo. He felt sure that he had superiority of numbers, despite a Spanish intelligence report which assessed Marmont's strength as 48,000.[16] His confidence was shared by the rest of the army; 'Hitherto,' wrote Captain Kincaid of the 95th Rifles, 'we had been fighting the description of battle in which John Bull glories so much – gaining a brilliant and useless victory against great odds. But we are now about to contend for fame on equal terms.'[17] This was just what Marmont wanted to avoid and so on 16 June he evacuated Salamanca and withdrew north-east to Fuentesauco to await the reinforcements he had summoned from Generals Bonet and Louis Marc Caffarelli.

His retreat was the first stage in a sequence of complex manoeuvres and skirmishes which continued until 22 July. Marmont was playing for time in which to consolidate his forces, while Wellington was seeking an engagement on advantageous terms. To start with he had to detach forces to capture three fortalices on the outskirts of Salamanca, which were finally overcome on 27 June. Taking advantage of this distraction, Marmont staged an unexpected offensive on 20 June which forced Wellington to abandon temporarily the sieges and concentrate his forces on the San Cristobal ridge. Marmont and his staff examined his position from the foot of the escarpment, coming under artillery fire, but, no doubt remembering Busaco and Fuentes, chose not to offer battle. So too did Wellington, who as he watched the advancing columns below, remarked, 'Damn tempting! I have a great mind to attack 'em,' and considered ordering a cavalry charge.[18]

What he had seen had severely shaken his confidence for it was now clear that Marmont's army was larger than he had previously thought. During the next few days, Marmont executed a number of probing movements across the Tormes to discover whether he could penetrate behind Wellington's eastern flank and force him back along the Ciudad Rodrigo road, but they came to nothing. After the loss of three small forts on 27 June, he decided to fall back to Tordesillas, demolishing bridges as he went, and make a junction with Caffarelli and Bonet.

Wellington now realized that he was losing control of the situation. 'Matters have not gone as I could wish at Salamanca,' he wrote to Liverpool on 25 June, but nevertheless he split his army into two columns and set off after Marmont in the belief that Bonet and Caffarelli would feel bound by Napoleon's instructions and remain in the north. He was partly correct; on 1 July Bonet joined Marmont with 7,000 men, but Caffarelli felt constrained to keep all his infantry and sent only some cavalry and artillery, much to Marmont's disgust.

As matters stood at the beginning of July, Marmont with 50,000 men lay in the vicinity of Tordesillas with his mind full of doubts. He had no clear picture of his enemy's strength and movements, imagining that Wellington was about to be reinforced by Hill's corps, which in fact was still in Estremadura, and had no idea how many, if any, reinforcements he could expect in the following weeks.[19] Wellington was in no better position. His army of just over 50,000, including 3,000 Spanish, was concenetrated around Medina del Campo and, while he was aware that he still enjoyed parity of strength, he feared that the opportunity for a decisive offensive was past. So, when on 15 July Marmont began an advance towards Salamanca, Wellington fell back along a parallel route.

A day later he heard, via an intercepted message, that Joseph was preparing to march from Madrid with 14,000 hastily gathered men to assist Marmont.[20] There was no way of telling whether Marmont knew of this, although Wellington rightly guessed that he did not, but this did not matter since once the two forces were united he would have no choice but to slip away back to Ciudad Rodrigo. For five days, and often within musket shot of each other, the two armies trudged back to Salamanca. Wellington, who showed amazing composure in the face of what appeared to be the collapse of his plans, maintained a constant vigilance, scanning the reports of subordinate commanders and patrols for any indication that Marmont might attack or cut him off from Salamanca.[21]

By the evening of 21 July, the Anglo-Portuguese army had passed through Salamanca and was occupying a defensive position on the San Cristobal heights to the south of the city. Wellington had relinquished his hopes of fighting a decisive battle and, having been outmanoeuvred, was anxious to withdraw to Ciudad Rodrigo with his army intact. The night of 21/22 July witnessed a spectacular thunderstorm which terrified men and horses, and the following morning, having slept in the open wrapped in a cloak, Wellington ordered his baggage train to start its journey to Ciudad Rodrigo.

Marmont was still close on his heels. The French had crossed the Tormes the day before and on the morning of the 22nd were edging southwards in a manoeuvre designed to swing around Wellington and severe his escape route. Throughout the campaign Marmont's thinking had been shaped by two assumptions. First, Wellington was a defensive commander of consummate skill and therefore not to be attacked on ground of his own choosing. Second, he would instinctively shrink from any offensive action. At the same time Marmont's reputation and moral pressure from his subordinates demanded that an attempt be made to prevent Wellington's escape. The chance to do this offered itself on the morning of 22 July as Marmont surveyed the British army from a hillside close to the hamlet of Calvarrasa de Arriba.

In the far distance he saw clouds of dust which he immediately interpreted as evidence that the bulk of Wellington's army was hurrying westwards towards the Ciudad Rodrigo road. This impression was confirmed by the presence of the British 7th Division opposite, which he immediately took to be a rearguard. In fact he had been deceived by the lie of the land; the high ground in front of him concealed the rest of Wellington's army. In ignorance of its closeness, he ordered three divisions (14,000 men) to advance rapidly westwards in a sweep which would cut off what he imagined to be a retreating army. Contact had already been made with what Marmont supposed to be the rearguard when the French attacked two high points, the Greater and Lesser Arapile, between the armies, taking the former and being repulsed from the latter.

Wellington received intimation of the westward movement of Marmont's three divisions while he was enjoying an impromptu luncheon of a chicken leg. An ADC announced, 'The enemy are in motion, my

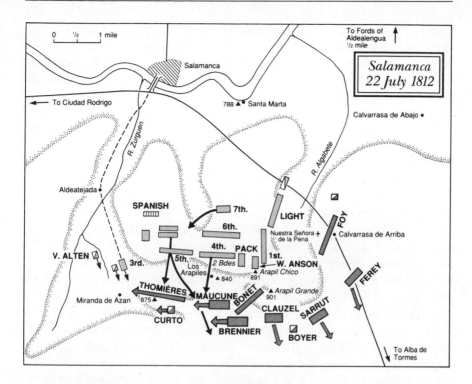

lord.' 'Very well,' he answered. 'Observe what they are doing.' 'I think they are extending their left.' 'The Devil they are! Give me my glass quickly.' With his telescope he rode to the Lesser Arapile and scanned the French columns now separated from Marmont's right and in a vulnerable, extended order. 'By God!' he exclaimed. 'That will do!' Within a few moments he had improvised a battle-plan and was riding towards his divisional commanders with instructions.

What he had in mind was a series of more or less simultaneous knock-out blows against the columns which, thanks to the undulating ground between them and their attackers, would be taken by surprise. The first, delivered by Pakenham's 3rd Division and Colonel Benjamin D'Urban's Anglo-Portuguese cavalry, sliced into General Thomières' leading division and scattered it. Half a mile to the east, the British 5th Division, inspired by General Leith, who had spoken with the 'eloquence of a Caesar', struck the second French division. It had no chance to recover before it was hit by Cotton's cavalry. Lieutenant-General John Le Marchant's heavy dragoons, tall men on big horses, spear-headed the charge and rode on to hack and trample under hoof the terrified Frenchmen of Brennier's division. Afterwards, an exuberant Wellington congratulated Cotton: 'By God, Cotton, I never saw anything so beautiful in my life; the day is *yours*.'

In a short time, two French divisions had been shattered and a third, Brennier's, was crippled. Nearly a quarter of Marmont's army was out of action and he, watching the débâcle from the Greater Arapile, had been badly wounded by shrapnel. Soon after, his second-in-command, Bonet, was killed. It was left to an able and determined officer, General Bertrand Clauzel, to rally what was left of the army and withdraw north across the Tormes. Some French made for the Huerta crossing, chased by cavalry, while others crossed the bridge of Alba de Tormes, which was open thanks to the chicken-hearted General España, who had fled to the nearby castle, taking the Spanish garrison with him. The pursuit lasted three days and was marked by an extraordinary incident in which Hanoverian heavy dragoons, whom civilians imagined to be all officers because of their cocked hats, charged a French square. A dying horse fell on the defenders and opened a gap through which the horsemen rode, capturing or killing at least 400.

Salamanca was an impressive victory which marked the beginning of the end of French power in Spain. Fourteen thousand Frenchmen were dead, wounded or taken prisoner, while Anglo-Portuguese losses were about 5,000. For Wellington it was a personal triumph; he had shown an astonishing combination of presence of mind and resourcefulness. In less than half an hour from receiving intelligence of his enemy's movements he had recognized the opportunity open to him, devised a plan and set it in motion. And, for the first time in the Peninsula, he had shown that he could fight and win an offensive action.

The political and military implications of Salamanca were enormous. French authority in Spain was temporarily in disarray as Joseph and his subordinate commanders regrouped their armies and faced up to the crisis. Joseph, who, ignorant of Marmont's exact position, had been on the Madrid-to-Valladolid road when he heard the news of Salamanca, hurried south-eastwards to the safety of Suchet's army in Valencia, abandoning Madrid on the way. When he joined Suchet on 17 August he was already convinced that the survival of French power in Spain depended on the concentration of all available armies in Valencia for a counter-offensive against Wellington.

Soult, who received instructions to evacuate Andalucía on 12 August, refused to comply and proposed instead a plan based on bringing Joseph's, Suchet's and the remnants of Marmont's army into the province, which would serve as a springboard for an offensive towards Portugal. Only after some debate did Soult concede, abandon the siege of Cádiz and march his men across southern Spain to Almansa, where he joined forces with Joseph on 2 October. With a combined army of 60,000 Joseph proceeded northwards towards Madrid. An army had also sprung up in the north-west, where Clauzel and the survivors of the Army of Portugal had combined with Caffarelli to create a force of 45,000 which was placed under the command of General Joseph Souham.

Thanks in great part to the energy of Clauzel, Caffarelli and Soult, who reluctantly accepted the loss of Andalucía, the French had staged a remarkable recovery and, by mid-October, were poised for a two-pronged offensive to retake Madrid and expel Wellington from north-western Spain.

Wellington was unaware of the speed and scale of the French counter-measures, although at the end of August he had correctly assumed that Soult and Joseph would join forces.[22] This did not worry him unduly since he had set in motion a number of activities designed to tie down French troops and distract their commanders. None achieved very much. Soult's progess across southern Spain was not impeded by Ballasteros's Spanish army; Anglo-Sicilian operations on the Catalan coastline gave few problems to Suchet; and lightning raids by guerrillas, supported by Royal Navy men-of-war, did not prevent Souham from mustering troops in Asturias and Biscay. Nor were the French deterred by Hill's 40,000-strong Anglo-Portuguese and Spanish army spread out along the upper Tagus and covering the approaches to Madrid. Embittered but wiser, Wellington blamed the Spanish. 'I have never yet known the Spaniards do anything, much less do anything well,' he wrote in November. 'Ballasteros has sometimes drawn the attention of a division or two for the moment [and] A few rascals called guerrillas attack one quarter of their numbers and sometimes succeed, and some-times not.'[23]

The failure of his diversionary measures placed him in a vulnerable position. After occupying Madrid, he had left its security in the hands of Hill's division and shifted the rest of his forces (20,000 Anglo-Portuguese and 16,000 Spanish) northwards to eliminate what was left of the Army of Portugal. Its commander, Clauzel, skilfully avoided an unequal engagement and withdrew northwards, leaving Wellington the task of taking Burgos. The encirclement began on 19 September and, lacking siege artillery, the besiegers were soon in serious difficulties.

There was also a breakdown in intelligence which meant that the information about the numbers and movement of enemy forces was fragmented and vague. An intercepted despatch written by Souham on 2 October confirmed Wellington's prediction that Soult and Joseph would attempt to retake Madrid, but until the middle of the month he remained convinced that Hill and Ballasteros would frustrate them.[24]

At the same time he underestimated the strength of French forces to the north, which was calculated at 34,000 when in fact Souham's full muster was 45,000.[25]

It was the approach of Souham during the third week in October which finally alerted Wellington to the danger he was in and drove him to withdraw from Burgos on 20 October. As the army fell back in two parallel columns towards Tordesillas, he hoped that he could make a stand where the road crossed the Pisuerga just south of Torquemada. It was here, on 27 October, that for the first time he realized that Souham's army more than matched his. In normal circumstances the French advantage in numbers might not have mattered, but Wellington was handicapped by the fact that a third of his army were Spaniards. Offering battle was out of the question for, as he frankly admitted, 'I cannot reckon upon these troops in a field of battle.'[26]

The only way out of what he called 'the worse scrape I was ever in' was a fighting retreat and the recall of Hill. He fell back to Rueda on the Tordesillas–Madrid road and commanded Hill to retire from the Tagus and join him in the vicinity of Salamanca. Hill was already on the move, having left Aranjuez on 27 October in the face of Soult's advance. His army passed through Madrid and on 3 November had reached Arévalo, where he received Wellington's orders to turn west and head for Alba de Tormes.

Four armies were converging on Salamanca. Wellington's from Rueda, Hill's from Arévalo, Soult's from Vilcastín, where he had arrived hot on Hill's tail on 4 November, and Souham's from Medina del Campo. Wellington and Hill reached the city first and combined on 7/8 November. Six days later, as the French were crossing the Tormes, Wellington withdrew south of Salamanca to the ground where he had engaged Marmont. Even though, as he feared, the French with a combined force of at least 90,000 were 'more than a match for us', he felt 'no hesitation in trying the issue of a general action on ground which I have selected'.[27]

No battle followed. As its army prepared for action on 14/15 November, the French High Command suffered a bout of nervousness. Joseph, the titular Commander-in-Chief, turned to Soult for professional advice and was offered a battle-plan for an offensive the next day. It was not implemented because of the heavy rain that fell unceasingly during the night and the following morning. The ground between the armies had become a quagmire over which an extremely hesistant Soult was reluctant to advance and with good reason, given the setbacks which had befallen other French commanders who had challenged Wellington in unpromising conditions. By two in the afternoon, Wellington realized that no attack was imminent and ordered his baggage train to begin a withdrawal along the Ciudad Rodrigo road. On 19 November the army had reached safety after a fifty-four-mile march during which it had been harassed, somewhat half-heartedly, by French cavalry.

Wellington had once been heard to exclaim, 'I am the luckiest fellow in the world; I must have been born under some extraordinary star.' His good fortune had been stretched to the limit during October and November 1812, which, he freely admitted, had been among the most unnerving periods of his life. He had been aware, during the siege of Burgos, that his men were becoming more and more disheartened. They 'behaved very ill' and were 'not all the style they were', which was to some extent explained by the fact that they had not been paid since April.[28] Matters were not helped by the fatigue and long marches in cold, wet weather, distempers and, during the final stage of the retreat, starvation thanks to Colonel James Gordon's bungling, which had separated the army from its supply train. Undismayed by his own maladroitness, this worthless officer proceeded to press the Horse Guards for an appointment as Wellington's Chief of Staff. He ended up as Quartermaster-General of the British army!

The deterioration in spirit and discipline was noticed by others and there was, as the army retreated, much sullen talk 'blaming Lord Wellington for not having sufficient confidence in us to hazard a battle'.[29] For his part, Wellington feared that the army was on the verge of disintegration and his reprimands to officers became increasingly intemperate; in one splenetic but understandable rage, he described his troops as 'the greatest knaves and worst soldiers' he had ever encountered or read about. Behind this public anger was private anxiety. During October and November the news from Russia was discouraging; Wellington knew Moscow had been occupied and there were unconfirmed reports that the Czar might capitulate.[30] The Marquess alone was responsible for the preservation of the only army in the Peninsula that was capable of defeating the French, and, as far as he knew, the only one on the continent which had not yet thrown in the sponge. As ever, Wellington was also aware that his defeat would not only shatter the backbone of Britain's army but could bring down the government, which had upheld the policy of intervention in Spain and Portugal. As it was, news of the retreat from Burgos had reawakened the government's critics, who were as quick as ever to condemn Wellington's strategy as cowardly.

Wellington was defiant in the face of such censure. At the end of November he described the past eleven months' operations as 'the most successful campaign' with 'more important results than any ... in which the British army has been engaged for the last century'.[31] The French had been expelled from southern Spain and Portugal; their army had lost a major battle; and Joseph's political pretensions looked increasingly threadbare. For these reasons Wellington felt more confident than ever in making demands on the government, for 'Commanding a successful army in the field he is the main support of the present administration.'[32]

The year 1812 had seen the appearance of a new ministry in Britain after the assassination of Spencer Perceval in May. For a time it seemed that the Prince Regent might invite the Opposition to form a government, and Wellington made it clear that he would be content to serve it. In the end the Regent chose Liverpool, who became Prime Minister with Castlereagh at the Foreign Office and Lord Bathurst as Secretary for War. One casualty of the upheaval has been the Marquess of Wellesley, who for the past two years had been neglecting his duties at the Foreign Office in favour of womanizing. His lustfulness dismayed Wellington, who bluntly told William Wellesley-Pole, 'I wish that Wellesley was castrated; or that he would like other people attend to his business and perform too. It is lamentable to see Talents and character and advantages such as he possesses thrown away on Whoring'.[33]

Wellesley's disappearance from the Foreign Office had no repercussions on affairs in the Peninsula. Henry Wellesley remained Ambassador at Cádiz, handling relations with the Spanish Council of Regency and Cortes with what his elder brother considered saintlike forbearance. This was needed since there was still a considerable body of opinion within both the Council and the Cortes which believed that the British wanted to use the Anglo-Spanish alliance as a means of taking over Spain's internal and external commerce and stripping her of her Latin American colonies. The predominant liberal element within the Cortes was also deeply suspicious about British demands for extensive reforms of the Spanish army which, they imagined, would create a powerful, professional Praetorian force that could overthrow the new constitution introduced in 1812. Liberal nightmares became reality in September 1812 when Ballasteros attempted a military coup in protest against Wellington's appointment as commander-in-chief.

Wellington had no wish to become entangled in Spanish politics. He wanted a centralized military administration with himself at the top as commander-in-chief. His revitalized Spanish army would be free of what he regarded as the meddling of politicians in Cádiz and capable of playing a significant part in operations on Spanish soil. Under his direction and supported by an efficient logistical machinery, it would become the equivalent of the Indian army, although he never went so far as to insist that the Spanish, like the Portuguese army, should accept a leavening of British officers.

His appointment as commander-in-chief was agreed in September 1812 but discussion of terms was postponed until the end of December, when he visited Cádiz. He had already strengthened his bargaining position by persuading the British Treasury to give him control over that part of the Spanish subsidy which was allocated for military expenditure. Half the £1 million despatched to the Spanish government for 1812 was diverted into Wellington's war chest to cover the costs of the Spanish contingents under his command. There was, of course, a practical reason for this arrangement since these soldiers relied entirely on British sources for their uniforms, weaponry and food. Nevertheless, Wellington appreciated that his grasp on the purse-strings would give him considerable political leverage in Cádiz.

He was welcomed with wild jubilation when he entered the city, something which he despised; a year earlier he had written contemptuously of how the Spanish expended their martial spirit 'in *vivas* and vain boasting'.[34] Despite the cheers and showers of roses, old misgivings were deeply rooted and he had to proceed tactfully, suppressing his patrician distaste for what he called 'the Democracy of Cádiz'. But he was firm, sticking to his demands for powers which a wartime commander-in-chief might reasonably expect such as a veto over appointments and promotion, budgetry control and a commitment to the creation of an efficient system of supply and transport. The Cortes conceded, but with little enthusiasm. For his part, Wellington left Cádiz on 9 January 1813 believing that the spread of democratic influence would undermine the Spanish war effort. There was, he concluded, 'no authority in the state', and he added, 'I wish that some of our reformers would go to Cádiz to see the benefit of a sovereign assembly.'[35]

For reasons he never fully comprehended, the Spanish were unable to fulfil their obligations. In the first place, after five years of war and two on the verge of bankruptcy, Spain lacked the wherewithal to support her armed forces. Nor was there the willpower to force through the reforms Wellington had demanded. The liberal patriots continued to harbour fears that Wellington might subvert the new constitution even though he scrupulously avoided being drawn into conservative intrigues against the Cortes. Relations deteriorated during 1813 until the end of August when he resigned as commander-in-chief after a quarrel over the dismissal of two conservative generals, his hunting companions Castaños and Girón. Popular rumours alleged that he was plotting to make himself 'King Arthur the First of Spain' and that he had ordered the sack of San Sebastián on 31 August in order to promote British commercial interests.[36]

By this time Wellington had discovered, painfully, that no progress had been made in the regeneration of the Spanish army. 'The Spaniards will not', he wrote in March 1813, 'allow … us to interfere much in their concerns, and will adopt, but unwillingly, any suggestion that we may be able to make for their improvement.'[37] So, as he ruefully observed, unfed Spanish soldiers continue to spread 'rapine and confusion' wherever they marched and, like the French, brought 'misery and distress' to their countrymen.[38] Some were sustained, like the Portuguese, by the British commissariat, but many fended for themselves or starved; a British officer noticed that they assuaged hunger by endlessly smoking cigarillos. Despite the £1.4 million allowed by the Treasury for Spanish troops, they were a burden which, by the autumn of 1813, Wellington was anxious to shed. By the end of the year 20,000 had been demobilized.

'Those who trust to the Spaniards trust to a broken reed,' wrote Colonel Bingham in March 1813.[39] It was a widespread opinion, based somewhat unfairly on stories of battles lost and disorderly, ill-clothed soldiers who shrank from a fight and, of course, on xenophobia. Wellington agreed, although his judgements, widely advertised after Talavera, were afterwards uttered privately. Yet, while the Spanish army was dismissed as a fighting force, the guerrillas remained invaluable. Since 1808 there had been a steady flow of British cash and munitions which had yielded useful military dividends in terms of the disruption of French communications, intelligence and tying down large bodies of soldiers. By the beginning of 1813, when it seemed that the French were at last on the defensive, guerrilla activity in northern Spain increased, with bands now well organized and backed by their own light artillery.

As a coalition commander, Wellington presided over what he knew to be an unequal alliance between three nations with a long history of mutual hostility. His politeness and tact could never obscure these facts nor his impatience with what he regarded as native incompetence and slackness. Seen from the other side there were times when his behaviour seemed very close to arrogance, although he believed that he was popular among the Spanish people, if not among their politicians.[42] It would have been impossible to ignore the fact that Britain was the paymaster and armourer of Spain and Portugal and that he was therefore the representative of the senior partner in the alliance. His disdain for the political views of the Spanish liberals was no secret; what they considered a struggle for national freedom and emancipation he believed was a war to restore the ultra-conservative Ferdinand VII.

In the end what mattered was that the common bond of a loathing for Napoleon and his tyranny (by 1812 Catalonia and Aragon had been annexed as départements of France) proved strong enough to hold the allies together until the end of 1813, when Spain and Portugal had been cleared of French troops.

2

The First General of Our Present Age: Spain and France, 1813–April 1814

At the beginning of 1813 Wellington was full of confidence. The tide of the war was now flowing in his direction; he had a clear idea of what he wanted to do and the means to do it. Since November 1812, when he had set up his winter HQ at Freineda, he had been rebuilding his army for a spring offensive designed to expel the French from Spain and open the way for an invasion of southern France. By early May, when the first advance was scheduled to begin, he was sure that his reorganized, reinforced and disciplined army was up to the task. 'I shall not be stronger throughout the campaign, or more efficient than I am now,' he wrote to Bathurst, adding, 'I cannot have a better opportunity for trying the fate of a battle, which, if the enemy should be unsuccessful, must oblige him to withdraw entirely.'[1]

In six months the army had been regenerated. With discretion, so as not to bruise their pride, Wellington had sent home dud commanders and replaced them by able veterans such as Picton, who had been recuperating from wounds and sickness. One, Brigadier-General Walker, who had been shot in the chest at Badajoz, demanded to be recalled notwithstanding 'one wound open in his breast'. Other invalids were recovering from active service in hospitals which had been reorganized and newly staffed through the initiative of Dr James McGrigor, the Inspector-General of Hospitals, who, with Wellington's backing, sliced his way through the bureaucratic inertia of the army's medical department. The results were impressive in terms of men returning to their units, and in May Wellington observed, 'I never saw the British army so healthy or so strong.'[2]

Strength came through numbers, and the government had strained every sinew to send reinforcements even though it was faced with an

American offensive against Canada and the need to keep troops at home to police the disaffected manufacturing districts in the North where the Luddite riots were at their height. After several years of pleading, Wellington at last had been given an adequate force of cavalry. Among the newcomers were the Blues and Life Guards, who, fittingly for a royal bodyguard in an age which took its aesthetics from the Classical past, wore huge crested helmets like those of the hoplites of Ancient Greece. This handsome headgear had been foisted on them by the Prince Regent, an enthusiastic designer of military costume and millinery. Wellington, whom the Prince had appointed their colonel, reviewed these elegant horsemen and was impressed, although in private he wondered whether they could endure the rigours of the forthcoming campaign.[3] At least, like the rest of the army, they would sleep in the tents which Wellington was introducing, partly for the men's comfort and partly to keep them away from the temptations found in town or village billets.

His personal standing in the army had never been higher. Some officers hailed him as a second Marlborough and the men's feelings were revealed by his reception at a review of the entire army before Salamanca in November.[4]

> The spirit of enthusiasm was however raised to the highest pitch by the electric effect of the words – 'Here he comes', which spread from mouth to mouth with the rapidity of lightning. The noble commander passed the columns in review, as usual, unaccompanied by any mark of distinction or splendour; his long cloak concealed his undergarments; – his cocked hat soaked and disfigured with rain.[5]

The same enthusiasm was stirring throughout the army early in 1813. On 24 April, a friend told the newly arrived Lieutenant-General Sir Thomas Graham that a campaign was in the offing which would be 'the last on this side of the Pyrenees'. 'No one knows the *Lord's* designs', but 'Conjecture' (that is, camp rumours) expected a flank attack through northern Portugal soon.[6] For once gossip was correct, although Wellington had gone to some trouble to keep his plans secret.

Underlying this eagerness for a decisive engagement was his knowledge of developments in eastern Europe, news of which was reaching his HQ during January and Feburary. On 13 December 1812 Napoleon has returned to Paris having abandoned his stricken army to its terrible fate on the Russian plains. The disastrous Russian campaign and the Czar's declaration that he would continue the war against France in the spring encouraged Napoleon's unwilling German subjects to break free. Reports of the upsurge of German nationalism, particularly in Prussia, and of the Russian advance on Dresden reached Freineda early in April.[7] Meanwhile Napoleon, having lost perhaps half a million men in Russia and Poland, was creating a new army, mostly teenagers and superannuated officers and NCOs, with which to regain supremacy in Germany. Spain now took second place in his plans and at the end of April he warned Joseph to expect no more reinforcements.[8] A month later, having fought two inconclusive slogging-matches at Lützen and Bautzen, Napoleon secured a truce, during which he negotiated to salvage something from the wreckage of his empire.

These events gave Wellington the deepest satisfaction. His prediction that the great powers would eventually discover the will and energy to rid Europe of Napoleon was at last being fulfilled. The Peninsular War was now what he had always hoped it would become, part of an international struggle to restore the peace and harmony of Europe's *ancien régime*.

This grand design demanded a swift victory in Spain. His army and now the Russians had finally broken the spell of French invincibility and what was now needed was an example of one subject nation liberating herself. Beyond this, Wellington believed it was necessary to carry the war into the heart of the nation which had hitherto exported it to the rest of Europe. By August 1813 his objective was to 'diminish the power and influence of France, by which alone the peace of the world could be restored and maintained'.[9] And yet in purely military terms his own resources for such an operation were limited in comparison to the hundreds of thousands of men available to Russia, Prussia and Austria, which joined the alliance in August. Nevertheless, he and the British government were well aware that victories gained in Spain and on the French border would stiffen the will of their allies and encourage them to press ahead and invade France from the east.

The crisis in eastern Europe had exposed the precariousness of French power in Spain. As the details of the Russian catastrophe became known in Madrid there was widespread dismay; Leith Hay, then a POW in Toledo, overheard officers predict that their army would be expelled from Spain by the summer.[10] There were good reasons for this prognosis. All that Joseph could now hope to achieve was an armed presence along the main roads between Madrid and Bayonne and to launch largely ineffective sorties against the guerrillas, particularly those in the north who were threatening to sever his links with France. By the beginning of May and in accordance with his brother's orders, he had gathered together the armies of the Centre, the South and Portugal and distributed them along the roads which radiated from Valladolid to Zamora in the west, Salamanca in the south, Madrid in the south-east and Miranda de Ebro in the north. On the frontier, Clauzel with 13,000 men was barely holding his own against the

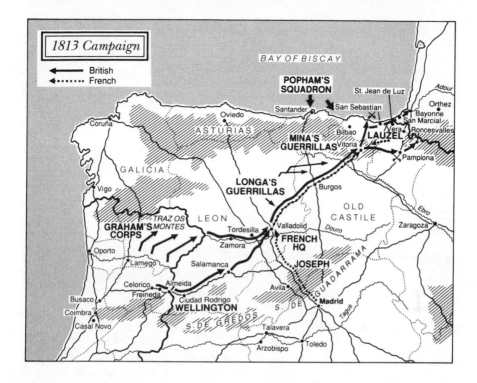

1813 Campaign

⬅ British
◀······· French

BAY OF BISCAY

POPHAM'S SQUADRON

St. Jean de Luz

Santander   San Sebastian   Adour

Orthez
Oviedo   Bayonne
San Marcial

Coruña   ASTURIAS   Bilbao   Vera   Roncesvalles

MINA'S GUERRILLAS   Vitoria   LAUZEL

GALICIA   ✕ Pamplona

LONGA'S GUERRILLAS   Burgos

Vigo   OLD CASTILE

GRAHAM'S *TRAZ OS MONTES*   LEON   Valladolid   Ebro
CORPS   Tordesilla   Douro   Zaragoza

Oporto   Zamora   FRENCH HQ

Lamego   Salamanca   JOSEPH

Celorico   Almeida   Avila   GUADARRAMA
Busaco   Freineda   Madrid
Coimbra   Ciudad Rodrigo   S DE
Casal Novo   WELLINGTON   S. DE GREDOS   Tagus
Talavera

Arzobispo   Toledo

---

partisans and no help could be expected from eastern Spain, where Suchet had his hands full keeping down Catalonia and Aragon.

Wellington intended to prise the French from their strongholds by a massive two-pronged offensive and then manoeuvre them into a position where they would either have to fight or else risk being cut off from France. His largest striking force of 50,000 under Graham was to advance from its winter quarters in Portugal, cross the Douro and, in four columns, head north-east over the highlands of the Traz os Montes. At the end of the march this army would occupy a line stretching between Bragança and Miranda do Douro and so outflank all the French units between Zamora and Valladolid.

Simultaneously, Wellington would move forward with an army of 30,000 towards Salamanca. The French were given every cause to believe that this force represented the entire allied army, a pretence whose success was guaranteed by an inpenetrable cavalry screen spearheading the advance. Strict operational security and the deficiency of French intelligence ensured that their High Command knew nothing of Graham's strength and movement.

This ambitious and complex offensive needed not only secrecy but methodical preparation. For this Wellington relied on the invaluable George Murray, who had rejoined his staff as Quarter-Master-General at the end of March. Immediately he threw himself into this work; during April his scouting officers scoured the districts through which Graham was to march and returned with exhaustive topographical reports of river-crossings; maps of roads with assessments of their suitability for cannon, wagons and horses; and estimates of the amount of fodder available locally.[11]

This was a masterpiece of thorough staff work which paid enormous dividends. On 13 April the first units of Graham's army left their billets at Coimbra and started to move towards the Douro. Progress was slow, there were plenty of minor snags, especially when scouting officers had been over-optimistic about the durability of road surfaces, and river-crossings were protracted. The passage of the 6,700 men of the 5th Division over the Douro at Pêso da Regua began at 7 a.m. on 13 May and was completed by 4.30 p.m. the following day. Using muscle-power and ferryboats which carried no more than a dozen men and often leaked, it took ten and a half hours to get the artillery over, seven for the baggage and ten and a half for the men. At one stage the ferrymen collapsed from fatigue and were grudgingly given a few hours' rest.[12] One onlooker, an officer, was stirred by what he saw. 'Every soldier', he thought, 'saw at a glance the collective strength of the great military machine of which he formed a part' and 'the glow of pride within him' swelled.[13]

By 27 May, this ponderous operation was over and Graham's army was in place. To the south-east Wellington was already pressing on to Salamanca, which he occupied, unopposed, on 27 May. Leaving Hill in charge, he rode across to Miranda do Douro and supervised the transit of Graham's force over the Esla. Within two days, and after some anxious moments during the search for a ford, Graham was advancing on Zamora and Toro, both of which had been abandoned by the bewildered French. Everywhere surprise was total and resistance was desultory: one of Graham's units captured an astonished French officer in bed with his Spanish mistress.[14] There had been a few skirmishes when French patrols tried to infiltrate Wellington's cavalry screen. After one of these, the body of a woman in French hussar uniform was discovered; apparently she had been the wife of an officer who had chosen to follow her husband into battle.[15] There were said to have been tragic examples of such fidelity at Waterloo.

The sheer scale and daring of Wellington's advance left the French dumbfounded and their response was fumbling and panicky. Soult, the only man who might have rallied the army, had been recalled to Paris for service in Germany, so responsibility for strategy had passed to

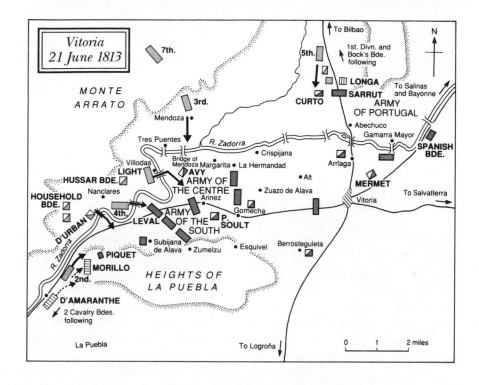

Jourdan. Joseph still remained nominal commander-in-chief, but few of his subordinates took much notice of what he had to say, which is not surprising since his brother had once observed that he would never make a soldier. Joseph's first reaction to the news of Wellington's advance was to flee Madrid. He left on 2 June, followed by a cumbersome train of staff officers, courtiers, Spanish collaborators, their wives, mistresses and children and wagons stuffed with the considerable spoils of his five-year reign.

When he joined Jourdan, the two men decided that the only option open to them was a retreat, during which their 60,000-strong army would be reinforced by Clauzel, who was summoned on 9 June. That he received the message on 15 June was a stroke of luck since the ubiquitous guerrillas had gained an iron grip over nearly every road in the region. Almost as soon as Joseph and Jourdan reached Vitoria on 18 June, they had to detach General Honoré Reille with three divisions to clear the way north.

As the French dragged their way along the Vitoria road, Wellington followed them by a parallel route which ran to the north. His objective was to swing around, cut off Joseph from Bayonne and attack his trapped, outnumbered army. There was nothing to check the allied advance, save the need for rest and refreshment. In twenty-nine days it covered 300 miles, marching at an easy pace with halts every six miles. Bands played as the troops passed through towns (a favourite tune, well liked by Wellington, was 'The Downfall of Paris') and in the countryside some men amused themselves by setting their greyhounds on rabbits and hares started in fields by the road.

By 19 June Wellington was ready to spring his trap. His army had divided, and Graham's 5th Division edged itself around to the north of Vitoria in readiness to block the roads which radiated to Bilbao and the French frontier. The rest of the army was concentrated along the road from Burgos and in the Monte Arrato, which rose to the north-west of the town. In outline, Wellington's plan called for these forces to launch four independent offensives against the French, who were strung out on low ground west of Vitoria between the River Zadorra and the heights of La Puebla. If these attacks succeeded, the French would be shepherded back into the town and then encircled by Graham, who would cut off their escape routes. This battle-plan was drawn up during 20 June for execution the following day, since a local spy, employed by Longa, had reported evidence which suggested that Joseph was about to evacuate the town.[16]

This was not so; Joseph intended to stay put and await Clauzel. What the spy had not noticed was the sclerosis which had taken hold of the French High Command and had transmitted itself to the rest of the army. Jourdan had taken to his bed with a fever on the 20th and in his absence no one bothered to take even the simplest precautions against an attack. The intelligence department had now broken down completely, for no patrols were sent out to ascertain the numbers or whereabouts of the allied army. Nor, and this deficiency was soon apparent the next day, had there been a systematic attempt to safeguard or demolish the bridges over the Zadorra. As Hay had noticed during his few weeks' captivity, fatalism and defeatism were spreading through the French army and there was, in many quarters, a strong urge to get clear of Spain with as much plunder as possible. Throughout the short campaign the hordes of hangers-on and the distended baggage train had been a nuisance; later one French officer remarked to Wellington, 'Le fait est, Monseigneur, que vous avez une armée, mais nous sommes un bordel ambulant.'[17] It is interesting to note that after the battle, some of the more enterprising courtesans attached themselves to British officers.[18]

Wellington's four formations struck the disorganized and unready French army at daybreak on 21 June. Hill's division thrust up from the south and established a foothold on the heights of La Puebla; the 4th and Light Divisions pressed across the Zadorra, the latter guided to an undefended bridge by a Spanish patriot, who was later killed; and the 3rd and 7th Divisions went for the French centre. To the north, Graham moved cautiously into position, but was warned by Wellington not to act precipitately. Only when it was clear that the main body of the French was beaten and in flight was he to make 'a wide movement to cut off [the] retreat and road beyond Vitoria'.[19]

The allied offensives faced dogged opposition. Wellington, in a message sent to Graham at 2 p.m., drew his attention to the 'strong and persevering' resistance of the French.[20] Such courage was worthy of a better general, for a confused Jourdan quickly lost control of events. At first he dismissed the assaults on his left and centre as a feint and predicted that the full weight of the offensive would fall on his right, nearest Vitoria. Then he changed his mind and began to shift men to the south to meet a non-existent blow from that direction. His dithering transmitted itself downwards; having crossed the Zadorra, men of the Light Division were astonished to find that their advance was ignored by some nearby French dragoons.

Wellington was often in the midst of the fighting, having attached himself to the centre column. He showed all his usual imperturbability under fire. As Captain Kincaid struggled to control his prancing horse, which had been scared by an exploding shell, he heard a voice behind call out, 'Look to keeping your men together, sir.' It was Wellington, and Kincaid was embarrassed since he thought he had been mistaken for 'a young officer, cutting a caper, by way of bravado', in front of his commander.[21] Another rifleman, Edward Costello, also encountered Wellington in the thick of battle.

> I now observed the Duke come riding up with some of his staff; and, seeing the confusion the enemy were in, cried out to one of his aides-de-camp, 'Send up a few of Ross's guns; here is work for them': saying to us at the same time, 'That's right, my lads: keep up a good fire', as he galloped to our rear.... [22]

By this stage in the battle, the French were crumbling and fugitives were pouring back towards Vitoria, closely pursued. This was the moment which Wellington had been waiting for and he was determined to press home his advantage. He rode up to Colonel Bingham and the 53rd and ordered them to advance. 'In column or line?' queried Bingham. 'Any how, but get on!' Bingham noted, 'Never shall I forget the animation of his countenance.'[23]

And yet, as he drove his men forward to destroy or capture the débris of the French army, his own began to fall apart. As the allied troops swarmed into Vitoria they discovered an Aladdin's cave of treasure, the accumulated plunder of Joseph and the French army. Among the first to be seduced from their duty by this temptation were the 18th Hussars, whom an apoplectic Wellington later encountered wildly rummaging through the French baggage. As the French poured helter-skelter along the Pamplona road, allied soldiers settled down to help themselves to riches beyond the dreams of avarice. Afterwards it was commonly accepted, even by Wellington, who was never given to hyperbole, that £1 million in cash, including the French army's pay chest, had disappeared into the pockets and knapsacks of his soldiers.[24] There was so much that the more discerning looters left silver dollars untouched and grabbed only gold.[25] Brandy was of course highly prized and quickly consumed, and Spanish and Portuguese muleteers were seen to drape the insignia of the Légion d'Honneur around the necks of their beasts. Lieutenant Woodberry, whose regiment had taken a lead in this enterprise, contented himself with eating Joseph's cold meats and stealing 'a French dog' which joined his two greyhounds.[26]

The distraction of so many of his men deprived Wellington of the victory he wanted. The French had lost 8,000 (two-thirds prisoners) but the bulk of the army escaped along the road to Pamplona with the ex-King Joseph setting the pace. To Wellington's profound dissatisfaction, the fugitives eventually rallied and were drafted into the army being created to defend the Pyrenees. With the road north closed by Graham, Wellington might have been able, had he the men available, to have pursued the French closely and prevented their reassembly.

Vitoria, while not the strategic masterstroke Wellington had intended, had far-reaching consequences. News of it and of the downfall of Napoleon's satrapy in Spain stiffened Russian and Prussian resolve and gave the German states a shining example of a successful movement for self-liberation. It also changed the attitude to the war of Austria, from where there had hitherto been what Bathurst described as 'little hope of any real goodwill, and almost none of any manly decision'.[27] Now, reassured by events in Spain, the Austrian government shed its neutrality and declared war on 12 August, bringing 200,000 men into the fray and tipping the balance decisively against Napoleon. In a jubilant Vienna, Beethoven composed a lively celebratory piece in which the strains of 'Rule Britannia!' and 'God Save the King' mingled. Wellington was now an international celebrity; in November his former ADC, Lord Burghersh, then attached to allied HQ at Frankfurt, wrote, 'You cannot conceive of the admiration which is felt here at the brilliant exploits you have achieved.'[28]

Vitoria had been a personal triumph for Wellington. Created a marquess after Salamanca and a Knight of the Garter early in 1813 (he was unsure whether the sash was worn over the right or left shoulder) he was promoted field-marshal in July. Among the items recovered from the mass looting had been Jourdan's baton, which was sent as a trophy to the Prince Regent, who returned the courtesy with a flourish in the form of a British field-marshal's baton. Some time later, Wellington paid two sovereigns to a hussar corporal who possessed two ornaments from Soult's baton and who claimed to have taken them from a French prisoner. The honours were well deserved and few would have contradicted Torrens's conclusion that Wellington had shown himself 'the first General of our present age'. He added, perhaps over-optimistically, 'There is such a military spirit in this country just now owing to your success that even conscription would, I believe, be tolerated.[29]

The Peninsular War, now in its final phase, had become a small sector of an international conflict. Its outcome and the future of Europe would be decided by a sequence of battles fought in Germany during the summer and autumn of 1813 by huge armies. At Lützen the Russians and Prussians totalled 83,000, at Bautzen 93,000 and at Dresden, where they were joined by the Austrians, 200,000. Against them Napoleon mustered between 100,000 and 167,000. This was warfare on a grand scale. By contrast Wellington never commanded more than 60,000 men during 1813 and early 1814, usually far less. Nevertheless while his campaign was a sideshow, its political importance remained considerable, as he was the first to appreciate.

There was no combined allied strategy in 1813 nor any clear, shared political objectives. All the great powers wanted a European peace, but there was no agreement about whether this was possible or desirable so long as Napoleon continued to rule France. Wellington believed he would have to go because of his record of constant aggression and deceit, and that it was therefore imperative to accelerate his departure by an invasion of France. And yet in September Bathurst warned Wellington that Austria had misgivings about this policy since Napoleon had married Marie Louise, the daughter of the Emperor Franz I. The British government, like Wellington, urged Napoleon's overthrow and since Britain was again the coalition's cashier, Castlereagh was able to exert powerful pressure. It was Napoleon who finally convinced all the allied sovereigns that he could never be allowed to stay ruler of France; twice in 1813 he had been offered generous terms and on each occasion he equivocated and used the negotiations as a breathing-space in which to raise new armies.

Wellington was kept in close touch with these developments by the government. He needed to know as soon as possible how the war was proceeding in central Europe and in particular the state of the allies' resolve. If, and this was vital during his French campaign of 1814, an armistice was signed, it would give Napoleon the chance to transfer troops from the northern and eastern fronts to the south, where Wellington could be overwhelmed.

An immediate consequence of the new, international dimension of the war was the forestalling of a crisis which, during mid-1813, threatened to undermine his commissariat system. Before the summer of 1812, when the United States declared war on Britain, the army in Portugal had been kept alive by imports of American grain. Clandestine imports continued for a few months and an ample stockpile was built up, but once the trade had been suppressed the government had to look hurriedly for fresh sources.[30] Egypt was proposed, but it was the reopening of Baltic commerce which saved the army, which for the rest of the war was fed on grain imported from the Prussian wheatlands.

A second consequence of the widening of the conflict was the reshaping of Wellington's overall strategy. Operations in Spain were by no means over after Vitoria; the French still clung to San Sebastián and Pamplona and in the east the Anglo-Sicilian and Spanish campaigns against Suchet had run out of steam, leaving at least 30,000 French troops free for service against Wellington. It was obviously imperative to take San Sebastián, whose harbour facilities were essential for supplies, and Pamplona, and there was a strong case, based on caution, to eliminate Suchet. However, in terms of the greater allied war effort, an invasion of France took priority. Its attractions were political and pyschological; the world would witness a blow to Napoleon's prestige as war was brought home to his country and the allies in the east would be encouraged. In some but not all respects it was akin to the opening of a Second Front in 1944.

As a soldier, Wellington was unhappy about the prospect, but he had to bow to government demands. He feared stubborn resistance in a country where he imagined 'everybody is a soldier' and there was a pool of trained veterans who would answer a call to arms.[31] He was even more troubled by the likelihood that he could be embroiled in a partisan war of the kind which had been fought in Spain and had crippled the French army there. His anxieties were well founded, since in January 1814 an intercepted despatch from Soult revealed details of a defence plan that involved a pattern of well-defended strongholds scattered across the countryside and supported by mobile guerrilla units.[32]

In fact nothing of the sort emerged. The French, weary of the tax collector and recruiting officer, offered very little oposition to soldiers who, by and large, respected property and paid in gold and silver rather than notes. These things mattered to the French peasant and

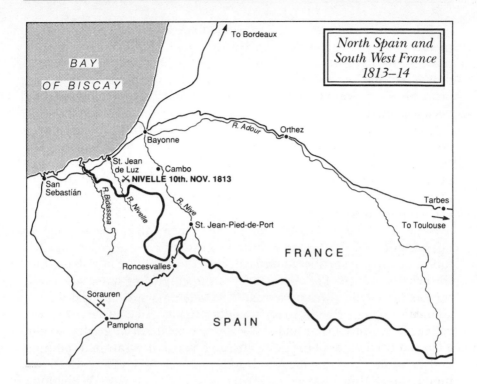

To Bordeaux

North Spain and South West France 1813–14

BAY
OF BISCAY

R. Adour · Orthez

Bayonne

St. Jean de Luz · Cambo
✕ NIVELLE 10th. NOV. 1813

San Sebastián

R. Bidassoa · R. Nivelle · R. Nive

St. Jean-Pied-de-Port

Tarbes
To Toulouse

FRANCE

Roncesvalles

Sorauren ✕

Pamplona

SPAIN

businessman who, after twenty-three years of war, shrugged off frantic appeals from Paris for a new *levée-en-masse*. Nevertheless, Wellington prepared the political ground carefully. His proclamation to the people of south-western France, issued on 1 November 1813, stated that the war was being waged solely because Napoleon had rejected peace. Those who feared that Portuguese and Spanish troops would take reprisals for the outrages committed in their countries were reassured: 'Il serait inhumain et indigne des nations auxquelles le Général en Chef s'addresse, de venger cette conduite sur les paisibles habitans de la France.'[33]

Before France could be attacked, Wellington had first to secure his grip on northern Spain, the base for his invasion. Operations commenced on a sour note for Wellington, whose patience snapped after a prolonged outbreak of indiscipline during the last week of June and the first of July. He relieved his feelings with a flurry of intemperate memoranda in which he branded his men as 'the scum of the earth' and their officers as irredeemable backsliders. In all likelihood men, newly enriched by the spoils of Vitoria, were keen to preserve their gains and their lives and there was an upsurge in desertions.[34] At Wellington's request, a special act that extended summary military jurisdiction was rushed through Parliament; a proto-military police force was formed; and draconian justice dispensed. Commissary Schaumann heard tales, probably exaggerated, that at least 200 Spaniards and Portuguese had been executed.

By the second week in July there was relative calm. The army was now concentrated in a triangle of land bounded by the Biscayan coast, the Pyrenees and Pamplona. San Sebastián was closely besieged, Pamplona was blockaded by Spanish troops and the 2nd, 3rd and 4th Divisions covered the Maya and Roncsevalles passes to block any French relief forces.

Sieges always stretched Wellington's patience and San Sebastián was no exception. The Ordnance Board's customary negligence had left him short of siege artillery and he accused the navy of not giving him the help he needed. The commander of the supporting naval squadron, Sir George Collier, was perplexed by receiving a surly official note of complaint together with 'a very friendly private letter'. An exasperated colleague regretted that soldiers 'seem to consider a large ship within a few hundred yards of the shore off San Sebastián as safe in its position and as immovable by the wind and waves as one of the Pyrenean mountains'.[35] Inter-service bickering could not obscure Wellington's debt to the navy, which he acknowledged later; ships and landing parts had helped drive the French from the coast of northern Spain and had secured Santander, through which the army's supplies had flowed since midsummer.

While allied efforts concentrated on San Sebastián, Soult, newly appointed commander of the optimistically titled Army of Spain, had been consolidating the remnants of its predecessors at Bayonne. After recuperation and rearming his army (all but one of Joseph's cannon had been abandoned at Vitoria), he struck across the Pyrenees towards Pamplona with 60,000 men. His twin thrusts were resisted but his forces, outnumbering the three British divisions guarding the Maya and Roncesvalles passes, pushed them back, and by 26 July Soult was approaching his goal.

Wellington rushed over from San Sebastián, took control, withdrew his forces beyond Pamplona and improvised a defence on a steep-sloped ridge near Sorauren. Lusty British cheers alerted Soult to Wellington's presence and made him nervous. His army attacked on 27 July without much conviction and made little headway. Rather than fight and lose another Busaco Soult called off the offensive and retired to Bayonne. The French reappeared on 31 August, this time under Reille, and made a dash for San Sebastián, then in its final extremities.

Forewarned by an intercepted despatch, the allies were prepared and Reille was repulsed by a 13,000-strong Spanish army at San Marçial, which must have been a rude shock since the French despised all Spanish soldiers. One officer, captured at this time, assured Larpent that they never 'fought like men'.

This was the final French offensive in Spain. On the same day the town of San Sebastián yielded and was ransacked, although the citadel's garrison held out for a further fortnight. Its fall and Soult's offensive in late July had given Wellington what he admitted were unnerving moments at a time when the government was demanding a start to operations inside France. The past three months of non-stop campaigning made this impractical since his men were spent. The corrosive effects of fatigue, a poor and sometimes irregular diet, extremes of climate and too much alcohol undermined the stamina of even the hardiest veteran: 14,500 men, a third of all British troops, and one in seven of the Portuguese were unfit for duty on 8 August and the proportions of invalids remained high for the next two months.[36]

During September and early October the army recuperated. While Wellington awaited news of events in central Europe, his soldiers relaxed in the foothills of the Pyrenees. 'Our life here is a very idle one,' commented one, while another, with a Romantic temperament, admired a landscape which combined 'the sublime, the beautiful, and the picturesque'.[37] It would not remain so for long as winter was hurrying on and by early October equinoctial storms brought heavy rain and snow from the Atlantic. At the same time the process of invigoration was slow and there were still 16,000 men off sick.[38] The number would rise if the army remained in its present positions, so Wellington was forced to make a move across the Bidassoa, even though he was still ignorant of the outcome of the campaign in Germany.

On 7 October allied troops crossed the Bidassoa and stormed the earthworks on its northern bank. Wellington's strongest thrust was over the river's estuary, where it was well over half a mile wide. For this reason the defences here were weakest, but a staff officer had secured, under threat, the services of some Basque fishermen who revealed paths where the estuary was passable at low tide.[39] It was a difficult crossing with men wading in mud which dragged at their shoes and water which reached their armpits. As they struggled over, under fire, an officer heard some Irishmen shout at the defenders, 'Oh! by Jesus! We'll give you it by and by, you French beggars! Damn your eyes, we'll sort you out!'[40] They did, and Soult fell back on his prepared positions on the rivers Nive and Nivelle.

Wellington did not immediately press home his advantage. His numbers were still depleted by sickness, and Pamplona remained

defiant and a threat to his communications. On 31 October it surrendered and, in the first week of November, he received details from
Liverpool of the four-day battle of Leipzig, where Napoleon had been
decisively beaten with estimated losses of 150,000.[41] As the remains of
his army trudged back to the Rhine, Napoleon's empire began to fall
apart. On 9 November, Wellington felt it was safe to start the next
stage of the invasion and ordered his army across the Nive.

Once the Spanish were on French soil their fragile discipline fell
apart. The action on the Nive was followed by plunder and Wellington
foresaw that such behaviour would antagonize the French as it had the
Spanish seven years earlier. He was also conscious that in Cádiz the
liberals were calling for his dismissal as commander-in-chief of the
Spanish army. Throughout the summer and autumn he had needed
Spanish troops, although, as he told his brother Henry, they were 'sad
vagabonds' whom he retained only because 'the state of Europe, and
of the world, and Spain required it'.[42] Relations deteriorated further
after the taking of San Sebastián, when the Spanish liberal press accused
the British of deliberately firing the town.[43] The outrages in November
convinced Wellington that his Spanish units were an operational nuisance and he began to discharge them. Those who remained continued
to cause trouble. 'The conduct of the Spanish is terrible,' he told
Beresford in February 1814, for their officers refused to stop their troops
from acts of revenge against the French and brazenly justified them as
the satisfaction of 'National Honor'.[44]

This unavoidable process of whittling down the numbers of Spanish
had its dangers. Early in December, when Wellington made a two-
pronged advance on Bayonne, he had only 60,000 men, about the same
number as Soult. The battle, subsequently known as Nive, lasted
three days and was fought across muddy ground often in heavy rain.
According to his battle-plan, Wellington intended the bulk of his forces
to march along the southern bank of the Nive towards Bayonne, while
Hill's division, having crossed upstream, would push northwards to the
Adour. Rather than be penned in, Soult counter-attacked Hill, who
was now isolated after the swollen waters of the Nive had washed away
two bridges. What followed was a soldier's battle in which generals
played a limited part and the issue was settled by hard-fought, small
actions. Everything depended on the courage and determination of
individual officers. This was admitted by Wellington, who afterwards
commented, 'I will tell you the difference between Soult and me: when
he gets into a difficulty, his troops don't get him out; mine always do.'[45]

They did at Nive and Wellington now had a firm foothold in France.
The weather closed in and there was a two-month pause in operations.
He had, he later told Croker, shaken off all his doubts about the future

of the war. After the fight on the Nive, he had interviewed a 'very sulky' French colonel who after a good dinner and some Madeira became talkative. Wellington observed that Napoleon must have had many sleepless nights lately and asked, 'where was his quartier général [HQ] when you last heard of him?' 'Il n'a pas de quartier général,' he replied. The answer gave Wellington the 'greatest pleasure I ever felt in my military life' for 'I then saw my way clearly to Bordeaux and to Paris'.[46]

There was more good news during the battle of Nive when the colonel of two Nassau battalions offered to surrender his men, asking that they and others from their country serving in eastern Spain be sent to Germany.[47] Their mood, if not their wish to turn their arms against Napoleon, spread to their French colleagues, who had shown a poor spirit during the fighting in November and December.[48] Many were green conscripts who deserted, often to the allies, at the first opportunity. Intercepted letters from Soult to the War Ministry in Paris, which were delivered to the British HQ at St Jean-de-Luz, revealed his despair over the spiralling desertion rate and his complaints that his men lacked '*élan*'. There were fewer of them too. Again relying on intercepted correspondence, Wellington learned that Soult had been ordered to send a cavalry division, two dragoon regiments, two horse batteries and two infantry divisions to Paris and Orléans to join Napoleon for his last-ditch resistance.[49]

Only Napoleon's will now sustained the war. The odds against him were enormous: by the beginning of 1814 over 200,000 Prussian, Russian and Austrian troops were edging into France on three fronts, opposed by 60,000 defenders, many of them schoolboys hurriedly mobilized. To repel the invaders Napoleon relied on a characteristic mixture of duplicity and daring. Negotiations were opened with the allies at Châtillon-sur-Seine while he prepared a counter-offensive. Having rejected an offer of France's pre-1792 frontiers, he masterminded a series of lightning counter-attacks and between 10 and 14 February stunned Marshal Gebhard Blücher's Prussians and forced an alarmed Prince zu Schwarzenberg to retreat on Troyes. It was a brilliant piece of improvisation which ultimately counted for nothing since the allies regrouped and then converged on Paris during the second and third weeks of March.

For Napoleon February's successes were a clear sign that his old genius had returned. 'I am still the man of Wagram and Austerlitz,' he boasted and immersed himself in plans to fight back from a new base at Orléans. While, like Hitler in the spring of 1945, he manoeuvred phantom armies, Marmont surrendered Paris on 30 March and, four days later, the French Senate declared him dethroned. Reality, in the shape of his former marshals and generals, confronted him at his palace at Fontainebleau and he abdicated on 11 April. There were histrionics and weeping from his now unemployed and unemployable Old Guard, but as he headed south to exile in his mini-kingdom of Elba his former subjects hailed his entourage with threats and abuse.

Wellington followed every turn of these developments. Letters now took between six and seven days to reach him from London and so he usually heard of events in eastern France ten days later.[50] Their course now determined his strategy for he was committed to do everything in his power to support the allies.[51] There were touch-and-go moments during early March when he was warned of the possibility that Austria might defect and force Russia and Prussia to pull back their forces. Only by the middle of the month, when Castlereagh assured him that the Châtillon conference had broken up and that a mass battle on the Marne was imminent, did Wellington feel confident enough to press ahead to Toulouse.

His customary strategic cautiousness now went by the board. In order to keep up the momentum of his advance, he had to bypass pockets of French resistance. At the end of February, Lieutenant-General Sir John Hope's division was detached and left to bottle up the garrison of Bayonne which, despite encirclement, held out until 27 April thanks to an obdurate Bonapartist commander who demanded to see Soult's written orders before he surrendered. The elimination of Soult's army was now Wellington's objective and he began his pursuit at the end of February.

On 27 February he pushed aside the French rearguard at Orthez and then moved to St Sever. Still unsure of what was happening in the east, he snatched the opportunity to occupy Bordeaux, Frances's second city and home to a sizeable royalist faction, which was entered by the 4th and 7th Divisions. Following closely behind them was the Count of Angoulême (later Charles X of France), the nephew of the exiled Louis XVIII who for some time had been an embarrassing addition to Wellington's HQ. Legitimist hopes had soared once the invasion of France was under way and the British government was offered pledges of armed assistance from a hidden army of Bourbon partisans. These were treated coolly since the allies had not yet decided on Napoleon's replacement.

Wellington, despite privately favouring a Bourbon restoration, had discreetly distanced himself from Angoulême, although he was well aware of the groundswell of legitimist sentiments in the region he was occupying. At Tarbes a crowd, largely made up of women, greeted the army with shouts of 'Vive l'Angleterre! Vives les Bourbons!' but the mainspring of such exclamations may have been war-weariness as much as an urge to bring back the *ancien régime*.[52] Soult took advantage of the British army's apparent attachment to the Bourbons, and his propaganda charged Wellington with hypocrisy since he was stirring up a civil war rather than, as he claimed, bringing peace to France. This was unfair since whenever possible Wellington had, as in India, officially backed the established local authorities and encouraged them to continue the administration of their districts. There was no civil war although after Napoleon's final banishment in 1815 south-western France was gripped by a White Terror in which former Revolutionaries and Bonapartists were persecuted, including a general who was assassinated in Toulouse.

As he pushed north-eastwards into Languedoc and towards Toulouse, Wellington had to keep in mind the possibility that he might find himself stranded and confronted with a French army enlarged by forces brought down from the north. Equally worrying was the chance that substantial reinforcements might reach Toulouse from eastern Spain, from where Suchet was extricating himself during March. Both considerations forced him to advance cautiously and a further break on his movement was imposed by heavy rains which delayed his ammunition convoys and the wagons that carried his pontoon bridges. There were also the inevitable rearguard actions by small French detachments and the problems created by damaged bridges.

On 26 March his cavalry patrols approached Toulouse, where Soult had concentrated his Army of Spain. What they reported and what he saw for himself convinced him that the city was 'inexpugnable'.[53] The old city was surrounded by its walls and beyond them to the north and east ran the Languedoc canal, which joined the Garonne a mile downstream. The bridge over the Garonne was fortified, as were those over the Languedoc canal. Wellington lacked the resources to lay siege to the city and an attack by escalade was out of the question against defences held by 42,000 men. He was certain, however, that by manoeuvre he could force Soult to withdraw.[54]

What followed was an untidy battle in which Wellington gained his objective although Soult would later, unconvincingly, claim a victory. Wellington's only hope of exerting pressure on the garrison lay in a combination of encirclement and occupation of the Calvinet Heights, which overlooked the eastern side of the city. To achieve this he deployed his troops as a screen to the north and east and ordered his pontoneers to place a bridge across the Garonne just below its confluence with the Arriège at Pinsaguel. On the night of 30/31 March the bridge was in place and the next morning 13,000 men crossed, the same day as the allied sovereigns were riding into Paris.

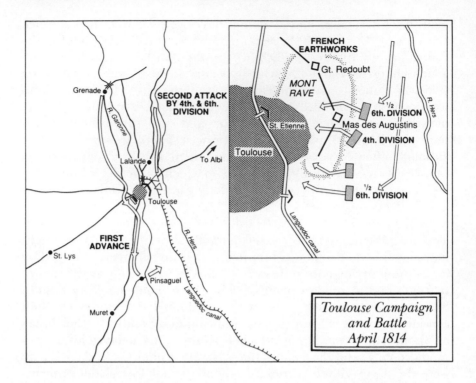

FRENCH EARTHWORKS

Gt. Redoubt

MONT RAVE

SECOND ATTACK BY 4th. & 6th. DIVISION

St. Etienne

Toulouse

½ 6th. DIVISION

Mas des Augustins

4th. DIVISION

½ 6th. DIVISION

R. Hers

Grenade

R. Garonne

Lalande

To Albi

Toulouse

FIRST ADVANCE

St. Lys

R. Hers

Pinsaguel

Languedoc canal

Muret

Languedoc canal

Toulouse Campaign and Battle April 1814

Wellington's next step was uncharacteristically rash. He replaced the pontoon with a flying bridge and sent the pontoneers and their wagons trundling ten miles north to Grenade, where a bridge was in place by 4 April. Hill's corps was dangerously isolated and for a time seemed in peril as Soult made a sally towards Vieille Toulouse. He then withdrew, leaving Hill to recross the Garonne and take up a position opposite the fortified St Cyprien bridgehead. Meanwhile snags were occurring at Grenade, where the pontoon bridge was disabled by swollen rivers and French sabotage in the form of logs and dead horses floated down from Toulouse. Three days later the bridge was repaired and Wellington was free to position his forces for an attack on the Calvinet Heights. So far he had enjoyed an astonishing run of luck because Soult had resolutely sat tight and failed to exploit all the advantages presented by his adversary's mischances.

He had however anticipated the point where Wellington would make his attack and three-quarters of his forces were concentrated on the Calvinet Heights, supported by four earthwork redoubts. By 8 April Wellington had evolved his scheme of attack: Hill's corps, the 3rd and Light Divisions, would distract the defenders of the bridgeheads over the Garonne and the canal, while the 4th and 6th Divisions would march south in the narrow strip of land between the River Hers and the heights and then storm them.

The assault was launched on 10 April, Easter Sunday. Picton misunderstood his orders and made a full-scale attack on the Pont Jumeux defences and was very roughly handled, losing 500 men. There were heavy losses and nerve-wracking moments during the advance on the Calvinet Heights. At the beginning the Spanish corps panicked and prompted Wellington to remark, 'Well damn me, if I ever saw ten thousand men run a race before!' After several hours' fighting, some of it with the bayonet, the French were dislodged and pushed back to their inner defences along the canal. A stalemate followed until the night of 11/12 April during which Soult withdrew from Toulouse, retreating along the Carcasonne road.

His departure was marked by a mass conversion to the Bourbon cause and the next morning a white flag was raised. Dr MacGrigor and his Portuguese orderly dragoon were among the first into the city, where he was hysterically mobbed by people who assumed that a mounted officer in a red coat and cocked hat must be Wellington. A few hours later a staff officer arrived from Bordeaux with the news of Napoleon's abdication. Wellington was amazed: 'How, abdicated? Ay, 'tis time indeed. You don't say so, upon my honour. Hurrah!'

The campaign was over and within a few weeks arrangements were in hand for the army's disbandment. It was not the end for Wellington, who on 21 April accepted the appointment as ambassador in Paris. 'Although I have been so long absent from England,' he wrote, 'I should have remained so as much longer if it be necessary; and I feel no objection to another absence in the public service.'[55] Soon after he was in Madrid, attending to unfinished military and diplomatic business, including arrangements for the return of paintings stolen from the Spanish royal palaces and recovered from Joseph's plunder at Vitoria. They included a Raphael, and Wellington, after examining them, had concluded that since so many were Italian in style they must have been spoil from Italy.[56] Between 11 and 14 June he was in Bordeaux and from there he sailed to England. He had been away for just over five years.

On 10 May the Prince Regent had promoted him Duke of Wellington and he took his seat in the House of Lords on 24 June, where he heard fulsome formal eulogies. After some debate Parliament had rejected a scheme to award him a £10,000 annuity from government stock and instead voted him £300,000 (raised to £500,000) to purchase an estate. The precedent was that of Marlborough who, after Blenheim, had been given the extensive royal estate of Woodstock, where he later had a palace built. Everywhere Wellington was lionized, but he took the fuss with good humour and found it at times amusing. As a crowd parted to let him through at the opera, he remarked to Lady Shelley, 'It's a fine thing to be a great man, is it not?'[57] She noticed that at a fête given in his honour by the Prince Regent he seemed to think the pompous toasts and speeches 'nonsense and fun'. When asked to speak himself he was diffident, beginning, 'I want words to express ...' and was then interrupted by the Prince who said, 'My dear fellow, we know your *actions*, and we will excuse your *words*, so sit down.' Within a few weeks he was on his way to Paris.

3

The Finger of God: Waterloo, 1815

Waterloo was Wellington's most famous battle. He and many of those who fought on either side shared a profound belief that their actions would change the course of history. Even Wellington shed his characteristic professional detachment and confessed to a feeling that 'The finger of God was upon me.'[1] Contemporaries and the generations which grew up during the long period of unparalleled international peace that followed his victory agreed and saw Wellington as an instrument of Divine Providence.

This interpretation of the events of 1815 was to a large extent the outcome of the propaganda of the past dozen or so years which had represented Napoleon as a creature of demonic cunning and uncontrollable destructive energy. Only the hand of God, acting through a chosen agent, could check his mischief and send him, like Satan, to distant banishment:

> Tyrant! thy hour is come! by Heaven's decree
> The British Scipio, WELLINGTON, is there
> To mar thy plots.[2]

Another contemporary poem, 'The Shades of Waterloo', repeated the theme and proclaimed 'Heaven is with his Arms'. The words 'saviour' and 'deliverer' were generously broadcast through the sheaves of official, press and literary testimonials which were addressed to Wellington in the weeks and months after the battle.

For the recipient of these encomiums the deepest satisfaction came from having commanded the army which finally restored the old order and confined, for a time, the inflammatory passions released by the French Revolution. Until his death, Wellington presided over annual celebratory Waterloo dinners where he was reunited with his brother officers. After the 1831 dinner, the Whig Lord John Russell wrote percipiently, 'It is strange how his political feelings have absorbed his military feelings,' for, while he had shown true brilliance in Spain, 'at Waterloo he displayed none, not even foresight'.[3] Leaving aside the military judgement, it was striking that Wellington had dropped his custom of holding anniversary dinners for Peninsular victories, won in a war of liberation, and chose instead religiously to commemorate a battle that had marked the triumph of conservatism in Europe.

For Wellington what was at stake in the battle was 'the public law of Europe'.[4] First as British Ambassador in Paris and then, during the winter of 1814/15, as Castlereagh's replacement as British delegate to the Congress of Vienna, he had been intimately involved in making that law. It rested upon the Treaty of Chaumont, signed the previous year, under which Napoleon accepted deposition and exile, while the allied powers agreed to support Louis XVIII as the legal ruler of France and maintained an army of occupation in Belgium which, under the provisions agreed at Vienna, would become a province of the Netherlands.

On 26 February 1815, Napoleon challenged the right of the Vienna powers to legislate for Europe. He left Elba, landed in southern France, and, accompanied by a handful of his Old Guard, set off northwards for Paris. He relied on his old magic and it did not fail him as soldiers and generals sent to arrest him laid down their arms and took up the cry 'Vive l'Empereur!' By 20 March he went back in Paris and Louis XVIII was hurrying across the Belgian frontier to set up a court in exile, shielded by allied troops. The princes of Europe were horrified and on 21 March Wellington added his signature to a treaty which bound the allies to a joint invasion of France and the overthrow of its new ruler, now branded an international outlaw.

As Wellington was the first to appreciate, politics dictated the strategy and direction of the Waterloo campaign. Napoleon had set his will, backed by force of arms, against the collective wisdom of the great powers, who were forced to put the issue to the test of battle. He was also aware that in order to survive he would have to convince a battered and war-weary French people that he was still the only man who could channel their aspirations and secure them their rightful place as masters of Europe. 'I shall have them all with me if I prove the strongest,' he proclaimed at the beginning of April as mobilization began for the invasion of Belgium.[5]

The forthcoming campaign, as he knew, would require a superhuman effort by a no means enthusiastic French people and a reawakening of the old audacity and genius that he had shown in 1796/7 when his

Italian campaigns had dazzled Europe. For the moment he could rely only on his natural constituency within France, the thousands of discharged soldiers and former POWs who were kicking their heels and the legions of ambitious officers now living in comparative poverty who saw a chance to make a profit and regain their former prestige. These were his greatest asset and he decided they would be most effectively employed in Belgium.

Obviously the recovery of Belgium, which had been French territory since 1794, would boost Napoleon's standing inside France. But there were other tempting prizes to be won. Napoleon realized, as did Wellington, that British public opinion was not wholeheartedly behind the war and a peace party was emerging that included the Marquess Wellesley. While the pro-government *Courier* had likened the French people's rejection of Louis XVIII for Napoleon to that of the mob which had spurned Christ in favour of Barabbas, the Opposition presented the war as a waste of men and money.[6] In a Lords debate on 23 May, Lord Grey argued that Britain had no moral right to reverse the French nation's choice of a ruler and added that, to date, Napoleon had shown no signs of aggression.[7]

It was clear to Napoleon, who closely followed the twists and turns of British politics, that Liverpool's government could not survive even a partial defeat of Wellington's army. It would be replaced, he believed, by a ministry of pacific inclinations which would disengage from the coalition and withdraw the £5 million annual subsidy that Castlereagh had promised Russia, Austria and Prussia. This gold bound the alliance together, and its members, deprived of their monthly injections of sovereigns, would be forced to negotiate. For these reasons Napoleon had to concentrate his strength on the Belgian border and bring Wellington and the Prussians to battle. Even if a victory did not bring him the political dividends he hoped for, Napoleon would be free to thrust southwards and intercept the Austrian, Russian and German Confederation armies as they crossed the Rhine and defeat them piecemeal.

Everything hung on time. On 22 March, a week before he left Vienna and assuming, perhaps naively, that the Russians and Austrians could meet their mobilization deadlines, Wellington predicted that 700,000 men would be assembled on France's borders by 1 June.[8] This was Napoleon's nightmare and, since his arrival in Paris, he had worked with an energy fuelled by desperation to raise an army of unprecedented size. Nothing like it had been seen since the *levée-en-masse* of 1792/3: on 21 March the Old Guard was reformed; old soldiers and sailors were recalled to the colours; and, on 10 April, a decree ordered every Frenchman between twenty and sixty who was not in uniform to join the National Guard, which, on paper at least, would soon number 2.5

million. Conscription was reintroduced, but the results were discouraging. Officials of the département of Bouches-du-Rhône reported that out of 3,200 youths liable for service 137 had been assembled, and nine out of ten called up in Tarn-et-Garonne vanished. Those who did not escape the gendarmes deserted in swarms.[9] There was a shortfall too in the number of weapons available for all those being swept into the new armies; by June, and after intensive efforts by workshops, only 340,000 muskets were available.[10]

Nevertheless, by the end of May Napoleon believed that he had stolen a march on his enemies. The Armée du Nord, the force earmarked for the invasion of Belgium under his command, numbered 124,000 men and the greater part of them were willing veterans captivated by the Napoleonic spell.

Wellington, who followed through intelligence reports the course of French mobilization, respected the man who was its mainspring. What impressed him most about Napoleon's generalship was his ability to react quickly and exploit to the full his opponents' mistakes. 'There certainly never existed a man', he wrote later, 'in whose presence it was so little safe to make what is called a false movement.'[11] When asked in 1814 how he would feel if he had to do battle with him he answered that given the choice he would prefer to fight any other French general with an extra 20,000 men than Napoleon on equal terms.[12]

In public at least, Napoleon had nothing but contempt for his adversary. On the eve of the Waterloo campaign, he announced in *Le Moniteur* that Wellington was 'un présomptueux, un téméraire, un ignorant, destiné à essuyer de grandes catastrophes'. Just before Waterloo and in the same blustering vein, he taunted Soult with the observation that he only regarded Wellington as a great general because he had been beaten by him. Napoleon's more considered opinion was given during a conversation with a British officer at Fontainebleau a year before when he remarked of Wellington, 'C'est un homme de grand vigeur. Il faut avoir cela comme lui dans le guerre.' This was said after he had been examining accounts of Soult's recent reverses.[13] Again, in January 1815, he was full of praise for Wellington during an interview given to an English visitor to Elba, although his remarks may have been coloured by the fact that he was day-dreaming about an Anglo-French alliance.[14]

Among British soldiers there was widespread sympathy for Napoleon. 'They thought of him, not as a foe but as a hero standing alone; a soldier to be hailed by soldiers,' Charles Napier remembered. He had watched, approvingly, as British sentries spat tobacco juice at the 'courtier soldiers' of Louis XVIII's escort as they rode into Paris, much to the delight of onlookers.[15] Private Wheeler shared these sentiments and mocked the eighteen-stone Bourbon as 'an old pantaloon, the Sir John Falstaff of France'.[16] It was rumoured in France that these feelings even extended to Wellington, who wanted Napoleon to be conveyed to England, where he would be treated with the respect due to his achievements. This was wishful thinking; Wellington backed his removal to St Helena and supported the reinstatement of Louis XVIII, despite the objections of those, including Czar Alexander, who thought it imprudent since the events of the past two months had demonstrated how unwelcome their king was to the French people.

The question of France's future government had to be postponed until after Napoleon had been beaten. Ever since his flight from Elba, informed opinion had feared that he would express his defiance of the Vienna Congress by a pre-emptive attack on Belgium. This threat was given substance by the dangerous presence of the Armée du Nord in positions within a week's march of the frontier, so, with British backing, the Congress appointed Wellington to command the Anglo-Dutch–Hanoverian–Brunswick army based on Brussels. He was perhaps the ablest and certainly the most successful allied general and he had experience of commanding heterogeneous armies, in India and the Peninsula. He replaced a nominal commander who had none of these qualities; Prince William of Orange was young, untried and, as events were to prove, a headstrong bungler who sacrificed men needlessly. Unfortunately Wellington had to find him a subordinate command to soften the blow of his demotion and to assuage the feelings of his father, King William of the Netherlands.

When he arrived at HQ in Brussels on the night of 4/5 May Wellington immediately set about putting his stamp on an army which fell far short of his standards of efficiency. It was deficient in equipment such as hospitals, lacked cohesion and was too weak either to withstand a French offensive or, when the time was right, to deliver its own. In the short term, remedy lay in the creation of mixed divisions, each with its stiffening of British troops who, Wellington believed, would add steadiness under fire as they had in India and Portugal. They were needed, because Wellington was only moderately impressed with the foreign units. There were too many green Hanoverian militia battalions, the Belgians seemed 'very small' and their officers' loyalty was suspect since nearly all had recently been in the French service. The seriously under-strength British detachments did not inspire confidence, for he described them as 'not what they ought to be to enable us to maintain our military character in Europe.'[17] A Ghent landlord put it more bluntly when he told a Highland officer that the allied army was 'little more than a rabble'.[18]

Wellington's first task was to raise the numbers and quality of his army. Britain ought to have been able to send enough men, but a cost-conscious government had already demobilized 47,000 and once the French campaign was over, 13,400 Peninsular veterans had been shipped to America.[19] Although the American War had ended inconclusively in December 1814 it was impossible to get men back to England in large numbers, although at the beginning of April forces which had been assembled in the Gulf of Mexico for the ill-fated New Orleans expedition were being hurriedly embarked for Ostend. Only a small proportion reached Belgium by mid-June. Such penny packets were not what Wellington had in mind. He estimated that operational needs and pledges made to the allies in Vienna required him to field 40,000 infantry and 15,000 cavalry, so he demanded large drafts from the home militia and the paring down of Irish garrisons. Torrens, who was doing all he could to muster reinforcements, confessed that he was faced with 'almost insurmountable difficulties' and while Castlereagh was willing to release 5,200 men from Ireland, he was nervous that a temporarily weakened garrison might encourage 'Paddy' to 'prepare for mischief'.[20] In the end and after drafting men from Gibraltar, Liverpool promised the full quota of 40,000 infantry, but not until September.[21]

Not for the first time, Britain's far-flung battle-line was stretched to breaking point. As it was, Napoleon would not wait and, when he mounted his offensive on 15 June, Wellington had at his disposal 69,000 men, of whom 20,000 were British infantry, 6,000 British cavalry, 5,800 King's German Legion and 37,000 Hanoverians, Brunswickers, Dutch and Belgians, supported by a naval squadron he had requested to stand by off the Scheldt. He had been sadly disappointed by the slowness of British mobilization.[22]

When he had arrived in Brussels, Wellington carried with him the knowledge that his strategy would remain defensive until all the allies were ready for a simultaneous invasion of France. For the next two months he kept in close contact with his fellow commanders, who provided him with details of their movements, plans and most importantly the projected timetable for the combined offensive. All that was required of him was to place his forces in positions from which they could quickly coalesce to meet a French advance on Brussels. He assumed that Napoleon could take two routes, thrusting through the gap between the Scheldt and Sambre, or, alternatively, between the Sambre and Meuse. He deployed his forces in readiness to block both paths; one Hanoverian detachment held Nieuport on the Channel coast while the bulk of his army occupied the towns and villages within a semi-circle which swung south from Gramont to Mons and east towards Charleroi. Beyond Charleroi and eastwards as far as Liège the defensive line was held by the 116,000 Prussians in four army corps.

Close co-operation between Wellington and the Prussian Commander-in-Chief, Field-Marshal Blücher, was absolutely vital throughout the campaign and, in the end, it proved the key to allied victory. Blücher was seventy-three years old, a tough professional soldier, a remorseless Francophobe and a general whose leadership stemmed from a dogged determination that earned him the nickname Marshal 'Vörwarts' (Forward). He struck Lord Byron, who, like Wellington, had first encountered him in London during the summer of 1814, as having the 'voice and manners of a recruiting sergeant'. Above all, he wanted to beat Napoleon and would have hanged him if he had caught him, and this driving passion cemented his friendship with Wellington, although the Duke never shared his urge for vengeance against France. From their first discussions in May the two commanders were resolved to act in tandem if faced with a French offensive. Relations between Wellington and Blücher's Chief of Staff, General von Gneisenau, were less cordial, for the Prussian mistrusted the British, who, he believed, might slip back across the Channel if the going got hard.

One of the first and most important fruits of the concert between the two commanders was a westward shift by General von Zeiten's corps, which took up positions around Charleroi adjacent to the eastern extremity of Wellington's line. This junction was, for Napoleon, the weakest point in the allied defences and therefore the first target of his forthcoming offensive. He assumed, mistakenly as it turned out, that once having split the Prussians from their allies all co-operation between the two would cease.

Throughout May staff at both HQs had been collating and sharing intelligence about French preparations. Information came from a variety of sources: there were plenty of talkative deserters; spies inside France; cross-border smugglers; and sources inside Louis XVIII's court at Ghent with French contacts.[23] Since the great powers, anxious not to appear the aggressors, had forbade premature irruptions into French territory, Wellington was deprived of the valuable intelligence which could only be provided by cross-border cavalry patrols. Nevertheless, enough material was flowing into his HQ for Wellington to make an assessment of French strength on 20 May.[24]

Of most significance were the dispositions of the six army corps in north-eastern France which were already destined to form Napoleon's striking force. The total strength was given as 140,000, an overestimate by 12,000 of the army which concentrated on the Belgian border on 14

June. What was missing from this report and the others that were reaching Brussels during the last week of May and the first of June were clues about Napoleon's intentions and his timetable for drawing together the dispersed corps. Nevertheless, there was enough evidence to suggest that something was about to happen.

By 10 June the signs that Napoleon was making his opening moves were unmistakable, even if they were largely based on latrine rumours repeated by deserters or on reports of indiscreet soldiers who boasted to civilians that they would soon be in action.[25] There were hints too that mobilization was now in full swing; on the 12th there was news that Soult, Napoleon's Chief of Staff, was on the road to Valenciennes, and two days later a traveller revealed that he had seen 100,000 French soldiers between Philippeville and Mauberge (in fact General Gérard's corps on the march from Thionville). The presence of these troops and others, from General Vandamme's corps, near Beaumont was confirmed the same evening by Prussian HQ, where there was a strong feeling 'that Bonaparte intends to commence offensive operations'.[26]

Prussian instinct was sound. On 6 June Napoleon had ordered his six army corps to assemble on the southern bank of the Sambre above Charleroi. The patchy intelligence reports collected by the British and Prussian HQs were evidence of a masterstroke that astonished Wellington.[27] Within seven days the Imperial Guard and six army corps had taken up their battle positions on the frontier without alerting their opponents. That they had moved with such stealth was a tribute to Napoleon's tight operational security, which had squeezed the flow of intelligence to a trickle. Wellington later admitted to amazement; he had not expected the big push until the end of the month and had even planned a commemorative ball for the anniversary of Vitoria on 21 June.[28] Final confirmation of Napoleon's plans and the first news of this breakthrough at Charleroi only reached Wellington at ten on the evening of the 15th while he was attending a ball given by the Duchess of Richmond.

Napoleon had laid out a plan which depended upon surprise, which he obtained, and on the ability of his forces to drive a wedge between the Prussians and the allies. Communications between the two armies would be severed, the Prussians would be driven north-east towards the Meuse while Wellington would fall back towards Brussels to defend his lifeline to the Channel ports. To work, this strategy demanded clear intelligence of enemy movements; precise direction by Napoleon; total subordination from his corps commanders; and the maintenance of an offensive momentum. All proved elusive. The morning of 15 June marked the beginning of three days' intermittent fighting in which four

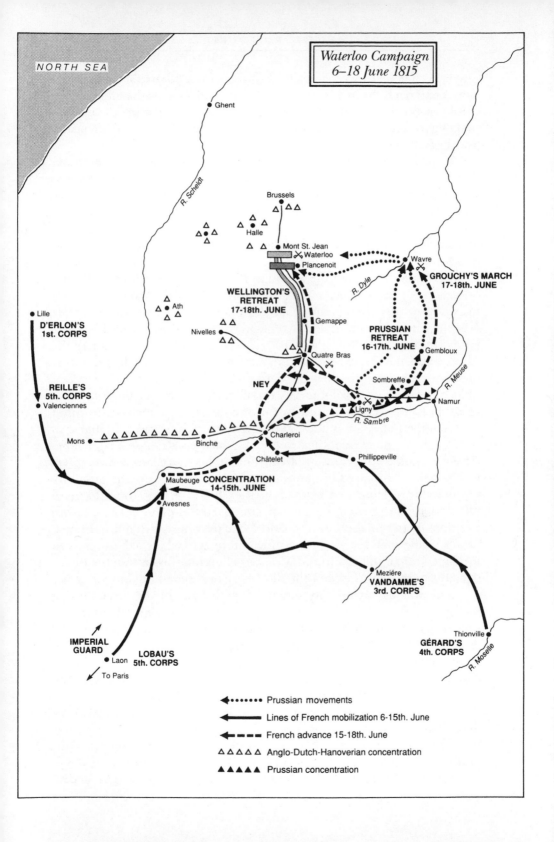

Waterloo Campaign
6–18 June 1815

NORTH SEA

Ghent

R. Scheldt

Brussels

Halle

Mont St. Jean
Waterloo
Plancenoit

Wavre

R. Dyle

**GROUCHY'S MARCH
17-18th. JUNE**

**WELLINGTON'S
RETREAT
17-18th. JUNE**

Ath

Gemappe

**PRUSSIAN
RETREAT
16-17th. JUNE**

Nivelles

Gembloux

Lille

**D'ERLON'S
1st. CORPS**

Quatre Bras

Sombreffe

R. Meuse

NEY

Ligny

Namur

**REILLE'S
5th. CORPS**

Valenciennes

R. Sambre

Mons

Binche

Charleroi

Châtelet

Phillippeville

**CONCENTRATION
14-15th. JUNE**

Maubeuge

Avesnes

Meziére

**VANDAMME'S
3rd. CORPS**

Thionville

**IMPERIAL
GUARD**

Laon

**LOBAU'S
5th. CORPS**

**GÉRARD'S
4th. CORPS**

R. Moselle

To Paris

- Prussian movements
- Lines of French mobilization 6-15th. June
- French advance 15-18th. June
- △ △ △ △ △ Anglo-Dutch-Hanoverian concentration
- ▲ ▲ ▲ ▲ ▲ Prussian concentration

major engagements were fought at Quatre Bras, Ligny, Waterloo and Wavre. In each the French attacked and found themselves faced with stubborn resistance. Napoleon had hoped for a campaign of brilliant manoeuvre and decisive victory; instead he found himself drawn into a war of attrition.

The nature of the forthcoming campaign was quickly revealed. At dawn on 15 June D'Erlon's and Reille's corps rolled up the Prussians west of Charleroi while Vandamme's and Lobau's broke into the town and then pushed north-eastwards towards Fleurus. The going was not easy; there had been rumours that neither side would take prisoners and the Prussians fought back fiercely. By the evening and after a series of savage contests, the remains of von Zeiten's corps had retired to Fleurus while the rest of the Prussian army was converging on Ligny. Somewhat to the west, Marshal Ney with a substantial force was feeling his way towards Quatre Bras and the vital high road which ran from Nivelles towards Namur. This area was thinly held by the 2nd Netherlands Division, but Prince William, who commanded this section of the front, had been alerted to the danger and during the night reinforcements were hurried to the crossroads.

Reports of these developments travelled slowly to Wellington's HQ at Brussels. Between four and five in the afternoon he was aware that an offensive had been made against various points around Charleroi but there was no clear indication of the enemy's strength or purpose. At six he took the precaution of warning all his divisional commanders to bring their dispersed brigades to their respective HQs and stand by for marching. He dared not go further for fear that the Charleroi offensive might prove to be a decoy contrived to lure forces away from positions between the Sambre and Scheldt where the main French attack would materialize. None came and by ten, when he had received messages from outposts around Mons, Wellington was certain the thrust over the Sambre was in fact the first stage of a general offensive.

There was as yet no way of knowing the size of the force closing on Quatre Bras nor whether it posed a serious danger. Despite his precautionary measures, Prince William felt the situation was safe enough for him to quit his HQ at Binche to attend the Duchess of Richmond's ball. When Wellington asked for news, he answered casually, 'No! Nothing but that the French had crossed the Sambre and have had a brush with the Prussians. Have you heard of it?'[29]

Wellington was up at five on the morning of 16 June after three hours' sleep. All the intelligence he had received in the past twelve hours indicated that Napoleon's intention was to eliminate the Prussians and it was therefore imperative that Wellington offered them as much assistance as he could. Orders had been transmitted overnight to divisional commanders asking them to rendezvous at Quatre Bras to safeguard the Prussian right and forestall any French attempt to cut communications between the two armies. Picton's division had already left Brussels, and Wellington rode ahead to see for himself what was happening. His effort to survey the ground was handicapped by a lack of cavalry, and the presence of French mounted pickets screening Ney's forces, which were three or four miles to the south.

As there were no signs of activity by the French, Wellington rode off towards Ligny, where Blücher was already laying out his battle-lines. The two met by a windmill near Byre and in full view of the French, who were forming up for an attack. Wellington expressed surprise that the Prussian formations were in the open and wondered why Blücher had not placed them behind slopes. He was told that the Prussians liked to see their enemies and he observed afterwards that they would be 'damnably mauled'. Nevertheless he pledged all the help he could to protect and support the Prussian right, although he was uncertain when it would be available. By two in the afternoon he had ridden back to Quatre Bras, where it was clear that Ney was preparing to attack.

Napoleon had demanded much of Ney, too much in fact. At eight he had been ordered to detach D'Erlon's division, which was to be thrown against the Prussian right and roll it up, and six hours later he was instructed to engage the Anglo-Dutch at Quatre Bras and then bring his forces towards Ligny, where they would work their way behind the Prussian right flank. This order with the exhortation 'Le sort de la France est dans vos mains' was delivered again just over an hour later. By this time Ney's forces were entangled in a desperate struggle from which they could not disengage. Already aware that the numbers facing him were higher than anticipated, Ney had recalled D'Erlon to redress the balance. Of developments at Ligny he knew nothing.

The attack on Quatre Bras started well for the French. Poor-spirited, raw Dutch troops were slowly flushed from the Bossu Wood while the assault on the centre of the allied position at Quatre Bras was making good headway. Wellington, who took command at three, immediately realized that this advance had to be stemmed at all costs since if the French occupied the crossroads they could prevent the deployment of the reinforcements expected later in the afternoon. Hanging on depended on his own leadership and the grit and tenacity of his British infantry, for his artillery was outmatched by the French, his cavalry were few in number and unreliable, as were the Dutch infantry and the Brunswickers, who had been disheartened by the death of their commander, Duke Frederick-William, who had been shot early in the engagement.

Throughout the battle Wellington personally directed units, moving them wherever they were needed to plug a gap or reinforce a threatened position. Once he was almost overwhelmed by a swarm of chasseurs à cheval, whom he escaped by clearing a ditch in which the 92nd Highlanders were sheltering. Soon after, when that regiment was charged by cuirassiers, he formed it into line and asked with characteristic politeness, 'Ninety-second, I will be obliged to you for a little fire.'[30]

These horsemen were among the reinforcements which reached Ney, along with the second order to proceed to Ligny, during the first phase of the fighting. Cavalry used as a sledgehammer was, he mistakenly imagined, the key to the battle. And so they should have been, but for all their high-spirited bravery and dash the French horsemen failed to shake the morale of their adversaries or ride them down. Wherever possible the British infantry formed defensive squares and shot down the cavalry in droves. Even when some regiments were taken unawares it was found that the firepower of the line was enough to deflect or throw back mounted men. To meet cavalry in this way needed nerve and was always dangerous. The 69th (South Lincolnshire Regiment) was ridden down after it failed to form a square in time, thanks to orders fumbled by Prince William.

Despite the weight of French cannon fire, which was especially lethal against squares, and despite some extraordinarily vigorous attacks, the allies held their ground. At times they seemed close to complete collapse but were saved by continual injections of fresh troops, including the Foot Guards, who reached the field at six-thirty. By nightfall Wellington had accumulated 30,000, men nearly twice those available to Ney. Unable to penetrate the allied position or meet the counter-attack which gathered momentum as the new troops arrived, Ney withdrew as darkness fell. At nine he was rejoined by D'Erlon's corps, which had through the confusion of orders been unable to exert its influence either at Ligny or at Quatre Bras.

In terms of the overall campaign Quatre Bras was a serious setback for Napoleon. Ney had prevented Wellington from giving help to Blücher, but at the cost of his corps' absence from Ligny, where Napoleon had cast it in a decisive role. Muddled orders, for which Ney unfairly took the blame, deprived Napoleon of D'Erlon's corps. Descending into the subjunctive which so many French soldiers then and later used for the campaign, Soult wrote on 17 June, 'Si les corps des comtes Reille et D'Erlon avaient été ensemble ... l'armée prussienne était totalement détruit et nous aurions peut être trente mille prisonniers.'[31] Whether these extra men would have so radically changed the course of Ligny is another matter; what was certain and of enormous importance for the future was that Wellington held Quatre Bras. Napoleon was no nearer his vital objective, the separation of the allied and Prussian armies.

It took some time for this fact to emerge. Wellington spent the night of 16/17 June at Genappe, where he picked up some vague details of how the Prussians had fared at Ligny and had the reassurance of hearing the arrival of the British cavalry.[32] At daybreak he returned to Quatre Bras, where there were no indications that the French were about to relaunch their offensive. It was now imperative to get accurate intelligence about what had passed at Ligny, so a reliable staff officer, Colonel Sir Alexander Gordon, rode eastwards with a hussar escort to make contact with the Prussians. He was back by seven with an account of a conversation he had just had with von Zeiten at the village of Tilly. It appeared that Blücher, after a ferocious resistance, had abandoned his position, was retreating north-eastwards and would concentrate his army at Wavre by the end of the day. He was in the process of being reinforced by Count Bülow von Dennewitz's 4th Corps of over 20,000 fresh troops.

This was the news that Wellington wanted to hear. The Prussian army was intact and close at hand, and, as he soon heard from von Müffling, its commander was in bullish temper and keen to co-operate in any forthcoming action. (The Marshal had been unhorsed and stunned at Ligny but had been revived by the generous use of brandy as both embrocation and stimulant.) Wellington no longer faced the hazard of taking on a stronger Napoleon single-handed or even, if the odds looked unfavourable, of having to give up Brussels and retreat to the coast. He was now free to seek a holding action on ground that he had selected in the knowledge that he could rely on Prussian help, which he hoped would take the form of Bülow's and one other corps. What he did not know was that, as he had predicted, Blücher had been mauled at Ligny and had taken 16,000 casualties, just over a fifth of his strength. Nor could he calculate with any degree of accuracy when and where the Prussians would arrive. This would depend to some extent on the attitude of von Gneisenau, who, despite von Müffling's explanation of how Wellington had tied down 30,000 French at Quatre Bras, was sore about the allies' absence from Ligny and even more mistrustful of their commander.[33]

Wellington's mind was now set on the imminent battle. By ten he was issuing orders to all his subordinates to converge on a position just south of the village of Waterloo. It had earlier been surveyed by engineers at his request on the ground that it was an ideal site for a defensive action to safeguard Brussels. An extended ridge crossed the main road from the south, and its northern slope offered protection from artillery fire and the means to shift men out of sight of the enemy.

It was also just under ten miles west of Wavre, where the Prussian army was mustering, although the connecting roads were of very poor quality.

For the rest of the day the main body of the allied army fell back from Quatre Bras. A sultry and airless morning promised a thunderstorm, which broke in mid-afternoon, and those moving on tracks or across fields were soon trudging through mud, and horses sank to their girths. Men, some of whom had been marching intermittently for the past twenty-four hours, collapsed with exhaustion.

Behind were French cavalry, held in check by a screen of British horsemen under Wellington's direction. Skirmishes were frequent and savage: one was recalled by Sergeant-Major Cotton of the 7th Hussars, who for the next forty or so years remained behind in Belgium as a guide to the battlefield:

> The head of the French column now appeared debouching from the town [Genappe], and Lord Uxbridge [later the Marquess of Anglesey] being present, he ordered the 7th Hussars to charge.
>
> The charge was gallantly led by the officers and followed by the men, who cut aside the lances, and did all in their power to break the enemy: but our horses being jaded by skirmishing on heavy ground, and the enemy being chiefly lancers, backed by cuirassiers, they were rather awkward customers to deal with, particularly so, as it was an arm with which we were unacquainted. When our charge first commenced, their lances were erect, but upon our coming within two or three horses' length of them, they lowered the points and waved the flags, which made some of our horses shy. Lord Uxbridge, seeing we could make no impression on them, ordered us about: we retired, pursued by the lancers and the cuirassiers intermixed....[34]

After this tussle there was a nasty incident which indicated that an ugly fanaticism had taken hold of some of the French, who were generally generous-spirited fighters. Major Hodge of the 7th, who had been wounded and taken prisoner, was murdered by the lancers.[35] Reports of such outrages circulated during the next day, draining compassion and chivalry from many British soldiers, who were strongly inclined to pay back the French in kind.

Farce was played out alongside tragedy. At another stage in the retreat, horse-artillerymen fired a Congreve rocket at a French gun position and scored a direct hit, scattering the gunners. The next rocket soared and then turned round on its terrified firers to the delight of the French, who returned to their piece and reopened fire.

Napoleon's reaction to the events of 16/17 June seemed to some of those around him inexplicable. He seemed in the grip of a fatal lassitude and showed none of that alacrity of mind which had made Wellington nervous. 'Le Napoléon que nous avons connu n'existe plus,' wrote a disappointed General Vandamme; 'notre succès d'hier restera sans résultat.' Others blamed Napoleon's ill-health for his apparent inertia and complacency; he was suffering from stomach and urinary distempers and probably piles. General Gérard was nearer the truth when he blamed 'irrémédiable lenteurs' for the army's failure to follow up the advantages it appeared to have secured.[36] Some units had been on the march for up to ten days and all had been in more or less continuous action for two. Soldiers were tired and scattered, and stocks of ammunition and provender had to be replenished. Napoleon's army needed a breathing-space and got one during the morning of 17 June.

The real weakness in the French position was caused not by unavoidable operational delays, but by a breakdown in Napoleon's intelligence apparatus which lasted throughout the 17th and much of the following day. During this time virtually no contact was made with the Prussian army and French HQ remained more or less in the dark about its location and strength. Much of the blame must rest with Napoleon, who convinced himself that he had inflicted an overwhelming defeat on Blücher, but efficient staff work might have brought him to reality. There was some encouraging news: a hysterical Prussian officer announced that 'Blücher had destroyed the Prussian monarchy for the second time', which was no doubt what Napoleon wanted to hear. It was however no substitute for the reports that would have followed careful reconnaissance of all the possible Prussian lines of retreat.

In fact the remains of the Prussian 1st and 2nd Corps had abandoned their positions between Tilly and Gentinne in the small hours of the 17th and were falling back towards Wavre, just as von Zeiten had told Sir Alexander Gordon. At the same time von Thielemann's 3rd Corps was retiring from Sombreffe on its way to Gemblouz, where it rested before heading towards Wavre to rendezvous with Bülow's 4th Corps, which was hurrying west from Namur. These manoeuvres by isolated units went undetected by French patrols and no attempt was made to interrupt their progress.

Nevertheless, Napoleon was conscious that von Thielemann might still constitute a threat and so at half-past eleven in the morning he ordered Marshal Grouchy to proceed towards Gembloux, collect information and then drive on towards the Prussian bases at Namur and Liège, where it was thought they would seek refuge. Grouchy had to conduct both a reconnaissance in force and a pursuit, so he was given 33,600 men, of whom a high proportion, one-fifth, were cavalry.

Grouchy advanced at a leisurely pace, setting off at three in the afternoon. His early reports to HQ were misleading and only at six the following morning did he have enough details to suggest that Blücher was on his way to Brussels 'so as to concentrate there, or give battle after joining Wellington'. For the rest of the day he stuck resolutely to the commission he had been given by Napoleon and continued his march to Wavre, where at four he made contact with the Prussian rearguard holding the north bank of the Dyle. His behaviour then and later aroused passionate criticism; at midday when he heard the sound of the opening bombardment at Waterloo, his bolder subordinates pleaded with him to march to the sound of the guns, but he kept to the letter of his orders, which were to find and engage the Prussians. As he later said in his defence, they were never countermanded.

One reason for the slowness of Grouchy's march had been the torrential rain which poured unrelentingly on all the armies from the afternoon of 17 June to nine the following morning. It was a 'dismal and dreary' dawn for men who had slept in the open and awoke, like Private Wheeler, 'drenched with rain, benumbed and shaking with cold'. 'You often blame me for smoking,' he told his family, 'but I must tell you if I had not a good stock of tobacco this night I must have given up the Ghost.'[37] Smoking calmed empty stomachs, and food was in short supply. Ensign Leeke of the 52nd faced a chunk of dried biscuit and broth which he tried to gulp, earning a rebuke from a superior: 'Master Leeke, I think you have had your share of that.'[38] Standards were high in the Light Infantry.

Despite these discomforts morale was high and, among the British, faith in their commander was absolute. His battle-plan had been devised on the assumption that he would fight a holding action until the arrival of Prussian reinforcements and then, with numerical superiority assured, counter-attack. He commanded an army of 68,000 men made up of 29,800 British and King's German Legion, 11,200 Hanoverians, 6,000 Brunswickers and nearly 21,000 Dutch, Belgians and Nassauers, backed by 140 cannon. Of these, many of the Dutch and Belgians had little heart for the fight and some secretly sympathized with the French. Against Wellington was an army of largely more experienced troops which totalled about 75,000 and was supported by 240 cannon.

Wellington hoped to redress the imbalance. The lie of the land offered some protection from artillery fire and he deployed his men in such a way as to facilitate their transfer to points where his line was in danger of snapping. It stretched along a ridge which crossed the Nivelles and Charleroi roads and was bounded to the north by the edge of the Soignies forest, to which men could be withdrawn if there was a risk of a complete collapse. To frustrate any outflanking sweep towards Brussels and to protect his own line of retreat, Wellington had detached 17,000 to hold Halle. His greatest strength lay in three groups of substantial buildings immediately in front of his position which had been transformed into fortalices. The small château, walled enclosures and outhouses of Hougoumont on his right flank, the farmhouse of La Haie Sainte in the centre and the smaller farms of Papellote and La Haie on the left were breakwaters which would reduce the impact of the French onrushes. Their capture was a prerequisite for a French victory and would, during the next few hours, divert thousands of men and dozens of cannon in a series of three, miniature sieges. By the end of the battle, the Hougoumont garrison, which had been increased from 500 to 2,000, had tied down over six times that number. Inevitably the attackers lost far more than the defenders.

All Wellington's dispositions rested on his assumption that Waterloo would be a contest of attrition. His men were placed where they could absorb shocks with as little damage as possible. How they reacted, particularly when the pummelling intensified, depended ultimately on their will to fight. That of the French was strong, verging at times on suicidal fanaticism. They fought with what one Highland officer considered 'too much ferocity'.[39] Another participant, Colonel de Lacy Evans of Wellington's staff and a future radical MP, characterized the battle as 'the struggle of enthusiasm and despair, on the one hand, of courage and duty on the other.'[40]

These last qualities manifested themselves in resilience and 'steadiness', a word widely used in all subsequent accounts, usually as a description of the British. General Sir James Kempt praised the 'invincible spirit and steadiness' of the men in his division and his own example was remembered by Captain Kincaid, who admired the way he rode along the ranks 'animating the men to steadiness'.[41] Ensign Leeke, for whom this was his first battle, quickly learned how to behave as he carried his regimental colours. 'I caught sight of a ball which appeared to be in direct line for me. I thought, shall I move? No! I gathered myself up, and stood with the colour in my right hand.' The cannonball struck some men close by.[42] A few moments before he had noticed an officer reprove a wounded man who was crying aloud, 'Oh man, don't make a noise.' He fell silent and Leeke was amazed that others in the same condition suffered quietly.

These qualities of stoicism and fortitude were stretched to breaking point once the battle was under way. It was opened just before midday by the French, who had waited for the sun to dry out the ground to a hardness that would enable cannon balls to bounce and make the going better for the infantry and cavalry who would attack across the valley which separated the armies. Napoleon's plan was simple: his massed

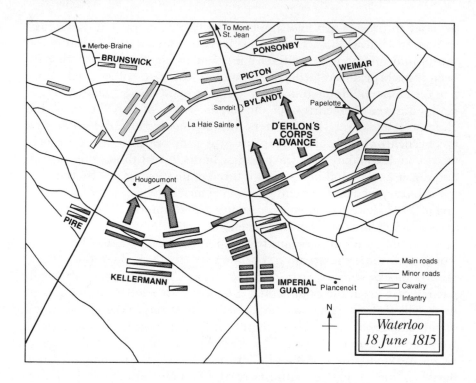

Merbe-Braine
BRUNSWICK
To Mont-
St. Jean
PONSONBY
PICTON
WEIMAR
Sandpit
La Haie Sainte
BYLANDT
Papelotte
D'ERLON'S
CORPS
ADVANCE
Hougoumont
PIRE
KELLERMANN
IMPERIAL
GUARD
Plancenoit

Main roads
Minor roads
Cavalry
Infantry

N

*Waterloo
18 June 1815*

infantry and cavalry columns would deliver a series of hammer-blows which, he felt assured, would fragment the allied line.

The first fell on Hougoumont and followed a bombardment whose intensity amazed even Peninsular veterans. This isolated surge by three divisions ran into heavy resistance, and a savage struggle developed around the buildings, which were held by the 1st and 3rd Foot Guards. At one-thirty, a second and more formidable attack by infantry and cavalry was thrown against the allied centre. Over 20,000 infantry, including the whole of D'Erlon's corps, came forward in waves supported by the fire from seventy-four cannon. This was too much for a Dutch regiment, which ran off the field in blind terror; as they ran past Picton's division they were hissed by the Highlanders. In front, part of D'Erlon's force enveloped La Haie Sainte and were drawn into a desperate fight for control of the building and its enclosures.

The rest of the attackers came on in tightly packed, unwieldy columns of between 150 and 200 men across and twenty-seven ranks deep. As they closed, an ill-timed attempt to redeploy gave Picton's division an opportunity for volley fire followed by a charge in which its commander was shot dead. The faltering French had no chance to recover their equilibrium; they were struck unexpectedly by a cavalry charge by the Royal Scots Greys and Inniskilling Dragoons. It was a dramatic and stirring incident immortalized in Lady Butler's *Scotland for Ever*, in which the Greys in their bearskins gallop furiously out of the canvas. It was a regiment which had not seen action for nearly twenty years and which the night before had cut notches in its swords so as to inflict jagged rather than clean-edged wounds.[43] As the horsemen prepared to charge they were cheered on with shouts of 'Scotland for ever!' from the 92nd Highlanders. 'I never saw soldiers of this regiment so very savage,' one of its officers remarked, 'they repeatedly called to the cavalry to spare none of the French.'[44] The approach of the cavalry threw the recoiling French into a panic: some cast off their sword belts as a token of surrender and others, in the words of a trooper, 'ran like hares' to the safety of their own lines.[45] The horsemen followed, overran one battery and sliced down the gunners. The tables were suddenly turned and the French cavalry counter-charged the by now dispersed dragoons whose horses were winded. The Greys and Inniskillings escaped, but only just and with heavy losses. As they struggled back, their brigade commander, Major-General Sir William Ponsonby, was unhorsed and killed by a French lancer as he lay helpless.

The French cuirassiers who had supported D'Erlon's offensive were seen off by the Life Guards. Undeterred by their adversaries' breast-plates, the Lifeguardsmen cut at reins and horses' legs, stabbed at their riders' thighs, groins and armpits and, as one boasted after, 'killed them with as much ease as we would have done rabbits'.[46]

In just over three hours the French had launched two massive offen-sives against Wellington's centre and right, gained no advantage and taken heavy losses. So too had the allies and, anxious to reduce casualties from cannon fire, Wellington ordered exposed units to fall back beyond the ridge. Ney interpreted this movement as the first stage of a general withdrawal and decided to press home the advantage with a massed cavalry charge. It was a suicidal move since the 5,000 horsemen were squeezed into a 1,200 yard front and had to charge across muddy fields that were thick with rye. As they gathered pace the French horse came under artillery fire and, as they galloped over the ridge, they rode into volleys of musketry from the infantry squares.

These held firm. Some horsemen 'walked their horses on all sides of the square to look for an opening, or dashed madly on, thinking to carry everything by desperation. But not a British soldier moved; all personal feeling was forgotten in the enthusiasm of such a moment. Each person seemed to think the day depended on his individual exertions.'[47] This was the view from inside the squares; outside it was frustration and rage. Cuirassiers shook their swords, challenged officers to individual combat or hacked at the wounded and dying.[48] Driven off, they rode away and the gunners who had taken shelter in the square ran back to their pieces and fired grape into the backs of the retreating horsemen. Wellington had ordered his artillerymen to detach a wheel from each of their cannon to prevent them from being hauled away and no senior French officer had bothered to issue hammers and spiking nails to the cavalrymen. Napoleon was appalled by Ney's rashness and commented to Soult, 'Voilà un mouvement prématuré qui pourra avoir des résultats funestes pour la journée.' Nonetheless he ordered fresh squadrons to join the attack, but they were thrown back into the others.

By six the stamina on both sides was waning, although the will to fight remained remarkably strong. The hours of attrition had reduced Wellington's numbers to a dangerously low level and it was less and less easy to find the men to plug gaps in his by now thinly spread line. 'Never before was I obliged to take such pains for victory,' he wrote later, 'and never before was I so close to being beaten.' The tension showed, for when, at about six-thirty, he took refuge in a square formed by the heavily depleted 30th (Cambridgeshire Regiment) and 73rd Highlanders, officers were struck by his strained features and anxious manner.[49]

His mind was on the Prussians. Overnight he had been given Blücher's assurances that his army would begin its march to the battlefield by daybreak, and soon after dawn a Prussian cavalry patrol had been spotted near Ohain. This encouraged Wellington to believe that the first substantial reinforcements would be joining his line in the early afternoon.[50] He was over-optimistic, for foul roads and operational hitches caused delays and the Prussians moved cautiously, fearing the sudden appearance of Grouchy on their flanks. Moreover, the advance guard of Bülow's 4th Corps headed towards Plancenoit to the east of Napoleon's army rather than in the direction of Wellington's left, where it was needed. Reports of its approach and deployment were in Napoleon's hands by two and for some time he was so dumbfounded that he refused to believe them.

Once contact had been made between Bülow's corps and French reserves, hastily thrown against him, Napoleon realized that he would now have to fight on two fronts and that his resources would become increasingly stretched. It was imperative that Wellington be eliminated as soon as possible and Ney was ordered to intensify pressure on the allied centre. He succeeded; by seven and after desperate fighting the French secured possession of La Haie Sainte, La Haie and Papellote. The way was now open for a final, all-out push against what remained of Wellington's centre, which was now under close-range bombardment.

The courage and enthusiasm of his men remained at a high pitch. 'It's a damned unfair fight,' one rifleman concluded. 'They are above two to one of us, and Wellington won't let us charge or we'd beat them now, we are obliged to stand in squares and be mown down like rotten sheep. They keep looking for the Prussians, but no Prussians are to be seen. Never mind, we've lost no ground and we'll beat them yet.'[51] An officer shared his impatience: 'Lord Wellington has won the Battle, if we could get the damned — to advance.'[52]

Such a move was out of the question. At this stage Wellington was preoccupied with finding ways to conserve and deploy his remaining forces. Since six he had been aware that the Prussians were in action at Plancenoit, but he had no way of knowing with what numbers or success. By seven, the first units of von Zeiten's corps had appeared on his left and for a few minutes engaged adjacent allied units, neither side being familiar with the other's uniforms.

Napoleon had watched the Prussians' progress and what he saw made him realize, slowly at first, that time was running against him. Nevertheless, he remained confident that he had the wherewithal to deliver a final, irresistible blow against what he thought was a wavering and distended allied line. This knock-out punch would be delivered in the grand manner by his best infantry, the untouched, 6,000-strong Imperial Guard. Advance warning of this offensive was carried to the allied command by a cuirassier officer who deserted across the lines with shouts of 'Vive le Roi!'[53]

Alerted to the attack, Wellington immediately shifted his best troops, Maitland's Brigade of Foot Guards, to the threatened point, ordering them to form a four-deep line and take cover in a cornfield. The Imperial Guard's advance was a splendid, awesome sight; the tall, moustached veterans in black bearskins kept rigid formation, indifferent to the hail of grape and roundshot which struck them. When the first column of chasseurs à pied came within sixty paces, Wellington called out, 'Now, Maitland! Now's your time!' Up sprang the guardsmen and within a minute their volleys had cut down 300 men. Unable to change formation, the entire column 'convulsed' as men shrank from the fire.[54] It intensified as guardsmen supported by the 52nd and 95th Rifles took up positions on the columns' flanks. Raked by crossfire, the Imperial Guard flinched, surged back, slowly to begin with, chased in what Peninsular veterans called 'the old style' by British bayonets.

The horrified cry 'La Garde receuil!' passed through the rest of the French army and drained men's will to fight. The odds had tipped decisively against the French: their final assault had been repulsed; a secondary battle was raging at Plancenoit; more and more of von Zeiten's Prussians were shoring up Wellington's line, which still held.

Soldiers, at first paralysed by the Imperial Gaurd's overthrow, lost heart, panicked and began to run. Ney tried to rally them: 'Venez, suivez-moi, mes camarades … je vais vous montrer comment meurt un maréchal de France, sur le champ de bataille.' But for most the old rhetoric no longer intoxicated and within half an hour Napoleon's army was dissolving.

Now certain that it was in its death throes, Wellington gave the order for a general advance and those units still intact moved forward, cheering wildly. It had been, in his famous words, 'a close run thing'. A few moments earlier many of his soldiers had been on the point of despair; a Scottish officer wrote afterwards that 'the men were so completely worn out, that it required the greatest exertion on the part of officers to keep up their spirits. Not a soldier thought of giving ground; but victory seemed hopeless.'[55]

Looking back over the day, Wellington observed, 'By God, I don't think it would have been done if I had not been there,' and few present with him would have dissented. And yet, in the hours after the battle, his mood was 'sombre and dejected'. He told one of his staff officers, 'The losses I have sustained have quite broken me down, and I have no feelings for the advantages I have gained.'[56] A few weeks later and in the same temper he expanded on his reactions to what was, for the world, his greatest victory. 'I hope to God that I have fought my last battle. It is a bad thing to be always fighting. While I am in the thick of it I am too much occupied to feel anything; but it is wretched just after. It is quite impossible to think of glory.… I am wretched even at the moment of victory, and I always say that, next to a battle lost, the greatest misery is a battle gained.'[57]

The intensity of his emotions owned much to the heavy cost of victory. The losses at Waterloo far outstripped those of his earlier battles; the allies suffered 16,000 casualties (over a fifth of the army), the Prussians 6,800, and the French, for whom no accurate tally was made, perhaps 25,000. The field itself was a ghastly sight. A hussar officer remembered how 'wounded or mutilated horses wandered or turned in circles. The noise was deafening, and the air of ruin and desolation … could give no inspiration of victory'. Colonel Seaton of the 52nd, when asked twenty years on to set down his version of events, answered that it was 'a most unpleasant task to refer to our past military operations, which are connected with many painful recollections'.[58]

Those who overcame such feelings and put their impressions on paper, and there were many, were united in their praise of Wellington, and all paid tribute to his bravery and nonchalance throughout the battle. A staff officer, who was close to him, remembered this coolness and detachment:

> His look and demeanour were always perfectly calm; and he rarely spoke to any one, unless to send a message or an order: indeed he generally rode quite alone – this is, no one was at his side; appearing unconscious even of the presence of his own troops, while his eye kept scanning intently those of his opponent. Occasionally he would stop, and peer for a few seconds through the large field-telescope he carried in his right hand: and this the docile Copenhagen permitted, without testifying a symptom of impatience.[59]

This had always been his style of leadership, although the writer ignored the many occasions when he intervened directly in the fighting. Once, when directing the fire of the 92nd, his customary humanity briefly deserted him. A solitary French cavalry officer, left in the lurch by his men who had galloped off, rode towards the Highlanders, and Wellington exclaimed, 'Damn it, 92nd, will you allow that fellow to escape?'[60] He did, for, although his horse was killed, a Highlander officer rescued him and the two later became friends.

In the end what mattered was Wellington's generalship. His army needed both the inspiration of his self-assured, unruffled presence and a guiding intelligence. His interpretation of his enemy's movements and detached calculations of how best his limited forces could be deployed and protected were exactly what were needed in a battle of attrition. To these qualities were added his understanding of the inner forces which drove his officers and men. All his judgements rested ultimately on knowing what his soldiers could endure and for how long.

The immediate consequence of Waterloo was the final collapse of Napoleon's state. The defeated and discredited Emperor found himself politically isolated when he returned to Paris, his broken army closely pursued by the Prussians. In eastern France other allied armies were crossing the frontiers and converging, almost unopposed, on Paris. On 22 June Napoleon abdicated under pressure from the representatives of a country sick of war.

In exile on St Helena Napoleon retreated into that comfortable world of what-might-have-been and in time convinced himself that he had really beaten Wellington, but that victory had been snatched from him by the Prussians. When his self-indulgent inquest on Waterloo was published shortly after his death in 1820, Wellington's friends were indignant. Not so the Duke, who dismissed French critics with good-humoured contempt. 'Damn them. I beat them and, if I was surprised, if I did place myself in so foolish a position, they were the greater fools for not knowing how to take advantage of my fault.'[61]

Part Eight
1815–1852

1

The Nation's Servant-of-All-Work: 1815–1852

Wellington insisted that every survivor of Waterloo received a medal from the government. This was an unusual step, for during the Peninsular War the award of medals had been confined to senior officers, who were given, on Wellington's recommendation, richly engraved gold crosses with clasps naming the battles at which they had served.[1] The Waterloo medal was of silver, weighed an ounce and was designed by Wyon, the foremost engraver of the age. It showed on the obverse the Prince Regent, firm-jawed and Caesar-like, and on the other, winged Victory holding an olive palm between the words 'Waterloo' and 'Wellington'. Wellington prized his own Waterloo medal above his more flamboyant decorations, often from foreign potentates, took great care of it and repaired its suspender clip with his own hands.[2] Peninsular veterans were not so well treated by their former commander and had to wait until 1847/8 for medals; some were hurt by this oversight.[3]

The news of Waterloo reached London during the evening of 21 June and the following morning special newspaper editions carried Wellington's despatch. The details were transmitted across the country with astonishing speed; on 24 June the victory was announced in Aberdeen, where the news spread through the town 'like lightning' and was greeted with 'joy unspeakable'.[4] This jubilation was universal, far in excess of that which had followed Trafalgar ten years earlier, when the simultaneous report of Nelson's death had dulled the edge of public celebration. Within a few hours of the release of Wellington's despatch the newsheets began to receive the first letters with eyewitness accounts of the fighting. All were full of praise for Wellington: 'the Duke has done all this,' ran one printed in the *Courier* on 23 June which proudly asserted that the battle was 'the severest and most bloody action ever fought, and the conduct of the British infantry had surpassed its former glory'.

There was a quick rush by entrepreneurs of all kinds to cash in on Waterloo and its victor. The new fast coach from London to Ramsgate was named 'Wellington'; 'Wellington' cloaks were advertised by a St James's tailor; 'Wellington' rings in gold with busts of 'this immortal Hero' were offered to *Courier* readers; and by 1 August artists were already on the spot making sketches of the battlefield in preparation for prints of the action in which the 'scourge of Europe' had met his fate.[5] Prints were also on sale of the latest portrait of Wellington, a full-length study which was recommended to those 'Public Bodies, corporations, Military Establishments and others desirous of erecting testimonials to the honour of this truly Great Man'.

Poets hurried after artists to view the battlefield, which had quickly become a popular tourist attraction, complete with gift shops selling souvenirs such as epaulettes, cuirassiers' breastplates and crested helmets which had been salvaged in the few days after the battle. Sir Walter Scott was an early visitor and shopper and, like other pilgrims, he passed on to Paris to pay homage to Wellington, who was there as a commander of the allied army of occupation. What he saw and what he heard were the raw material for a poem on Waterloo in which Napoleon was revealingly likened to the rebel slave Spartacus who had challenged the ordered empire of Rome and been destroyed. Wellington was portrayed as 'his country's sword and shield' and, inevitably for the romantic medievalist, there were comparisons with the earlier epic victories of Crécy and Agincourt.

Another literary tourist, Southey, had first celebrated the battle in grand if eccentric style by a crepuscular feast on the summit of Skiddaw, where, with Wordsworth and a gathering of Lakeland patriots, he ate roast beef and plum pudding and sang 'God Save the King'. His 'Poet's Pilgrimage to Waterloo' had an introduction in which he explained why he and his countrymen exulted over the victory and why it would continue to have a special place in the national consciousness throughout the nineteenth century. According to Southey, 'The peace which she [Britain] has won by the battle of Waterloo, leaves her at leisure to pursue the great objects and duties of bettering her own condition, and diffusing the blessings of civilization and Christianity.' His vision of national destiny embraced the commercial, humanitarian and imperial and would be repeated and expanded by subsequent seers who proclaimed Britain as the banner-bearer of enlightenment.

This is instructive because it helps explain why Wellington enjoyed such immense respect and prestige after 1815; Waterloo, his victory, opened an era of international peace during which British inventiveness, business acumen and moral high-mindedness dominated the world. It was not accidental that the most impressive public statues of Wellington were erected in those cities which were the powerhouses of the new commercial expansion. In 1844 an equestrian statue was placed in London's Cornhill and another in Glasgow's Royal Exchange; a Wellington on a rearing horse was set up at the end of Prince's Street, Edinburgh in 1852; and in 1853 Manchester's city fathers allocated £7,000 for a bronze statue and London's £5,000 for one in Carrara marble for the Guildhall. Gentlemen in Liverpool commissioned Benjamin Haydon to paint a life-sized, full-length portrait of the Duke in 1839, much to his pleasure.[6]

Commemoration of a national hero in bronze and marble was natural for a people who considered themselves the inheritors of Graeco-Roman civilization. They were also permanent reminders of a war in which Britain had endured perils and privations and had finally triumphed despite odds that at times had seemed overwhelming. The string of victories which stretched from Vimiero to Waterloo were an enormous boost to national self-esteem. According to Pierce Egan, the chronicler of the new and highly popular sport of boxing, the British had gained a reputation for 'heroic courage blended with humanity which has made them so renowned, terrific and triumphant in all parts of the world.'[7] In an age when 'game' and 'bottom' were terms of high praise, the nation and its armed forces had shown these qualities in abundance and patriotic self-confidence, damaged by setbacks in America and during the lacklustre campaigns of the 1790s, was restored and enlarged.

For these reasons and because Nelson had died, Wellington, the architect of victory, was assured of a position as a national hero. And yet his apotheosis was delayed until the 1840s. His reputation, which had been high in the years immediately after Waterloo, was quickly tarnished after his re-entry into domestic politics.

After supervising the allied occupation of France, Wellington returned to Britain in 1818 and joined Liverpool's cabinet as Master-General of the Ordnance. The years 1816–20 witnessed a recession, and a government struggling to keep the lid down on popular unrest was glad to secure the services of such an illustrious and experienced figure. And yet, then and later, there was public disquiet about a professional soldier holding high political office, especially at a time when the army was the only means available to preserve public order. These feelings were forcefully expressed by a London cheesemonger in a row with a newly commissioned officer in 1809: 'Ve dont vant sodgers in London – thank God! we can do without 'em. Ve vant no military government

here, my lad!'[8] Furthermore, anti-Bonapartist propaganda had portrayed France and her client states as military despotisms where soldiers
did as they liked, unlike Britain where the constitution guaranteed a
subject's rights.

Wellington, the first soldier since Cromwell to have used his military
career as a springboard for a political one, therefore attracted much
suspicion, which he did little to allay. In 1828, when asked by George
IV to form a ministry, he did so reluctantly and alarmed public opinion
by appointing two former brothers-in-arms, Sir George Murray and
Sir Henry Hardinge, to the cabinet. A cartoon pictured the new administration as a squad of fierce, moustached officers lined up behind the
Duke and there were mutterings about a military dictatorship. He
could not understand such reactions; ruling a country, like running an
army, was best undertaken by trustworthy, hard-working men of ability
and it did not matter that they happened to be soldiers.

The very qualities which distinguished Wellington as a soldier were
encumbrances in an age when political attitudes and forms of behaviour
were changing. His often bitter experiences in the Peninsula had intensified his loathing for political factions and parties. Then, he had been
a servant of the Crown conducting an enterprise for the public good
continually distracted by the carping criticism of politicians who knew
nothing of the difficulties he was facing and were motivated solely by
a partisan spirit. He grumbled then about party spirit and continued
to do so for the rest of his life.

In office, as Prime Minister between 1828 and 1830, again for nine
days in 1831, as a caretaker for Sir Robert Peel in 1834–5 and briefly
as Foreign Secretary in 1835, he always behaved as if he were a servant
of the Crown and not the leader of a party. After Victoria's accession in
1837, whenever he spoke of himself or his fellow ministers he deliberately
used the expression 'Her Majesty's servants' and, although his ministries
were dominated by Tories, he described himself as politically neutral,
attached to no party. When the Whigs were in power, as they were for
most of the 1830s, he freely offered advice based on his military experience to the government.

In general he disliked all forms of popular political association and
condemned the anti-slavery campaign, the Political Unions of 1831/2,
the Chartists and the Anti-Corn Law League. In his eyes each was
a dangerous unrepresentative conspiracy designed to intimidate the
government. Behind these fears were his memories of the Irish secret
societies and the French political associations of the 1790s. In 1832 he
likened the pro-Reform Political Unions to the Jacobin Clubs which
Napoleon had crushed by force of arms and predicted that something
of the same sort might have to be undertaken in Britain. 'The whole

question of the British monarchy now depends on the discipline and efficiency of the British army.' Earlier, when there was a possibility of rioting in London, he gave detailed suggestions about where soldiers were to be stationed, and added grimly, 'If the troops are to be turned out, let it be to act; and that at once and efficiently.'[9]

Not surprisingly, opponents like Russell believed that Wellington the statesman was in fact the soldier in disguise. He was a cavalier in his adherence to the Crown and a soldier in his respect for higher authority. His view of the relationship between the state and the subject was revealed in his observations on a court-martial in 1809. 'I consider a Sentry a Repository of Public Authority at his station and that all men however high in Rank are bound to obey the orders he has given them.'[10] Take away or challenge that authority and society would dissolve into chaos.

And yet, as a strategist, Wellington had shown remarkable flexibility and always adhered to that common-sense principle that what could or could not be done on the battlefield depended on the means to hand. He carried this pragmatism into political life. In 1829, when faced with the possibility that Ireland would become ungovernable, he relented on the issue of political rights for Roman Catholics and introduced the Emancipation Act. It was passed despite the bitterest opposition from those Tories and Anglicans who preferred to risk a civil war rather than abandon the principle that only loyal communicants of the established Church could be trusted with political power.

Catholic emancipation lost Wellington much support within the Tory Party, his implacable hostility to Parliamentary reform made him into the demon king of reaction between 1830 and 1832. He was mobbed in the streets of London and fourteen policemen guarded Apsley House, which he fortified with bullet-proof iron shutters. When the Reform Act was passed, he gloomily predicted the onset of 'mobocracy' and an era of levelling. He appeared – and his public outbursts supported this conclusion – a man who was out of temper with his times.

He had been an unwilling statesman, impelled to hold public office out of a sense of duty. In 1827 he had been appointed commander-in-chief, a post he was most sorry to relinquish a year later when he became Prime Minister, and which he returned to again in 1841. He was perhaps happiest managing the affairs of the army and he saw himself as its guardian, defending it from the assaults of outsiders, particularly politicians of a reforming bent.

At the same time he compiled memoranda and offered advice on operational matters. Although this was a period of European peace, the army was engaged in a large number of colonial campaigns mostly conducted to extend or pacify frontiers. This was a sort of warfare that Wellington fully understood from his Indian days and he offered plenty of suggestions to those engaged in it. Many, like Viscount Combermere (formerly Sir Stapleton Cotton), Lords Gough and Hardinge and Sir Harry Smith, had served under him in the Peninsula and at Waterloo. 'I have been fortunate indeed to be reared in the military school of the great Duke,' Smith wrote and in 1850/1 he consulted his old mentor about operations against the Xhosa and other tribesmen on the borders of Natal and the Cape Colony. After a mass mutiny and defection to the enemy by the locally recruited native gendarmerie, Smith remembered the advice he had been given by Wellington who had cautioned him to 'take care of these gentlemen, they may carry swords which cut two ways.'[11] Like so many others, this frontier war was condemned by missionary societies and humanitarians at home who claimed that the colonial government had behaved brutally. Wellington defended Smith in the Lords in February 1852, but felt obliged to censure him for not having penetrated the borderlands with roads, no doubt remembering his own measures in Mysore fifty years before.

Unusually for this period, Wellington was a senior statesman who possessed at intimate knowledge of India. He recognized, more clearly than most, that control over India was more than a valuable commercial asset. It provided Britain with a reservoir of first-class soldiers which enhanced the country's status as a world power and could be deployed outside India. But he was worried by the threat to India's security posed by Russia, which, throughout the 1820s and 1830s, was pushing her frontiers deep into central Asia and seeking political influence in Persia. In 1834, as the stage was set for what would be called 'The Great Game', Wellington wrote, 'if we are ever to come to blows with the Russians in India we must rely on the sepoys', whom he rated better than the Spanish and equal to the Hanoverian militia he had commanded at Waterloo.[12] Despite his forebodings about Russian ambitions, he did not favour an aggressive forward policy in India and expressed misgivings, based upon the risks involved, about the annexation of Sind, Afghanistan and the Punjab.[13] He was right about Afghanistan, where in 1840/1 the Anglo-Indian army of occupation was thrown out of Kabul and destroyed as it retreated down the Khyber Pass.

Taking the army as a whole, Wellington was extremely cautious about tampering with the machine which he had fine-tuned to perfection in Spain. He strenuously defended flogging as a punishment; objected to proposals designed to amalgamate administrative departments, strangely perhaps in the light of the problems he had encountered in the Peninsula; and insisted that the officer corps be filled by gentlemen who conducted themselves accordingly. He was furious when, in 1827, he read court-martial proceedings which revealed how two officers of the 53rd had sworn at a sentry and threatened him with a flogging after he had attempted to stop them bringing a woman into barracks. Such behaviour, Wellington wrote, would 'impair the respect of the Soldiers for the impartiality and justice of their superiors'. Soon after Wellington had left the Horse Guards his successor Lord Hill issued a public admonition in terms which would have pleased the Duke. The miscreants were reminded that 'they are not commissioned for their Amusement or to pass their lives in Idleness'.[14] Both Wellington's sons were officers and, much to his regret, fell into the wastrel category. The eldest, Lord Douro, was a great disappointment. 'As a Man, he is exactly what his Mother was as a woman ... I am convinced that if ever I am re-employed again, in the command of an Army for instance, I shall be under the necessity of disgracing them both'.[15] Nothing, not even natural affection, could interfere with the performance of public duty.

Wellington's lasting legacy to the army was his example. Its officer corps remained what it had been in the Peninsula, an aristocratic brotherhood bound together by a common code of honour. Like their commander they led because they could show their men how to behave and were willing to share their discomforts. 'It is incumbent on us in high situation', he had once written, 'to set an example of patience and perseverance in the performance of our duty, of which we have witnessed such signal instances in the lower classes of society and in inferior ranks in the army.'[16] His belief in the natural leadership of the gently born and talented had been under continuous assault since his youth, but, by what he had achieved on the battlefield, he had shown its value. The army and the nation it served shared that belief until the 1914–18 war, but afterwards confidence in aristocratic leadership withered. No commander of Wellington's energy and genius had emerged during that war and the British army had, at great cost, to make do with generals of markedly inferior quality.

By the early 1840s, when he was in his early seventies, deaf and increasingly crippled by rheumatism, Wellington had become a revered national institution. He had become a patriarchal figure, a repository of wisdom and experience whose past political attitudes were forgotten or excused on account of his age. He was now 'the best known man in London' and the 'object of universal royal-like homage which he neither courted or shunned'.[17] One of those who came to stare in June 1850 was Charlotte Brontë, who had been an ardent admirer for years.[18] She was not disappointed by the sight of 'a real grand old man' and purchased a picture of him for her brother.

There were plenty of reminders of the Duke's heroic and by now far distant past: a re-enactment of Waterloo was held in the Vauxhall pleasure gardens during the summer of 1850; there was a huge model of the battlefield with thousands of model soldiers in the United Services Institute; and in the summer of 1852 visitors to the Regent Street Gallery of Illustration could see 'Dioramic Paintings' of all Wellington's campaigns. All around the Duke's residence at Apsley House were 'articles of triumph and statues symbolic of power and command'.[19] Most imposing was the enormous equestrian statue of the Duke in high-crowned cocked hat, his arm outstretched as if to command an advance, which had been placed on top of Constitution Arch by Hyde Park in 1846. (Sadly, it was removed to Aldershot in 1888.) Near by and just north of the Duke's residence at Apsley House was a massive figure of Achilles, cast from French cannon taken at Waterloo, which had been set up as a tribute in 1822.

The object of this reverence and display was still to be seen making his way on horseback to Whitehall and his desk in the Horse Guards. He considered himself still on call in any national emergency and 'the nation's servant-of-all-work' in spite of his infirmities.[20] He was the greatest living Englishman, an Olympian, detached figure whose opinions were sought and commanded authority and respect. 'I am the Duke of Wellington and must do as the Duke of Wellington doth,' he would sometimes remark in acknowledgement of his uniqueness.

He had prospered during his long career; he returned from India £40,000 better off, took a £50,000 share of the Peninsular prize-money, had received estates and the title of Duke of Ciudad Rodrigo from the Spanish government, and, in 1817, had been given in perpetuity the estate of Stratfield Saye in Hampshire. Although he played to the full the public duties of a country landowner, he found the Hampshire climate exacerbated his rheumatism so his preferred out-of-town residence was Walmer Castle on the Kent coast, of which he had the use as Warden of the Cinque Ports.

Here he died, quite suddenly, on 14 September 1852, aged eighty-three. Tributes were abundant and fulsome, none more so than that of *The Times*. This revealed Wellington as far more than a victorious general and, to be honest, moderately successful statesman. 'There is none with whom the valour and worth of this nation were so incorporate' ran the editorial on 15 September and, on 18 November, a day after the Duke's magnificent funeral, the writer returned to the same theme. He had been the 'highest incarnation of English character'. 'Who can tell what would have been the state of Europe or of England during the last half century or at this moment had Arthur Wellesley never lived?' The author believed that a clue to the answer might have been found among the mourners who prayed that, should 'this land of freedom' ever again be threatened, then another Wellington would emerge to save it from destruction.

These were all rather high-flown sentiments, although natural enough for a prosperous, flourishing and buoyant country proud of its heroic past and aware how narrowly it had survived the test of war. How far the clear-headed, acerbic, cynical, hard-swearing, highly intelligent and supremely self-confident aristocrat embodied that elusive abstraction 'national character' is another matter, although Victorian schoolmasters and preachers made much of that Wellingtonian virtue, service before self. His own reaction to his achievements was characteristically diffident. 'I am the luckiest fellow in the world; I must have been born under some extraordinary star.'[21]

NOTES & SOURCES

All books listed were published in London unless otherwise stated.

Abbreviations

ADM: Admiralty
BL: British Library
HMC: Historic Manuscripts Commission
HO: Home Office
IOL: India Office Library
JRL: John Rylands Library
JSAHR: *Journal of the Society for Army Historical Research*
NAM: National Army Museum
NLS: National Library of Scotland
PRO: Public Record Office
SD: *Supplementary Despatches, Correspondence and Memoranda of the Duke of Wellington*
SRO: Scottish Record Office
SU: Southampton University
WO: War Office
WP: Wellington Papers

Notes

Part One: 1769–1793

I: A SPRIG OF THE NOBILITY: 1769–1790

1. Lochée, 17–18.
2. HMC, *Fortescue*, I, 287; Buckingham, I, 334–5, 348.
3. BL, Add. Mss. 37, 315, 50–1; 37, 416, 21.
4. HMC, *Fortescue*, I, 296.
5. SRO, Melville, GD 51/1/349, 9.
6. Croker, I, 342.
7. *Dispatches*, VI, 287.
8. Croker, I, 41, 42–3.
9. Lochée, 14.
10. Croker, II, 205, 218.
11. IOL, Strachey, Mss. Eur. F 163, Elphinstone to Strachey, 23 August 1803; printed in Wills, 172.
12. Scott, *Letters, 1815–17*, 97.
13. Blakiston, II, 373.
14. Croker, I, 345.
15. *SD*, VII, 171–2.
16. BL, Add. Mss. 29, 238, 30d.
17. Larpent, I, 93.
18. *Ibid.*, 92.
19. NAM, Woodberry, 98.
20. Gomme, 373–4.
21. Anon, *Military and Naval Magazine*, 195.
22. PRO, WO 71/217.
23. Harris, 28; Donaldson, I, 199.
24. Cooke, 172–3.

II: GALLIC BREEZES: 1790–1793

1. Wellington, *Speeches*, I, 4.
2. Buckingham, II, 205.
3. HMC, *Fortescue*, III, 149.
4. Hansard, 3rd Series, VII, 1197; Gleig, 68.
5. BL, Add. Mss. 37, 308, 16.
6. *Dispatches*, VI, 17.
7. Hansard, 3rd Series, IV, 645.
8. BL, Add. Mss. 37, 308, 170–5.
9. Larpent, I, 119.
10. *Quarterly Review*, XXV (July 1815), 275.

Part Two: 1793–1795

I: FORCE AND MENACE, AIDED BY FRAUD AND CORRUPTION

1. PRO, WO 3/598, 309–10.
2. PRO, WO 6/34, 18–19.
3. *SD*, VIII, 94.
4. HMC, *Fortescue*, IX, 41–4.
5. Rath, 22.
6. Bond, 113–14.
7. Holland, 367–8.
8. Larpent, II, 5.
9. Rath, 23.
10. Bond, 115.
11. Lejeune, I, 39.
12. Cadell, 142.
13. NAM, Bingham, III, 63.
14. *Dispatches*, VI, 67, 79, 88.
15. PRO, WO 1/267, 283, 299, 319.
16. PRO, WO 25/3225.
17. PRO, WO 90/1, 77d.
18. Larpent, II, 42; Buckham, 232, 259, 272.
19. Quoted in Napier, *Lights and Shades of Military Life*, 7–8.
20. Batty, 111.
21. Ellenborough, I, 179.
22. Lynn, 148.

23. Gomme, 248–9.
24. Croker, II, 287–8.
25. Gomme, 248.

26. Croker, I, 339–40.
27. HMC, *Wellington*, I, 346.
28. Von Müffling, 252–3.

II: THE MECHANISM AND POWER OF THE INDIVIDUAL SOLDIER

1. Croker, I, 337.
2. Gleig, 3.
3. *Ibid.*, 333.
4. Anon, 'Memoir of Field-Marshal the Duke of York', *Naval and Military Magazine*, 2–3; Blakiston, I, 43.
5. Webb-Carter, *passim*.
6. Dundas, 53.
7. Paret, 43.
8. Dundas, 13–14.
9. Oman, *Moore*, 324; *Historical Records of the 71st Regiment*, 65–6.
10. Cadell, 3–4.
11. Donaldson, I, 85.
12. PRO, WO 71/229.
13. Costello, 59–60.
14. Croker, I, 345.
15. Gleig, 304–5.
16. HMC, *Wellington*, I, 156, 393.

17. NAM, Woodberry, 16.
18. PRO, HO 50/437.
19. HMC, *Fortescue*, I, 287; Buckingham, I, 335; PRO, WO 40/7.
20. PRO, WO 1/1066, 287; WO 40/3.
21. SRO, Melville, GD 51/1/729.
22. Brown, *The Campaign*, 18.
23. Donaldson, I, 84–5.
24. *Ibid.*, 81.
25. Larpent, II, 5, 43.
26. PRO, WO 25/2906, 58; 2907, 675.
27. *SD*, VIII, 38.
28. *Dispatches*, IV, 417–19; 486.
29. Lynn, 94–5; Bertauld, 149, 220.
30. Von Müffling, 212.
31. Croker, I, 13.

III: HOW NOT TO WAGE WAR: BELGIUM AND HOLLAND, 1794–1795

1. SRO, Melville, GD 51/1/650/2.
2. Sherwig, 18–19; 78.
3. Combermere, I, 31.
4. PRO, WO 1/170, 465–9.
5. *Ibid.*, 285.
6. PRO, WO 1/1096, 453–5, 471, 473.
7. BL, Add. Mss. 37, 308, 15.
8. *Ibid.*, 15.
9. PRO, WO 1/1096, 581–3.
10. SRO, Melville, GD 51/1/605.
11. PRO, WO 1/172, 97–8.
12. *Ibid.*, 337–41.
13. BL, Add. Mss. 46, 706, 176.
14. *Ibid.*, 224d.
15. PRO, WO 40/7.

16. Brown, *An Impartial Journal*, 224.
17. PRO, WO 4/291, 120.
18. PRO, WO 40/7.
19. Thomas, 26–9.
20. *Ibid.*, 17–18.
21. BL, Add. Mss. 46, 706, 224d.
22. Thomas, 27.
23. PRO, WO 1/170, 285.
24. PRO, WO 1096, 730–1.
25. NAM, White 29.8.93; PRO, WO 1/1096, 743d.
26. Cornwallis, III, 274.
27. Wellington, *Speeches*, I, 5.
28. *Minutes of Evidence*, 479–80.
29. E.g. Francis Jeffrey in *Edinburgh Review*, 18 (April 1807), 15ff.

Part Three: *1795–1805*

I: A CERTAIN FORTUNE: 1795–1798

1. Thorn, 9.
2. Stanhope, 130.
3. Combermere, I, 73.
4. *SD*, I, 16.
5. NLS, Walker, 13605, 105–6d; *SD*, I, 223–5.
6. Peers, 20.
7. Blakiston, I, 229–30.
8. *Dispatches*, I, 47, 51.
9. Gupta, xxxii–xxxiii.
10. Carver, 14.
11. Webb-Carter, 77.
12. Elers, 57.
13. *SD*, IV, 29.
14. *Ibid.*, III, 185; Hickey, IV, 172; Elers, 121.
15. NLS, Brown, MS. 1855, 1; Elers, 116, 121, 123–4; Blakiston, I, 105–6.
16. Elers, 55–6, 124.
17. BL, Add. Mss. 37, 416, 2d.
18. Metcalfe, I, 54; HMC, *Fortescue*, IV, 382–3.
19. HMC, *Fortescue*, IV, 383.
20. *SD*, I, 250–1.
21. *Dispatches*, I, 35; Wellesley sent the mechanical tiger to his brother.
22. Wellesley, I, 3–5: also HMC, *Fortescue*, IV, 384.
23. *SD*, I, 13, 54–5.
24. *Ibid.*, I, 70–1, 113.
25. Lenman, 42–3.
26. *SD*, I, 16–17.
27. *Dispatches*, I, 66.
28. SRO, Melville, GD 51/1/764, 20.
29. Wellesley, I, 63.

II: LIGHT AND QUICK MOVEMENTS: 1799

1. Stanhope, 182.
2. *SD*, III, 13–14.
3. Elers, 117.
4. BL, Add. Mss. 29, 238, 18; Elers, 122.
5. *SD*, III, 432–3.
6. *Ibid.*, I, 157.
7. MacKenzie, II, 23–5.
8. Scott, 65.
9. *SD*, I, 433.
10. Kirmani, II, 230, 258; Wellesley, I, 442.
11. BL, Add. Mss. 29, 238, 2.
12. PRO, WO 1/854, 336–9.
13. Wellesley, V, 163.
14. Wellesley, III, 395.
15. Blakiston, I, 234.
16. Malcolm, I, 219, 222.
17. BL, Add. Mss. 37, 416, 2d.
18. *SD*, I, 208; Stanhope, 103.
19. Stanhope, 102.
20. IOL, Strachey, Mss. Eur. F 163, Elphinstone to Strachey, 12 August 1803.
21. *SD*, IV, 29.
22. PRO, WO 1/357, 285.
23. Stanhope, 130.
24. NLS, Walker, Ms. 13, 605, 101.
25. *SD*, I, 208.
26. NLS, Walker, Ms. 13, 605, 98d.
27. *SD*, I, 208–9.
28. *Ibid.*, I, 209–10; Elers, 102–3; Blakiston, I, 83.
29. Wellesley, I, 578; NLS, Walker, Ms. 13, 605, 103.

III: SOMETHING MORE THAN A FIGHTING MACHINE: 1799–1802

1. *SD*, I, 273.
2. *Ibid.*, 506.
3. NLS, Walker, Ms. 13, 605, 17.
4. *Ibid.*, 3d–4.

5. NLS, Walker, Ms. 18, 55, 56, 82.
6. BL, Add. Mss. 17d–18.
7. *SD*, III, 21.
8. NLS, Walker, Ms. 13, 605, 8–9.
9. *Ibid.*, 24–5; 13, 602, 49.
10. NLS, Brown, Ms. 1855, 1.
11. NLS, Walker, Ms. 13, 605, 12d–13; BL, Add. Mss. 29, 238, 48d–9.
12. NLS, Walker, Ms. 13, 605, 21d.
13. *Ibid.*, 13, 603, 78.
14. IOL, Scott, Mss. Eur. D 828, 1, 4d, 5.
15. *SD*, II, 167.
16. BL, Add. Mss. 23, 239, 5–5d.

17. IOL, Munro, Mss. Eur. D 151/1, Summary of Daundia Campaign; NLS, Walker, Ms. 13, 605, 24.
18. IOL, Munro, Mss. Eur. D 151/1, Summary of Daundia Campaign, 19–25 June 1800.
19. *Ibid.*, 30 August 1800.
20. NLS, Walker, Ms. 13, 605, 33d; *Dispatches*, 1, 72.
21. *Ibid.*, I, 72–3; NLS, Walker, Ms. 13, 605, 33d.
22. *SD*, II, 103.
23. Gleig, 278.

IV: WELLESLEY SAHIB BADAHUR: 1803–1805

1. *Dispatches*, I, 66.
2. Wellesley, III, 182–3; V, 174.
3. Wellesley, V, 174.
4. Wills, 187, 188, 192–4; Pemble, 382–3.
5. Wellesley, III, 190, 192.
6. Pemble, 393.
7. Broughton, 46.
8. IOL, Bell, 46.
9. *SD*, IV, 128.
10. *Ibid.*, 213.
11. *Dispatches*, II, 444.
12. *SD*, IV, 128, 213.
13. Malcolm, I, 203.
14. *Dispatches*, II, 373–4.
15. PRO, WO 1/854, 519.
16. Blakiston, I, 90.
17. *SD*, III, 361.
18. *Ibid.*, IV, 98.
19. *Ibid.*, 163; *Dispatches*, II, 217.
20. NLS, Brown, Ms. 1855, 3d–4; Blakiston, I, 93.
21. NLS, Brown, Ms. 1855, 4.
22. *SD*, IV, 55, 81, 95, 109–10.
23. *Ibid.*, 171, 187.
24. *Ibid.*, 107.
25. *Ibid.*, 210.
26. *Dispatches*, II, 464–5.
27. *Ibid.*, I, 346.

28. IOL, Strachey, Mss. Eur. F 163, Elphinstone to Strachey, 17 August 1803.
29. Blakiston, I, 144.
30. IOL, Strachey, Mss. Eur. F 163, Elphinstone to Strachey, 17, 21, 30 August 1803.
31. Stanhope, 57.
32. *SD*, IV, 184, 210.
33. *Dispatches*, I, 355.
34. IOL, Strachey, Mss. Eur. F 163, Elphinestone to Strachey, 3 October 1803.
35. Stanhope, 57; Wills, 170 [from Elphinstone's letter of 27 September].
36. Blakiston, I, 160.
37. Wills, 172; IOL, Strachey, Mss. Eur. F 163, Elphinstone to Strachey, 3 October 1803.
38. *SD*, IV, 186.
39. Malcolm, I, 233.
40. Thorn, 296.
41. Wellesley, IV, 285.
42. Wills, 183–4; Blakiston, I, 229–30.
43. HMC, *Fortescue*, VII, 381–2.
44. Malcolm, I, 238–9.
45. *Ibid.*, 257.

46. *Ibid.*, 263.
47. Thompson, *The Making of the Indian Princes*, 97.
48. *Ibid.*, 98.
49. *SD*, I, 246–7.
50. *The Times*, 2 April 1804.
51. Thompson, *The Making of the Indian Princes*, 64.

52. HMC, *Fortescue*, IX, 353.
53. George, Prince of Wales, VI, 335.
54. Von Müffling, 212.
55. Quoted in Peers, 20.
56. Quoted in Thompson, 'The Uses of Adversity', 20.

Part Four: 1805–1808

I: AN END TO THE OLD WORLD: 1805–1808

1. SU, WP 1/4.
2. Thorne, II, 173; V, 473, 504–5.
3. HMC, *Fortescue*, X, 149.
4. Croker, II, 232–3.
5. Arbuthnot, I, 168–9; II, 5–6.
6. HMC, *Fortescue*, VIII, 353.
7. *SD*, VI, 35–82; HMC, *Fortescue*, IX, 479–85.
8. *Ibid.*, 48–9.
9. HMC, *Fortescue*, VIII, 419.
10. *Dispatches*, IV, 156.
11. HMC, *Fortescue*, IX, 128–9.
12. PRO, WO 3/603, 9–10.
13. Arbuthnot, I, 141.

14. *SD*, VI, 2.
15. NAM, Gordon, Alexander to Alicia Gordon, 25 July 1807.
16. *SD*, VI, 5.
17. PRO, WO 1/188, 195–6.
18. SU, WP 1/175, 18 August.
19. *SD*, VI, 9–10; PRO, WO 1/188, 179–85.
20. PRO, WO 1/188, 143.
21. *SD*, VI, 12–13; SU, WP 1/175, Beckwith to Wellesley, 30, 31 August 1807.
22. PRO, WO 44/642, 399.
23. Napier, *Life and Opinions*, I, 77.

II: I AM NOT AFRAID OF THEM: PORTUGAL, 1808

1. Sherwig, 198–9.
2. *Dispatches*, IV, 16.
3. Glover, *Britannia Sickens*, 41: PRO, ADM 1/340, Cotton to Admiralty, 14 August 1808.
4. Castlereagh, VI, 386–8.
5. SU, WP 1/214, Wellesley to Castlereagh, 5 September 1808.
6. Castlereagh, VI, 389–90.
7. PRO, ADM 1/340, Cotton to Admiralty, 4 July 1808.
8. Castlereagh, VI, 396.
9. PRO, WO 1/240, 362–3.
10. Croker, I, 13.
11. Glover, *Britannia Sickens*, 83.
12. *Ibid.*, 102–3.
13. Harris, 35.
14. NAM, Anon, 4d.

15. Warre, 27.
16. Burghersh, 24–5; *SD*, VI, 126, 165, 176; *Dispatches*, IV, 100.
17. Oman, *Moore*, 511.
18. Glover, *Britannia Sickens*, 49.
19. PRO, ADM 1/340, Siniavin to Cotton, 2 September 1808.
20. SRO, Melville, GD 51/1/742, 1; see also, *SD*, VI, 157.
21. SRO, Melville, GD 51/1/742, 1.
22. *Ibid.*, 11.
23. *SD*, VI, 122–3; 126–7.
24. *Dispatches*, IV, 153.
25. *SD*, VI, 124.
26. SU, WP 1/214, Wellesley to Castlereagh, 5 September 1808.
27. *Ibid.*
28. *SD*, VI, 155–6; 161–3.

29. Schneer, 98–9.
30. SRO, GD 51/1/743, 1; 744.
31. *SD*, VI, 186–7.

32. *Ibid.*, 153, 161.
33. *Cobbett's Parliamentary Debates*, XII, 178.

Part Five: 1809–1812

I: ACUTE AND DECISIVE TALENTS FOR COMMAND: THE ROAD TO TALAVERA, 1809

1. Scott, 139, 159.
2. *SD*, VI, 232.
3. NAM, Bingham, I, 3; PRO, WO 37/6, 2.
4. PRO, WO 28/343, 1.
5. Quoted in Napier, *Lights and Shades of Military Life*, 286.
6. Castlereagh, VI, 429.
7. Napier, *History*, II, 92–3.
8. NAM, Bingham, I, 29 April 1808.
9. Munster, 158.
10. Wilkie, 100; NAM, Gordon, Alexander to Alicia Gordon, 4 December 1808.
11. E.g. HMC, *Hastings*, III, 284–6.
12. *Dispatches*, IV, 424–5.
13. *Ibid.*, 265–6; 261.
14. PRO, WO 37/9, 9 May 1808: informaton about French negligence came from deserters.
15. Munster, 163–4.
16. SU, WP 1/269, 42.
17. *Dispatches*, IV, 281; 341; 346–7; 350–1.
18. *Ibid.*, 384–5.
19. *Ibid.*, 445.
20. *Dispatches*, IV, 445.
21. Schaumann, 158–9.
22. NAM, Bingham, I, 8 June 1809.
23. PRO, WO 90/1, 68–68d.
24. PRO, WO 71/218.
25. *Dispatches*, IV, 399–400; 405–6; 407.
26. SU, WP 1/269, 38.
27. Costello, 35.
28. Munster, 194–5.
29. NAM, Bingham, I, 47.

II: NO BRILLIANT EVENT: SPAIN AND PORTUGAL, AUGUST 1809–SEPTEMBER 1810

1. SRO, Leith Hay, Bundle 26, n.d.
2. NAM, Bingham, I, 43.
3. *Dispatches*, V, 15.
4. SU, WP 1/286, 55; NAM, Gordon, Alexander Gordon to Lord Aberdeen, 25 August and 19 October 1809.
5. SU, WP 1/286, 16.
6. *Dispatches*, V, 8–9.
7. *SD*, VI, 373.
8. JRL, Clinton, Box 14, Wellington to Bentinck, 9 August 1813.
9. *SD*, VI, 479.
10. Raikes, 347–8.
11. Bald, 105.
12. Boutflower, 17.
13. SRO, Leith Hay, Bundle 26, n.d.
14. SU, WP 1/286, 55.
15. HMC, *Hastings*, III, 277.
16. Horward, 97–8.
17. SU, WP 1/286, 57.
18. *Ibid.*, 285, 24.
19. *Ibid.*, 286, 57.
20. *SD*, VI, 465–7; PRO, WO 6/50, 7–10.
21. *Cobbett's Parliamentary Debates*, XV, 106–7, 109, 281, 285, 287.
22. *Gentleman's Magazine*, LXXX (1810), 256.
23. PRO, WO 6/50, 181–2.
24. *SD*, VI, 515.

25. PRO, WO 57/9, I, Kennedy to Castlereagh, 10 July 1810.
26. Carss, 9.
27. *SD*, VI, 219.

28. Croker, I, 347.
29. *Dispatches*, VI, 172–3, 179, 234, 257–8.

III: LIONS AT BAY: PORTUGAL, SEPTEMBER 1810–DECEMBER 1811

1. Douglas, 104.
2. Ward, 151–2; PRO, WO 37/7A, 9–11.
3. WO 37/7A, 40.
4. SRO, Leith Hay, Bundle 26, 17 October 1810.
5. *Ibid.*
6. Marbot, II, 115–16, 177–8.
7. SRO, Leith Hay, Bundle 26, 4 October 1810.
8. Boutflower, 149.
9. Andrews, 488n.
10. Carss, 11.
11. E.g. Anon, 'Campaigns of 1811', *Quarterly Review*, May–August 1811, 409; HMC, *Hastings*, III, 286, 288.
12. SU, WP 1/334, Wellington to Stuart, 1 June 1811.
13. PRO, WO 57/39/2.II.
14. *Dispatches*, VII, 192; Sherwig, 244–5.
15. PRO, WO 28/343, 38.
16. PRO, WO 1/926, 62–3.
17. *SD*, VII, 11–12.

18. *Ibid.*, 46.
19. PRO, WO 3/598, 309–11; WO 25/3224; *SD*, VI, 41, 91.
20. *Ibid.*, 245–6.
21. *Ibid.*, 69–70; PRO, WO 6/50, 181–3; WO 6/34, 96–97A.
22. *SD*, VII, 93.
23. *Ibid.*, VII, 103–5.
24. Gomme, 219; Nightingall, 151.
25. Anon, *Seventy-First*, 60.
26. PRO, WO 37/7A, 5 May 1811; Larpent, I, 105.
27. PRO, WO 37/7A, 5 May 1811; Cocks, 108.
28. PRO, WO 37/7A, 5 May 1811.
29. *SD*, VII, 176.
30. SU, WP 1/335, Dunlop to Wellington, 1 July 1810.
31. *SD*, VII, 176.
32. *Ibid.*, 167, 221, 228, 237.
33. SU, WP 1/335, York to Wellington, 5 July 1811.
34. De Melito, II, 448.
35. PRO, WO 28/343, 25 March 1811.

Part Six

I: LORD WELLINGTON DON'T KNOW HOW TO LOSE A BATTLE: THE COMMANDER AND HIS MEN

1. Wheeler, 161.
2. Heeley, 115.
3. Croker, I, 352.
4. E.g. Larpent, I, 105, 157–85.
5. Anon, *Colburn's United Service Magazine*, 184.
6. Croker, I, 330.
7. *Ibid.*, 346.
8. *SD*, VI.

9. PRO, WO 3/37, 449–50; WO 3/51, 75.
10. SU, WP 1/285, 20.
11. PRO, WO 71/236.
12. Larpent, I, 154.
13. SU, WP 9/1/1/8, 94.
14. *Dispatches*, VI, 325.
15. PRO, WO 3/597, 263–79.
16. SU, WP 1/286, 58; Ward, 173.

17. *SD*, VII, 486.
18. *Ibid.*, 213.
19. *Ibid.*, 527; SU, WP 1/334, Wellington to Erskine, 22 June 1811.
20. Larpent, II, 181.
21. SU, WP 9/2/2/37; Larpent, II, 181.
22. Johnson, 95.
23. Stanhope, 87.
24. Larpent, I, 78–9; 229; Tylden, *passim.*
25. Barnard, 136–7.
26. Larpent, I, 150.
27. *Ibid.*, II, 247.
28. *Ibid.*, 77; Anon, *Letters from Spain*, 191–2.
29. Larpent, I, 182.
30. Tylden, *passim*; Johnson, 100.
31. *SD*, VI, 84–5; 88–9.
32. *Ibid.*, VII, 468.
33. *Ibid.*, XIV, 329.
34. NAM, Woodberry, 186–7.
35. *Ibid.*, 202.
36. Croker, I, 352–3.
37. Larpent, I, 133.
38. *Ibid.*, 175.
39. NAM, Gordon, Alexander to Alicia Gordon, 3 November 1810.
40. Anon, *Letters from Spain*, 9;
Napier, *Life and Opinions*, I, 173.
41. Carss, 9.
42. NAM, Bingham, III, 16; Woodberry, 12.
43. NAM, Whitman, 8 July 1812.
44. Gunn, 116.
45. Donaldson, II, 131.
46. Cooke, I, 32–3, 159.
47. Heeley, 116.
48. NAM, Anon, 38th, 20d–21.
49. Anon, *Personal Narrative*, 302; Donaldson, I, 201.
50. NAM, Gairdner, II, 10 December 1813.
51. NAM, Anon, 38th, 21.
52. Donaldson, I, 220–1.
53. Quoted in Anon, *The Battle of Waterloo*, II, 66.
54. Gomme, 188; Rice-Jones, 94–5.
55. Cooke, I, 75.
56. NAM, Whitman, 5 July 1812.
57. Hennell, 54–5; Gunn, 110.
58. Wheeler, 49–50.
59. Warre, 6.
60. NAM, Woodberry, 147–8.
61. Anon, *Seventy First*, 53, quoted in Anon, *The Battle of Waterloo*, II, 51; Anon, *Letters from Spain*, 22–3.
62. Kincaid, 62, quoted in Davies, 97.

II: LABORIOUS ATTENTION: WELLINGTON'S LOGISTICS
1. *Dispatches*, X, 614.
2. Croker, I, 42–3; Chad, 7.
3. Anon, *The Principles of War*, xvii; Stanhope, 182.
4. *SD*, XIV, 49.
5. PRO, WO 3/603, 62.
6. NAM, Sullivan, 56; Davies, 99–100; Schaumann, 256–7, 265, 335.
7. Larpent, I, 175.
8. PRO, WO 3/605, 171–2.
9. *Dispatches*, X, 604.
10. *SD*, VII, 318–19; *Dispatches*, IX, 421.
11. *Ibid.*, X, 367–8.
12. Ward, 86; *SD*, VII, 179.
13. Picton, I, 383; Anon, *Military Sketch-Book*, 154.
14. PRO, WO 57/38, 1, I; WO 1/244, 433; WO 57/39, 1, 4.
15. Batty, 13–14.
16. SU, WP 1/392, 'List of all Transports'.
17. *Dispatches*, X, 273, 400; *SD*, VIII, 273.
18. PRO, ADM 1/643, Admiral Berkeley to Admiralty, 5 August 1811.

19. *Dispatches*, X, 605.
20. Quoted in Ward, 101.
21. PRO, WO 25/1569; *SD*, VII, 523.
22. PRO, WO 25/1382; JRL, Clinton, Box 14.
23. *Dispatches*, IX, 335–6, 452, 577; X, 5, 77, 473.
24. PRO, WO 6/50, 84, 245; SU, WP 1/392, York to Wellington, 10 January 1814; JRL, Clinton, Box
25, Wellington to Sir Henry Clinton, 18 May 1812.
25. PRO, WO 25/3225, York to Bathurst, 20 October 1813.
26. Daniel, 69–70.
27. *SD*, XIV, 247; *Dispatches*, X, 183–4.
28. NAM, Whitman, 23 March 1813.
29. *SD*, XIV, 3, 27.

III: THE OTHER SIDE OF THE HILL: INTELLIGENCE AND WEAPONS

1. Quoted in Ward, 117; Croker, III, 275.
2. SRO, Leith Hay, Bundle 27, 13 April 1813.
3. *Dispatches*, VI, 290–1.
4. Hyden, 101.
5. SRO, Leith Hay, Bundle 26, 18 June and 20 November 1812.
6. Ellenborough, I, 186; Smith, 38–9.
7. PRO, WO 28/343, 28.
8. *Dispatches*, IX, 34; X, 248.
9. JRL, Clinton, Box 13, Account Book 1813.
10. SU, WP 9/4/1/1, 3, 4, 7; Ward, 126–7.
11. SU, WP 1/335, Cocks to Stapleton, 5, 6, July 1811.
12. Gomme, 168.
13. SRO, Leith Hay, Bundle 27, 31 January 1812.
14. *Ibid.*, Memoirs 1812/13.
15. SU, WP 1/335, Cocks to Stapleton, 7 July 1811.
16. SRO, Leith Hay, Bundle 27, 7 July 1813.
17. JRL, Clinton, Box 13, Account Book 1813.
18. SRO, Leith Hay, Bundle 27, Memoirs 1812/13.
19. *SD*, XIV, 27.
20. NLS, Murray, 46.2.18, 145–7; 46.2.20, 227; PRO, WO 28/343,
37, 18 February 1811, 26 October 1811.
21. PRO, WO 28/343, 37, 2–6, 26 and 28 October 1811.
22. Hyden, 97.
23. SU, WP 9/4/1, 5, 6; PRO, WO 37/12, 8, 29.
24. *SD*, VII, 459; *Dispatches*, X, 237, 255–6.
25. PRO, WO 37/12, 9, 41.
26. *SD*, VII, 596.
27. PRO, WO 37/57, 72–109.
28. Quoted in Ward, 107.
29. *Ibid.*, 111.
30. SU, WP 1/286, 40.
31. *SD*, VII, 62.
32. *Dispatches*, VI, 287.
33. *SD*, 457; Creevey, I, 173.
34. *Dispatches*, X, 198.
35. Holt, 173; Napoleon, II, 245.
36. Buckham, 269.
37. PRO, WO 44/642, 473.
38. Anon, *Seventy First*, 61.
39. Rothenburg, 65.
40. Surtees, 290.
41. *SD*, VII, 179.
42. Anon, *Letters*, 312.
43. Heeley, 114; Fortescue, VIII, 599; Surtees, 290.
44. Johnson, 93; NAM, Woodberry, 101.
45. *SD*, VII, 587; Fortescue, VIII, 452–3; *Dispatches*, IX, 240.

46. Ompteda, 280; Schaumann, 395; Costello, 41–2.

47. *SD*, VIII, 280; Larpent, II, 257–8; Gleig, *The Subaltern*, 298.

Part Seven: 1812–1815

I: THE MOST SUCCESSFUL CAMPAIGN: SPAIN, 1812

1. *SD*, VII, 305.
2. *Dispatches*, VII, 482–3; IX, 457.
3. *Ibid.*, 485.
4. *Ibid.*, 557, 560.
5. Fortescue, VIII, 365–6.
6. SU, WP 12/1/5, 67.147.
7. SU, WP 9/1/1/2, 28; *Dispatches*, VIII, 571, 575, 579, 607.
8. See p. 183.
9. PRO, WO 28/345.
10. *Dispatches*, IX, 7, 12; Fortescue, VIII, 381.
11. *Dispatches*, IX, 24, 33; Daniel, 86.
12. NAM, Whitman, 51–2.
13. Arbuthnot, II, 143.
14. Buckham, 23–6.
15. Costello, 176, 180.
16. *Dispatches*, IX, 238–9, 242.
17. Kincaid, 74.
18. Fortescue, VIII, 467.
19. *SD*, XIV, 52.
20. *Ibid.*, 75–6, 99.
21. Gomme, 290–1; JRL, Clinton, Box 25, Wellington to Henry Clinton, 16 July 1812.
22. *Ibid.*, Box 14, Wellington to McDonnell, 28 August 1812.
23. *SD*, VII, 477–8.
24. *Ibid.*, XIV, 124; VII, 451–2, 458.
25. *Ibid.*, VII, 459, 477.
26. *Dispatches*, IX, 515, 519, 523.
27. *Ibid.*, 554, 561.
28. *Ibid.*, 421, 466.
29. Donaldson, II, 120.
30. *Dispatches*, IX, 525; *SD*, VII, 463, 469–70.
31. *Dispatches*, IX, 565.
32. *SD*, VII, 423.
33. Longford, 268.
34. *Dispatches*, VIII, 483.
35. *Ibid.*, X, 54.
36. Mazar, 53; Esdaile, 81–2.
37. JRL, Clinton, Box 14, Wellington to Bentinck, 9 August 1813.
38. *Ibid.*, 20 July 1813.
39. NAM, Bingham, III, 16.

II: THE FIRST GENERAL OF OUR PRESENT AGE: SPAIN AND FRANCE, 1813–APRIL 1814

1. *Dispatches*, X, 372.
2. Fortescue, IX, 90; McGrigor, 336; *Dispatches*, X, 357.
3. Larpent, I, 178–9.
4. D'Urban, 304.
5. Burroughs, 69.
6. NLS, Graham Ms. 3611, 41.
7. *SD*, VII, 593.
8. Napoleon, II, 251.
9. *Dispatches*, X, 640.
10. SRO, Leith Hay, Bundle 27, 22 April 1813.
11. NLS, Murray, 42.2.16, 17, *passim*.
12. *Ibid.*, 42.2.17, 119–20.
13. Anon, *Military Sketch-Book*, 14.
14. Wheeler, 113.
15. NAM, Woodberry, 119.
16. NLS, Graham Ms. 3611, 87.
17. Stanhope, 144.
18. Larpent, II, 5.
19. NLS, Murray, 47.2.19, 37.
20. *Ibid.*, 48.
21. Kincaid, 108–9.
22. Costello, 231–2.
23. NAM, Bingham, III, 43.
24. *Dispatches*, X, 472–3.
25. Anon, *Military Sketch-Book*, 135.

26. Schaumann, 354.
27. *SD*, VIII, 17.
28. *Ibid.*, 349.
29. *Ibid.*, 198–9.
30. Watson, 869.
31. *Dispatches*, IX, 614.
32. *SD*, XIV, 339.
33. *Ibid.*, VIII, 67–9, 332.
34. Fortescue, IX, 197; *SD*, VIII, 194; SU, WP 9/1/1/8, 187.
35. Keith, III, 300.
36. *Dispatches*, X, 576, 605, 614, 628, 630; *SD*, VIII, 321.
37. Hennell, 133; Batty, 321.
38. *SD*, VIII, 321.
39. Batty, 31–2.
40. Anon, *Military Sketch-Book*, 153.
41. *SD*, VIII, 321.
42. *Ibid.*, 176–7.
43. Mazar, 53.
44. SU, WP 1/404, Wellington to Beresford, 7 February 1814.
45. Quoted in Glover, *Peninsular War*, 306.
46. Croker, I, 340.
47. JRL, Clinton, Box 14, Wellington to Clinton, 11 December 1814.
48. D'Urban, 312–13; *SD*, XIV, 296, 339, 362.
49. *SD*, XIV, 362, 364.
50. SU, WP 1/401, *passim*.
51. *SD*, VIII, 743.
52. Daniel, 300.
53. *SD*, VIII, 754.
54. *Ibid.*, 748.
55. *Dispatches*, XI, 668.
56. *Ibid.*, 586.
57. Shelley, 71.

III: THE FINGER OF GOD: WATERLOO, 1815

1. Shelley, 96.
2. Gilmour, 13.
3. Russell, 309–10.
4. *SD*, X, 514.
5. Guizot, I, 175.
6. *Courier*, 27 March 1815.
7. Hansard, XXXI, 335.
8. *SD*, IX, 606.
9. Charras, 24–5.
10. *Ibid.*, 31.
11. *SD*, IX, 519.
12. Shelley, 69.
13. PRO, WO 1/318, 18d.
14. *SD*, 554–5.
15. Napier, *Life and Opinions*, I, 267.
16. Wheeler, 177.
17. *Dispatches*, XII, 288–9; 291–2; *SD*, X, 167–8.
18. Anon, *Letters from Spain*, 210.
19. *SD*, IX, 82.
20. *Ibid.*, X, 27, 42, 43, 49–50, 66–7.
21. *Ibid.*, 75–6.
22. *Ibid.*, 169.
23. *Ibid.*, 336, 345, 348, 354–5, 412.
24. *Dispatches*, XII, 394–6; *SD*, X, 451.
25. *SD*, X, 424–5, 439.
26. *Ibid.*, 456–7, 470–1, 476.
27. Greville, I, 182.
28. *Waterloo Letters*, 147.
29. *Ibid.*, 2, 23.
30. Anon, *Letters from Spain*, 236.
31. Quoted in Morris, 161.
32. *SD*, X, 526.
33. Von Müffling, 238.
34. Cotton, 22.
35. Anglesey, *passim*.
36. Quoted in Morris, 162.
37. *Waterloo Letters*, 326; Wheeler, 170.
38. Leeke, I, 19.
39. Anon, *Letters from Spain*, 265.
40. NLS, Murray, 46.9.19 [report on the battle of Waterloo by Major de Lacy Evans, Assistant Quartermaster-General], 115–115d.
41. *SD*, X, 536; Kincaid, 166.

42. Leeke, I, 33.
43. Somerville, 163.
44. Anon, *Scots Magazine*, 650–1; Anon, *Letters from Spain*, 254–5; *Waterloo Letters*, 77, 81.
45. Quoted in Caird, 36, 41–2.
46. Anon, *Letters from Spain*, 274.
47. Anon, *Scots Magazine*, 649.
48. *Waterloo Letters*, 381; Anon, *Letters from Spain*, 258.
49. *Waterloo Letters*, 330, 339.
50. *SD*, X, 528; *Dispatches*, XI, 528.
51. Heeley, 115.
52. *Waterloo Letters*, 179–80.
53. Leeke, I, 41.
54. *Waterloo Letters*, 254, 255, 257, 258, 276, 293.
55. Anon, *Scots Magazine*, 650.
56. Anon, *Colburn's United Service Magazine*, 349.
57. Shelley, 102.
58. *Waterloo Letters*, 179, 281.
59. Anon, *Colburn's United Service Magazine*, 184.
60. *Waterloo Letters*, 386–7.
61. Arbuthnot, I, 234–5.

Part Eight

I: THE NATION'S SERVANT-OF-ALL-WORK: 1815–1852

1. See SU, WP 1/392, Col. Canning to Wellington, 11 January 1814; WP 1/402, Wellington to Torrens, 10 Feburary 1814.
2. Anon, *Quarterly Review*, 92, 91–2.
3. Wheeler, 185.
4. *Courier*, 22 June 1815; *Aberdeen Chronicle*, 28 June 1815.
5. *Courier*, 5, 6, 7, 14 July, 18 August; *The Times*, 1 August.
6. George, 236.
7. Egan, 3.
8. Anon, *Military Sketch-Book*, 30.
9. Wellington, *Despatches, Correspondence and Memoranda*, VIII, 26, 368.
10. SU, WP 1/286, 62.
11. PRO, WO 135/2, 8; Smith, 562, 627, 642–3.
12. HMC, *Wellington*, I, 457.
13. *Ibid.*, 456–7; Hardinge, 73, 184.
14. PRO, WO 91/4, 47, 53–6, 102–3.
15. *Wellington and His Friends*, 111.
16. *Dispatches*, X, 439.
17. Brontë, I, 191; III, 116–17, 130–1.
18. Anon, *Quarterly Review*, 92, 447.
19. *Ibid.*
20. *Ibid.*, 476.
21. Scherer, *Military Memoirs*, 216.

Sources

This list includes the materials referred to in the Notes.

Unpublished

LONDON, PUBLIC RECORD OFFICE
ADM 1; WO 1, 2, 3, 4, 5, 6, 27, 30, 31, 37 [Papers of General Sir
George Scovell], 40, 44, 57, 71, 92, 130 [Papers of Sir Harry Smith].

LONDON, BRITISH LIBRARY
Additional Manuscripts 13, 772–8; 29, 238; 37, 308; 37, 416; 46, 706.

LONDON, INDIA OFFICE LIBRARY
Letters and papers of General Robert Bell, Sir Thomas Munro, Major-
   General Sir James Scott and Edward Strachey [including letters from
   Mountstuart Elphinstone]

LONDON, NATIONAL ARMY MUSEUM
Letters, diaries and papers of Anon [Private, 38th Regiment]; Sir George
   Bingham; Lieutenant James Gairdner; Sir Alexander Gordon;
   Lieutenant Sullivan; Lieutenant Taylor White; Charles Whitman.
Lieutenant W. P. Woodberry, 'The Idle Companion of a Young Hussar during
   the Year 1813'.

EDINBURGH, NATIONAL LIBRARY OF SCOTLAND
Letters and papers of Major John Brown; General Sir Thomas Graham [Lord
   Lydenoch]; General Sir George Murray; Brigadier Alexander Walker.

EDINBURGH, SCOTTISH RECORD OFFICE
Letters and papers of General Sir John Leith Hay; Henry Dundas, 1st
   Viscount Melville.

MANCHESTER, JOHN RYLANDS LIBRARY
Letters and papers of General Sir Henry Clinton.

SOUTHAMPTON UNIVERSITY LIBRARY
Wellington papers.

Published

T. J. Andrews, 'Masséna's Lines of March in Portugal and French Routes in
   Northern Spain', *English Historical Review*, XVI (1901).
Marquess of Anglesey, 'The Correspondence Concerning the Death of Major
   Hodge, 7th Hussars at Genappe, 17 June 1815', *JSAHR*, 43 (1965).
Anon, 'Campaigns of 1811', *Edinburgh Review*, 18 (May–August 1811).
——, *The Principles of War exhibited in the practise of the Camp ... of the Duke of
   Wellington* (1815).

Anon, [excerpts from various letters from Waterloo], *Scots Magazine*, 77 (September 1815).

——, 'An Account of the Mahrattas', *Asian Journal*, I (1816).

——, [A Near Observer], *The Battle of Waterloo* (2 vols, 1817).

——, [Officer of 92nd Highlanders], *Letters from Spain and Portugal &c.* (1819).

——, [An Officer of the Line], *The Military Sketch-Book: Reminiscences of Seventeen Years in the Service Abroad and at Home* (2 vols, 1827).

——, 'Memoir of Field-Marshal the Duke of York ... and a Narrative of his Campaigns', *Naval and Military Magazine*, I (March 1827).

——, 'Recollections of a Staff-Officer', *Colburn's United Service Magazine* (1847, Part III).

——, Review of *Apsley House, Piccadilly, the town residence of His Grace the Duke of Wellington*, *Quarterly Review* 92 (March 1853).

——, *A Soldier of the Seventy-First*, ed. C. Hibbert (1975 edn).

The Journal of Mrs Arbuthnot, ed. F. Bamforde and the Duke of Wellington (2 vols, 1950).

'The Letters of John Bald, 91st Regiment', ed. S. G. D. Ward, *JSAHR*, 50 (1972).

'The Letters of Lt Colonel, later General Sir Andrew Barnard', ed. M. C. Spurrier, *JSAHR*, 47 (1969).

R. Batty, *The Campaign in the Pyrenees and Southern France, 1813–1814* (1823).

A. S. Bennett, 'Arthur Wellesley as Political Agent', *Journal of the Royal Asiatic Society*, 2 (1987).

J.-P. Bertauld, *The Army of the French Revolution* (Princeton, 1988).

G. Best, *War and Society in Revolutionary Europe, 1770–1870* (1982).

R. Blakiston, *Twelve Years' Military Adventure* (2 vols, 1829).

C. Boutflower, *The Journal of a Surgeon during the Peninsular War* (Manchester, 1912).

A. Brett-James, *Life in Wellington's Army* (1972).

The Brontës: Their Lives, Friendships and Correspondence, ed. J. J. Wise and A. J. Symington (3 vols, Oxford, 1980).

T. B. Broughton, *Letters from a Maratha Camp*, ed. M. E. Duff (1892).

R. Brown, *An Impartial Journal of a Detachment from the Brigade of Guards* (1795).

——, *The Campaign: A Poetical Essay* (1797).

H. A. Bruce, *The Life of Sir William Napier K.C.B.* (2 vols, 1864).

D. H. Buchan, *The Battle of Waterloo: A Poem* (Edinburgh, 1816).

E. W. Buckham, *Personal Narrative &c. during the War in 1812 and 1813* (1827).

The Duke of Buckingham and Chandos, *Memoirs of Courts and Cabinets of George III* (2 vols, 1853).

Lord Burghersh, *Memoir of an Early Campaign of the Duke of Wellington in Spain and Portugal* (1820).

G. F. Burroughs, *A Narrative of the Retreat of the British Army from Burgos in a series of Letters with an introductory sketch of the Campaign of 1812 and Military Character of the Duke of Wellington* (Bristol, 1814).

I. Butler, *The Eldest Brother: The Marquess of Wellesley, the Duke of Wellington's Eldest Brother* (1973).

C. Cadell, *Narrative of the Campaigns of the 28th Regiment* (1835).

A. Mcl. Caird, *The Battle of Waterloo from the Traditions of the Scots Greys and Highlanders* (Glasgow, 1850).

J. Cannon, *Aristocratic Century* (Cambridge, 1984).

'The 2nd/53rd in the Peninsular War: Contemporary Letters from an Officer of the Regiment [John Carss]', ed. S. H. F. Johnston, *JSAHR*, 26 (1948).

Lord Carver, *Wellington and his Brothers* (Southampton, 1989).

Memoirs and Correspondence of Viscount Castlereagh, ed. the Marquess of Londonderry (12 vols, 1848–53).

The Conversations of the First Duke of Wellington with George William Chad, ed. 7th Duke of Wellington (Cambridge, 1956).

Lt-Col. Charras, *Histoire de la campagne de 1815* (Leipzig, 1857).

Cobbett's Parliamentary Debates.

Intelligence Officer in the Peninsular. Letters &c. of Edward Cocks, ed. J. Page (New York, 1986).

Memoirs and Correspondence of Field-Marshal Viscount Combermere, ed. Viscountess Combermere (2 vols, 1866).

J. H. Cooke, *Memoirs of the Late War* (2 vols, 1831).

R. G. S. Cooper, 'Wellington and the Marathas in 1803', *Journal of International History*, XI, i (February 1989).

The Correspondence of Charles, first Marquis of Cornwallis, ed. C. Ross (3 vols, 1859).

E. Costello, *The Adventures of Edward Costello, K. S. F.* (1841).

Sergt-Major Cotton, *A Voice from Waterloo* (1862).

The Creevey Papers, ed. H. Maxwell (2 vols, 1903).

The Croker Papers: Correspondence and Diaries of John Wilson Croker (3 vols, 1884).

J. E. Daniel, *Journal of an Officer in the Commissariat Department of the Army* (1820).

J. Donaldson, *Recollection of an Eventful Life* (2 vols, Glasgow, 1825).

'The Diary of Captain Neil Douglas, 79th Foot, 1809 to 1810', ed. A. Brett-James, *JSAHR*, 41 (1963).

D. Dundas, *Principles of Military Movement chiefly applied to the Infantry* (1787).

P. Egan, *Boxiana, or Sketches of Antient and Modern Pugilism* (2 vols, 1818).

The Memoirs of George Elers, ed. Lord Monson and G. Leveson-Gower (1903).

Lord Ellenborough, *A Political Diary, 1828–30*, ed. Lord Colchester (2 vols, 1881).

C. Elmsley, *British Society and the French Wars, 1793–1815* (1979).

A. T. Embree, *Charles Grant and British Rule in India* (1962).

C. J. Esdaile, 'The Duke of Wellington and the Command of the Spanish Army', in N. Gash (ed.), *Wellington: Studies in the Military and Political Career of the First Duke of Wellington* (Manchester, 1990).

'The Peninsular and Waterloo Letters of Captain Thomas Charles Fenton', ed. C. W. fforde, *JSAHR*, 53 (1975).

'With the Tenth Hussars in Spain: Letters to Edward Fitzgerald', ed. D. J. Haggard, *JSAHR*, 44 (1966).

J. Ford, 'A Journal of the Pyrenees in 1813', *Colburn's United Service Magazine* (1844), Part 1.

J. W. Fortescue, *A History of the British Army* (13 vols, 1899–1930).

'A Subaltern in the Peninsular War: Letters of Lieutenant Robert Garrett, 1811–1813', ed. A. S. White, *JSAHR*, 13 (1934).

N. Gash (ed.), *Wellington: Studies in the Military and Political Career of the First Duke of Wellington* (Manchester, 1990).

E. George, *The Life and Death of Benjamin Robert Haydon* (Oxford, 1948).

Correspondence of George, Prince of Wales, 1787–1812, ed. A. Aspinal (10 vols, 1963–71).

R. Gilmour, *The Battle of Waterloo: A Poem* (1816).

G. R. Gleig, *Personal Reminiscences of the Duke of Wellington*, ed. M. E. Gleig (1904).

——, *The Subaltern* (1825).

M. Glover, *Britannia Sickens: Sir Arthur Wellesley and the Convention of Cintra* (1970).

——, *The Peninsular War, 1807–1814* (Newton Abbot, 1974).

R. Glover, *Peninsular Preparation: The Reform of the British Army, 1795–1809* (Cambridge, 1963).

The Greville Diary, ed. P. W. Wilson (2 vols, 1927).

The Letters and Journals of Field-Marshal Sir William Maynard Gomme, ed. R. C. Carr-Gomme (1881).

'The Memoirs of Private James Gunn', ed. R. H. Roy, *JSAHR*, 49 (1971).

F. Guizot, *Memoirs to illustrate the History of my times* (2 vols, 1858).

P. C. Gupta, *Fort William–India House Correspondence*, XIII; *1796–1800*, India Records Society (Delhi, 1959).

The Letters of the First Viscount Hardinge of Lahore to Lady Hardinge and Sir Walter and Lady James, 1844–1847, ed. B. S. Singh, Camden Society, 4th Series, 32 (1986).

Recollections of Rifleman Harris, ed. C. Hibbert (1970).

'The Journal of Edward Heeley, Servant to Lieutenant-Colonel Sir George Scovell K.C.B., Q.M.G. to the British Army in the Campaign of 1815', ed. D. C. Chandler, *JSAHR*, 64 (1986).

A Gentleman Volunteer: The Letters of George Hennell from the Peninsular War, ed. M. Glover (1979).

The Memoirs of William Hickey, ed. A. Spencer, vol. IV: *1790–1809* (1948).

Historical Records of the 52nd Regiment, ed. W. S. Moorsom (1860).

Historical Records of the 71st Regiment (1852).

Historical Records of the 74th Regiment (Highlanders), ed. R. Cannon (1850).

Historical Records of the 79th Queen's Own Highlanders, ed. T. A. MacKenzie, J. S. Ewart and C. Findlay (1887).

HMC, *Report on the Manuscripts of J. Fortescue Esquire* (9 vols, 1900–15).

HMC, *Report on the Manuscripts of Reginald Rawdon Hastings* (3 vols, 1928–47).

R. B. Holtman, *Napoleonic Propaganda* (New York, 1969).

D. D. Horward, 'Wellington as a Strategist', in N. Gash (ed.), *Wellington: Studies in the Military and Political Career of the First Duke of Wellington* (Manchester, 1990).

J. S. Hyden, 'The Sources, Organisation and Use of Intelligence in the Anglo-Portuguese Army', *JSAHR*, 62 (1984).

E. Ingram, 'The Defence of British India: The Invasion Scare of 1798', *Journal of Indian History*, 48 (1970).

——, 'A Further Confidential Letters from Wellesley', *Journal of Indian History*, 50 (1972).

[H. A. Johnson], 'Letters from Headquarters, 1812–1813', ed. M. Glover, *JSAHR*, 43 (1965).

P. Jupp, *Lord Grenville, 1759–1834* (Oxford, 1985).

The Keith Papers, III: *1803–1815*, ed. C. Lloyd, Navy Records Society, (1955).

J. Kincaid, *Adventures in the Rifle Brigade and Random Shots from a Rifleman* (1981 edn).

Mir Hussein Ali Kirmani, *The History of the Reign of Tipu Sultan*, trans. W. Miles (2 vols, 1844).

F. S. Larpent, *The Private Journal of F. S. Larpent, Judge-Advocate-General* (3 vols, 1853).

W. Leeke, *The History of Lord Seaton's Regiment at the Battle of Waterloo* (2 vols. 1866).

Memoirs of Baron Lejeune, trans. A. Bell (2 vols, 1897).

B. Lenman, 'The Weapons of War in Eighteenth-Century India', *JSAHR*, 46 (1968).

L. Lochée, *An Essay on Military Education* (1773).

Elizabeth Longford, *Wellington: The Years of the Sword* (1971 edn).

J. A. Lynn, *The Bayonets of the Republic* (Urbana, Ill., 1984).

R. Mackenzie, *A Sketch of the War with Tipoo Sultan* (2 vols, Calcutta, 1792).

The Life and Correspondence of Sir John Malcolm, ed. J. W. Kaye (2 vols, 1846).

The Memoirs of Baron Marbot, trans. A. Butler (2 vols, 1892).

J. Marcus, *A Naval History of Britain*, vol. II: *The Age of Nelson* (1971).

Lt Mazar, 'Les Divisions Espagnols de l'armée du Wellington', *Révue des Pyrénées*, XV (1913).

J. McGrigor, *The Autobiography of Sir James McGrigor* (1861).

T. H. McGuffie, 'The Significance of Military Rank in the British Army between 1790 and 1820', *Bulletin of the Institute of Historical Research*, 30 (1957).

Memoirs of Count Miot de Melito, ed. General Flieschmann (2 vols, 1881).

C.-F. de Meneval, *Memoirs to serve for the History of Napoleon I* (3 vols, 1895).

C. Mercer, *Journal of the Waterloo Campaign* (1927 edn).

The Life of Correspondence of Charles, Lord Metcalfe, ed. W. Kaye (1854).

Minutes of Evidence taken before the Committee of the whole House upon the Conduct of H.R.H. the Commander-in-Chief (1809).

G. C. Moore Smith, *A Life of John Colborne, Field-Marshal Lord Seaton* (1903).

W. O'C. Morris, *The Campaign of 1815* (1900).

F. R. von Müffling, *Passages of my life*, trans. P. Yorke (1853).

Earl of Munster, *An Account of the British Campaign of 1809* (1831).

[Sir George Murray] Reviews of W. Napier's *History of the Peninsular War*, *Quarterly Review*, 56 (1836) and 61 (1838).

C. Napier, *Lights and Shades of Military Life* (1850).

C. Napier, *The Life and Opinions of General Sir Charles James Napier*, ed. W. Napier (4 vols, 1857).

W. Napier, *History of the War in the Peninsula* (6 vols, 1828–40).

The Confidential Correspondence of Napoleon Bonaparte with his brother Joseph (2 vols, 1853).

'The Nightingall Letters: Letters from Major-General Sir Charles James Nightingall in Portugal, February to June 1811', ed. M. Glover, *JSAHR*, 51 (1973).

Carola Oman, *Sir John Moore* (1953).

Charles Oman, *A History of the Peninsular War* (7 vols, Oxford, 1902–30).

In the King's German Legion: Memories of Baron Ompteda (1894).

R. Paret, 'Colonial Experience and European Military Reform at the End of the Eighteenth Century', *Bulletin of the Institute of Historical Research*, 27 (1964).

——, *York and the Era of Prussian Reform, 1807–1815* (Princeton, 1966).

D. M. Peers, 'The Duke of Wellington and British India during the Liverpool Administration, 1819–1827', *Journal of Imperial and Commonwealth History*, 27 (October 1988).

J. Pemble, 'Resources and Techniques in the Second Maratha War', *Historical Journal*, 19 (1976).

Memoirs of Lieutenant-General Sir Thomas Picton, ed. H. B. Robinson (2 vols, 1835).

Private Correspondence of Thomas Raikes with the Duke of Wellington, ed. H. Raikes (1861).

R. R. Rath, *The Fall of Napoleon's Kingdom of Italy* (New York, 1941).

Lt Rice-Jones RE, 'Letters from the Peninsula during 1812–1813', ed. H. N. Shore, *Journal of the Royal United Service Institute*, 61 (1916).

G. E. Rothenberg, *The Art of Warfare in the Age of Napoleon* (1977).

A. Schaumann, *On the Road with Wellington*, ed. and trans. A. M. Ludovici (1924).

M. Scherer, *Recollections of the Peninsula* (1823).

——, *Military Memoirs of Field-Marshal the Duke of Wellington* (2 vols, 1832).

R. M. Schneer, 'Arthur Wellesley and the Cintra Convention: A New Look at an Old Puzzle', *Journal of British Studies*, 19 (1979).

The Letters of Sir Walter Scott, 1808–1811, ed. H. J. L. Grierson (1932).

J. K. Severn, 'The Wellesleys and Iberian Diplomacy', in N. Gash (ed.), *Wellington: Studies in the Military and Political Career of the First Duke of Wellington* (Manchester, 1990).

J. Shaw Kennedy, *Notes on Waterloo* (1865).

The Diary of Lady Shelley, ed. R. Edgecumbe (2 vols, 1912).

J. W. Sherwig, *Guineas and Gunpowder: British Foreign Aid in the War with France, 1793–1815* (Harvard, 1969).

W. Siborne, *The Waterloo Campaign, 1815* (1895 edn).

L. Simon, *Journal of a Tour and Residence in Great Britain during the years 1810 and 1811* (2 vols, Edinburgh, 1815).

Autobiography of Lt-General Sir Harry Smith, ed. G. Moore Smith (1901).

A. Somerville, *The Autobiography of a Working Man* (1967 edn).

T. S. Sorell, *Notes of the Campaigns of 1808 and 1809* (1828).

P. H. Stanhope, *Notes on Conversations with the Duke of Wellington, 1831–1851* (1888).

H. Strachan, 'The British Army and "Modern War": The Experience of the Peninsula and Crimea', in T. A. Lynn (ed.), *Tools of War: Instruments, Ideas and Institutions of Warfare, 1445–1871* (Chicago, 1990).

W. Surtees, *Twenty-five Years in the Rifle Brigade* (1833).

R. N. W. Thomas, 'Wellington in the Low Countries, 1794–1795', *International History Review*, 11 (February 1989).

E. Thompson, *The Making of the Indian Princes* (Oxford, 1943).

N. Thompson, 'The Uses of Adversity', in N. Gash (ed.), *Wellington: Studies in the Military and Political Career of the First Duke of Wellington* (Manchester 1990).

W. Thorn, *Memoir of War in India* (1818).

R. G. Thorne (ed.), *The House of Commons, 1790–1820* (5 vols, 1986).

G. Tylden, 'The First Duke of Wellington as a Horseman', *JSAHR*, 43 (1965).

S. P. G. Ward, *Wellington's Headquarters: A Study in the Administrative Problems in the Peninsula, 1809–14* (Oxford, 1957).

W. Warre, *Letters from the Peninsular, 1802–1812*, ed. E. Warre (1909).

Waterloo Letters, ed. H. Siborne (1891).

G. E. Watson, 'The United States and the Peninsular War', *Historical Journal*, 19 (1976).

B. W. Webb-Carter, 'Colonel Wellesley's Standing Orders to the 33rd Regiment', *JSAHR*, 50 (1972).

J. Weller, *Wellington in India* (1972).

The Despatches, Minutes and Correspondence of the Marquess of Wellesley, K. G. (5 vols, 1836).

Wellington, 1st Duke of, *Dispatches of the Duke of Wellington, 1799–1818*, ed. and compiled by R. Gurwood (13 vols, 1834–9).

——, *Speeches of the Duke of Wellington in Parliament*, ed. R. Gurwood (2 vols, 1854).

——, *Supplementary Despatches, Correspondence and Memoranda of the Duke of Wellington*, ed. by his son (14 vols, 1858–72).

——, *Despatches, Correspondence and Memoranda of the Duke of Wellington, 1818–1832*, ed. by his son (8 vols, 1867–80).

——, *Political Correspondence*, vol. I: *1833–34*, vol. II. *1834–35*, Historic Manuscripts Commission, Prime Ministers' Papers Series (1975 and 1986).

——, *Wellington to His Friends* [various private letters], ed. 7th Duke of Wellington (1965).

H. Westergaad (ed.), *Epidemics Resulting from Wars* (Oxford, 1916).

C. U. Wills, *British Relations with the Nagpur State in the Eighteenth Century* (Nagpur, 1926).

M. Younge, *The Shadow of Waterloo* (1817).

INDEX

W. stands for Arthur Wellesley, Duke of Wellington.